Critical Essays on William Faulkner

Critical Essays on
William Faulkner

Robert W. Hamblin

University Press of Mississippi / Jackson

The publication of this book was made possible in part by a generous donation by the Center for Faulkner Studies at Southeast Missouri State University.

The University Press of Mississippi is the scholarly publishing agency of the Mississippi Institutions of Higher Learning: Alcorn State University, Delta State University, Jackson State University, Mississippi State University, Mississippi University for Women, Mississippi Valley State University, University of Mississippi, and University of Southern Mississippi.

www.upress.state.ms.us

The University Press of Mississippi is a member of the Association of University Presses.

First printing 2022
∞

Library of Congress Control Number: 2022942379
ISBN 9781496841124 (hardback)
ISBN 9781496841131 (trade paperback)
ISBN 9781496841148 (epub single)
ISBN 9781496841155 (epub institutional)
ISBN 9781496841162 (pdf single)
ISBN 9781496841117 (pdf institutional)

British Library Cataloging-in-Publication Data available

In Memoriam
Kaye Smith Hamblin 1938–2020
L. D. Brodsky 1941–2014
John Pilkington 1918–2012

Contents

Preface

I first read a Faulkner novel—it was *As I Lay Dying*—in an undergraduate Southern Literature class taught by Thomas Daniel Young at Delta State University in 1959. Later, as a graduate student at the University of Mississippi, I continued reading Faulkner in the seminars led by John Pilkington, who would soon publish his outstanding study of Faulkner, *The Heart of Yoknapatawpha*. Subsequently, I wrote a master's thesis and a doctoral dissertation on Faulkner, both directed by Dr. Pilkington.

In my early years of teaching, first at the high-school level and then at Southeast Missouri State University, selected Faulkner novels or stories almost always found their way into my course syllabi. Then, in 1978, I had the good fortune to meet Louis Daniel Brodsky, a native of St. Louis, who was in the process of amassing one of the world's finest collections of Faulkner books, manuscripts, letters, documents, photographs, and other memorabilia. Over the next ten years, L. D. and I collaborated on books, articles, lectures, and public exhibits based on the materials in his private collection. In 1988, through a combination gift/purchase arrangement, L. D. placed his Faulkner collection at Southeast Missouri State University, and the university established the Center for Faulkner Studies, which I directed for the next twenty-five years. Throughout those years, until his death in 2014, L. D. continued his active involvement with the Center, acquiring additional items for the collection, working with me on various programs and projects, and assisting the visiting scholars, American and international, who came to conduct research at the Center.

My work with L. D. and the Faulkner Center has afforded many opportunities to be involved in the field of Faulkner studies. I have authored or coedited twenty-one books on Faulkner, including *Myself and the World: A Biography of William Faulkner*; *Faulkner: A Comprehensive Guide to the Brodsky Collection*; *A William Faulkner Encyclopedia*; *Teaching Faulkner: Approaches and Methods*;

and *My Life with Faulkner and Brodsky*. I've served on the program staff of the annual Faulkner and Yoknapatawpha Conference at the University of Mississippi, directed Faulkner seminars for the National Endowment for the Humanities and the Missouri Humanities Council, and lectured on Faulkner throughout the United States and in England, the Netherlands, Romania, Japan, China, and Taiwan. In *Light in August* Faulkner has Lena Grove say, "My, my, how a body does get around," as he takes her from Alabama to Mississippi and Tennessee. He has taken me much, much farther.

The essays in this volume date from 1980 to 2020. Except for a few changes to make the language gender neutral and race sensitive, update endnotes and referenced time spans, and minimize redundancy, I have resisted the temptation to revise the early essays. Some of my observations and conclusions have been validated, some opposed, by later scholars; but all criticism, like all literature, belongs to a particular time and place, and (except for the changes noted above) I have decided to let the essays stand as they were originally written. One of the pet peeves of scholars as old as I is to read or hear an interpretation or conclusion without attribution to the individual who had already made the point decades previously. Perhaps one advantage of including my earliest essays in this volume is to recognize and acknowledge some of the pioneering scholars who paved the way for so many of us in our study of Faulkner.

As readers will quickly discover, my study of Faulkner has led me down a variety of paths, some of which are quite different from those traveled by other scholars. For example, while I acknowledge that in many ways Faulkner is the quintessential southern writer, I also seek to place his work in the broader context of American, and even international, settings. In addition to discussions of his techniques and meanings, I explore some of the psychological underpinnings of both the origin and the form of his art. I explore intertextual linkages of his fiction with that of other writers. Perhaps most significantly, I argue that his film work in Hollywood is much better and of far greater value than most scholars have acknowledged. (In this connection, I've been pleased to note that Carl Rollyson's recent biography of Faulkner takes a giant step in remedying this neglect.)

In recent decades Faulkner studies have focused largely on the specialized areas of race, class, and gender. Such studies are valid and significant, but my approach has always been more general, more broadly humanistic, even universal. To illustrate, I cite my explorations of Faulkner's use of myth, as well as my view that the overarching themes of all of Faulkner's works relate to time and consequent change. The history of Faulkner's Yoknapatawpha stretches from the arrival of the white settlers on the Mississippi frontier in the early 1800s to the beginnings of the civil rights movement in the 1940s. In between are stories that relate to the antebellum plantation world supported by chattel slavery, the Civil War and emancipation, Reconstruction, Jim Crow, the decline of the old aristocracy and the rise of the yeoman farmers of the middle and lower classes, World Wars I and II, the Great Depression, and the intrusion of industrialization into the agrarian economy.

Caught in this world of continual change that produces a great degree of uncertainty and ambivalence, the Faulkner character (and reader) must weigh the traditions of the past against the demands of the present and the future. Faulkner's tragic characters—such as Quentin Compson, Gail Hightower, Emily Grierson, Thomas Sutpen, Temple Drake, and Ike McCaslin—are those who cannot escape the past, cannot accept the changes required to adapt to a new world, or—like Joe Christmas and Caddy Compson—are victimized by those who cannot accept change. Other characters, the successful ones it seems to me—like Dilsey Gibson, Lena Grove, Byron Bunch, V. K. Ratliff, Sarty Snopes, Chick Mallison, Linda Snopes, and Lucius Priest—prove willing and able to navigate the sometimes turbulent waters caused by the conflict of the past and present, tradition and progress.

In his novels and stories, William Faulkner sought to explore, honestly and faithfully, the ambivalent and delicate relationship that exists between every individual and his or her society. Although Faulkner recognizes that the specific issues and questions will change from one generation or culture to the next, he believed there are certain general principles that apply to all situations. The overriding principle is that all issues must be considered in the context of a genuine concern for ethical, moral values, for what Faulkner called "the old verities and truths of the heart," specifically, "love and honor and pity and pride and compassion and sacrifice." Thus, it is not enough just to be able, like Jason Compson and Flem Snopes, to adapt to a changing world; one must be careful not to forfeit one's soul in doing so. In order to be faithful to such "verities," we must never allow our allegiance to our society to blind us to its shortcomings and failings. At the same time, a hatred for those traditions and practices that are contemptible should never seduce us into betraying those elements in our personal and cultural history that are positive and good. As the content and form of Faulkner's fiction imply, only the individual can decide which aspects of any culture are deemed worth preserving; it is left to each of us to discover, even to fashion, as best we can, our own voice out of the many voices that float through our minds and experiences. As Faulkner acknowledges, this process of discovery and growth is a difficult and sometimes painful one; yet to engage in that quest is to realize the very essence of what it means to be human.

As we know from the several biographies of Faulkner, including the latest excellent one by Carl Rollyson, Faulkner suffered numerous physical, emotional, and psychological ailments. Given his trying circumstances, how he was able to produce so many magnificent novels and stories is quite remarkable. In his Nobel Prize Acceptance Speech he spoke of "the agony and sweat of the human spirit" that goes into artistic creation, and for him that struggle was particularly acute. Poor and neglected for much of his life, suffering from chronic depression and the disease of alcoholism, unhappy in his personal life—Faulkner overcame tremendous obstacles to achieve his success. One of the major themes of his novels and stories is endurance, and his biography exhibits that quality in abundance. Like the most admirable of his characters, Faulkner as both man and artist endured, and ultimately prevailed. Not only his books, but also his life, can inspire others to do the same.

Acknowledgments

Listed below are the places where several of these essays were first published. I am grateful to the publications for permission to reprint the essays in this volume.

"*As I Lay Dying*: The Oprah Book Club Lectures," *Teaching Faulkner*, no. 26 (Fall 2008).

"Beyond the Edge of the Map: Faulkner, Turner, and the Frontier Line," in *Faulkner in the Twenty-First Century: Faulkner and Yoknapatawpha, 2000*, ed. Robert W. Hamblin and Ann J. Abadie (Jackson: University Press of Mississippi, 2003).

"Carcassonne in Mississippi: Faulkner's Geography of the Imagination," in *Faulkner and the Craft of Fiction*, ed. Doreen Fowler and Ann J. Abadie (Jackson: University Press of Mississippi, 1989).

"'A Casebook on Mankind': Faulkner's Use of Shakespeare," *Teaching Faulkner*, no. 15 (Fall 1999).

"The Curious Case of Faulkner's 'The De Gaulle Story,'" *Faulkner Journal* 16 (Fall 2000/Spring 2001).

"'Did You Ever Have a Sister?': Salinger's Holden Caulfield and Faulkner's Quentin Compson," *Teaching Faulkner*, no. 14 (Fall 1998).

"Faulkner and Hollywood: A Call for Reassessment," in *Faulkner and Film*, ed. Peter Lurie and Ann J. Abadie (Jackson: University Press of Mississippi, 2014).

"Faulkner's Hucks and Jims," in Robert W. Hamblin and Melanie Speight, eds., *Faulkner and Twain* (Cape Girardeau: Southeast Missouri State University Press, 2009).

"'A Fine Loud Grabble and Snatch of AAA and WPA': Faulkner, Government, and the Individual," *Arkansas Review* 31 (April 2000).

"Homo Agonistes, or, William Faulkner as Sportswriter," *Aethlon: The Journal of Sport Literature* 13 (Spring 1996).

"The International Faulkner," in *East-West Cultural Passage*, Lucian Blaga University, Sibiu, Romania, 13 (July 2013).

"'Like a Big Soft Fading Wheel': The Triumph of Faulkner's Art," in *Faulkner at 100: Retrospect and Prospect*, ed. Donald M. Kartiganer and Ann J. Abadie (Jackson: University Press of Mississippi, 2000).

"'Longer than Anything': Faulkner's 'Grand Design' in Absalom, Absalom!" in *Faulkner and the Artist*, ed. Donald M. Kartiganer and Ann J. Abadie (Jackson: University Press of Mississippi, 1996).

"Mythic and Archetypal Approaches," in *A Companion to Faulkner Studies*, ed. Charles A. Peek and Robert W. Hamblin (Westport, CT.: Greenwood Press, 2004).

"No Such Thing as Was": William Faulkner and Southern History. Cape Girardeau, MO: Center for Faulkner Studies, 1994.

"'Saying No to Death': Toward William Faulkner's Theory of Fiction," in *"A Cosmos of My Own": Faulkner and Yoknapatawpha 1980*, ed. Doreen Fowler and Ann J. Abadie (Jackson: University Press of Mississippi, 1981).

"Teaching *Intruder in the Dust* through Its Political and Historical Context," in *Teaching Faulkner: Approaches and Methods*, ed. Stephen Hahn and Robert W. Hamblin (Westport, CT: Greenwood Press, 2000).

"The World Is like an Enormous Spider Web": The Contrasting Legacies of Thomas Sutpen and Cass Mastern," in Christopher Rieger and Robert W. Hamblin, eds., *Faulkner and Warren* (Cape Girardeau: Southeast Missouri State University Press, 2015).

"Faulkner and Steinbeck" was presented at the Steinbeck Centennial Celebration at the National Steinbeck Center in Salinas, California, in 2002. "The Artistic Design of *The Sound and the Fury*" was presented at Willamette University in Salem, Oregon, in 2007. "Contextual Readings of *The Sound and the Fury*" was presented at National Taiwan University, Taipei, 2008. "The International Faulkner" was presented at the 2013 "International Faulkner" conference at Lucian Blaga University in Sibiu, Romania. I'm grateful, respectively, to the National Steinbeck Center, Michael Strelow, Wen-ching Ho, and Didi-Ionel Cenuser for the invitations to present these papers.

Given that my involvement in Faulkner studies has now spanned more than a half century, it would be impossible for me to thank all of the individuals who have assisted me along the way. But I must name at least a few. Principal among those are the three listed on the dedication page—my wife, Kaye; my friend and collaborator L. D. Brodsky; and my mentor and friend John Pilkington. I have also benefited greatly from my interactions over the years with my colleagues on the Teaching Faulkner panels at the Faulkner and Yoknapatawpha conferences: Jim Carothers, Chuck Peek, Arlie Herron, Terrell Tebbetts, Theresa Towner, and Brian McDonald. I offer special thanks to Ann Abadie, Gerald Walton, and Jay Martin, who have encouraged and supported not only my Faulkner work but also my other writing endeavors. I also wish to acknowledge the support of a succession of administrators at my home institution, Southeast Missouri State University: Bill Stacy, Les Cochran, Robert Foster, Fred Goodwin, Henry Sessoms, Martin Jones, Jane Stephens, Robert Burns, Carol Scates, Kayla Stroup, Charles Kupchella, Dale Nitzschke, Kenneth Dobbins, and Frank Barrios.

Abbreviations

Unless otherwise noted, citations are to Random House Vintage Books editions.

AA   *Absalom, Absalom!* (Vintage International)
AILD   *As I Lay Dying* (Vintage International)
CS   *Collected Stories*
EPP   *William Faulkner: Early Prose and Poetry*, ed. Carvel Collins (Boston: Little, Brown, 1962)
ESPL   *William Faulkner: Essays, Speeches, and Public Letters*, ed. James B. Meriwether (New York: Random House, 1965)
F   *A Fable* (New York: Random House, 1954).
FB   *Faulkner: A Biography* by Joseph Blotner (New York: Random House, 1974)
FCF   *The Faulkner-Cowley File: Letters and Memories, 1944–1962* (New York: Viking Press, 1966)
FID   *Flags in the Dust/Sartoris* (Vintage International)
FIU   *Faulkner in the University: Class Conferences at the University of Virginia, 1957–1958*, ed. Frederick L. Gwynn and Joseph L. Blotner (Charlottesville: University of Virginia Press, 1959)
FR   *The Faulkner Reader* (New York: Random House, 1954)
FWP   *Faulkner at West Point*, ed. Joseph L. Fant III and Robert Ashley (New York: Random House, 1964)
GDM   *Go Down, Moses* (Vintage International)
H   *The Hamlet*
IID   *Intruder in the Dust*
KG   *Knight's Gambit*
LIA   *Light in August*
LIG   *Lion in the Garden: Interviews with William Faulkner, 1926–1962*, ed. James B. Meriwether and Michael Millgate (New York: Random House, 1968)
M   *The Mansion*
MF   *The Marble Faun* (New York: Random House, 1965)
Mos   *Mosquitoes* (New York: Liveright, 2011)
P   *Pylon* (Vintage International)
PF   *The Portable Faulkner*, ed. Malcolm Cowley, rev. ed. (New York: Penguin Books, 1967)
R   *The Reivers*
RFN   *Requiem for a Nun*

S	*Sanctuary*
SF	*The Sound and the Fury* (Vintage International)
SL	*Selected Letters of William Faulkner*
SP	*Soldiers' Pay*
T	*The Town*
U	*The Unvanquished* (Vintage International)
US	*Uncollected Stories*
WP	*The Wild Palms/If I Forget Thee, Jerusalem* (Vintage International)

Critical Essays on William Faulkner

Faulkner, Myth, and Archetype

Any consideration of the role of myth and archetype in Faulkner's work must examine two related but quite distinct aspects of mythic practice. The first involves an author's use of mythological plots, characters, and themes in writing his or her own novels, stories, poems, or plays. In this essay this approach will be identified by the name given it by T. S. Eliot—"the mythical method." The second approach concerns an author's invention of an original set of characters, places, events, and beliefs that, taken together, create the semblance and significance of ancient myth. Modern examples of such authorial myths include the visionary works of William Butler Yeats, the Poictesme novels of James Branch Cabell, the "Myth of America" poetry of Hart Crane, the Narnia novels of C. S. Lewis, and the symbolic fantasies of J. R. R. Tolkien. Over the decades scholars have found both of these classifications of myth relevant to Faulkner. His works have been carefully analyzed in relation to ancient myths, specifically Greco-Roman and Christian; and he has been heralded for creating, in his extended series of interlocking novels and stories, a mythical world of his own, the one now universally known as Yoknapatawpha.

THE MYTHICAL METHOD

In his extraordinarily prescient review of James Joyce's *Ulysses*, T. S. Eliot gave a name to a relatively new literary trend that would become increasingly prominent in the years and decades to come. Eliot asserts that in using Homer's narrative of the epic journey of Ulysses in the *Odyssey* as the framework for the twentieth-century story of Leopold Bloom, "Mr. Joyce is pursuing a method which others must pursue after him. . . . It is a method for which the horoscope is auspicious. Psychology . . . , ethnology, and *The Golden Bough* have concurred to make possible what was impossible even a few years ago. Instead of narrative method, we may now use the mythical method."[1]

As Eliot defines the term, "the mythical method" involves an author's "manipulating a continuous parallel between contemporaneity and antiquity," the purpose being to provide "a way of controlling, of ordering, of giving a shape and a significance to the immense panorama of futility and anarchy which is contemporary history." Clearly, Eliot saw the use of myth as one means of understanding and resisting the chaotic conditions dramatized by World War I. While other writers, including Faulkner, would direct the application of myth away from the political and philosophical agenda of Eliot, the fact remains that Eliot correctly identified the literary technique that would come to dominate the practice of writers of his, and the next, generation.

Eliot could write so knowingly about Joyce's use of the mythical method, of course, because Eliot himself was employing the same principle in his work. *The Waste Land*, published one year earlier than his review of Joyce's novel, similarly draws heavily upon mythic sources, as Eliot explains in the copious footnotes to the poem. Eliot specifically cites Jessie L. Weston's study of the Grail legend, *From Ritual to Romance*, and Sir James George Frazer's *The Golden Bough* as major influences upon his poem.

Just as Weston and Frazer sought to demonstrate that many aspects of western civilization have actually evolved from pagan rituals and beliefs, so Eliot merged the Christian myth of death, burial, and resurrection with corresponding details from primitive vegetation myths. Woven into these blended myths are also quotations from or allusions to nearly three dozen authors representing various historical epochs. All such elements, mythic and literary, become for the narrator of Eliot's poem "fragments" to be "shored against [the] ruins" of contemporary chaos.

As Eliot notes in his review of *Ulysses*, recent developments in psychology and anthropology had laid the foundation for the mythical method of writing. In his reference to psychology, Eliot was undoubtedly alluding to the pioneering work of Sigmund Freud and Carl Jung, both of whom were engaged in analyzing the role of the subconscious mind in human behavior. Indeed, Freud's utilization of the term *Oedipus complex*, applying the actions in Sophocles' ancient play to the behavior of certain patients, parallels Joyce's reprise of Homeric materials. Even more than Freud, Jung would become crucial to the development of mythic literary practice because of his insistence, in a significant extension of Freudian theory, that individuals possess not only a personal but also a "collective" unconscious, or "racial memory," in which are stored "archetypes" that embody the memories and experiences of the entire human race. According to Jung, these archetypes, which he calls "primordial images," have supplied the characters, situations, symbols, and themes of stories from primitive societies onward throughout history. Examples of archetypes may be found in the symbolism typically associated with such images as water (creation, purification, redemption), circles (wholeness, unity), gardens (paradise, fertility), and various colors (red: blood, sacrifice; green: hope, progress; black: evil, melancholy, death; white: purity, innocence), as well as such universal character types as the Innocent, the Serpent, the Great Mother, the Wise Old Man, the Hero, the Trickster, and the Scapegoat. Writers being individuals in whom the working of the collective unconscious is particularly strong, these archetypal symbols, motifs, and character types will naturally find expression in literary works, quite independent of the conscious awareness or intention of the writers themselves.[2]

While Jung's theory of the collective unconscious provides one of the major underpinnings of the mythical method, giving it a psychological and even pseudo-scientific validity, it is important to recognize that writers and critics quickly broadened the definition of "archetype" to include cultural and conscious—as well as personal and unconscious—derivatives of older materials. It is this wider definition that Eliot alludes to in his mention of the importance of ethnology and *The Golden Bough*. Here his reference is almost certainly to the Cambridge Hellenists, an influential group of British scholars, including F. M. Cornford, Gilbert Murray, and Jane Harrison, as well as Frazer, who were busily applying recent anthropological findings to the examination of the mythic and ritualistic origins of Greek drama. Their aim was to discover the essential and universal truths of existence buried, like treasures in ancient tombs, in the narratives embraced by early cultures.

A conscious (or at least semiconscious) use of literary archetypes would be further explored by Maud Bodkin, a British psychologist and literary critic whose *Archetypal Patterns in Poetry: Psychological Studies of Imagination* represents another important contribution to the development of mythic criticism. Bodkin applied Jung's theories to wider cultural and linguistic considerations. For Bodkin archetypes are located not so much within the individual consciousness as in "the common nature lived and immediately experienced by the members of a group or community." While not denying a "biological inheritance" of archetypes, Bodkin argues for a "social inheritance" as well, one that is passed down from generation to generation through language and the recycling of narrative and poetic patterns.[3]

This idea of a "social inheritance" best interpreted by anthropologists and archaeologists explains the importance to Eliot and other mythic writers and critics of Frazer's *The Golden Bough*. An encyclopedia (eventually comprising twelve volumes) of primitive man's beliefs and practices, *The Golden Bough* documents Frazer's notions of how the superstitions and magic rituals of pre-historic cultures evolved into the religious practices of the civilized, Christian world. Specifically, Frazer investigated the practice of primitive societies in ritualistically slaying an aging king, thought to be divine, and replacing him with a younger, more vigorous successor. Only by so doing, the ancients believed, could the vitality and health of their culture be ensured. In such primitive concepts, Frazer argued, could be found the origins of the basic tenets of Judeo-Christian theology, as well as many modern secular behaviors such as hero worship and scapegoating. Perhaps the most famous literary expressions of Frazer's notions are the uses of the Fisher King motif in Eliot's *The Waste Land* and Hemingway's *The Sun Also Rises* and of the scapegoat motif in Shirley Jackson's "The Lottery," but one has only to place the text of Faulkner's "The Bear" alongside Frazer's chapter on "Killing the Sacred Bear" to understand the relevance of Frazer to Faulkner studies as well.

Predictably in a culture heavily influenced by Judeo-Christian thought, biblical myths have provided especially fruitful material for writers seeking to import older narratives into their contemporary works. This pattern is clearly illustrated by such works as Thomas Mann's *Joseph and His Brothers*, Robinson Jeffers's *Tamar*, Archibald MacLeish's *J. B.*, Thornton Wilder's *The Skin of Our Teeth*, and John Steinbeck's *East of Eden*, as well as several works by Faulkner.

As demonstrated by Eliot's allusions in *The Waste Land* to earlier writers such as Dante, Chaucer, Spenser, Shakespeare, and Goldsmith, and even more recent authors such as Baudelaire, the mythical method quickly came to embrace the use of any literary predecessor (particularly authors of "classics" well known to the reading public) a writer would find useful to his or her purposes. Thus, the mythical method may be understood to apply not only to such works as Eugene O'Neill's retelling of the classical myths of Oedipus (*Desire under the Elms*) and Agamemnon (*Mourning Becomes Electra*) or Robert Bly's employment of an ancient folk tale in *Iron John* but also to such literary adaptations and restatements as Joseph Conrad's use of Dante's *Inferno* in *Heart of Darkness*, Robert Penn Warren's recycling of Shakespeare's *Julius Caesar* and Milton's *Paradise Lost* in *All the King's Men*, William Golding's ironic employment of island utopias from Sir Thomas More's to R. M. Ballantyne's in *Lord of the Flies*, and Jane Smiley's retelling of *King Lear* in *A Thousand Acres*. The process is ongoing, of course, so that by now Faulkner's texts have also become a "mythic" pattern for later writers: *The Sound and the Fury*, for example, provides much of the design for William Styron's *Lie Down in Darkness*, and Graham Swift's *Last Orders* is modeled on *As I Lay Dying*.

Building upon the psychological theories of Freud, Jung, and Bodkin, the anthropological materials provided by Frazer and the other Cambridge Hellenists, and the literary practice of Joyce, Eliot, and others, a number of influential thinkers and critics have applied and extended the tenets of mythic literary theory. Joseph Campbell, in *The Hero with a Thousand Faces* and the multivolume *Masks of God*, greatly expanded comparative mythology to include studies of Native American, Eskimo, Australian, and Oriental as well as Greek and Christian stories, finding in all of them the same recurring myths and archetypes, especially that of the "monomyth," the story of the hero's journey, initiation, and return that, according to Campbell, supplies the single pattern that undergirds all mythic structures. Northrop Frye, in his seminal *Anatomy of Criticism*, argues that the seasonal cycles of the year stand as archetypes for the major literary genres: spring for comedy, summer for romance, fall for tragedy, and winter for irony. Frye has been particularly influential in incorporating literary antecedents as myth, calling attention to the "reverberating significance, in which every literary work catches the echoes of all other works of its type in literature, and so ripples out into the rest of literature and thence into life."[4] Claude Lévi-Strauss, the generally acknowledged founder of structuralism, is equally important as a mythic theorist. His *Structural Anthropology* seeks to identify the basic structural features in myth ("mythemes") that are comparable to the fundamental components of language (for example, phonemes and morphemes) identified by structural linguists such as Ferdinand de Saussure. Like other myth critics, Lévi-Strauss is concerned to decode the essences that are embedded within all narratives.

All of the individuals cited above would tend to agree that the aim of mythical and archetypal criticism is "to see beneath the surface of 'story' to essential and lasting concerns of the human race, to recognize the repetitions of man's history and the commonality of the human condition throughout man's life, and to realize the craftsmanship of the author in weaving his creation with the very stuff of all men's lives."[5] As this observation reveals, the mythic writer or critic is primarily concerned with two principal aspects of life and literature: universality and repetition. The two characteristics are mutually dependent: the same old stories are told over and over again because they are universally true, and one knows that they are true because they are repeated in all times and places.[6]

FAULKNER AND THE MYTHICAL METHOD

While Faulkner seems to have had little direct involvement with the works or ideas of Freud, Jung, or any of the mythic or archetypal critics except Eliot, he clearly identified with the basic principles of the mythical approach to literature. On at least one occasion Faulkner discussed the symbolic aspects of his work in language that almost exactly parallels Jung's notion of the collective unconscious. "What symbolism is in the books," Faulkner told one interviewer, "is evidently instinct in man, not in man's knowledge but in his inheritance of his old dreams, in his blood, perhaps his bones, rather than in the storehouse of his memory, his intellect" (*LIG* 126). More often, however, Faulkner spoke of artistic genesis in language resembling Maud Bodkin's theory of socially embodied archetypes. The writer, Faulkner said, "collects his material all his life from everything he reads, from everything he listens to, everything he sees, and he stores that away in a sort of filing cabinet" (*FIU* 116). Speaking of the Christian elements in his fiction, Faulkner explained,

> The Christian legend is part of any Christian's background, especially the background of a country boy, a Southern country boy. My life was passed, my childhood, in a very small Mississippi town, and that was a part of my background. I grew up with that. I assimilated that, took that in without even knowing it. (*FIU* 86)

Such statements as these invite one to identify the role of Quentin Compson and his use of memory in *Absalom, Absalom!* with the function of the artist.

If Faulkner tended to agree with the mythic critics regarding the genesis of a writer's work, he was similarly persuaded of their opinions concerning the universals and repetitions of human history. This latter point explains Faulkner's tendency to downplay his regionalism, his southernness. For Faulkner regionalism was only a means to a greater end. He wrote to Malcolm Cowley:

> I'm inclined to think that my material, the South, is not very important to me. I just happen to know it, and don't have time in one life to learn another one and write at the same time. Though the one I know is probably as good as another, life is a phenomenon but not a novelty, the same frantic steeplechase toward nothing everywhere and man stinks the same stink no matter where in time. (*FCF* 14–15)

At Virginia he said: "I feel that the verities which these [characters] suffer are universal verities—that is, that man, whether he's black or white or red or yellow still suffers the same anguishes, he has the same aspirations, his follies are the same follies, his triumphs are the same triumphs. . . . And in that sense there's no such thing as a regional writer" (*FIU* 197). At West Point, just weeks before he died, Faulkner reiterated this point: "The writer is simply trying to use the best method he possibly can find to tell you a true and moving and familiar old, old story of the human heart in conflict with itself for the old, old human verities and truth, which are love, hope, fear, compassion, greed, lust" (*FWP* 59).

Given the developing interest in myth and its literary uses among the writers and thinkers of Faulkner's generation, as well as his own statements on the subject, it is not at all surprising that a considerable amount of criticism has been devoted to Faulkner's use of myth. A number of early reviewers, most notably Evelyn Scott, who produced an insightful monograph to accompany the publication of *The Sound and the Fury*, and André Malraux, who wrote the preface for the French edition of *Sanctuary*, called attention to Faulkner's affinity with ancient myths, both Greco-Roman and Christian; and later critics would develop these parallels in greater depth. During the 1950s, when Faulkner's international reputation as a Nobel laureate encouraged scholars to emphasize the universality of his work, mythic criticism provided a highly useful approach. The publication of *A Fable* in 1954 gave further impetus to mythical approaches to Faulkner. Even those reviewers who disliked the book (and there were many) could not ignore the centrality of the Christ myth to Faulkner's novel of modern warfare.

THE INITIATION MOTIF

Faulkner's fondness for mythic correspondences is nowhere more apparent than in his use and reuse of the "initiation" motif. Like Dickens, time and again Faulkner returns to the fate of innocence in a tragic world. "I am telling the same story over and over," Faulkner wrote to Cowley, "which is myself and the world" (*FCF* 14); and he observed of his use of the stream image in *The Sound and the Fury*, "I saw that [the] peaceful glinting of that branch was to become the dark, harsh flowing of time sweeping [Caddy] to where she could not return."[7] As in the works of Milton and Blake, Innocence and Experience represent the essential oppositions in Faulkner's world.

Consistent with the ironic pattern of the mythical method, however, Faulkner usually excludes from his "monomyth" of initiation any type of heroic return or triumph (the Lena Grove story in *Light in August* and the

Lucius Priest narrative in *The Reivers* are notable exceptions). In Faulkner's world the Fall is seldom fortunate.

"That Evening Sun" stands as the prototype of Faulkner's many treatments of initiation.[8] Faulkner develops his theme by ironically juxtaposing the adult world of sex (including adultery and prostitution) and of death (including suicide and anticipated murder) with the ignorance and innocence of children. These contrasting extremes come together, though only barely, in the person of Quentin, the oldest child and narrator of the story. In Quentin's characterization Faulkner dramatizes the moment when childhood innocence gives way to the beginnings of mature perception and understanding. Quentin's initiation thus serves to bridge the opposing worlds of innocence and awareness and, further, to foreshadow the impending fate of the other children.

The adult world of "That Evening Sun" is a tragic one permeated with real and imagined evil. In Mr. Stovall's abuse of Nancy, in Jesus's expressed antagonism toward white men, in Nancy's promiscuity, drug addiction, and paranoia, in Mr. Compson's indifference to Nancy's possible fate, in Mrs. Compson's selfishness, one perceives a problematic world in which cruelty and a propensity to violence pervade both individual and societal relations. Though the starkness of these details is somewhat muted by the limited perspective of the child-narrator's viewpoint, the reader can hardly miss the bleakness of the situation. Without question the overriding tenor of the story is one of hopelessness and despair.

The sinister threat that hovers over all the characters of the story is personified by Jesus, Nancy's husband. Appropriately, Jesus exists primarily as an abstraction. His one brief appearance, "with his razor scar on his black face like a piece of dirty string" (*CS* 292) and his vengeful remarks about white men, while supporting the identification of Jesus with evil, hardly accounts for the degree of fear and repulsion that the other characters feel toward the man. Faulkner makes Jesus (his name, by the way, is one of the clearest examples of irony in all of Faulkner's works) more than a wronged black man harboring revenge; he becomes an unseen but unavoidable presence, a spectral figure linked with forebodings of doom. Significantly, Nancy identifies him with Satan: "He say I done woke up the devil in him" (294–95).

The children have strict instructions to stay away from Jesus. As Quentin observes, "We would stop at the ditch, because father told us to not have anything to do with Jesus . . . and we would throw rocks at Nancy's house until she came to the door" (290). Mrs. Compson objects to her husband's willingness to "leave these children unprotected, with that Negro about" (294). However, all such attempts to shield the children are bound to fail. When Dilsey, the regular housekeeper, becomes ill, Nancy enters the Compson household, bringing with her Jesus and all he symbolizes.

If Jesus is the personification of a general and pervasive evil, Caddy serves as the principal embodiment of childhood innocence. Throughout the narrative she constantly displays ignorance and naiveté—as well as a compulsive curiosity—about the adult situation. "Off of what vine?" "Talking what way?" "Let what white men alone? How let them alone?" "Slit whose belly, Nancy?" "All right from what, Nancy? Is Jesus mad at you?" "What's the matter with you, Nancy?" "What, Father? What's going to happen?" (292ff.) All such questionings dramatize a child's inability to penetrate or comprehend the world of adults.

Only Quentin among the children comes to discern something of Nancy's pitiful plight. There are three instances in the story that suggest Quentin's unique understanding, limited though it be, of Nancy's dilemma. The first occurs early in the narrative when Nancy, in acknowledgment of Quentin's being the oldest child, attempts to justify her behavior to him: "I aint nothing but a n——r. It aint none of my fault" (293). The second is found in the scene in which Quentin clarifies for a miscomprehending Caddy the nature of Nancy's desperate prayer: "It's the other Jesus [that is, not her husband] she means" (297). Finally, and most importantly, toward the end of the story, after he has viewed the disabling effect of Nancy's fear and paranoia, Quentin asks, "Who will do our washing now, Father?" (309) Like the other children, Quentin is a long way from being an adult in this story; but, appropriately for the oldest child, he is the youngster who comes closest to understanding Nancy's predicament.

Viewing "That Evening Sun" as an initiation story about childhood innocence invites a further consideration of the title of the story. As various critics have noted, the title seems to derive from the lyrics of W. C. Handy's "St. Louis Blues": "I hate to see that evenin' sun go down / 'Cause that man of mine done left this town." Linked with Nancy, the title is highly ironic, since Nancy's blues result from her fear, even conviction, that her man has *not* left her town. But the title surely relates to the children as much as to Nancy; and the opening line of the title's source, "I hate to see that evenin' sun go down," fairly echoes Faulkner's regret, expressed many times but perhaps most poignantly in his reference to Caddy and the stream imagery (quoted above), concerning the inevitable fate of childhood innocence.[9]

Faulkner's narratives of initiation take many different forms, and not all of them involve children. *Soldiers' Pay*, Faulkner's contribution to the Lost

Generation novel, traces the painful adjustment that Donald Mahon and other soldiers must make in returning to a homeland largely unaffected by the tragic experiences of war. *Sartoris/Flags in the Dust* extends the Lost Generation motif to make Bayard Sartoris's story representative of the displacement of a traditional, rural society (symbolized by the horse and the hunt) by a modern, mechanized society (symbolized by the airplane and the automobile). *The Sound and the Fury*, which continues the initiation of the Compson children begun in "That Evening Sun," and *As I Lay Dying* both register a growing cynicism and disillusionment concerning familial relationships—brother-sister, child-parent, and husband-wife. *Sanctuary* and its sequel, *Requiem for a Nun*, trace the Fall experience of Temple Drake, an Ole Miss student who must cope with both rape and confinement in a Memphis brothel—and with her own willful collusion in her tragic circumstances. In *Light in August* Joe Christmas is initiated into, and destroyed by, a southern society ruled by excessive Puritanism and racial bigotry. Racial conflicts also provide the context of the coming-of-age stories of Thomas Sutpen, Isaac McCaslin, and Chick Mallison in *Absalom, Absalom!*, *Go Down, Moses*, and *Intruder in the Dust*. *The Unvanquished* traces the maturation process of Bayard Sartoris. *The Wild Palms/If I Forget Thee, Jerusalem* presents disillusioning experiences in relation to dual quests for romantic love and human freedom. The Snopes trilogy follows the destructive influences of the Snopes clan upon Frenchman's Bend and Jefferson. *A Fable* recounts the crucifixion of a Christ figure who tries to stop a war. Not insignificantly, Faulkner's last novel, *The Reivers*, returns to the treatment of childhood, recounting the initiatory experiences of eleven-year-old Lucius Priest during his first trip to Memphis.

THE CHRIST STORY AND *A FABLE*

Faulkner's most ambitious use of the mythical method is to be found in *A Fable*, published in 1954. Conceived in Hollywood during the mid-forties, labored at for more than a decade, called by Faulkner his "big book" (*SL* 328ff.) and by Random House his "crowning achievement" (dust jacket flap), *A Fable* has been generally regarded as Faulkner's hugest novelistic failure. Lawrance Thompson's judgment is typical: "Perhaps the worst artistic fault is that the allegorical skeleton sticks through the flesh unpleasantly, and the characters come too near to being types who seem created too largely for purposes of illuminating the thinly-concealed allegorical meaning."[10] As more sympathetic critics have argued, however, such negative judgments are mistaken, deriving largely from a misunderstanding of Faulkner's intention in his application of Christian myth.

A Fable merges the Christ story into the account of an obscure French corporal who leads a mutiny during the latter stages of World War I. This soldier, who is born in a stable and is the illegitimate son of the Supreme Commander of the Allied Forces, gathers around himself a squad of twelve disciples and travels with them throughout the front lines encouraging both French and German troops to lay down their arms. For a brief time it appears that the idealistic scheme of the corporal and his followers will succeed, as the refusal of one French regiment to attack leads to a temporary cessation of fighting all across the battlefront. However, the corporal and the other rebellious soldiers are arrested, and high-level Allied and German commanders conspire to ensure the resumption of the war.

On Thursday of Faulkner's modern-day Passion Week, the jailors serve a meal to the corporal and his squad. They have been imprisoned because Polchak, a fellow soldier, has betrayed the corporal into the hands of the authorities. Another companion, appropriately named Pierre Bouc, denies his leader. Following the reenactment of the Last Supper, the corporal is called away to a private meeting with his father, the Supreme Commander. From a point overlooking the city of Paris, in a scene that recalls both Christ in the Garden of Gethsemane and Satan's temptation of Christ in the wilderness, the old Marshal offers the corporal secret passage to safety. The corporal, however, refuses the offer, and returns to his cell. The next day he is tied to a post between two criminals and executed by a firing squad. When he is shot, he falls into a coil of barbed wire—Faulkner's equivalent of the crown of thorns. Following the execution the corporal's half-sisters, Marthe and Marya, claim the body for burial on the family home site; but shortly after the burial an artillery shell hits the area, destroying any trace of the corporal's grave or body.

After the war some soldiers are assigned to locate an unidentified corpse to be placed in the Unknown Soldier's tomb under the Arc de Triomphe. Ironically, they unwittingly secure the body of the disgraced corporal and deliver it to Paris, to lie under the eternal flame as the symbol of the heroic sacrifice made by a common soldier for all humanity. In addition to this natural type of "immortality," the corporal also lives on in the memory and example of the British runner, a Saul-turned-Paul-type disciple whose defiance of the military in the concluding scene of the novel perpetuates the message and actions of the doomed corporal.

As noted earlier, most reviewers and critics panned *A Fable* mercilessly, and, despite the author's and publisher's pride in it, the novel quickly found its way to the bottom of the list of Faulkner's works. And the critics unwilling to leave it there have been few indeed: for example, Dayton Kohler, Heinrich Straumann, Keen Butterworth, Noel Polk, Joseph R. Urgo, Richard Godden. On occasion invited lecturers at the annual Faulkner and Yoknapatawpha Conference have admitted, sometimes even boasted, that they have never bothered to read the novel.

While it is not necessary to defend the novel as an artistic success in order to demonstrate that it clearly shows Faulkner's fondness for biblical myth, it is arguable that an accurate understanding of the nature and function of the mythical method would serve to refute most, if not all, of the objections to the work. First of all, readers should recognize that they are reading a post–World War II novel that is set during World War I and uses the Passion Week of Christ as an analogue for twentieth-century events and issues. As Urgo properly notes, "The corporal . . . is not a *symbolic* Christ, nor is the story an *allegory* based in the life of the historical Jesus."[11] In other words, *A Fable* is not about Christ, or even primarily World War I, but rather the world situation as Faulkner saw it in the late forties and early fifties. In addition, readers must remember that the technique of the mythical method, as Eliot defined it, requires the old myth to be inverted, thereby creating an ironic contrast to the contemporary application. Arguments, therefore, that Faulkner's handling of the Christ story is inconsistent with New Testament accounts are quite beside the point. If readers and critics would take more seriously Faulkner's explanation of his design and purpose, they would understand that the novel is a modern fable and not a literal retelling of the life and death of Christ. As Faulkner explained in a 1944 letter to Robert Haas,

> The argument is (in the fable) in the middle of that war, Christ (some movement in mankind which wished to stop war forever) reappeared and was crucified again. We are repeating, we are in the midst of war again. Suppose Christ gives us one more chance, will we crucify him again, perhaps for the last time. That's crudely put; I am not trying to preach at all. But that is the argument: We did this in 1918; in 1944 it not only MUST NOT happen again, it SHALL NOT HAPPEN again. i.e., ARE WE GOING TO LET IT HAPPEN AGAIN? Now that we are in another war, where the third and final chance might be offered us to save him. (*SL* 180)[12]

As Faulkner already knew from the repetitions of history and the old myths, the answer to that question is Yes. Unlike the gospel accounts, Faulkner's narrative does not end with a divine miracle of resurrection. The ending of

A Fable is just as ironic and no more hopeful than that of *The Sound and the Fury*. "I am not laughing," the old soldier says in the final lines. "What you see are tears" (437).

There are numerous clues planted in the text of *A Fable* that fix the present tense of the narrative in the post–World War II era, and, coincidentally, these are no less accessible than the ones that orient Benjy in the present tense in *The Sound and the Fury*. Among such clues are the direct quotations from Faulkner's 1950 Nobel Prize acceptance speech and allusions to the Marshall Plan, atomic bomb shelters, and house trailers. There are also passages like the following, which seems far more descriptive of totalitarian regimes like Hitler's and Stalin's and Franco's than of the Axis powers during World War I:

> "Bah," the corps commander said again. "It is man who is our enemy: the vast seething moiling spiritless mass of him. Once to each period of his inglorious history, one of us appears with the stature of a giant, suddenly and without warning in the middle of a nation as a dairymaid enters a buttery, and with his sword for paddle he heaps and pounds and stiffens the malleable mass and even holds it cohered and purposeful for a time. But never for always, nor even for very long: sometimes before he can even turn his back, it has relinquished, dis-cohered, faster and faster flowing and seeking back to its own base anonymity." (30)[13]

The military, however, merely substitutes one type of anonymity for another; and it is against all faceless anonymity and in defense of individual freedom that the corporal raises his rebellion and sacrifices his life. This is the conflict, in Faulkner's view, in the secular, political, and militaristic modern world that finds its analogue in Christ's struggle against the religious and cultural establishment of his day.

Readers who approach *A Fable* as a retelling of the New Testament story of Christ are understandably perplexed and even offended by many of Faulkner's alterations in the biblical narrative,[14] perhaps most of all by the fusion of the God figure of the novel, the Supreme Commander, and Satan. Adding to the confusion of this pairing is the fact that it is the satanic figure, the Tempter, who voices the sentiments of Faulkner's Nobel Prize speech: "Oh yes, he will survive . . . [he later adds "prevail"] because he has that in him which will endure even beyond the ultimate worthless tideless rock freezing slowly in the last red and heatless sunset" (354). Such ambiguous attribution of moral and ethical values is hardly biblical, but it is very much the context of the modern world. Cold War readers should have been better able to recognize their contemporary world in the pages of Faulkner's novel; today's readers—post-Vietnam, post-Watergate, post-Clinton, post-terrorism, post-WorldCom—cannot fail to recognize theirs. [Today we could add conspiracy theories, fake news, and "the Big Lie" to this list.]

THE MYTH OF YOKNAPATAWPHA

While Faulkner clearly employed the mythical method by borrowing materials from ancient stories in creating his own fiction, he was also keenly aware that he was inventing his own all-embracing "myth" of people, places, and events in an imaginary Mississippi county he called Yoknapatawpha. It is this inventive, *myth-making* dimension of his art that he had in mind when he spoke of "sublimating the actual into apocryphal" and of creating "a cosmos of [his] own." "I like to think of the world I created," Faulkner continued, "as being a kind of keystone in the Universe; that, as small as that keystone is, if it were ever taken away, the universe itself would collapse" (*LIG* 255). The same intent is captured in the signature Faulkner added to one of his maps of Yoknapatawpha: "William Faulkner, sole owner & proprietor" (*AA* back flyleaf).

Critics have long debated the point at which Faulkner became consciously aware of the overall design of his Yoknapatawpha narratives. It is indisputable that early on, following the advice of Sherwood Anderson, he recognized the literary potential in his "little postage stamp of native soil" (*LIG* 255) and that, almost as soon, he began recycling characters like Horace Benbow, Gavin Stevens, Quentin Compson, the Sartorises, and the Snopeses. Nevertheless, the idea of a highly integrated series of novels and stories spanning several historical epochs and presenting a select number of overarching themes (somewhat on the order, Faulkner said, of Honoré de Balzac's *Comédie humaine*) seems to have been a product of Faulkner's later life and career.

George Marion O'Donnell is generally credited with being the first scholar to call attention to an interlocking pattern in Faulkner's works. O'Donnell's 1939 essay, "Faulkner's Mythology," subsequently challenged as being too reductive, interprets Faulkner's novels as recurring treatments of a southern ethical tradition, symbolized by the Sartorises, being threatened and overrun by an amoral modernism, represented by the Snopeses.[15] But O'Donnell's approach, despite his title, was more allegorical than mythological. The notion that Faulkner was deliberately creating a myth of the South seems primarily (some would say solely) the product of Malcolm Cowley's compilation of *The Portable Faulkner* in 1946.

The promotional blurb on the dust jacket makes clear Cowley's intent in selecting and organizing more than seven hundred pages from Faulkner's various works: "the saga of Yoknapatawpha County, 1820–1945, being the first chronological picture of Faulkner's mythical county in Mississippi." In his introduction to the volume, Cowley argued that Faulkner's work presents "a mythical kingdom" (5) that should be viewed as "an organic unity" (24). Cowley's selection of materials, dating from antebellum and Civil War times through the closing of the frontier and the rise of the poor whites to the racially torn modern South, is chosen to present Faulkner as "an epic or bardic poet in prose, a creator of myths that he weaves together into a legend of the South" (23).

Early readers and reviewers of *The Portable Faulkner* could not know what Cowley would reveal two decades later in *The Faulkner-Cowley File*: that Faulkner had at first been reluctant to accept Cowley's suggestions about a controlling design in his books, particularly one that purported to be "a legend of the South," but that he gradually acceded to Cowley's thesis and eventually even cooperated in the project by supplying a new "Appendix" to *The Sound and the Fury* for inclusion in the text and by drawing a revised map of Yoknapatawpha County to be printed inside the front and back covers of the volume. More significantly, one may argue, once the idea of a Southern "saga" or "legend" had been planted in Faulkner's mind, and long after the appearance of Cowley's book, Faulkner seized opportunities to create missing pieces of the pattern. For example, the historical interchapters of *Requiem for a Nun*, the pseudo-autobiographical essay "Mississippi," and even such political and cultural essays as "On Privacy" and "Address to the Delta Council" strike one as attempts to fill in gaps in the mytho-historical chronicle suggested by Cowley.

Following Cowley's lead (and perhaps Faulkner's own endorsement of Cowley's project), other scholars emphasized the mythic quality of Faulkner's work, particularly as it related to the history of the American South. Irving Howe's influential study defines Faulkner's "Southern myth" as "the fate of a ruined homeland," pitting "[Faulkner's] pride in the past against his despair over the present."[16] Other critics, including Robert Penn Warren, Carvel Collins, William Van O'Connor, Hyatt H. Waggoner, and Richard P. Adams, questioned a too-close identification of Faulkner's works with the South, arguing that Faulkner's myth is not regional but universal.

These last critics were right, of course; and they had the advantage in the ongoing debate because Faulkner agreed with them. On numerous occasions (and as he initially tried to inform Cowley), Faulkner sought to explain that the actual South, both historical and contemporary, was a microcosm, a synecdoche, for a larger Faulknerian cosmos. For example, in 1955 in Manila he stated:

> I think that the setting of a novel is just incidental, that the novelist is writing about truth; I mean by truth, the things that are true to all people, which are love, friendship, courage, fear, greed; that he writes in the tongue which he knows, which happens to be the tongue of his own native land. I doubt if environment or country can be enough inspiration to write a book about, that the writer is simply using the tool which he knows. I write about American Mississippi simply because that is what I know best. (*LIG* 202)

Faulkner undoubtedly felt that he had already explained all of this in "The Bear," if readers had only paid closer attention. There he presents a detailed overview of southern history but makes it unequivocally clear that that history is representative of a far broader experience. "Dispossessed of Eden," the refrain that runs throughout part four of the story, expresses the central theme of the narrative; and that theme is applied to a series of situations that range from the personal to the universal. At the simplest level "The Bear" presents the initiation of a young woodsman, Isaac "Ike" McCaslin. The deaths of Sam Fathers, Old Ben, and Lion and the corresponding disappearance of the wilderness expose Ike to the tragic realities of time and change and loss, of life's defeats and limitations. Simultaneously, Ike discovers sin and guilt when he reads in the old family ledgers of his grandfather's miscegenation, incest, and inhumanity. Through this double initiation Faulkner intensifies Ike's loss of childhood innocence and his emergence into adult awareness and responsibility.

To extend this bildungsroman beyond the individual and the immediate, Faulkner places Ike's story within a framework of symbolic allusions and parallels. The pattern of the work may be diagrammed as a series of five concentric circles, with the inner one representing Ike's personal experience and the succeeding ones symbolizing, in order, the southern experience, the American Dream, European history, and the archetypal Eden myth. Thus, in its broadest allegorical application, "The Bear" becomes an interpretation of the history of humanity. Ike sees all of history as a continual rise and fall of empires, each founded on romantic dreams of permanence and perfection and each in its turn falling prey to human folly and weakness.[17] This view accounts for the many historical and biblical allusions within the work—not only to the discovery of America and the settlement of the Old South but also to the rise and fall of the Roman Empire, the destruction of Noah's world by flood, the quest of the Hebrews for Canaan, and, most importantly, the loss of Eden. The history of all nations and cultures is a cyclical reenactment of the loss of Eden and the quest to reclaim the Garden experience in some "promised land" of the future. Thus caught between a lost Eden and a dreamed-of Canaan, human beings exist in a paradoxical state of ambition and failure, hope and memory: like old L. Q. C. McCaslin, they are "capable of anything any height or depth" (270).

While Yoknapatawpha presents, in its detailed record of people and events, an essentially tragic view of human history, in another important respect Faulkner's invented cosmos makes an altogether affirming statement. This characteristic of Faulkner's myth, the product of what might be termed his religion of art, posits the maker of Yoknapatawpha as an imitator of God, the divine creator, and the world thus created, that is, the art, as immortal. Much of the critical commentary on Faulkner's mythology concerns Yoknapataw-pha as *mimesis*, a copy of the actual world, whether southern, American, or universal. Faulkner, however, more typically spoke of his fictional creation as *poiesis*, emphasizing not the end result but the act of creativity itself. For Faulkner, Yoknapatawpha is only secondarily a mirror of objective reality; it is first and foremost an imaginary process, a fleshing out of the artist's genius and inner vision.

For this reason Faulkner tended to subordinate the mimetic aspects of Yoknapatawpha. "The artist's prerogative," he once said, "is to emphasize, to underline, to blow up facts, distort facts in order to state a truth" (*FIU* 282). Such has always been the case with the best writers, Faulkner insists. As he has Julius say in *Mosquitoes*, "Dante invented Beatrice, creating him-self a maid that life had not had time to create, and laid upon her frail and unbowed shoulders the whole burden of man's history of his impossible heart's desire" (358). "There's probably no tribe of Snopeses in Mississippi or anywhere else outside of my own apocrypha," Faulkner stated. "They were simply an invention of mine to tell a story of man in his struggle" (*FIU* 282). Concerning the writers of the Southern Renaissance, he said, "They had to invent a world a little different from the shabby one they lived in so they took to writing" (*FIU* 43). Not altogether joking, he claimed that in the creation of his characters in *Flags in the Dust*, he had "improved on God who, dra-matic though He be, has no sense, no feeling, for theatre" (*FB* 532). In his later years this association of the maker of Yoknapatawpha with the divine creator would become a staple of his public appearances. As he told the students at Virginia, "I think that any writer worth his salt is convinced that he can cre-ate much better people than God can," and, again, "No writer is satisfied with the folks that God creates. He's convinced that he can do much better than that" (*FIU* 118, 131–32). The Nobel Prize speech contains a veiled allusion to the god of the Genesis story in Faulkner's description of his own "life's work" as an endeavor "to create out of the materials of the human spirit something which did not exist before" (*ESPL* 119). Jean-Paul Sartre once remarked that, to the youth of France, "Faulkner is a god" (*FB* 1187); and, though not in the way the French meant, that is precisely the way Faulkner thought of himself in relation to Yoknapatawpha.[18] He was quite in character when he referred to his artistic creation as "a cosmos of [his] own" and identified himself as the "sole owner & proprietor."

Not only, in neoromantic fashion, does Faulkner imbue the artist with divinity, but he also insists, as a logical corollary, that the product of that creativity may earn for its creator a type of immortality. Such is certainly Faulkner's expressed hope for Yoknapatawpha. Writing, Faulkner said on numerous occasions, was his way of "saying No to death" (*FR* ix); and he wrote to Joan Williams, "That's the answer, the reason for it all, the one and only way on earth you can say No to death: the best, the strongest, the finest, the most enduring: to make something" (*FB* 1461). "Since man is mortal," Faulkner told Jean Stein, "the only immortality possible for him is to leave something behind him that is immortal since it will always move. This is the artist's way of scribbling 'Kilroy was here' on the wall of the final and irrevocable oblivion through which he must someday pass" (*LIG* 253).

Faulkner's views on the divinity of the author and the immortality of art properly belong to the realm of myth because such views are long-cherished, heroic, idealistic imaginings that are clearly beyond the boundaries of all that is known about time and history—as unreal and visionary as any fictional character, place, or event. Longinus is certainly right in his observation that "Time is fleeting," but the first half of his aphorism, "Art is long," is more problematic. The vast majority of authors and works do not outlast the pitiless parade of decades and centuries, and there is no guarantee that Faulkner will continue to prove one of the exceptions. Indeed, some readers, teachers, and critics already want to dismiss Faulkner's works as dated and irrelevant. As Ian Hamilton has demonstrated, many esteemed authors, including a surprising number of twentieth-century poets who were considered great during their lifetimes, have lost their fight against oblivion.[19] But all such observations merely serve to prove that Faulkner's exalted views of art and the artist are mythic, reaching, like all myths, beyond empirical fact and logic to embrace, as Faulkner put it, "the whole history of the human heart" (*FIU* 144). As a chronicle of repetitious and unresolved human experience

Yoknapatawpha may be a tragedy, but as an artistic creation it is a human comedy that is very nearly divine. And it is just such polarities that comprise the myth of Yoknapatawpha.

CONCLUSION

Recent critics such as feminists, deconstructionists, and neohistoricists have persuasively argued the political nature of all literary discourse, even those approaches that purport to be apolitical.[20] Without question the "mythical method" is similarly based upon a number of presuppositions about human nature, institutions, and experience. That human beings share an identical psyche, that all national, regional, and local differences are ultimately sub-sumed into oneness, and that history is inevitably cyclic, ever repeating the past, are views that, no longer privileged as absolute, have fallen out of criti-cal fashion; and there can be little doubt that the will to believe such "truths" was prompted at least in part, as Eliot understood and enunciated, by a felt need to restore unity and order to a modern world that seemed to be moving toward chaos. In this regard the study of myth and its literary applications in the first half of the twentieth century may be paralleled with concomitant searches for one-world government and a single, worldwide language. Like these other dreams of universal unity, the mythical method would come to be viewed as seriously flawed and dated, not the Truth it claimed to be but merely another "truth" among many. Nevertheless, the fact remains that it provided the underlying theory and working materials for the generation of writers who are arguably the best that the twentieth century produced. And Faulkner, as evidenced by his own statements as well as his literary practice and achievement, must be counted as one of the movement's most ardent and accomplished members.

NOTES

1. T. S. Eliot, "Ulysses, Order and Myth," *Dial* 75 (November 1923): 483.

2. For a good summary of Freud's and Jung's influence on literature, see Wilfred L. Guerin and others, *A Handbook of Critical Approaches to Literature*, 3rd ed. (New York: Oxford University Press, 1992), 118–26, 166–71.

3. Maud Bodkin, *Archetypal Patterns in Poetry: Psychological Studies of Imagination* (New York: Vintage Books, 1958), 19, 23.

4. Northrop Frye, *Fables of Identity: Studies in Poetic Mythology* (New York: Harcourt, Brace and World, 1963), 37.

5. David J. Burrows and others, eds., *Myths and Motifs in Literature* (New York: Free Press, 1973), xiii.

6. For a good demonstration of these principles, see David Leeming, *Myth: A Biography of Belief* (Oxford: Oxford University Press, 2002).

7. David Minter, ed., *The Sound and the Fury: A Norton Critical Edition*, 2nd ed. (New York: W. W. Norton, 1994), 222.

8. What follows is a condensation of my article "Before the Fall: The Theme of Innocence in 'That Evening Sun,'" *Notes on Mississippi Writers* 11 (Winter 1979): 86–93.

9. See Faulkner's comment to Buzz Bezzerides about Jill's childhood: "It's over very soon. . . . This is the end of it. . . . She'll grow into a woman" (*FB* 1169).

10. Lawrance Thompson, *William Faulkner: An Introduction and Interpretation*, 2nd ed. (New York: Holt, Rinehart and Winston, 1967), 13.

11. Joseph R. Urgo, *Faulkner's Apocrypha: "A Fable," "Snopes," and the Spirit of Human Rebellion* (Jackson: University Press of Mississippi, 1989), 95.

12. Faulkner's view of this matter did not change over the decade of composition of the novel. See, for example, his remarks at the University of Virginia (*FIU* 27).

13. A remarkably similar passage, which is a description of Hitler, appears in *Battle Cry*, the unproduced screenplay Faulkner wrote in 1943. See Louis Daniel Brodsky and Robert W. Hamblin, eds., *Faulkner: A Comprehensive Guide to the Brodsky Collection, Volume IV: Battle Cry* (Jackson: University Press of Mississippi, 1985), 252–54.

14. Faulkner is not the only writer who has been taken to task for such "errors." Consider the response of much of the Christian community to Andrew Lloyd Webber and Tim Rice's musical *Jesus Christ, Superstar*, and Nikos Kazantzakis's *The Last Temptation of Christ*.

15. George Marion O'Donnell, "Faulkner's Mythology," *Kenyon Review* 1 (Spring 1939): 285–99.

16. Irving Howe, *William Faulkner: A Critical Study*, 2nd ed. (New York: Vintage Books, 1962), 27, 29.

17. With regard to the dialogue between Ike McCaslin and Cass Edmonds, some critics side with Ike, others with Cass. It is important to note, however, that Ike and Cass do not disagree on the nature of history, but rather on what the appropriate response to that history should be—Ike arguing for renunciation, Cass for engagement.

18. Interestingly, Faulkner also referenced the divine in his remarks about James Joyce's *Ulysses* and *Finnegans Wake*: "That was a case of a genius who was electrocuted by the divine fire" (*FIU* 53).

19. Ian Hamilton, *Against Oblivion: Some Lives of the Twentieth-Century Poets* (New York: Viking, 2002).

20. Concerning this last point, see Lawrence H. Schwartz, *Creating Faulkner's Reputation: The Politics of Modern Literary Criticism* (Knoxville: University of Tennessee Press, 1988).

"Saying No to Death"
Toward Faulkner's Theory of Fiction

Undoubtedly many critics even today agree with Henry Nash Smith's contention in 1932 that William Faulkner "has no theory of fiction" (*LIG* 32). Other readers, surveying the multitude of books and articles which analyze Faulkner's fictional techniques, may conclude that the Nobel laureate held many different, even contradictory theories. The truth, of course, lies in neither of these extremes. Faulkner, as he acknowledged many times, was not "a literary man," that is, one formally schooled in aesthetics and criticism; and he never developed, in the manner of Henry James or William Dean Howells, an elaborate definition of his aims and practices as a writer. Nevertheless, as revealed by even a cursory examination of his letters, essays, speeches, interviews, and fiction, Faulkner was more than mildly interested in literary theory throughout his career. Moreover, although he went through several phases as an author, producing poetry as well as prose and embracing varying combinations of realism, naturalism, and romanticism, and although he never offered an underlying premise for his art until the 1950s, that basic premise had been operative, though perhaps subconsciously, from the very beginning of his career. At the risk of appearing to adopt a reductionist approach, I suggest that the key to Faulkner's theory of fiction is to be found in his statement, repeated many times after 1951 but implicit in even his earliest work, that writing was his way of "saying No to death."[1] This impulse, I believe, accounts not only for the origin of Faulkner's art but also for the principal features in the design of that art.

An initial demonstration of my thesis is provided by section five of "The Bear," one of those remarkable passages which communicate the very essence of Faulkner's views on life and death, and, by implication, on art. In this section Isaac McCaslin returns for one last time to the big woods in which he has served his hunting novitiate under Sam Fathers.

Though Ike identifies with the "baseless and illusory hope" (*GDM* 301) that Major de Spain will revoke his agreement to sell the property to a Memphis lumber company, the youth knows that the wilderness is doomed. That doom, already foreshadowed by the deaths of Old Ben, Lion, and Sam, is now confirmed beyond doubt by the construction of the planing-mill at Hoke's Junction. As Ike rides the logging train into the wilderness, he perceives that even his clothes convey an awareness of death, "as garments carry back into the clean edgeless blowing of air the lingering effluvium of a sick-room or of death" (306).

Submerged once more in the deep woods, however, Ike is able to convince himself, at least momentarily, that nothing has changed or will change, that the woods are timeless and "death [does] not even exist" (312). Revisiting the grave sites of Lion and Sam Fathers, Ike observes

> the knoll which was no abode of the dead because there was no death, not Lion and not Sam: not held fast in earth but free in earth and not in earth but of earth, myriad yet undiffused of every myriad part, leaf and twig and particle, air and sun and rain and dew and night, acorn oak and leaf and acorn again, dark and dawn and dark and dawn again in their immutable progression and, being myriad, one: and Old Ben too, Old Ben too; they would give him his paw back even, certainly they would give him his paw back: then the long challenge and the long chase, no heart to be driven and outraged, no flesh to be mauled and bled. (313)

This vision of immortality, though, at least insofar as it relates to personal immortality, seems merely wishful thinking, an illusion, as the following incident suggests. Ike's hopeful reflections are interrupted by a "sharp shocking inrush" (313) of fear caused by the intrusion of a rattlesnake into the idyllic scene. Faulkner leaves no doubt as to the identity and the significance of this invader: the snake is "the old one, the ancient and accursed about the earth, fatal and solitary and [Ike] could smell it now: the thin sick smell of rotting cucumbers and something else which had no name, evocative of all knowledge and an old weariness and of pariah-hood and of death" (314). That "all knowledge" equates with death, not immortality, is further emphasized when Ike assigns to the serpent those titles of respect he learned from Sam Fathers: "Chief . . . , Grandfather" (314).

If the concluding segment of "The Bear" dramatizes Ike's initiation into the tragic realities of mutability and death, the section also demonstrates Ike's reluctance, even refusal, to accept these realities. Against his dual enemies, time and annihilation, Ike aligns the creative powers of memory and imagination. Ike's entry into the heart of the now-doomed wilderness is paralleled by a three-page flashback in which the youth recalls the killing of his first buck and Uncle Ash's subsequent demand for equal rights. The comic element in this episode (desirable since the humorous tone enables Faulkner to avoid sentimentality) in no way lessens the point that the recollection of the past provides Ike with one means of negating time and death. The same intent may be identified with the wistful dream-passage, cited previously, in which Ike envisions an ideal realm in which Old Ben will once again participate in the chase. Ike's imaginative leaps in this section, both backward and outward, seem obvious (though probably unconscious) attempts to deny or at least compensate for the inadequate present which is tyrannized by death. That this initiation in the wilderness is intended as a paradigm of all of Ike's subsequent experiences is indicated by the conjecture about his future marriage: "he would marry someday and they too would own for their brief while that brief unsubstanced glory which inherently of itself cannot last and hence why glory: and they would, might, carry even the remembrance of it into the time when flesh no longer talks to flesh because memory at least does last" (311). Ike has learned from the wilderness experience the age-old truth that happiness and joy are fleeting, transient qualities, that "glory . . . cannot last"; but he protests such loss, and he registers his opposition through the exercise of both memory and imagination.

Faulkner could write movingly about Ike McCaslin's initiation in part because Ike's realizations were Faulkner's own. In fact, in Ike's confrontation with the harsh and inescapable reality of death, in his refusal to accept willingly this brutal fact, and in his employment of memory and imagination to deny death, one finds an almost exact corollary to Faulkner's theory of fiction.

Like Isaac McCaslin, Faulkner was extremely apprehensive concerning death.[2] This fear, even obsession, probably originated in early childhood and may have derived from what Faulkner later recalled as "those spells of loneliness and nameless sorrow that children suffer" (SL 20), or from his close brush with death from scarlet fever at age four, or from the successive deaths of his beloved grandmothers when he was nine years old. Whatever the basis for his anxiety, it seems clear that Faulkner's childhood was marked by a heightened awareness concerning death. One may be fairly certain that the reaction of the four-year-old boy to the hearse in "Sepulture South: Gaslight" is in some measure autobiographical:

"What?" I said. "A deader? What's a deader?" And they told me. I had seen dead things before—birds, toads, the puppies the one before Simon (his wife was Sarah) had drowned in a croker-sack in the water-trough . . . , and I had watched him and Sarah both beat to bloody shapeless strings the snakes which I now know were harmless. But that this, this ignominy, should happen to people too, it seemed to me that God Himself would not permit, condone. So they in the hearse could not be dead: it must be something like sleep: a trick played on people by those same inimical forces and powers for evil which made Sarah and her husband have to beat the harmless snakes to bloody and shapeless pulp or drown the puppies—tricked into that helpless coma for some dreadful and inscrutable joke until the dirt was packed down, to strain and thrash and cry in the airless dark, to no escape forever. So that night I had something very like hysterics, clinging to Sarah's legs and panting: "I won't die! I won't! Never!" (*US* 452)[3]

This boyhood abhorrence of death seems to have been intensified in the mature Faulkner by a corresponding disbelief, or at least a serious doubt, concerning immortality. There are many evidences of Faulkner's skepticism on this point, notably the early identification with the poetry of Swinburne and Housman, the dust-to-dust imagery of such apprenticeship works as "Mississippi Hills: My Epitaph" and "The Artist," the dramatic situation in the short story "Beyond," the handling of the Christ story in *A Fable*, and Faulkner's general preference for the word "oblivion" as a substitute for "death." Perhaps the most explicit statement of disbelief in an afterlife in all of Faulkner's writing is Harry Wilbourne's reflection upon rejecting suicide at the end of *The Wild Palms*: "*Between grief and nothing I will take grief*" (*WP* 273).[4] In any event, it seems safe to conclude that it was not merely death which Faulkner feared, but death as obliteration.[5]

Faulkner's attitude toward death, and toward the time-ridden world which eventuates in death, is crucial to an understanding of his perception of himself as an artist. Confronted with death as possible annihilation, Faulkner was inclined to view art as the principal means by which man might defy time and death and achieve at least a measure of immortality. This belief accounts for the elevated, even religious tone of many of Faulkner's pronouncements on art. "Since man is mortal," Faulkner told Jean Stein, "the only immortality possible for him is to leave something behind him that is immortal since it will always move. This is the artist's way of scribbling 'Kilroy was here' on the wall of the final and irrevocable oblivion through which he must someday pass" (*LIG* 253). Following the death of Albert Camus, Faulkner wrote: "When the door shut for him, he had already written on this side of it that which every artist who also carries through life with him that one same foreknowledge and hatred of death, is hoping to do: *I was here*" (*ESPL* 114). In a letter to Joan Williams, Faulkner observed: "That's the answer, the reason for it all, the one and only way on earth you can say No to death: the best, the strongest, the finest, the most enduring: to make something" (*FB* 1461). Given such views on art and time, one can easily understand Faulkner's attraction to Keats's "Ode on a Grecian Urn," which celebrates in both its content and its continuing acceptance the enduring power of all great art.[6]

If Faulkner's observations on art reflect an anxiety toward death and a corresponding desire for immortality, his comments also demonstrate the degree to which art, in his view, is interrelated with memory and imagination. Faulkner frequently identified the sources of his fiction as "observation, experience, and imagination."[7] The first two of these equate with memory. According to Faulkner, all that a writer has seen, heard, read, and done is unconsciously stored in his memory, from which he can draw forth images and details to suit his needs. "Memory believes before knowing remembers," Faulkner observes in *Light in August* (104); and he told the cadets at West Point:

> I think that every experience of the author affects his writing. He has a sort of a lumber room in his subconscious that all this goes into, and none of it is ever lost. Some day he may need some experience that he experienced or saw, observed or read about, and so he digs it out and uses it. . . . Everything that happens to him he remembers. And it will be grist to his mill. (*FWP* 96)

Since art derives partly from memory, it functions for the reader as a record of past experience. In his Nobel Prize acceptance speech, Faulkner declares that the poet's privilege is "to help man endure by lifting his heart, by reminding him of the courage and honor and hope and pride and compassion and pity and sacrifice which have been the glory of his past" (*ESPL* 120). In Japan Faulkner commented: "The reason that the books last longer than the bridges and the skyscrapers is that that is the best thing man has discovered yet to record the fact that he does endure, that he is capable of hope, even in darkness, that he does move, he doesn't give up, and that is not only a record of his past, where he has shown that he endures and hopes in spite of darkness, but it is a promise of the validity of that hope" (*LIG* 177–78). At West Point, Faulkner observed that the writer's purpose is "to uplift man's heart by showing man the record of the experiences of the human heart" (*FWP* 48). As Faulkner demonstrates with the account of the race of the locomotives in *The

Unvanquished, the past is "not gone or vanished either," as long as succeeding generations continue "to tell it or listen to the telling" (*U* 98).

In stressing the link between his art and memory of his own and humanity's past, Faulkner was not endorsing a mimetic theory of fiction. Though he has often been called both a "realist" and a "naturalist," Faulkner has little in common with the photographic realism of Howells or the scientific documentation of Zola and Dreiser. For reasons which will be discussed later, Faulkner always stressed "imagination" as the principal ingredient in his fiction. Indeed, as evidenced by the handling of the past in *Absalom, Absalom!*, even memory frequently becomes for Faulkner and his characters imaginative reconstruction rather than simple recall. "I dont care much for facts," Faulkner once noted (*FCF* 89); and he criticized John Steinbeck (mistakenly, one might add) for being "just a reporter, a newspaperman, not really a writer" (*LIG* 91). At Charlottesville, Faulkner observed, "The artist's prerogative . . . is to emphasize, to underline, to blow up facts, distort facts in order to state a truth" (*FIU* 282). Yoknapatawpha, as Faulkner told Jean Stein, may have evolved from his "little postage stamp of native soil," but it was produced "by sublimating the actual into apocryphal" (*LIG* 255). The Nobel Prize speech defines art not only as "the record of man" but also as "something which did not exist before," an artifact "create[d] out of the materials of the human spirit" (*ESPL* 120, 119). In other words, art, according to Faulkner, results from both memory and invention, fact and imagination.

Close examination of Faulkner's belief that literature provides the writer with a means of saying No to death, of recording the heroic struggle of man, and of exercising the power of invention reveals that the three ideas are actually interdependent. Denial of death, in Faulkner's view, is the end of art; memory and imagination are the means. As was noted in Ike McCaslin's response to the loss of the wilderness, both the reconstruction of the past and the imagining of an ideal "other" world are ways of counteracting death, of keeping the beloved lost object alive. It remains to demonstrate how these notions worked to influence Faulkner's fictional techniques, particularly his handling of subject matter and his style.

One can hardly overstate the degree to which Faulkner's fiction is intertwined with memory. Like a host of other American writers, for example, Cooper, Hawthorne, Twain, Anderson, Wolfe, and especially Cather, Faulkner indulges in more than a modicum of nostalgia. As Henry Nash Smith inferred from his conversation with Faulkner in 1932, the author "loved [Oxford] as it was in his boyhood, before billboards and electric signs invaded the quiet, when a two-story gallery had surrounded the square" (*LIG* 29). Faulkner himself was inclined to link his discovery of his true subject, the people and places and events of Yoknapatawpha, with the act of preservation through recollection. After producing scores of mediocre poems and two unsuccessful novels (both of which are significantly rooted in the present rather than the past), Faulkner wrote *Flags in the Dust* (*Sartoris*), the first of the Yoknapatawpha novels and the work which he said contains "the germ of my apocrypha" (*FIU* 285). In explaining the genesis of this work, Faulkner observed that he had been "speculating idly upon time and death" and had concluded that "nothing served but that I try by main strength to recreate between the covers of a book the world as I was already preparing to lose and regret, feeling, with the morbidity of the young, that I was not only on the verge of decrepitude, but that growing old was to be an experience peculiar to myself alone out of all the teeming world, and desiring, if not the capture of that world and the feeling of it as you'd preserve a kernel [or] a leaf to indicate the lost forest, at least to keep the evocative skeleton of the dessicated [*sic*] leaf." Faulkner further noted his concern that this world, his world, "should not pass utterly out of the memory of man," as well as his need to "reaffirm the impulses of [his] own ego in this actual world without stability." Thus, *Sartoris* derived from a protest against time and death and a consequent desire to preserve in print a passing scene. In fact, so strong was this impulse to oppose death through creativity that Faulkner could not be sure whether "I had invented the [fictional] world to which I should give life or if it had invented me, giving me an illusion of greatness."[8]

As these remarks on the composition of *Sartoris* suggest, the dramatic turnabout in Faulkner's career marked by the creation of Yoknapatawpha may be due as much to the discovery of art as a means of asserting the artist's ego in the face of death as to the discovery of native materials. In fact, the two discoveries can scarcely be distinguished. What better way, one perceives in retrospect, could Faulkner have dramatized the passing of his own world than by paralleling it with a previous generation which had already succumbed to time and death. Thus, one supposes, evolved the double timeframe and the dominant motif in *Flags in the Dust/Sartoris*. All of the elements of this work conjoin to produce one single refrain: *memento mori*. The plot involves two generations of Sartorises, one past and the other passing. The protagonist, young Bayard Sartoris, seems old beyond his years, having already accepted the grim reality of death and unable to escape that reality, as his counterpart Horace Benbow does, through fancied wanderings "beyond the moon, about meadows nailed with firmamented stars to the ultimate roof of things, where unicorns filled the neighing air with galloping, or grazed or lay supine in golden-hoofed repose" (*FID* 172). The action unfolds against the relentless progression of the seasons, from spring, to summer, to autumn, to winter, culminating in the cold December rain which "drop by drop . . . wore the night away, wore time away" (324). Even the occasional humor and the joyous descriptions of nature seem designed to accentuate, not relieve, the melancholy.

Appropriately, the family's name, Sartoris, is associated with the tragic theme: "For there is death in the sound of it, and a glamorous fatality, like silver pennons downrushing at sunset, or a dying fall of horns along the road to Roncevaux" (*FID* 404). Not surprisingly, one of the last scenes in the novel takes place in the cemetery, among the family's tombstones, the most prominent of which carries the inscription "Pause here, son of sorrow; remember death" (399).

But the course of history, as symbolized by the tragic fate of the Sartoris clan, is just one pole, the negative one, in this novel. The other, the positive pole, is art, not the subject matter of the book but the book itself, which, as Faulkner said, was written to capture and preserve between its covers his passing world. It is not quite accurate to say, as many critics do, that Faulkner's major theme is time; more precisely, his principal concern is *resistance* to time. In *Flags in the Dust/Sartoris* this positive, even heroic emphasis is symbolized by the marble statue of Colonel John Sartoris:

> He stood on a stone pedestal, in his frock coat and bareheaded, one leg slightly advanced and one hand resting lightly on the stone pylon beside him. His head was lifted a little in that gesture of haughty pride which repeated itself generation after generation with a fateful fidelity, his back to the world and his carven eyes gazing out across the valley where his railroad ran and the blue changeless hills beyond, and beyond that, the ramparts of infinity itself. The pedestal and effigy were mottled with seasons of rain and sun and with drippings from the cedar branches, and the bold carving of the letters was bleared with mold, yet still decipherable. (399)

This monument, seemingly impervious to time and capable of evoking memories of the bygone past, symbolizes the relationship Faulkner perceives between art and memory. Another monument to this concept is *Flags in the Dust/Sartoris* and the rest of the Yoknapatawpha novels and stories.[9]

The statue of John Sartoris is only one of many objects in Faulkner's fiction which are noteworthy for having survived the passing of time and which serve to evoke thoughts of persons and events from earlier years.[10]

These "relics," or "art surrogates" as they may be termed, take many forms. There is, for example, the pipe which old man Falls gives to aging Bayard Sartoris and which revives for Bayard memories of his father. Indeed, old man Falls is himself a relic, his sole purpose in *Sartoris* being to convey to Bayard and the reader the "far more palpable presence" of John Sartoris from "a dead period" (*FID* 3). One thinks also of the hunting horn cherished over the years by Ike McCaslin and of the slipper and the pasture which recall the past, however dimly, to Benjy Compson's restricted mind. Sometimes the relic assumes a communal rather than a personal significance, as with the Jefferson courthouse and jail in *Requiem for a Nun*. And occasionally the relic takes a written form, as with the old family ledger which Ike McCaslin discovers in the plantation commissary, or the letter from Charles Bon to Judith Sutpen, preserved and passed on three generations later to Quentin Compson. Significantly, Mr. Compson's explanation as to why Judith gave Bon's letter to Quentin's grandmother echoes Faulkner's own observations about the artist and death:

> Because you make so little impression, you see. You get born . . . and then all of a sudden it's all over and all you have left is a block of stone with scratches on it And so maybe if you could go to someone, the stranger the better, and give them something—a scrap of paper—something, anything, at least it would be something just because it would have happened, be remembered even if only from passing from one hand to another, one mind to another, and it would be at least a scratch, something. (*AA* 127)

Judith, according to Mr. Compson, is obsessed with the desire to communicate to others that she has existed, that she *was*; and this compulsion leads her, in Mr. Compson's words, "to make that scratch, that undying mark on the blank face of the oblivion to which we are all doomed" (129). In this instance, if not in others, there can be no doubt that Mr. Compson speaks for his creator.

Another art surrogate, Cecilia Farmer's signature scratched on the jailhouse window in *Requiem for a Nun*, bears even greater resemblance to Faulkner's definition of art and the artist.[11] This signature, "a few faint scratches apparently no more durable than the thin dried slime left by the passage of a snail, yet which has endured a hundred years" (218), survives to evoke in the twentieth-century stranger to Jefferson a vicarious participation in Cecilia's life and time. The way Cecilia's story "comes alive" as the stranger gazes at her signature parallels Faulkner's observations on art in the "Foreword" to *The Faulkner Reader* and elsewhere:

. . . suddenly . . . something has already happened: the faint frail illegible meaningless even inferenceless scratching on the ancient poor-quality glass you stare at, has moved, under your eyes, even while you stared at it, coalesced, seeming actually to have entered into another sense than vision: a scent, a whisper, filling that hot cramped strange room . . . : the two of them in conjunction—the old milky obsolete glass, and the scratches on it: that tender ownerless obsolete girl's name and the old dead date in April almost a century ago—speaking, murmuring, back from, out of, across from, a time as old as lavender, older than album or stereopticon, as old as daguerreotype itself. (*RFN* 219)

The capacity of Cecilia's signature to survive into the future and inspire imaginative, emotional responses in strangers reminds one of Faulkner's statement to Jean Stein: "The aim of every artist is to arrest motion, which is life, by artificial means and hold it fixed so that 100 years later when a stranger looks at it, it moves again since it is life" (*LIG* 253). Critics have paid considerable attention to the first half of this statement, the notion that art is arrested motion, but Faulkner may have been more concerned with the second part of his definition. Only when art "moves again" has the creator successfully said No to death and thus achieved immortality.

An interesting parallel to Faulkner's fondness for "relics" and "art surrogates" is his compulsion to return time and again to the same characters, incidents, and scenes in Yoknapatawpha. The resurrection of the Compson family in the "Appendix" to *The Sound and the Fury* and the continuation of the Snopes narrative over a period of thirty years are only the most prominent of the countless instances in which Faulkner retells and reworks previous stories. While such repetitions and extensions serve various narrative purposes—for example, suspenseful unfolding of plot, fuller characterization, and multiple viewpoints—one suspects that Faulkner's practice in this regard is dictated as much by psychological as by literary needs. Given his anxiety concerning time and death, and given his concern about (initially) the acceptance and (ultimately) the survival of his art, it seems reasonable to suggest that Faulkner's return to his earlier stories was at least partly motivated, though probably unconsciously, by his need to be assured of the vitality of his art. Faulkner's reluctance to reread his published work seems related to the same point. A completed work (for the artist, that is) belongs to the past, to (in one sense) death, a fact strongly to be resisted. One form of resistance is to depend upon sympathetic readers to respond vicariously to the work and thus cause it to "move again." Another approach is for the creator to ensure that his creation "move again" by the addition of appendices and extended chapters. Predictably, Faulkner's tendency to retell old stories increased with his advancing years. Most critics insist that Faulkner's late years are marked by a flagging creativity, but another possibility is that as Faulkner grew older, as he became more and more conscious of his own mortality, he felt more and more compelled (again subconsciously) to inject new life into his earlier creations. In any case, the fact remains that memory functions, within the confines of Yoknapatawpha as well as in the relation of Yoknapatawpha to actuality, to resist time and say No to death.

If such reasoning is correct, then *The Reivers* becomes a quite significant work in the Faulkner canon. Indeed, this last novel seems precisely the kind of book an artist who views memory as an antidote to death would produce during the late stage of his career. As the subtitle indicates, *The Reivers* is "a reminiscence," a nostalgic recounting by Lucius Priest, a grandfather bearing close resemblance to William Faulkner, of events which occurred more than a half century previously. In producing this novel Faulkner not only returned to the actual livery stable days of his own boyhood but also ranged freely throughout the fictional world of Yoknapatawpha. Elizabeth Kerr may be wrong in identifying *The Reivers* with "the Doomsday Book, the Golden Book, of Yoknapatawpha County" (*LIG* 255) which Faulkner predicted he would someday write, but she is certainly correct in calling attention to the extent to which the novel draws upon Faulkner's previous works.[12] The use of the Memphis setting from *Sanctuary*, the manipulation of the initiation motif prevalent in Faulkner's works, references to key events in the history of Jefferson and Yoknapatawpha County, and the mention of numerous characters from earlier books—all such features demonstrate that *The Reivers* stands as a valediction in which Faulkner celebrates, through memory, the total achievement of Yoknapatawpha.

The use of memory as a means of opposing time and death affected not only Faulkner's subject matter but also his style. As Robert Penn Warren has explained, "The style of a writer represents his stance toward experience";[13] thus it is to be expected that Faulkner's style mirrors a strong resistance to death through the desire to preserve the past. One suspects that Marcel Proust served as an important model in this regard. "After I had read *A la Recherche du Temps Perdu*," Faulkner once observed, "I said 'This is it!'—and I wished I had written it myself" (*LIG* 72). In any event, one finds in Faulkner's stream-of-consciousness prose the same obsession with the past, the same compulsion to preserve and restate it in terms of the present.[14] Various critics have noted how Faulkner's style functions to unite past and present time. Alfred Kazin, for instance, describes Faulkner's prose as "an attempt to realize continuity with all our genesis, our 'progenitors' . . . with all we have touched, known, loved. This is why he needs those long successive parentheses, and parentheses within parentheses. They exemplify the chain of human succession."[15] Faulkner said as much himself. He told Cowley, "My ambition is to put everything into one sentence—not only the present but the whole past on which it depends and which keeps overtaking the present, second by second" (*FCF* 112). At the University of Virginia, Faulkner stated: "To me, no man is himself, he is the sum of his past. There is no such thing really as was because the past is. And so a man, a character in a story at any moment of action is not just himself as he is then, he is all that made him, and the long sentence is an attempt to get his past and possibly his future into the instant in which he does something " (*FIU* 84). In a letter to Cowley, Faulkner wrote, "I'm still trying to put all mankind's history in one sentence" (*FCF* 17).

Readers will find this principle at work on almost any page of Faulkner's stream-of-consciousness prose, but the following passage from the opening of *Absalom, Absalom!* will serve as a case in point.

> *It seems that this demon—his name was Sutpen—(Colonel Sutpen)—Colonel Sutpen. Who came out of nowhere and without warning upon the land with a band of strange n——s and built a plantation—(Tore violently a plantation, Miss Rosa Coldfield says)—tore violently. And married her sister Ellen and begot a son and a daughter which—(Without gentleness begot, Miss Rosa Coldfield says)— without gentleness. Which should have been the jewels of his pride and the shield and comfort of his old age, only—(Only they destroyed him or something or he destroyed them or something. And died)—and died. Without regret, Miss Rosa Coldfield says—(Save by her) Yes, save by her. (And by Quentin Compson) Yes. And by Quentin Compson. (5)*

In this passage Quentin's rumination over the public legend of Thomas Sutpen's career a half century earlier is intermixed with the recall of Miss Rosa's recent interpretations and with Quentin's own present-tense emotional response. Throughout the passage Faulkner employs parenthetical interpolations and repetition of key phrases to dramatize the interrelationship of remote past, near past, and present time. The whole of *Absalom, Absalom!* is constructed on this principle, as are also the interior monologues of Benjy and Quentin Compson, Addie Bundren's deathbed reflections, Gail Hightower's reconstruction of his family's history, and Ike McCaslin's thoughts in "The Bear." The three prologues in *Requiem for a Nun*, the third of which is comprised of a single sentence extending to fifty pages, are only the most extreme forms of what is a common practice in Faulkner's fiction.

That in certain instances, perhaps most, the past is brought forward as burden rather than delight matters little. In Faulkner's metaphysic the question of existence is seldom one of suffering versus joy; it is rather a question of being versus nonbeing. And Faulkner's heroes more often than not are those individuals who, like the artist, say No to death, who choose life even when that choice entails a considerable amount of anxiety, guilt, or pain.[16]

As important as memory was for Faulkner, it could not, for demonstrable reasons, become the sole basis for his poetics. Merely to recall experience and to record it in stenographic fashion would be to duplicate, and thus to accept, the fallen world despoiled by time and death. And it is precisely this fallen world against which Faulkner rebels. To say No to death is ultimately to say No to life, since death is the culmination of the life process. Faulkner's uneasy relationship to actuality is evidenced in his sense of southern history, his disillusionment with his father, his rejection by Estelle Oldham and later by Helen Baird, his disappointment as an aviator during World War I, his struggle as a fledgling author, and even his misgivings about his smallish stature.[17] All of these disenchantments, however, these "little deaths," were mere earnest for what Faulkner had already accepted as the ultimate payment required by life. Whatever the effect on Faulkner's personality of his various frustrations, it is clear, as *The Marble Faun*, "Nympholepsy," and *Mayday* reveal, that Faulkner early on came to view the world through the jaundiced eye of the disillusioned romantic. And Faulkner never altogether recovered from his youthful disappointments. His oft-quoted comment about the reasons for the twentieth-century renaissance among southern writers is quite revealing of his own personal outlook: "I myself am inclined to think it was because of the bareness of the Southerner's life, that he had to resort to his own imagination, to create his own Carcassonne" (*FIU* 136).[18] Similarly, in commenting on the origin of "The Bear," Faulkner remarked, "There's a case of the sorry, shabby world that don't quite please you, so you create one of your own, so you make Lion a little braver than he was, and you make the bear a little more of a bear than he actually was" (*FIU* 59). As these quotations suggest, Faulkner has definite links with the Freudian definition of the artist as one who sublimates his frustrations and neuroses in symbolic projections and fantasies.[19] Art, in this view, serves as one form of compensation for the inadequacies of life; and imagination, the means of transcendence, becomes the principal ingredient in that art.

Here, as is so often the case in the study of Faulkner, one is confronted with a curious paradox. One impulse in Faulkner, his desire to say No to death, moved him to celebrate life and experience, even tragic experience, and to seek to preserve the world through an aesthetic of memory. But a stronger impulse, deriving from the ultimate recognition that life is ever subject to death, led Faulkner to oppose life as it is given and to transform it through an aesthetic of imagination.[20] This second impulse accounts for all those remarks in which Faulkner claimed to have "improved on God."[21] As he told the students at Charlottesville, "No writer is satisfied with the folks that God creates. He's convinced that he can do much better than that" (*FIU* 131–32). Such comments express not so much the attitude of an arrogant, egotistical artist as the felt need to embellish the "bareness" of "the sorry, shabby world" with imaginative fictions.

How deep-seated was Faulkner's compulsion to remake the actual world in his own image is demonstrated by the various personae Faulkner adopted throughout his lifetime. The most celebrated example, of course, is his pose as a returning war hero following World War I. Wearing his military uniform about Oxford and to nearby towns, posing for photographers with his Royal Flying Corps badge and wings displayed on his tunic, walking with a noticeable limp, Faulkner gave every appearance of being an experienced, war-wounded pilot. Other poses followed: bohemian poet, town character, simple farmer, Hollywood eccentric, romantic lover, English squire. While an innocent playfulness infuses much of Faulkner's role-playing (as when he told one interviewer, "I was born of a Negro slave and an alligator, both named Gladys Rock" [*LIG* 9]), one must acknowledge a degree of neuroticism in such behavior. In extreme cases the necessity to embroider actuality becomes a pathological mythomania; in Faulkner's case the tendency seems to have been limited to a mild form of what Jules de Gaultier has termed "the Madame Bovary complex," defined as "the power given man to see himself other than what he is."[22] Such a complex is hardly surprising in an individual who, like Faulkner, expresses, both in words and in his dependence upon alcohol, a deep aversion to the real world. Writing and drinking, as Faulkner's poses illustrate, are not the only ways "to invent a world a little different from the shabby one" (*FIU* 43) which man inhabits.

Faulkner's antipathy to the actual world is also reflected in such "nonfiction" pieces as the essay "Mississippi," which purports to be an autobiographical reminiscence tracing the formative influences upon Faulkner's mind and art. The first sentence establishes the interfusion of fancy and fact which characterizes the whole essay: "Mississippi begins in the lobby of a

Memphis, Tennessee hotel and extends south to the Gulf of Mexico" (*ESPL* 11). The piece goes on to summarize Mississippi history from the time of the Mound Builders to the mid-twentieth century. As in his Yoknapatawpha Saga, Faulkner oversimplifies a complex historical process to make it conform to his own particular version of *Paradise Lost*. Thus, the virgin wilderness and the numerous Native American tribes are assigned to a prelapsarian but doomed era, slaveholding cotton planters and carpetbagging lumbermen are portrayed as destroyers of Eden, and twentieth-century rednecks who support demagogues and join the Ku Klux Klan are depicted as symbols of the ultimate degradation which is the inevitable consequence of man's inhumanity and folly. Judgment and retribution periodically come to this fallen world, as with the Civil War in the nineteenth century and the raging Mississippi River flood in the twentieth. But Faulkner's narrative, like Milton's great epic, is not without its *felix culpa*. The tragedies, whether man-made or natural, serve "merely to give man another chance to prove . . . just how much the human body could bear, stand, endure" (25–26).

Into this highly stereotyped and mythologized frame of history, Faulkner inserts both actual and fictional personages. Murrell, Mason, Hare, the two Harpes, Forrest, Bilbo, Vardaman, and Caroline Barr are mentioned; but so are the Sartorises and De Spains and Compsons, the McCaslins and Ewells and Hogganbecks, "and now and then a Snopes too because by the beginning of the twentieth century Snopeses were everywhere" (12). "Mississippi" contains fact and fiction, and fact made fiction. An actual millionaire sportsman, Paul Rainey, is transformed into the fictional Sales Wells; and the Faulkner of the essay becomes "in his hierarchial turn Master of the [hunting] camp" (13), though the real Faulkner never did. Oxford does not appear, but Jefferson does. In its blending of historical fact, memory, and imaginative constructs, "Mississippi" epitomizes Faulkner's art. It is Yoknapatawpha in miniature, a cosmos of Faulkner's own making, in part suggested by and modeled upon actuality but created "by sublimating the actual into apocryphal." In such a cosmos not the mirrored world but the invented one is paramount: in this realm the imaginative artist, not God, is "Sole Owner & Proprietor."

There are several features of Faulkner's technique which may be linked to his aesthetic of imagination. One such feature is the propensity toward the grotesque and the marvelous.

Readers are quick to notice how Faulkner's characters often tend to be distortions of typical human beings, extremes rather than well-rounded, "realistic" figures. Walter Slatoff describes the Compson family—with its alcoholic failure for a father, a hopeless hypochondriac for a mother, and an idiot, a neurotic suicide, a nymphomaniac, and a ruthless materialist for children—as "utterly monstrous"; and he reaches a similar conclusion about the murderer, the suicide, the two schizophrenics, the bigot, and the madman who appear in the cast of *Light in August*.[23] In some cases Faulkner's grotesquerie approaches caricature: the loquaciousness of Gavin Stevens, the stubbornness of Lucas Beauchamp, the animality of the Snopeses, the greed of Jason Compson, the sexuality of Eula Varner. Faulkner's comment about Eula, "she was larger than life, she was too big for this world" (*FIU* 31), applies to many—indeed, most— of his characters. Like the figures with elongated bodies and noseless faces in Faulkner's early drawings, Faulkner's characters are grotesques drawn less from life than from the artist's creative vision. Apparently only such characters could provide their creator with a sense of control and even superiority over the deficient world of time and death.[24]

A tendency toward extravagance, even sensationalism, is also a marked characteristic of Faulkner's handling of incident and plot. Examples spring readily to mind: the macabre journey of the Bundrens, the rape of Temple Drake, the obsessive actions of Thomas Sutpen, the love affair of Ike Snopes and the cow, the gravedigging scenes in *Intruder in the Dust*, the insane behavior of Emily Grierson, the murderous act of Nancy Mannigoe, the escapades of the convict in *The Wild Palms*. Faulkner's comic incidents, like the horse-swapping antics of Pat Stamper or the deviltry of Byron Snopes's half-Indian children, have much in common with the "tall tale" tradition of the southwestern yarn spinners; but the use of exaggeration and willful distortion is not restricted to Faulkner's comedy. Nor is it limited to individual scenes. Faulkner's overall plot designs, marked as they are by violent disruptions of chronology, radical shifts of viewpoint, and startling innovations of form (as in *The Wild Palms* and *Requiem for a Nun*), likewise tend toward extravagance and sensationalism. Here, too, as in Faulkner's grotesque characterizations and shocking incidents, one perceives a need to escape the ordinary and the conventional and enter a realm of the ego's own making.

Faulkner's rejection of the actual world of time and death is likewise evidenced in his inclination toward mythologizing. Thomas Sutpen is not merely a nineteenth-century southern planter: he is (depending upon the viewpoint) a godlike creator bringing order out of chaos, "creating the Sutpen's Hundred, the *Be Sutpen's Hundred* like the oldtime *Be Light*," or a satanic being, "this Faustus, this demon, this Beelzebub . . . who hid horns and tail beneath human raiment and a beaver hat" (*AA* 9, 178). Or, as the title *Absalom, Absalom!* implies, Sutpen is a kingly David undone by his tragic flaw. Flem Snopes is more than a conniving, amoral businessman: he is, as a key scene in *The Hamlet* reveals, an archfiend capable of usurping the throne from the Prince of Hell. Eula Varner (possibly the only character in Faulkner's works for whom source critics, understandably, have not located a proto-type) is alternately Helen, Lilith, Semiramis, Eve, Venus—in short, the primal female whose "entire appearance suggested some symbology out of the old Dionysic times" (*H* 95). In *Go Down, Moses* the wilderness is Eden, the New South is Canaan, and Ike McCaslin is a Christ figure seeking to atone for the sins of his race. The idealistic Gavin Stevens is Don Quixote, frustrated and befuddled by the real world. And so on throughout the fiction. Indeed, almost every Faulkner character and event has a parallel in ancient myth, the heroic epic, or the chivalric romance.[25] While such correspondences serve to elevate Faulkner's fiction above its local and regional setting and give the work a uni-versal quality, the mythic elements also evidence Faulkner's compulsion to envelop drab, commonplace reality with an aura of romance and greatness. Through such conversions Faulkner could give meaning and significance to "the sorry, shabby world" of experience.

As in the case of his aesthetic of memory, Faulkner's aesthetic of imag-ination finds clear expression in his style. And the function is likewise the same: to protest and hopefully escape the tragic world of time and death. Rec-ognizing, as Wallace Stevens does, that man "cannot look at the past or the future except by means of the imagination,"[26] Faulkner utilizes the stream-of-consciousness method as a tool of transcendence. On one occasion, in noting his agreement with Henri Bergson's idea of "the fluidity of time," Faulkner observed, "There is only the present moment, in which I include both the past and the future, and that is eternity" (*LIG* 70). In other words, immortality, "eternity," equates with the imaginative leap from the present moment into either the past or the future. Conversely, to be trapped in any one of these dimensions—the dead past, the dying present, or the nonexistent future—is to be defeated by time and death. In the same interview statement, Faulkner went on to say that "time can be shaped quite a bit by the artist; after all, man is never time's slave" (*LIG* 70). In a physical sense, of course, as Faulkner well knew, man *is* time's slave; but through the exercise of his imagination, man can reshape time to his own purposes. In so doing he transcends the limita-tions of the physical world and makes contact with "eternity."

Readers will find in almost any stream-of-consciousness passage in Faulkner's books an application of this principle. One was cited at the begin-ning of this essay, Ike McCaslin's thoughts upon returning to the big woods at the end of "The Bear." Another good example is a seven-page passage in *Intruder in the Dust.* The time is Monday night shortly after ten o'clock, and

Chick Mallison and his uncle Gavin Stevens are "standing beside the sheriff's car in the alley beside the jail watching Lucas and the sheriff emerge from the jail's side door and cross the dark yard toward them" (211). As the sheriff and Lucas move toward the car, Chick turns and walks the short block to the edge of the town square, now empty after the frenzied excitement of the day. Feeling like an actor waiting in the wings to complete the last act of a drama, Chick notes "the square which was more than dead: abandoned" (211), illuminated only by the lights in an all-night cafe and Stevens's second-story law office. As he looks over "the whole dark lifeless rectangle" (211), Chick contrasts this Monday night with "the other the normal Monday nights when no loud fury of blood and revenge and racial and family solidarity had come roaring in from Beat Four" (212–13).

These other Monday nights are characterized by the various activities of moviegoers and livestock buyers. Next, Chick's thoughts turn to the appearance of the square on the previous night, Sunday, when the citizens of Jefferson sat quietly behind their doors anticipating the lynching of Lucas Beauchamp. As the narrative continues, the focus shifts back to the present scene, then briefly to Chick's projections of the coming week: "tomorrow it would be over, tomorrow of course the Square would wake and stir, another day and it would fling off hangover, another and it would even fling off shame" (214). The reflection concludes with a two-page italicized section which repeats Gavin's words to Chick—expressed presumably many times but most recently only thirty minutes earlier—about the future of Black and white southerners. Following this recollection, Chick leaves the square and returns to the alley to observe again "the sheriff and Lucas crossing the dark yard" (217).

The reader is surprised to learn that this entire seven-page narrative has occupied only a minute or two, perhaps only seconds, in actual time. Obviously, Faulkner's intent here is to capture in the slow-motion process of linear prose the rapid and kaleidoscopic thought patterns which can perhaps be rendered convincingly (if at all in art) only by the motion picture film. But one senses in such passages more than an attempt to capture what Faulkner once defined as "the whole complete nuance of the moment's experience" (*LIG* 107). One perceives also an urgency, even a desperation, a straining against the limits of time through the creative power of the imagination. All of Faulkner's characteristic stylistic devices—his penchant for stringing together a succession of coordinate, often synonymous terms; the extensive use of lengthy series of subordinate and parenthetical phrases and clauses; the pervasive reliance upon analogy, simile, and metaphor; and the attempt to utilize (and sometimes misapply) the whole range and scope of the English vocabulary—derive from this same urgency. Faulkner well understood his purpose in this regard, even if some of his readers have not. As he stated in Japan,

> I would say that that style is a result of a need, of a necessity. This is what I mean, man knows that he cannot live forever, he has only a short time to live, there could be in a man's mind, in his heart, a desire to express some universal truth and he knows he has only a certain number of years to express that truth in, and so in my own case anyway, it's the compulsion to say everything in one sentence because you may not live long enough to have two sentences. (*LIG* 141)

Thus, Faulkner's idiosyncratic style not only mirrors the interaction of human beings with time but also records a protest against its tyranny.

In considering Faulkner's style as a means of denying time and death, one should pay particular attention to one aspect of that style, the extensive use of figurative language. Faulkner readers are quite familiar with his proclivity to describe characters, actions, and objects not as isolated, independent entities but almost always in relation to other persons and things. Indeed, one might conclude that nothing in Faulkner's work has significance in and of itself, but only as it is transformed metaphorically by the creative imagination. The pattern is exemplified by *Intruder in the Dust*, not generally considered one of Faulkner's best novels but one of the most conspicuous in its use of figurative language. This work contains, by quick count, more than three hundred figures of speech, including similes, metaphors, personifications, and analogies.[27] It seems inadequate to account for such a preponderance of figures as merely a holdover from Faulkner's practice as a poet. To perceive the ultimate significance of this characteristic of Faulkner's style, one must look beyond such facile labels as "Faulkner's poetic prose" and consider the psychological basis for metaphoric language. As almost all theorists agree, writers resort to metaphor when ordinary language proves inadequate for their needs, when they desire to capture, through suggestion, an intensity or a significance which cannot be conveyed by direct treatment. In this regard, the inclination toward metaphor readily serves Faulkner's aesthetic of memory. As Rene Wellek and Austin Warren explain, "We metaphorize . . . what we love, what we want to linger over and contemplate, to see from every angle and under every lighting, mirrored in specialized focus by all kinds of like things."[28] But metaphor is not only a way of enhancing an object as object; it is also a reaching beyond, an attempt at metamorphosis. The root meaning of the word "trope," the generic term for all figures of speech, is "turning away"; thus, metaphoric language is basically an attempt to transcend the commonplace and the conventional. As

Philip Wheelwright insists, "What really matters in a metaphor is the psychic depth at which the things of the world, whether actual or fancied, are transmuted by the cool heat of the imagination."[29] And so it is with Faulkner. Like his use of mythic correspondence for character and incident, the employment of figurative language evidences a need to transcend "the sorry, shabby world" through the creative force of the imagination. Metaphor, then, in Faulkner's method becomes just one more means of "saying No to death."

I have sought to demonstrate that a desire, not always conscious, to protest the tragic realities of time and death provided both the impetus and the pattern for Faulkner's fictional creation. I have noted that Faulkner's twin aesthetics of memory and imagination, both clearly exhibited in his subject matter and style, are logical derivations of the compulsion to "say No to death." Now, in conclusion, I wish to identify one major inference to be drawn from this approach to Faulkner's work.

Critics have debated at length whether Faulkner's fiction, on balance, makes a positive or negative statement regarding the human condition. Some readers find in Faulkner's books an unrelieved pessimism; others find a strong assertion of humanistic values; still others find that Faulkner began in cynicism but ended in hope. These various judgments explain the conflicting reactions to Faulkner's Nobel Prize acceptance speech: one reader interprets the address as nothing more than empty rhetoric, while another insists that it is a statement of genuine belief and promise.

The disagreement about Faulkner's definition of humanity is bound to continue, but even the most emphatic naysayer concerning Faulkner's view of human behavior and potential must concede that the writer's feelings for art and the artist are extremely positive. In considering the crass materialism of the Snopeses, the pathetic fates of Quentin Compson, Addie Bundren, Joe Christmas, and Thomas Sutpen, and the noble but largely ironic deeds of Dilsey Gibson, Ike McCaslin, and the French corporal, one should remember that he is viewing the world through the refraction of art. The world that Faulkner mirrors may be one of tragedy and grief, but the art which images that world is a magnificent triumph, a thing of beauty. While Faulkner as historian, or politician, or psychologist, or philosopher, or theologian may despair, Faulkner as artist has supreme faith in the value of creativity and the nature of art. One suspects that the Nobel Prize address is only secondarily a statement about humankind and its destiny: it is first and foremost a declaration of faith in the creative act of the poet. Perhaps Faulkner was mistaken (though one hopes not) in viewing his own artistic struggle and triumph as emblematic of the fate of humanity,[30] but this question should not be allowed to obscure his characterization, in the Nobel Prize speech and elsewhere, of the poet's role as heroic. The poet is heroic because he is totally dedicated to his craft and will allow neither hardship nor success to distract him from his task. The poet is heroic because he risks the impossible and because he refuses to accept defeat, even though it is inevitable.[31] The poet is heroic because he matches his imagination against "the sorry, shabby world." Above all, the poet is heroic because through his creativity he "says No to death." In these ways, in its processes and not necessarily its content or message, art may be said to be "the salvation of mankind" (*LIG* 71). "The most important thing," Faulkner said, "is that man continues to create, just as woman continues to give birth. Man will keep writing on pieces of paper, on scraps, on stones, as long as he lives" (*LIG* 73). All individuals, of course, strive in their own ways to overcome time and death, but the artist, according to Faulkner, comes closest to success. As he observed at Nagano, "[Man] can't live forever. He knows that. But when he's gone somebody will know he was here for his short time. He can build a bridge and will be remembered for a day or two, a monument, for a day or two, but somehow the picture, the poem—that lasts a long time, a very long time, longer than anything" (*LIG* 103).

NOTES

1. The earliest use of this phrase which I find in Faulkner's work occurs in *Requiem for a Nun*, 185; but a virtually synonymous term, "saying No to time," appears in the unfinished manuscript of "Elmer" (unpublished typescript, Faulkner Collection at the University of Virginia, 60), written in 1925.

2. See Jerold Howard Stock, "Suggestions of Death-Anxiety in the Life of William Faulkner," unpublished dissertation (West Virginia, 1977). A few of Stock's arguments seem somewhat strained, but his work represents an important contribution to Faulkner scholarship.

3. Cf. Vardaman's boring holes in his mother's coffin in *AILD*.

4. Similar statements appear in *GDM*, 179, and *F*, 399.

5. Faulkner's anxiety about an afterlife is reflected in his remark to his brother Jack during their mother's final illness: "Maybe each of us will become some sort of radio wave." Murry C. Falkner, *The Falkners of Mississippi: A Memoir* (Baton Rouge: Louisiana State University Press, 1967), 189.

6. For an excellent discussion of the Keatsian influence, see Blanche H. Gelfant, "Faulkner and Keats: The Ideality of Art in 'The Bear,'" *Southern Literary Journal* 2 (Fall 1969): 43–65.

7. See, for example, *FIU*, 103, 123, 147, 181.

8. Joseph Blotner, "William Faulkner's Essay on the Composition of *Sartoris*," *Yale University Library Gazette* 47 (January 1973): 122–23.

9. Memory also plays an important role in the non-Yoknapatawpha works. For example, *The Wild Palms*, based in part on Faulkner's relationships with Helen Baird and Meta Carpenter, was originally entitled "If I Forget Thee, O Jerusalem." See *FB*, 978, 989–91.

10. Cf. Faulkner's tendency, as reported by his brother John, to "squirrel away" toys and other items. "All of us had special storage places for our possessions. Jack's and mine were never very interesting. We broke our toys or forgot them. But Bill's was always neat and seemed to have everything in it he had ever owned. He was still that way about saving curious mementos up until he died. His study had more objects stashed about in it and most of us wondered why in the world he kept them." John Faulkner, *My Brother Bill: An Affectionate Reminiscence* (New York: Trident Press, 1963), 76.

11. Michael Millgate similarly links Cecilia's legacy with Faulkner's comments on art. See *The Achievement of William Faulkner* (New York: Random House, 1966), 225.

12. See Elizabeth M. Kerr, "*The Reivers*: The Golden Book of Yoknapatawpha County," *Modern Fiction Studies* 13 (Spring 1967): 95–113. For a rejoinder, see James B. Meriwether, "The Novel Faulkner Never Wrote: His Golden Book or Doomsday Book," *American Literature* 42 (March 1970): 93–96.

13. Robert Penn Warren, "Why Do We Read Fiction?" *Saturday Evening Post* 235 (October 20, 1962): 84.

14. As Jean-Paul Sartre has written, "Proust really *should have* employed a technique like Faulkner's; that was the logical outcome of his metaphysic." "Time in Faulkner: *The Sound and the Fury*," in *William Faulkner: Three Decades of Criticism*, ed. Frederick J. Hoffman and Olga W. Vickery (New York: Harbinger Books, 1963), 229–30.

15. Alfred Kazin, "Faulkner's Vision of Human Integrity," *Harvard Advocate* 135 (November 1951): 33.

16. Cf. Louise's statement in "Dr. Martino" (*CS*, 577): "Then he told me one day, when I was big enough to understand, how there is nothing in the world but living, being alive, knowing you are alive. And to be afraid is to know you are alive, but to do what you are afraid of, then you *live*. He says it's better even to be afraid than to be dead." This is not to suggest that Faulkner honors life at any price. As Cass Edmonds observes in *Go Down, Moses* (179), "There is only one thing worse than not being alive, and that's shame." Flem Snopes, Jason Compson, and Popeye Vitelli are examples of Faulkner characters who choose shameful lives, while Eula Varner Snopes demonstrates (at least in the opinion of Charles Mallison) that not every suicide is dishonorable. Concerning the last point, see *The Town*, 337.

17. One suspects that Faulkner's comments about Sherwood Anderson's size (*FIU* 259–60) reflect Faulkner's own feelings of insecurity. See also Murry Falkner's observation in *Falkners of Mississippi*, 191–92.

18. Faulkner dramatizes this point, as well as other ideas he held concerning art and the artist, in the short story "Carcassonne." See my article "'Carcassonne': Faulkner's Allegory of Art and the Artist," *Southern Review* 15 (Spring 1979): 355–65.

19. Much of the conversation in Faulkner's second novel, *Mosquitoes*, centers around a Freudian approach to literature. Consider, for example, Dawson Fairchild's statement "That's about all the virtue there is in art: it's a kind of Battle Creek, Michigan [site of a renowned sanitarium], for the spirit" (337), and Julius's reflection, "Dante invented Beatrice, creating himself a maid that life had not had time to create, and laid upon her frail and unbowed shoulders the whole burden of man's history of his impossible heart's desire" (358). Bayard Sartoris (*U* 228) and General Gragnon's aide (*F* 44–45) also offer Freudian explanations for the creation of literature.

20. Strictly speaking, memory may be identified with realism, and imagination with romance. Significantly, Faulkner produces neither a literature which copies life nor a literature of escapism but "a living literature" which draws from both extremes. See Faulkner's prefatory note to *The Mansion*.

21. Blotner, "William Faulkner's Essay on the Composition of *Sartoris*," 123.

22. Jules de Gaultier, *Bovarysm*, trans. Gerald M. Spring (New York: Philosophical Library, 1970), 4. According to de Gaultier, the will-to-illusion is an essential faculty of man and becomes destructive, as in the case of Emma Bovary, only when it is sentimentalized.

23. Walter J. Slatoff, *Quest for Failure: A Study of William Faulkner* (Ithaca: Cornell University Press, i960), 80.

24. The same point might be made in relation to Faulkner's cavalier handling of dates and other details from one novel to another. As Faulkner explained at Charlottesville, "When you go to the trouble to invent a private domain of your own, then you're the master of time, too. I have the right, I think, to shift these things around wherever it sounds best, and I can move them about in time and, if necessary, change their names" (*FIU* 29).

25. For an extended treatment of this matter, see Lynn Gartrell Levins, *Faulkner's Heroic Design: The Yoknapatawpha Novels* (Athens: University of Georgia Press, 1976).

26. Wallace Stevens, "Imagination as Value," *The Necessary Angel: Essays on Reality and the Imagination* (New York: Alfred A. Knopf, 1951), 144.

27. Roughly one-half of the figures in *Intruder in the Dust* are similes; about one-third are metaphors or personifications. Strangely, Edwin R. Hunter (*William Faulkner: Narrative Practice and Prose Style* [Washington, DC: Windhover Press, 1973], 215) finds only twenty-eight similes and four metaphors in the novel.

28. Rene Wellek and Austin Warren, *Theory of Literature*, 3rd ed. (New York: Harvest Hook, 1963), 197.

29. Philip Wheelwright, *Metaphor and Reality* (Bloomington: Indiana University Press, 1962), 71.

30. I agree with Blotner's contention that "there was . . . probably an intensely personal component in the words of the speech" (*FB* 1367).

31. See, for example, *LIG*, 81, 88, 138, 221, 238.

"Longer than Anything"
Faulkner's "Grand Design" in *Absalom, Absalom!*

> [Man] can't live forever. He knows that. But when he's gone some-
> body will know he was here for his short time. He can build a bridge
> and will be remembered for a day or two, a monument, for a day or
> two, but somehow the picture, the poem—that lasts a long time, a
> very long time, longer than anything.
> —FAULKNER at Nagano, Japan, 1955[1]

Many critics have written extensive commentaries on Thomas Sutpen's "Grand Design" in *Absalom, Absalom!*[2] Indeed, one of the most thorough treatments of the topic, Dirk Kuyk, Jr.'s book-length study, carries the title *Sutpen's Design*.[3] Less has been written, however, about another "design" in the book that counters Sutpen's, providing an upward, transcendent movement that contrasts sharply with Sutpen's tragic fall. This second pattern is Faulkner's, the creator's; and to understand that design is to understand a great deal about Faulkner's views of art and the artist.

I begin with a rarely cited passage that characterizes not only the type of novel that *Absalom, Absalom!* is but also the kind of writer that William Faulkner is. The passage, which appears early in chapter 8, is, significantly, one of the few in the novel narrated by the omniscient author. The passage describes Quentin's and Shreve's reconstruction of the conversation between Thomas and Henry Sutpen in the library of the Sutpen mansion a half century earlier. As Quentin and Shreve imagine the scene, Henry, while he listens to his father speak, looks through the window and sees Judith and Charles Bon walking together in the garden, "the sister's head bent with listening, the lover's head leaned above it while they paced slowly on in that rhythm which not the eyes but the heart marks and calls the beat and measure for, to disappear slowly beyond some bush or shrub starred with white bloom—jasmine, spi-raea, honeysuckle, perhaps myriad scentless unpickable Cherokee roses" (236).

Then, abruptly, without even a sentence break, the omniscient narra-tor retracts what has just been said by pointing out that it would have been impossible for Henry to see what Quentin and Shreve want to believe he saw, because it was both wintertime (specifically Christmas Eve) and nighttime: "and hence no bloom nor leaf even if there had been someone to walk there and be seen there." Then, just as abruptly, three times in rapid succession, the narrator offers a judgment on the apparent contradiction by observing that Quentin and Shreve's misconceptions "did not matter," since what really mat-ters for Quentin and Shreve (and for Faulkner as well) is the power of the creative imagination to bridge the gap between present and past and thus to enable "the immortal brief recent intransient blood" (237) of the dead to "course" once again.

No passage better illustrates the degree to which the narrative strategy of *Absalom, Absalom!* turns upon the mythologizing tendency of the human imagination. For Quentin and Shreve the scene between Henry and his father is characterized by sunlight, blooming flowers, youth, idealism, and love—symbols of life and regeneration. For the narrator, whose role as realist is to demythologize, or deconstruct, the myth, the actual scene is one of winter and darkness—universal symbols of death. Thus are presented the polarities of Faulkner's greatest novel—death versus life, history versus myth, actuality versus art, the lost, irretrievable past versus the past as resurrected and revivi-fied in poetic fabulation.

Throughout his career Faulkner was interested in—even, one might justifi-ably argue, obsessed with—the paradoxical relationship between art and life. "The aim of every artist," he once said, "is to arrest motion, which is life, by artificial means and hold it fixed so that 100 years later when a stranger looks at it, it moves again since it is life" (*LIG* 253). At Charlottesville he spoke of the writer's goal in similar terms: "You catch this fluidity which is human life and you focus a light on it and you stop it long enough for people to be able to see it" (*FIU* 239). Such statements acknowledge that art is a created object, an artifact, a stoppage of life and motion and hence antithetical to the flux and mutability that characterize the human condition. In this sense, of course, all art is ultimately a divorcement from actuality; as Gail Hightower observes in *Light in August*, "How false the most profound book turns out to be when applied to life" (455). At the same time, however, Faulkner's statements also assert that whatever success is possible for the artist is directly proportionate to the degree that his art is interrelated with actual experience.[4]

Faulkner's fictional oeuvre may be viewed as an ongoing dialectic on the relationship between art and life. At times Faulkner seemed to favor the realists' theory of art as *mimesis*, a view which asserts the dependence of art on life and thereby implies a superiority of life over art; at other times, drawing upon the practice of the neoromantics, the Symbolists, he stressed art as *poiesis*, a position that emphasizes the artist's originality and creativity and thus argues for the supremacy of art over life. While a tension between these two positions is evidenced throughout his career, in general Faulkner may be identified with the life-over-art school of thought during his apprenticeship and with the art-over-life school after he reached his literary majority.

In one of his earliest essays, published in 1922, Faulkner characterizes Joseph Hergesheimer as an author who seeks to divorce his art from life. Faulkner claims that Hergesheimer is "afraid of living, of man in his sorry clay," and adds that *Linda Condon* is "not a novel" but "a lovely Byzantine frieze: a few unforgettable figures in silent arrested motion, forever beyond the reach of time and troubling the heart like music." Faulkner further observes: "One can imagine Hergesheimer submerging himself in *Linda Condon* as in a still harbor where the age cannot hurt him and where rumor of the world reaches him only as a far faint sound of rain" (*EPP* 101–2). Clearly, Faulkner views Hergesheimer's art as escapist, and therefore incompatible with the truth of actual experience.

Recognition of the paradoxical tension that exists between art and life seems to account in part for the characterization of the faun in Faulkner's first published book, *The Marble Faun*.[5] In this pastoral cycle of poems, a marble faun, reminiscent of both Praxiteles's statue in Rome and Hawthorne's novel based on the statue, is exposed to the changes wrought in nature by the advancing seasons of the year. The mutability observable in nature contrasts sharply with the "marble-bound" existence of the faun. One might expect such a contrast to be employed, as it often is in the poetry of the Romantics, to assert the superiority of art over nature, but just the opposite seems to be the case.

Why am I sad? I?
Why am I not content? The sky
Warms me and yet I cannot break
My marble bonds. That quick keen snake
Is free to come and go, while I
Am prisoner to dream and sigh
For things I know, yet cannot know,
'Twixt sky above and earth below.

The spreading earth calls to my feet
Of orchards bright with fruits to eat,
Of hills and streams on either hand;
Of sleep at night on moon-blanched sand:
The whole world breathes and calls to me
Who marble-bound must ever be. (12)

Although the faun exists in an immutable, deathless world, this realization, in a manner that recalls Calypso in Homer's *Odyssey*, occasions no joy.

And we, the marbles in the glade,
Dreaming in the leafy shade
Are saddened, for we know that all
Things save us must fade and fall. (31)

In the Epilogue the faun continues to lament the fact that he is forever excluded from both the ecstasies and sorrows of real life:

Ah, how all this calls to me
Who marble-bound must ever be
While turn unchangingly the years.
My heart is full, yet sheds no tears
To cool my burning carven eyes
Bent to the unchanging skies:
I would be sad with changing year,
Instead, a sad, bound prisoner.
For though about me seasons go
My heart knows only winter snow. (50–51)

Unlike Hawthorne's Donatello, Faulkner's faun is never allowed to become humanized, to exchange his innocence for experience in the actual world. He remains, at the end as in the beginning, trapped in his artificial, marble-bound existence.

Faulkner's most explicit treatment of the paradoxical relationship between art and life is found in his second novel, *Mosquitoes*. In fact, this book, in which Faulkner portrays a group of New Orleans artists, would-be artists, intellectuals, and socialites on a four-day outing aboard a yacht, may be viewed primarily as a colloquium which allows the author to examine various theories of art and the artist. As Michael Millgate pointed out in his seminal study, the novel contains "statements of artistic principle and belief which seem most fully to embody Faulkner's own position—almost as if the book, with its exploration and exposition of many different viewpoints, had been the means by which he had argued out his own uncertainties and arrived eventually at a clearer conception of his role as an artist."[6] Although many different topics (not all of them literary) are discussed, the principal concern, as in *The Marble Faun*, appears to be the relationship between life and art; and the characters may be grouped according to their views regarding this central concern.

At one extreme are such young people as Patricia, David West, Jenny, and Pete, who are intensely involved in living but utterly indifferent to art. As Julius, the Semitic man, observes, "Look at our books, our stage, the movies. Who supports 'em? Not the young folks. They'd rather walk around or just sit and hold each other's hands" (239). At the other extreme are the dilettantes like Ernest Talliaferro and Mrs. Maurier and such artist-pretenders as Mark Frost, Eva Wiseman, and Miss Jameson. Like J. Alfred Prufrock, with whom Talliaferro is specifically paralleled, these characters are all fearful of life (as with Prufrock, the revealing metaphor is sex) and prefer conversation to action. Their discussions, lengthy and often tiresome, are appropriately described as "talk, talk, talk: the utter and heartbreaking stupidity of words" (194). Ironically, Mrs. Maurier mistakes the detachment from life symbolized by such verbalization as a prerequisite to artistic endeavor: "To live within yourself, to be sufficient unto yourself. . . . To go through life, keeping yourself from becoming involved in it, to gather inspiration for your Work—ah, Mr. Gordon, how lucky you who create are" (157–58).

Standing alone as the one character who is capable of at least partially reconciling these extremes, of bridging the gap between life and art, is the sculptor Gordon. Not only is he the most perceptive and creative among the artist group (he manages to capture in the clay bust of Mrs. Maurier the very essence of her character, whereas Dawson Fairchild, who has been acquainted with the lady much longer, discovers that he hardly knows her at all), but he is also the least talkative.

Moreover, his involvement with Patricia, while not altogether satisfying, nonetheless suggests an openness to life denied the aesthetes and pseudo-artists. Gordon's refusal to withdraw from life in the manner of the other artists is symbolized by his encounter with the prostitute toward the end of the novel. "Gordon entered and before the door closed again they saw him in a narrow passageway lift a woman from the shadow and raise her against the mad stars, smothering her squeal against his tall kiss." This act of engagement with life is immediately juxtaposed with the image of Gordon's statue of the young virgin: "*Then voices and sounds, shadows and echoes change form swirling, becoming the headless, armless, legless torso of a girl, motionless and virginal and passionately eternal before the shadows and echoes whirl away*" (358). The point seems clear: only the artist with the courage and passion to engage life honestly and directly can hope to transform that experience into authentic art.

Faulkner wrote his review of *Linda Condon, The Marble Faun,* and *Mosquitoes* during a period of his life when art seemed rather poor compensation for missed adventures in living. Like the frustrated poet in "Carcassonne," that early story which reveals so much about its creator, Faulkner wanted "*to perform something bold and tragical and austere*" (*CS* 899). His recent disillusionments in military service and love doubtless contributed to a sense of unfulfillment, but he had not yet lost his youthful idealism. Despite his disappointments, he was still inclined to identify with Dawson Fairchild's tendency in *Mosquitoes* to "prefer a live poet to the writings of any man" (258). Indeed, as he had confessed in his 1924 essay "Verse Old and Nascent: A Pilgrimage," poetry was primarily a way of "furthering various philanderings in which [he] was engaged"; only, he continues, after he found his "concupiscence waning" did he turn to "verse for verse's sake" (*EPP* 115). As such statements evidence, to the young Faulkner life, not art, was the magical realm where happiness could best be found.

By the time he wrote *Absalom,* however, Faulkner's view of life had become much more jaded and cynical—and, conversely, as I shall subsequently demonstrate, his view of art much more positive. The former attitude derived partly, one suspects, from the time period in which the novel was written. In the mid-1930s the nation was in the midst of the Great Depression; and Faulkner, unlike his contemporary Margaret Mitchell, could find little encouragement in the situation. Whereas Mitchell's novel, *Gone with the Wind* (coincidentally published the same year as *Absalom, Absalom!*), stresses the popular theme of the resiliency of the human spirit to bounce back from defeat and hardship, Faulkner's politically incorrect novel offered no such hopeful vision. On the contrary, Faulkner's message was more akin to that of his Hollywood hunting companion Nathanael West, whose *Miss Lonelyhearts* (1933) depicted an America being overwhelmed by chaos, violence, alienation, and despair.

In addition to the Great Depression context of the novel, there was also, as Faulkner's biographers have helped us to realize, a personal element in the bitterly pessimistic view of life expressed in Faulkner's rendition of Sutpen's fate.[7] The approach of middle age, the failure to achieve the literary and financial success that he desired and felt he deserved, the growing conviction that he was trapped in an unhappy marriage, the chronic drinking—such factors contributed to Faulkner's discontent and malaise. Then, too, there was the cruel, untimely death of his brother Dean in the crash of the plane that Faulkner had provided. Given such developments, it is not at all surprising that the Faulkner of this period was coming to perceive human history in the terms he would employ at the end of *Absalom, Absalom!* to describe the collapse of Sutpen's dream: "it was all finished now, there was nothing left now, nothing out there now but that idiot boy to lurk around those ashes and those four gutted chimneys and howl" (301). The echoes of the famous quotation from *Macbeth*, from which Faulkner had taken his title for *The Sound and the Fury*, are unmistakable—and very likely intentional.

Even Faulkner's mail brought him suggestions that life and history are futile. As Joseph Blotner has documented, about the time Faulkner was beginning the work that would become *Absalom, Absalom!* he received from Hal Smith a copy of André Malraux's *Man's Fate* (*FB* 827). This novel, which traces the betrayal and defeat of a group of Chinese revolutionaries, depicts the ongoing but pathetic struggle of man's idealism in an indifferent and absurd cosmos. Faulkner's novel would develop much the same theme—but without Malraux's redeeming "beginning again" conclusion.

Viewed as history, Thomas Sutpen's story is exceedingly tragic, deterministically so. As we know from a number of other Faulkner works, particularly *The Sound and the Fury*, "The Bear," and *A Fable*, Faulkner's ultimate view of history was decidedly pessimistic. In fact, it could be called Spenglerian.[8] Individuals age and die, cultures rise and inevitably fall, dreams and ideals are constantly frustrated and thwarted, remaining alive only as hope and memory. As Harry Wilbourne, a character not altogether unlike Thomas Sutpen, comes to understand, the common lot of humanity is "grief," the only alternative, as Quentin Compson has already discovered, being "nothing" (*WP* 324).

It is, I think, to stress the inevitability of grief and loss that Faulkner accounts for Sutpen's failure to realize his design in deterministic terms. As every reader comes to recognize, Sutpen's defeat is inextricably tied to the question of race. Sutpen is undeniably and unapologetically "racist," but it becomes instructive to examine carefully the influences that make him so.

Faulkner treats Sutpen's first encounter with a Black almost casually—in fact, parenthetically—but the experience has profound ramifications, foreshadowing as it does Sutpen's subsequent career. The encounter occurs when Sutpen is a ten-year-old boy, accompanying his family as it migrates from the mountains of western Virginia to the Tidewater region to the east. As Sutpen recalls for General Compson, a good portion of that journey was spent sitting in the family's cart outside taverns waiting for the alcoholic father to complete his drinking binges. Frequently the father would become so drunk that he had to be physically carried from the tavern and loaded onto the cart. On one occasion that chore had been accomplished "by a huge bull of a n——r, the first black man, slave, they had ever seen, who emerged with the old man over his shoulder like a sack of meal and his—the n——r's—mouth loud with laughing and full of teeth like tombstones" (182).

Sutpen's Negrophobia has its origin in this scene. Readers should not underestimate the shocking and lasting effect of a young boy's watching his father's being manhandled and ridiculed by a large, powerful Black stranger. Significantly, the description of the scene conveys two images that symbolize forces that Sutpen will later contend against in his quest to build a family dynasty: the twin fears of dehumanization (the father is handled "like a sack of meal") and death (the Black's teeth look "like tombstones").

This negative experience, which made such a startling impression upon the young Sutpen that the adult would still recall and repeat it more than a quarter century later, is followed by others just as traumatic and influential. Once, as he and his sister walk along a dirt road, the young girl is nearly run down by a carriage driven by a "n——r coachman in a plug hat" (187). On another occasion he listens as his father, in a voice of "fierce exultation, vindication" (187), recounts the beating of a Black enslaved man by a group of night riders. Then, when he is about thirteen or fourteen years of age, Thomas is sent by his father with a message to the "big house," whereupon he is turned away from the front door and told to go to the back by a "monkey-dressed n——r butler" (187).

All readers agree, following Sutpen's own assessment of the incident, that the rejection at the door is the central experience of Sutpen's childhood. But most readers, I think, have been too quick to follow Sutpen's lead in affixing blame for the humiliation. Although Sutpen consciously insists that his anger and desire for revenge are directed toward the owner of the plantation and not the Black butler, it is hard to believe that his subconscious has completely exonerated the Black butler of guilt.[9] In fact, Sutpen's redundant reiteration that it was "not the n——r" who was at fault seems excessive, the futile effort perhaps of an uncertain man to persuade himself of a truth of which he is not altogether convinced. No reader takes Quentin's protestation, "*I dont hate it! I dont hate it!*" (303), at face value; neither should we necessarily believe everything that Sutpen says. As psychologists recognize, it is not at all unusual for individuals to find it extremely difficult, at least subconsciously, to separate a message from its deliverer. His use of the demeaning phrase "monkey n——r" certainly seems to suggest that Sutpen has been unable to do so.

The terrifying, near-death experience in Haiti further exaggerates the Negrophobia that Sutpen's early conditioning has already established. In fact, the Haiti episode merely repeats on a wider, adult scale the tragic initiation pattern of the young boy's Tidewater experience. As General Compson notes, Haiti is "a theatre for violence and injustice and bloodshed and all the satanic lusts of human greed and cruelty," located at "the halfway point between what we call the jungle and what we call civilization" (202). Compson associates Sutpen's journey to the island as a journey to "the heart of the earth" (202), a phrase that recalls the experience of another character from one of Faulkner's favorite books—Kurtz in Joseph Conrad's *Heart of Darkness*. Although Faulkner chooses to present Sutpen's Haitian terror indirectly, through suggestion and implication (as he does the terror element in such stories as "A Rose for Emily" and "Dry September"), his references to voodooistic ritual, the eight-day siege, the paralyzing fear of those under attack, and Sutpen's life-threatening wounds persuade most readers that Sutpen is not exaggerating when he characterizes the episode as "more than flesh should be asked to stand" (205).

Unlike Kurtz, Sutpen survives his Descent into Hell; but he does not escape unscathed: the horrors he saw and experienced there have a catastrophic effect upon his subsequent life and career. In fact, so intense is his association of those terrible days with his memory of the smell of burning sugar cane that "he had never been able to bear sugar since" (201). Undoubtedly, like Kurtz (and like Captain Delano in another horror story that Faulkner may have known, Melville's "Benito Cereno"), Sutpen also comes to associate such atrocities with black skin.

Sutpen's subsequent effort to create Sutpen's Hundred and establish a family dynasty in Yoknapatawpha County represents a heroic, though eventually maniacal, attempt to control the forces of dehumanization, disintegration, and death that he has come to associate, albeit perhaps subconsciously, with the condition of Blackness. To prove his superiority to and control over this condition, he coerces a subhuman "band of wild n——s like beasts half tamed to walk upright like men" (4) to build his mansion. For the same reason he engages in hand-to-hand combat with some of these "beastlike" creatures. Rosa Coldfield is right at least on this point, viewing Sutpen's motivation for the no-holds-barred fights "as a matter of sheer deadly forethought toward the retention of supremacy, domination" (21). The picture of Sutpen standing triumphantly over the body of a vanquished Black is an obverse image of his watching his father's being manhandled by a huge enslaved man, or his being turned away from the Tidewater plantation house by a "monkey n——r," or his being pinned down for days and nearly killed during the slave insurrection in Haiti. The desperate need for a plantation house and a family dynasty is merely a further extension of his desire to prove to himself and to the world that he is forevermore impervious to such threats.[10]

Ironically, in seeking to prove his invincibility, to escape his fear of powerlessness and dehumanization, he oppresses and abuses the very group in the novel with which he originally has so much in common, that is, the Blacks, three of whom are his wife, his son, and his daughter. While Sutpen's treatment of Eulalia Bon, Charles Bon, and even Clytie is sad and disgraceful, it is, given his past experience, altogether logical and predictable. The shrewd manipulation of Henry to prevent Bon's marriage to Judith is not merely consistent with Sutpen's character, it is inescapable. Given his personal history, the last thing that Sutpen could allow would be to have his "design" tainted by any trace of Black blood. The logic of the racist may appear to others to be confused and irrational, but to the racist it has the precision and inevitability of a mathematical equation.

I am aware that the explanation I have presented for Sutpen's behavior is not consistent with Sutpen's own understanding of his motives. He believes—and he is partly right—that it is the owner of the big house, not the Black butler, who is to blame for his youthful humiliation and thus responsible for the genesis of his "design." He also genuinely believes that on two crucial occasions in the pursuit of that design he has exercised free will in the making of choices: the first time, in Haiti, when he elects to set aside his first wife and child as incompatible with his life's purpose, and again, years later in Mississippi, when he rejects his mixed-race son a second time.

I believe, however, that Sutpen is at least partly mistaken on both counts. In the final analysis, Sutpen's adult behavior seems as rigidly predetermined as that, say, of Quentin Compson, Joe Christmas, or Popeye Vitelli. When the defining moment of his destiny presents itself in the person of Charles Bon at his door, Sutpen thinks that he makes a choice; but that choice has already been made for him long ago. Were he more self-aware, he might say with Joe Christmas, "I have never got outside that circle. I have never broken out of the ring of what I have already done and cannot ever undo" (*LIA* 321).

I have stressed the deterministic aspects of Faulkner's handling of the fate of Thomas Sutpen to suggest how thoroughly bleak and pessimistic is the view of history expressed in *Absalom, Absalom!* That pessimism is evidenced not only in the death of Sutpen, the destruction of his mansion, and the ironic survival of Sutpen's blood lineage only in the "idiot negro" (301) Jim Bond, but also in the degree to which Sutpen's fall is linked to circumstance, geography, and the ineradicable imperfections of human nature. Sutpen's "innocence," therefore, is in part his belief, his illusion, that history can be anything other than what it already, inexorably is.

But history is only one aspect, the negative one, of this great novel; art is the other, the redeeming feature. Whereas Sutpen's historical "design" plunges downward to defeat and death, Faulkner's artistic "design"—far grander than Sutpen's—moves upward and outward, defeating both time and geography through the immortality of art and the universality of myth. His faith in life diminishing, and not having the solace of a belief in an afterlife, Faulkner, like many of the Symbolists before him, elevated art into a religion, and the artist into a high priest. Years later he would speak of art as "the salvation of mankind" and "a proof of man's immortality" (*LIG* 71, 103). One of his earliest and most forceful dramatizations of this exalted view of art is *Absalom, Absalom!*

The point that *Absalom, Absalom!* is as much about art as it is about history is encoded in Faulkner's text in several significant ways. For example, there is the letter that Judith Sutpen passes on to Mrs. Compson. Like the statue of John Sartoris at the end of *Sartoris* or the McCaslin family ledgers in "The Bear" or the signature that Cecilia Farmer scratches into glass in *Requiem for a Nun*, Bon's letter to Judith serves as an art-surrogate that symbolizes the capability of works of art to withstand the ravaging effects of time. The artist's driving impulse, Faulkner repeatedly said, is "to say No to death," and he frequently cited his favorite poem, Keats's "Ode on a Grecian Urn," as both an expression and realization of that desire.[11]

It is hardly coincidental that Judith's explanation of why she wants to pass Bon's letter into another person's hands—someone who will live after her—almost exactly parallels Faulkner's statements on the artist's attempt to defeat time.

"Because you make so little impression [Judith says] . . . and then all of a sudden it's all over and all you have left is a block of stone with scratches on it. . . . And so maybe if you could go to someone, the stranger the better, and give them something—a scrap of paper—something, anything . . . at least it would be something just because it would have happened, be remembered even if only from passing from one hand to another, one mind to another, and it would be at least a scratch, something, something that might make a mark on something that *was* once for the reason that it can die someday, while the block of stone cant be *is* because it never can become *was* because it cant ever die or perish." (100–101)

Judith may be uncertain as to her motive for giving the letter to Mrs. Compson, but Faulkner is not. He knows that her attempt "to make that scratch, that undying mark on the blank face of the oblivion to which we are all doomed" (102) is akin to the artist's denial of death. "Since man is mortal," Faulkner told one interviewer, "the only immortality possible for him is to leave something behind him that is immortal since it will always move. This is the artist's way of scribbling 'Kilroy was here' on the wall of the final and irrevocable oblivion through which he must someday pass" (*LIG* 253).

Faulkner similarly links Thomas Sutpen's "design" to the artist's quest for immortality.[12] Carving Sutpen's Hundred out of a frontier wilderness becomes an analogue to what Wallace Stevens has called the artist's "Blessed rage for order."[13] Significantly, in this connection Sutpen is identified with the divine, ex nihilo creator of the Genesis myth: "Then in the long unamaze Quentin seemed to watch them overrun suddenly the hundred square miles of tranquil and astonished earth and drag house and formal gardens violently out of the soundless Nothing and clap them down like cards upon a table beneath the up-palm immobile and pontific, creating the Sutpen's Hundred, the *Be Sutpen's Hundred* like the oldtime *Be Light*" (4).[14] Even more revealingly, Sutpen is linked to the artist's resistance to time and death and to Carcassonne, Faulkner's personal symbol for artistic creation.[15] Conscious of "a need for haste, of time fleeing beneath him" (25), Sutpen is described in a key passage as "a madman who creates within his very coffin walls his fabulous immeasurable Camelots and Carcassonnes" (129). One need not, of course, be negatively influenced by the use in this passage of the word "madman." Like Shakespeare in his creation of King Lear or Melville in his characterization of Captain Ahab (characters with whom Sutpen has a great deal in common), Faulkner occasionally associates madness with special knowledge or insight.[16]

Even in his ruthlessness to realize his dream, Sutpen may be compared to Faulkner's notion of the artist. "They did not think of love in connection with Sutpen," the reader is told. "They thought of ruthlessness rather than justice and of fear rather than respect, but not of pity or love" (32). Faulkner, one recalls, made similar statements about artists. "The writer's only responsibility," he once said, "is to his art. He will be completely ruthless if he is a good one. . . . If a writer has to rob his mother, he will not hesitate; the 'Ode on a Grecian Urn' is worth any number of old ladies" (*LIG* 239). So too, Sutpen believed, was a dynasty. The comparison is underscored by the fact that Sutpen is continually identified as a "demon"—the same word Faulkner occasionally used to describe the artistic impulse within an individual (*FIU* 19, 159).

As noted at the very outset, however, the most significant statement on art in *Absalom, Absalom!* is to be found in the imaginative reconstruction of the Sutpen story by Quentin and Shreve in their Harvard dormitory room. Whereas the first five chapters of the novel present the characters' search for historical facts, the remaining four chapters abandon (necessarily, in Faulkner's view) a concern for fact in favor of intuition and imaginative invention. In these concluding chapters history is usurped by fiction; actuality is superseded by art. In repeating the ancient ritual of storytelling, in the shared act of narrating and hearing, in the dead of winter, a story about events that happened a half century previously, Quentin and Shreve dramatize the capability of art to defeat time and death. Faulkner would repeat the symbolism in his next novel, *The Unvanquished*. Like Drusilla's story to Bayard and Ringo of the Confederates who defy their conquerors by racing a locomotive along tracks supposedly controlled by the Yankees, the Sutpen story will never be "gone or vanished either, so long as there should be defeated or the descendants of defeated to tell it or listen to the telling" (*U* 98). Rosa Coldfield is linked to the same faith in the resurrectional power of storytelling when she tells Quentin, "So maybe you will enter the literary profession as so many Southern gentlemen and gentlewomen too are doing now and maybe some day you will remember this and write about it" (5). "*It's because she wants it told,*" Quentin thinks, "*so that people whom she will never see and whose names she will never hear and who have never heard her name nor seen her face will read it*" (6).

Reading *Absalom, Absalom!* as a celebration of the superiority of art over life contributes to an understanding of the significance of the map of Yoknapatawpha County which Faulkner drew and allowed to be tipped in to the back of his novel. Though the point has been generally ignored by readers and critics, the end of *Absalom, Absalom!* is not Quentin's tortured and passionate assertion that he doesn't hate the South. Nor is it the appendix listing the Sutpen "Chronology" and "Genealogy." The end of *Absalom, Absalom!* is Faulkner's map.[17] As I hope to demonstrate, that map functions in much the same way as the title does, that is, by extending the province of the novel beyond the regional to the universal, by converting the "facts" of history into the "truth" of myth. In fact, the title and the map serve as matching bookends, or, better, a symbolic parenthesis enclosing the tragic history of Thomas Sutpen. Taken together, they are the alpha and omega, the first word and the last, of the novel, and both express Faulkner's faith in the triumph of art over the inevitable, downward spiral of history.

Most critics have interpreted Faulkner's title as an ironic commentary on the Sutpen family history. As John Hagopian has pointed out, the Sutpen narrative parallels the biblical story of David and Absalom in its emphasis on "revolt, incest, and fratricide," but it differs in that Faulkner's David, unlike the biblical one, is unable to feel love and compassion for his rebellious son. Hagopian views this key difference as "the main point of the Sutpen story."[18]

While he is undoubtedly right in his point-by-point comparison of the two stories, Hagopian ignores the broader implications of Faulkner's biblical allusion. Faulkner's interest in the David-Absalom story, as in the Greek and medieval legends with which it is clustered, is rooted in its mythic dimension—the manner in which it captures and reiterates, in its retelling, important aspects of the universal human condition. Faulkner's view of the Bible is pertinent here. As he made quite clear, his reading of the Bible was always literary, mythic, never religious. Like Ike McCaslin, Faulkner viewed the authors of biblical myths as "human men" who "were trying to write down the heart's truth out of the heart's driving complexity, for all the complex and troubled hearts which would beat after them" (*GDM* 260). What impressed Faulkner primarily about the David and Absalom material was that it was a story that had been written and preserved through the centuries for generations of readers. That preservation had little to do with the religious significance or the historical accuracy of the story—in point of fact King David was a petty tyrant in a petty kingdom whose story would have been quickly forgotten had it not been recorded in "The Book." The real hero of the narrative is neither David nor Absalom but the anonymous bard/scribe who told/wrote a story that has outgrown and outlasted the author, the subject, and the historical era that produced it—that, in short, like Quentin and Shreve's retelling of the Sutpen myth, has conquered time and death to live on as art.

Just as the biblical allusion of the title extends Sutpen's regional, temporal story into the realms of the universal, the mythic, and the timeless, so too does the map that ends the novel. Like the title, the map functions at three different levels: the realistic, the ironic, and the symbolic.

As Jules Zanger has explained, one of the most obvious purposes of a literary map is to provide clarification and verisimilitude for the story it accompanies.[19] Faulkner, of course, would have been familiar with numerous maps employed in this manner: for example, biblical maps tracing the migration of the Hebrew people or the missionary journeys of Paul, Bulfinch's maps depicting the settings of the Greek and Roman myths and the wanderings of Ulysses, Sir Thomas More's map of Utopia, Jonathan Swift's maps of the travels of Lemuel Gulliver, Thomas Hardy's maps of Wessex, Sherwood Anderson's map of Winesburg. Like other authorial devices such as Hawthorne's "discovery" of the scarlet A and the papers of Jonathan Pue in the Salem custom house, or the "missing" parts of Henry Mackenzie's *The Man of Feeling*, the literary map enables the reader to suspend disbelief and momentarily accept a fictionalized world as authentic and actual. To visualize Sutpen's Hundred on a map makes it easier to view Thomas Sutpen as a historical character inhabiting a real world.

On this level Faulkner's map reiterates and extends the tragic view of life and history that the Sutpen narrative has already conveyed. Through the handwritten entries that Faulkner made, the landscape of Yoknapatawpha is presented primarily as a setting for grief, villainy, and death. At the top is the "fishing camp where Wash Jones killed Sutpen"; at the bottom is the place "where Popeye killed Tommy." In between are references to the deaths of other characters—old Bayard Sartoris, John Sartoris, Addie Bundren, Joe Christmas, Joanna Burden, Lee Goodwin.

The cemetery and the jail are highlighted, as also are the unscrupulous actions of Flem Snopes and Jason Compson. Even the courthouse, which sits at the center, as Faulkner says in another place, "laying its vast shadow to the uttermost rim of horizon" (*RFN* 35), and which ideally should be identified with order and stability and justice, is instead associated with Temple Drake's perjury and the pathetic fate of Benjy Compson. Like the story of Thomas Sutpen, Faulkner's map of Yoknapatawpha depicts history literally as a dead-end, or, to use the phrases that Faulkner later directed to Malcolm Cowley, a "pointless chronicle," "the same frantic steeplechase toward nothing every-where" (*FCF* 7, 15).

But a map is not merely a representation of place; it is also a guide, a means of assisting a traveler in getting from one point to another. "You are here," we read in the subway or museum and chart our intended destination, trusting the map to show us the way, to keep us from getting lost. In this regard a map serves as an ideal corollary to a novel of quest and initiation. *Absalom, Absalom!*, of course, is just such a novel, being filled with travel references and journeys of one kind or another: Thomas Sutpen's journey from the mountains to the Tidewater and thence on to Haiti and Mississippi; Charles Bon's migration from Haiti to New Orleans to Oxford to Sutpen's Hundred; Henry Sutpen's travels to Oxford, New Orleans, the war, Texas, and back to Mississippi; the various characters' trips back and forth between Sutpen's Hundred and Jefferson; Quentin Compson's trip to Harvard. All such journeys represent psychological quests as well: Sutpen's attempt to escape his threatening past by creating a "design" of safety and security, Bon's search for a father, Henry's search for personal and cultural identity, Quentin's desperate hope to understand both himself and the South.

In this connection, however, Faulkner's map, like his title, functions ironically. All of the personal quests in *Absalom, Absalom!* end in futility and failure. Bon dies, unacknowledged by his father; Sutpen dies, frustrated in his design; Henry dies, outcast and condemned; Quentin will soon die, still troubled and confused about the meaning of existence. Faulkner's map, like the plot of the novel it underscores and supports, is, so far as it is a map of history and the human condition, a map charting failed ambitions and pointing the way to death. Had Faulkner chosen an epigraph for his drawing, it might well have been the quotation from Shakespeare alluded to earlier, the one he used for the title of his second-greatest novel:

Tomorrow, and tomorrow, and tomorrow,
Creeps in this petty pace from day to day
To the last syllable of recorded time,
And all our yesterdays have lighted fools
The way to dusty death. Out, out brief candle!
Life's but a walking shadow, a poor player
That struts and frets his hour upon the stage
And then is heard no more: it is a tale
Told by an idiot, full of sound and fury,
Signifying nothing.

Any map, however, as Faulkner surely understood and appreciated, is more than a graphic representation of an actual place and a practical guide for travelers; it is simultaneously a metaphor. Despite its seeming verisimilitude, every map remains, like the familiar Mercator projection, a distortion of the actual, a substitution for the real, an evocation of an order and harmony that exists, finally, only in the mapmaker's mind and imagination. Cartography, therefore, is not only a science but also an art.

Moreover, even to the degree that a map may be considered metaphorically "true," as opposed to "factual," that truth is always temporary and partial. Thus, maps must be periodically redrawn, as medieval maps were rendered obsolete by the discovery of the New World and as celestial charts were altered by the invention of the telescope. Thus, too, maps must always be understood in relation to a larger whole. Maps end at their edges, but reality and meaning do not. Counties merge into states, states into nations, nations into continents, continents into hemispheres and worlds, and so on outward through the cosmos.

All such observations suggest why Faulkner's map of Yoknapatawpha County provides an appropriate ending for *Absalom, Absalom!* Just as the map blends both "factual" information and metaphor, the novel fuses actuality and art. Just as the map—with its roads, rivers, and railroad leading off the edge and its arrows pointing to Memphis and Mottstown and ultimately, as Faulkner claimed in *The Town*, "from Jefferson to the world" (*T* 315)—suggests a geography beyond Yoknapatawpha, the novel links local, time-bound history with universal, timeless myth. Just as Faulkner's map, like every map, must eventually be revised and redrawn,[20] the novel presents truth as partial and relative, changing with the addition of new information and constant shifts in perspective.

Faulkner's map of Yoknapatawpha is the artistic equivalent of the historical Sutpen's Hundred. Each is the result of its creator's great "design" to impose order and meaning on chaos. But whereas Sutpen's, as a part of what Faulkner considered to be a fatally flawed human history, is inevitably doomed to fail, Faulkner's, by being elevated to the level of great art, is timeless. On Faulkner's fictional "historical" map, Sutpen's Hundred is a tiny, finite circle, ending where it began. On Faulkner's real map, however—the one that depicts the mythical "Jefferson, Yoknapatawpha Co, Mississippi"—Sutpen's Hundred survives and endures, a lasting symbol of the redeeming power of art. Like the novel of which it is such an integral part, and the title which it complements, Faulkner's map both evidences and celebrates the artist's capacity to defeat time and death by crafting a work of art that will last "a long time, a very long time, longer than anything" (*LIG* 103).

NOTES

1. *LIG*, 103.

2. I have borrowed this term from Elizabeth M. Kerr, *Yoknapatawpha: Faulkner's "Little Postage Stamp of Native Soil"* (New York: Fordham University Press, 1969), 7; but numerous other critics, including Malcolm Cowley, Melvin Backman, Ilse Dusoir Lind, Eric Sundquist, and Frederick Karl have similarly referred to Sutpen's dream as a "grand" or a "great" design. The adjectives are supplied by the critics; in Faulkner's text the term employed is merely "design." My intent, as I hope my title conveys, is to contrast Sutpen's "design" with Faulkner's "grand design."

3. Dirk Kuyk, Jr., *Sutpen's Design: Interpreting Faulkner's "Absalom, Absalom!"* (Charlottesville: University Press of Virginia, 1990).

4. By the time he wrote the prefatory note to *The Mansion* (1959), Faulkner had discovered a happy oxymoron to express his notion of the ideal interrelationship between life and art. There he describes his entire life's work as an attempt to create "a living literature." He goes on to explain that "since 'living' is motion, and 'motion' is change and alteration and therefore the only alternative to motion is un-motion, stasis, death, there will be found discrepancies and contradictions in the thirty-four-year progress of this particular chronicle." This statement should be viewed not merely as an attempt to excuse the chronological errors in the successive

volumes of the Snopes trilogy (Abner Snopes's age, for example), but rather as another expression of Faulkner's conviction that great literature is both superior to and allied with the actual life process. The inconsistencies in the Snopes narrative, Faulkner says, are "due to the fact that the author has learned, he believes, more about the human heart and its dilemma than he knew thirty-four years ago; and is sure that, having lived with them that long time, he knows the characters in this chronicle better than he did then." In other words, the complexities and contradictions in the Snopes saga result from Faulkner's attempt to be faithful to his evolving definition of the human condition. Still, as Faulkner readily acknowledged, regardless of its degree of verisimilitude, ultimately art is art, not life. "Living literature," therefore, is a paradoxical literature that seeks to be faithful to both art-as-life and art-as-art.

5. For an extended discussion of this idea, see Robert W. Hamblin, "The Marble Faun: Chapter One of Faulkner's Continuing Dialectic on Life and Art," *Publications of the Missouri Philological Association* 3 (1978): 80–90.

6. Michael Millgate, *The Achievement of William Faulkner* (New York: Random House, 1966), 74.

7. Elisabeth Muhlenfeld, in "Introduction," *William Faulkner's "Absalom, Absalom!": A Critical Casebook* (New York: Garland, 1984), has also discussed the novel in the context of Faulkner's personal situation. She concludes: "A brief look at this period suggests, perhaps, that the intricacy, force and sustained intensity of *Absalom*, with its relative lack of humor and its overriding tragic vision, may be due in part to the very elements in Faulkner's life during the writing of the novel which he had to confront, to endure, and ultimately to control, at least to the extent that he was not shackled or defeated in his role as artist" (xii–xiii). See also Frederick Karl, *William Faulkner: American Writer* (New York: Weidenfeld and Nicolson, 1989), 549, 573n.

8. Oswald Spengler's monumental work on the philosophy of history, *Der Untergang des Abendlandes* (English title, *The Decline of the West*), one of the most influential books of the twentieth century, appeared in German from 1918 to 1923 and in English from 1926 to 1928. Spengler's ideas had a profound effect upon a number of American writers, including Eliot, Hemingway, Fitzgerald, and Faulkner.

9. In this regard it seems significant that in Faulkner's prototype of the scene of the boy at the door of the big house—appearing in an earlier, unpublished story entitled "The Big Shot"—the hostility is clearly directed at the servant as well as the owner. Faulkner's description there makes explicit the cultural antipathy between white and Black that is only implied in the corresponding passage in *Absalom, Absalom!* "There was a negro servant come to the door behind the boss, his eyeballs white in the gloom, and Martin's people and kind, although they looked upon Republicans and Catholics, having never seen either one, probably, with something of that mystical horror which European peasants of the fifteenth century were taught to regard Democrats and Protestants, the antipathy between them and negroes was an immediate and definite affair, being at once biblical, political, and economic: the three compulsions—the harsh unflagging land broken into sparse intervals by spells of demagoguery and religio-neurotic hysteria—which shaped and coerced their gaunt lives. A mystical justification of the need to feel superior to someone somewhere, you see" (*US* 508).

10. For broader applications of Sutpen's desire for power and control, see James Guetti, *The Limits of Metaphor: A Study of Melville, Conrad, and Faulkner* (Ithaca: Cornell University Press, 1967), 88–91, and Panthea Reid Broughton, *William Faulkner: The Abstract and the Actual* (Baton Rouge: Louisiana State University Press, 1974), 85–86, 105.

11. For an extended discussion of the centrality of this concept to Faulkner's view of art, see Robert W. Hamblin, "'Saying No to Death': Toward William Faulkner's Theory of Fiction," included in this volume.

12. For a helpful discussion of this point, see Ruth M. Vande Kieft, "Faulkner's Defeat of Time in *Absalom, Absalom!*," *Southern Review* 6 (1970): 1100–1109. Vande Kieft argues that the novel stands as "a comprehensive symbol of [Faulkner's] relationship to time as an artist," mirroring "not only his obsession with time, but his battle against the oblivion which threatens all human achievement" (1100).

13. Wallace Stevens, "The Idea of Order at Key West," *The Collected Poems of Wallace Stevens* (New York: Alfred A. Knopf, 1955), 130.

14. For an extended analysis of this analogy, see William D. Lindsey, "Order as Disorder: *Absalom, Absalom*'s Inversion of the Judaeo-Christian Creation Myth," in *Faulkner and Religion: Faulkner and Yoknapatawpha, 1989,* ed. Doreen Fowler and Ann J. Abadie (Jackson: University Press of Mississippi, 1991), 85–102.

15. I have previously discussed the influence of Carcassonne upon Faulkner's thought in "'Carcassonne': Faulkner's Allegory of Art and the Artist," *Southern Review* 15 (Spring 1979): 355–65, and "Carcassonne in Mississippi: Faulkner's Geography of the Imagination," included in this volume.

16. The best example, of course, is Darl Bundren of *As I Lay Dying*.

17. The most detailed treatment of Faulkner's map of Yoknapatawpha is Elizabeth Duvert, "Faulkner's Map of Time," *Faulkner Journal* 2 (Fall 1986): 14–28. Duvert's essay is an excellent discussion of the map in relation to the entire corpus of Faulkner's Yoknapatawpha fiction but says nothing of its function in *Absalom, Absalom!* To my knowledge, Pamela Dalziel, in "*Absalom, Absalom!*: The Extension of Dialogic Form," *Mississippi Quarterly* 45 (Summer 1992): 277–94, is the only previous critic to link the map to the text of *Absalom, Absalom!* She views Faulkner's drawing as "the final narrative" (292) of the novel and argues that it contributes to the pattern of inconsistency and ambiguity that characterizes the novel as a whole.

18. John V. Hagopian, "The Biblical Background of Faulkner's *Absalom, Absalom!*," *CEA Critic* 36 (January 1974): 22–24; reprinted in *William Faulkner's "Absalom, Absalom!": A Critical Casebook,* ed. Muhlenfeld, 131–34. See also Ralph Behrens, "Collapse of Dynasty: The Thematic Center of *Absalom, Absalom!*" *PMLA* 89 (1974): 24–33.

19. Jules Zanger, "'Harbours like Sonnets': Literary Maps and Cartographic Symbols," *Georgia Review* 36 (1982): 773–90.

20. Faulkner redrew his map in 1945 for Cowley's edition of *The Portable Faulkner*, published in 1946. A variant of that map is reproduced as the endpapers for volume I of *Faulkner: A Comprehensive Guide to the Brodsky Collection,* ed. Louis Daniel Brodsky and Robert W. Hamblin (Jackson: University Press of Mississippi, 1982).

Carcassonne in Mississippi
Faulkner's Geography of the Imagination

In Oxford, where the stately courthouse looms over the town square, "tall as cloud, solid as rock, dominating all" (*RFN* 35); where the Confederate statue faces exactly the way Faulkner says it does in the fiction, "not toward the north and the enemy, but toward the south, toward (if anything) his own rear" (*RFN* 206); and where even the most dedicated formalistic or mythopoeic critic slips easily into conversations about "Dilsey's cabin" or "Benjy's yard" or "Gavin Stevens's law office," it is impossible to escape or deny the local influences upon Faulkner's work. Still, as we all know, it is easy to overemphasize the regional and mimetic aspects of Faulkner's writings. In this essay I propose to examine the other side of Faulkner's art—that side represented not by Oxford and Lafayette County and Mississippi but by the fabled French city of Carcassonne.

As he made quite clear in one of his interview statements at the University of Virginia, Faulkner associated Carcassonne with the creative imagination. Asked to account for the twentieth-century renaissance among southern writers, Faulkner observed: "I myself am inclined to think it was because of the bareness of the Southerner's life, that he had to resort to his own imagination, to create his own Carcassonne" (*FIU* 136). A similar use of Carcassonne as a symbol of imaginative invention is found in *Absalom, Absalom!* in the identification of Thomas Sutpen (an artist-type whose grandiose "design" [*AA* 212] is not altogether unlike Faulkner's dream of creating "a cosmos of [his] own" [*LIG* 255]) with "a madman who creates within his very coffin walls his fabulous immeasurable Camelots and Carcassonnes" (*AA* 129). In both of these quotations, Carcassonne is identified not with the real world, with actuality, but with a private, inner vision that opposes and negates, respectively, the sterility of the southerner's life and the dying dream of Sutpen. In other words, art—at least the kind of art symbolized by Carcassonne—is here presented as

65

subjective, compensatory, and escapist, even otherworldly. This view of Carcassonne is consistent with Faulkner's definition of the artist in the Nobel Prize Acceptance Speech as one who strives "to create out of the materials of the human spirit something which did not exist before" (*ESPL* 119).

Why Faulkner came to identify Carcassonne with the artistic imagination has intrigued scholars but remains very much a mystery. Neither Joseph Blotner nor Carvel Collins, the early authorities on the details of Faulkner's biography, believes that he visited Carcassonne on his walking tour of France in 1925 or, for that matter, at any subsequent time.[1] Cleanth Brooks has linked Faulkner's interest in Carcassonne to the highly popular chanson by the nineteenth-century French poet Gustave Nadaud—the theme of which was, according to Brooks, well known in the South of Faulkner's youth.[2] Nadaud's poem, entitled "Carcassonne," records the poignant lament of a French peasant who, sixty years old and "bent with age," is greatly disappointed that he is nearing death without ever having realized his youthful dream of seeing the "fair" and "lovely" city. While the text of the poem makes clear that Carcassonne is a symbol of perfection and thus of man's unrealized hopes and dreams—and consequently a meaningful parallel to Faulkner's notion regarding his own "magnificent failure" (*FIU* 61) as an artist—there is nothing within the poem to suggest why Faulkner chose Carcassonne and not, say, Camelot or Xanadu or Byzantium to represent his artistic ideal. For this explanation, I suspect, one must turn to the imposing physical appearance and legendary history of the actual Carcassonne.

Located in southwestern France, some sixty miles southeast of Toulouse, Carcassonne is famous as the site of the finest remains of medieval fortifications in all of Europe. Actually, there are two Carcassonnes: the Ville Basse (lower town), which contains the city's business district, and La Cité, the ancient fortifications that occupy the summit of an isolated hill on the opposite bank of the Aude River. It is, undoubtedly, the picturesque La Cité that Faulkner identifies with the creative ideal. A strategic military fort dating from the fifth century BCE, this Carcassonne has played a significant role in the history of the Romans, Visigoths, Saracens, Franks, feudal lords, seneschals, and French kings who have successively ruled the city throughout its long and storied past. The most beautiful and distinctive features of the city—the massive walls punctuated by fifty rising towers and, within these ramparts, the mighty castle and cathedral—give Carcassonne an aura of enchantment and make-believe. One travel reporter of Faulkner's young manhood recorded this impression: "As you approach the city from the lower town beyond the river and lift up your eyes to the hill and behold its titanic wall with its cloud of towers and turrets surmounted by a citadel you will find it hard to convince yourself that what you see is not a phantom metropolis, a figment of some artist's imagination."[3]

Even if, as seems the case, Faulkner never actually visited Carcassonne, he probably had seen photographs, on postcards or in newspapers, of the town's famous skyline; and he may have read about the city in feature stories such as the one quoted above or in Baedeker's annual travel guides for tourists. He might conceivably have heard about Carcassonne in the French classes he took with Professor Calvin Brown at Ole Miss in 1919–20. Faulkner may even have been aware of the lingering public debate concerning whether Viollet-le-Duc's restorations of the Old Town fortifications during the nineteenth century had been based on authentic history or the subjective and fanciful desires of the architect.[4] In any event, whatever the source or extent of Faulkner's knowledge of Carcassonne, the city became for him a kind of art surrogate, embodying in its abiding presence and romantic history significant features that parallel Faulkner's characterization of his own fictional design. For example, the city's survival through centuries of war and empire-building mirrors the capacity of "saying No to death" (*FR* xi) that Faulkner identified with all great art. In addition, the city projects, in its contrast of the citadel and the lower town, a juxtaposition of the romantic past and the less-than-romantic present—an opposition that provides a dominant emphasis in several of Faulkner's major works. More pertinent to the present discussion, however, is the identification of Carcassonne with the power of the creative imagination to reshape and transcend the narrow world it inhabits. In this regard it seems safe to assert that Faulkner would hardly have been troubled by the claim that Viollet-le-Duc may not have been entirely faithful to historical fact in his restoration efforts.

Such associations as the above may be attributed to Faulkner with some degree of confidence because the features I have just listed are precisely those that Faulkner attaches to the French city in his remarkable and revealing short story "Carcassonne."[5] Presumably written during the mid-to-late 1920s, this work is virtually without plot and consequently has been labeled "a prose poem"[6] or a piece of "romantic prose,"[7] rather than a short story. In one of his few recorded comments on the story, Faulkner expressed a particular fondness for it, called it "fantasy" and not "simple realism," and defined its subject as "a young man in conflict with his environment" (*FIU* 22). The story presents, in stream-of-consciousness form, the thoughts of an aspiring poet who lives in poverty and a considerable degree of humiliation in a seaport town named Rincon. The protagonist resides in a tiny garret provided by a wealthy benefactress, Mrs. Widdrington, where he sleeps under a strip of tarred roofing paper and listens to the rats scurrying in the darkness.

Notwithstanding, however, his failure as a poet and his limited material circumstances—indeed, in counteraction to these conditions—the protagonist wildly dreams of escaping his impotence and despair "to perform something bold and tragical and austere" (CS 899). This ambitious desire, fused in the poet's consciousness with the bold deeds of Norman warriors and steeds during the First Crusade, merges with the poet's heroic view of himself "on a buckskin pony with eyes like blue electricity and a mane like tangled fire, galloping up the hill and right off into the high heaven of the world" (CS 895).

The principal content of "Carcassonne" is devoted to a dialogue between the poet and his skeleton. Somewhat reminiscent of a medieval debate between the body and the soul, the discussion contrasts the physical, inert, and earthbound values of the skeleton with the subjective, transcendent, and limitless fancies of the poet's imagination. In literary terms the skeleton represents realism, and the poet's consciousness romance or myth. The skeleton, identified with "that steady decay which had set up within his body on the day of his birth," rests "motionless" in the "dark," under a ceiling that "slant[s] in a ruined pitch to the low eaves," knowing "that the end of life is lying still" (896–97, 899). But the imagination, which transcends the actual world and is therefore subject to "neither insects nor temperature," gallops "unflagging on the destinationless pony, up a piled silver hill of cumulae where no hoof echoed nor left print" (895). Throughout the narrative the skeleton is associated with images of immobility, confinement, and impending death, while the imagination is linked, as in the central symbol of the flying horse and rider, with connotations of activity, escape, and resurrection. Though the skeleton serves the poet by "supplying him with bits of trivial information" (899), that is, with facts (as, for example, the term *chamfron*), such information has a limited use, since in Faulkner's view facts are not to be equated with truth. Hence, despite its empirical knowledge, the skeleton "know[s] next to nothing of the world" (899). Although the story leaves unresolved the verbal debate between the poet and the skeleton, the symbolic victory of the imagination in imposing its will upon the harsh reality of the setting represents one of Faulkner's strongest statements of the necessity and power of invention. This victory, albeit an ironic one, finds expression in the evocative prose passage that serves as a refrain throughout the story. Significantly the passage opens with the factual, even the prosaic ("and me on a buckskin pony"), and then proceeds, in its employment of two similes ("eyes like blue electricity and a mane like tangled fire") and a metaphor ("the high heaven of the world"), toward the poetic and the mythic. In *Requiem for a Nun* Faulkner defines the imagination as that quality "so vast, so limitless in capacity . . . to disperse and burn away the rubble-dross of fact and probability, leaving only truth and dream" (225). "Carcassonne" dramatizes just such a conversion process.

The celebration of the transcendent and transmutable power of the imagination in "Carcassonne" invites comparison with Faulkner's remarks about the sources of a writer's material. Time and again Faulkner identified these sources as "observation, experience, and imagination" (*FIU* 123). Faulkner listed these three influences in varying orders of emphasis, and he pointed out that sometimes each can function independently of the others. "A writer," he said, "needs 3 things: experience, observation, imagination, any two of which, at times any one of which, can supply the lack of the others" (*LIG* 248). Often, Faulkner noted, it is virtually impossible to distinguish a writer's use of the separate sources. As he observed at West Point, "It's difficult to say just what part of any story comes specifically from imagination, what part from experience, what part from observation. It's like having . . . three tanks with a collector valve. And you don't know just how much comes from which tank. All you know is a stream of water runs from the valve when you open it, drawn from the three tanks—observation, experience, imagination" (*FWP* 96–97).

Although Faulkner often conceded, as in this last quotation, that the genesis of art is complex and mysterious, taken as a whole his comments reflect a bias toward imaginative invention. This bias explains his frequently expressed hostility toward "facts" and mere "reporting" of actuality. In the amusing self-portrait that appears in *Mosquitoes*, Faulkner identifies himself as "a liar by profession" (149); and he told one group of students, "I don't have much patience with facts, and any writer is a congenital liar to begin with or he wouldn't take up writing" (*FB* 6). Faulkner frequently noted the writer's tendency, even compulsion, to embellish reality. "The writer is incapable of telling the truth," he said. "He couldn't take an actual human being and translate him onto paper and stick to the facts. He has got to change and embroider" (*FWP* 120). Faulkner laughingly told his students at the University of Virginia that he might conceivably use them in his fiction but added, "You'll be changed" (*FIU* 123). Because of this insistence upon the role of the creative faculty, Faulkner was inclined to criticize those who view writing as mere reporting. "Steinbeck," Faulkner once observed, "is just a reporter, a newspaperman, not really a writer" (*LIG* 91). A writer, Faulkner insisted, does not depend upon research. "I think if he does that he is not really a fiction writer" (*FIU* 116). Of his handling of characterization, Faulkner said, "I think that any writer worth his salt is convinced that he can create much better people than God can" (*FIU* 118). He told the West Point cadets: "Certainly I don't think that any writer ever wrote down or put down anything he actually saw or heard because a writer is congenitally incapable of telling the truth about anything. He has got to change it. He has got to lie. That's why they call it fiction, you see" (*FWP* 116). While it is evident that for Faulkner a work of literature is a complex alloyage of fact and fancy, history and myth, life and art—in his words, "experience, observation, and imagination"—it is equally evident that for Faulkner the principal component in this amalgam is the creative imagination of the artist.

Faulkner's ideas on the relationship of life and art become clearer upon examination of one source from which those ideas partly derived: Willard Huntington Wright's *The Creative Will: Studies in the Philosophy and the Syntax of Aesthetics.*[8] Wright, better known as the S. S. Van Dine of detective story fame, produced several works on literature and painting; and the one just named made a vivid impression on Phil Stone, who discussed its contents with his young protégé, Billy Falkner. Regarding the influence of *The Creative Will* on Faulkner, Stone has written: "The aesthetic theories set forth in that book, strained through my own mind, constitutes [*sic*] one of the most important influences in Bill's whole literary career. If people who read him would simply read Wright's book they would see what he is driving at from a literary standpoint."[9] Not all of Stone's judgments on Faulkner and his work can be trusted, but this one seems right on target. Indeed, many of Wright's views on art and the artist came to be those held by Faulkner.

Of particular interest are Wright's views on the relationship of life to art. Wright contrasts Balzac, in Wright's opinion one of the great masters of literature, with Zola and other "recorders of nature" (23) who think that mere documentation is art. "No one believes that a photograph of a clock will tell time," Wright argues. "Yet there are those who assert that imitation of nature is the life of art!" (202). This is not to say that the artist has no use for nature. "There can be no great ascetic artist," Wright insists (181); the artist's creativity evolves in part from contact with the objective world. The artist stores all of his experiences, according to Wright, in his "minute filing cabinet" (23) of a mind, and "out of his mass of data he evolves, by combinations ever new, a microcosmos" (23–24). Wright describes this cognitive process as follows:

> The artist's process of thought is like an arithmetical progression. He conceives a trivial idea from his contact with exterior nature. Something in this trivial idea, after a period of analysis, calls up another idea which, in turn, develops, through volitional association, into a group of ideas. And this group becomes,

for him, the basis of constructive thinking, replacing, as it were, the original
basis of objectivity. From his segregation and arrangement of these ideas, which
are no longer directly inspired by nature, there springs the great idea. (83)

Thus, Wright asserts, true art derives from "the imagination of him who has
understood and experienced life" (23); the genuine artist "takes the *essence*
of his special world of sound, colour or document, and creates a new world
of them" (24). In this endeavor the artist sacrifices "facts" and even distorts
"because he is ever after a profounder truth than that of the accuracy of
detail" (12). "Art," Wright proclaims, "has nothing to do with truth in the sense
of' 'verity' or 'accuracy'" (28). Wright concludes: "In all great and profound
aesthetic creation the artist is an omnipotent god who moulds and fashions
the destiny of a new world, and leads it to an inevitable completion where it
can stand alone, self-moving, independent, and with a consistency free of all
exterior help or influence. In the fabrication of this cosmos the creator finds
his exaltation" (221–22). This last statement, of course, sounds remarkably
similar to Faulkner's comments about his godlike creation of an independent
and self-generating cosmos that could stand as a "keystone in the Universe"
(*LIG* 255). The principal ingredient in the formation of such art, for Faulkner
as for Wright, is the creative imagination of the artist.

Faulkner's preference for a fabricated literature over a representational
one finds distinct, if at times amusing, expression in the record of his work
on *The De Gaulle Story*, an unproduced movie script he wrote for Warner
Bros. Pictures in 1942.[10] Between July and November of that year Faulkner
wrote, in rapid succession, a story outline, a treatment, a revised treatment, a
full-length screenplay, and a revised screenplay dramatizing the contemporary struggle of General Charles de Gaulle and the Free French underground
against the Nazi occupation of France. To retrace Faulkner's progress on this
project, intended as a propaganda film to promote de Gaulle's image in the
eyes of the American public, is to follow a debate on the fundamental conflict
inherent in the techniques of documentary and imaginative filmmaking—in
short, between fact and fiction. Assigned to assist Faulkner on the biographical and historical details of the story were Adrien Tixier, the Free French representative in Washington, DC, and de Gaulle's personal agent on the project;
and Henri Diamant-Berger, a French film director and producer who was the
principal Gaullist spokesman in Hollywood. Opposition between Faulkner
and these Free French consultants quickly surfaced, deepened as the project
continued, and eventually became a key factor in the studio's decision to can-
cel the proposed film.

In the initial stages of his work on *The De Gaulle Story*, Faulkner relied heavily upon documents and information provided by the Free French consultants. Demonstrating his typical disdain for facts, however, Faulkner quickly began to exercise his fertile imagination and to substitute fictional events and characters for the historical details. The response from the Frenchmen was immediate. When Tixier read Faulkner's story treatment, he responded with a long list of "Observations on Inexact Details" challenging Faulkner's accuracy and verisimilitude.[11] Diamant-Berger's evaluation of Faulkner's completed script echoed Tixier's call for closer adherence to the historical record.[12]

For a time Faulkner sought to placate the French consultants by making many of the changes in the script that they requested. In fact, on one occasion Faulkner demonstrated that he could be as much a stickler for accurate detail as anyone else. When an objection was raised to Faulkner's having a character allude to his task of "planting corn"—an objection based on the grounds (expressed in an attached note) that "the French don't eat corn; Coupe-Tête would be planting potatoes"—Faulkner inserted his rejoinder in the margin: "Planting potatoes in May??? What does horse eat?" But this notation was undoubtedly made as much in spite or anger as in jest. For soon afterward, exasperated by the unbending literal-mindedness of the Free Frenchmen and recognizing the impasse as having become insurmountable, Faulkner petitioned producer Robert Buckner for a free hand in structuring the screenplay. In an interoffice memorandum dated November 19, 1942, Faulkner suggested to Buckner: "Let's dispense with General De Gaulle as a living character in the story." The problem, as Faulkner stated it, was that the Frenchmen wanted to produce "a document" rather than "a story." As a consequence, they would "insist upon an absolute adherence to time and fact, no matter how trivial the incident nor imaginary the characters acting it, and regardless of the sacrifice of dramatic values and construction or the poetic implications and overtones." The matter was further complicated by the fact that de Gaulle was a living figure. According to Faulkner, any historical hero "becomes colorful and of dramatic value only after he has been dead for years, because only then can a dramatist make him dramatic without challenge from the people who knew him in the flesh and who insist on fact."[13]

Another work that exhibits Faulkner's contempt for facts and documentation is the short story "Artist at Home," published in 1933. Primarily a satirical treatment of popular notions of artists and their behavior, the story contains an interesting detail that relates to the question of fact versus imagination as a source for the writer's materials. When Roger Howes, a novelist of limited accomplishment, is confronted with the developing love affair between his wife Anne and his friend John Blair, a poet, Howes turns immediately to his typewriter: "Now get this. This is it. He came back down to the office and put some paper into the typewriter and began to write. He didn't go very fast at first, but by daylight he was sounding like forty hens in a sheet-iron corn-crib, and the written sheets were piling up" (CS 638). Throughout the next several days and weeks, interrupted only by Anne's exits to meet Blair and the discussions following her returns, Howes continues to type at a frantic pace. Each new development in Anne's affair enhances this "bull market in typewriting" (639). Toward the end of the story, the reader is told what it is that Howes has been working on so feverishly: "And what was it he had been writing? Him, and Anne, and the poet. Word for word, between the waiting spells to find out what to write down next, with a few changes here and there, of course, because live people do not make good copy, the most interesting copy being gossip, since it mostly is not true" (644). Given the comic tone of the story, one is inclined to view with amusement Howes's dependence upon a traumatic experience to resurrect his feeble art. "Artist at Home" provides an ironic reversal of the traditional literary plot: here the reader's haste to read the next fictional episode is transferred to a writer who must wait to see what happens in an actual situation before he can know what to write in his next scene. Faulkner's purpose appears to extend beyond a mere desire to satirize the Freudian notion (one, by the way, with which Faulkner basically agreed) that all art derives from suffering. In Howes's frantic, even futile, efforts to record the fast-developing events of his experience, one perceives the dilemma of any realist seeking to mirror a constantly changing life process. Not only, Faulkner seems to suggest, is such photographic rendering impossible; it is not even desirable. Thus it is that Howes cannot help but make "a few changes here and there" and fictionalize the actual. Even the most confirmed realist, Faulkner implies, cannot completely close off the workings of invention; besides, gossip makes better copy than fact. In this manner "Artist at Home" ridicules the notion that art is mere copying and underscores Faulkner's emphasis upon the necessity of imagination in the fictive process.

How different to the realistic, "word for word" approach of a Roger Howes is the imaginative handling of experience by Quentin Compson in *Absalom, Absalom!* Michael Millgate and others have perceived in the relationship of Quentin to the story he tells a dramatization of the problems of authorship.[14] Support for this view is found in Miss Rosa's remark that Quentin may one day utilize the Sutpen story as material for fiction: "So maybe you will enter the literary profession as so many Southern gentlemen and gentlewomen too are doing now and maybe someday you will remember this and write about it. You will be married then I expect and perhaps your wife will want a new gown or a new chair for the house and you can write this and submit it to the magazines" (5). The overall structure of *Absalom, Absalom!* further supports the view of Quentin as author-surrogate. The first five chapters relate Quentin's immediate, if principally second- and third-hand, involvement in the Sutpen narrative, but the remaining four chapters present the imaginative reconstruction of the story by Quentin and his Harvard roommate, Shreve McCannon. This shift from listening to telling, from assimilation to invention, reflects more than the creation of an aesthetic distance involving time and place: the shift mirrors also the play of imagination over experience.

In this visionary realm where the imagination interfuses and transforms fact, actual characters and events become unreal, fictional: "the two of them creating between them, out of the rag-tag and bob-ends of old tales and talking, people who perhaps had never existed at all anywhere, who, shadows, were shadows not of flesh and blood which had lived and died but shadows in turn of what were (to one of them at least, to Shreve) shades too, quiet as the visible murmur of their vaporizing breath" (243). Any reader who has sought to ascertain which of the characters in *Absalom, Absalom!* knew what, and when, recognizes the degree to which the novel is grounded in speculation and ambiguity. Such distortion of event and action, though, is not loss but gain.

> It seemed to Quentin that he could actually see them: the ragged and starving troops without shoes, the gaunt powder-blackened faces looking backward over tattered shoulders, the glaring eyes in which burned some indomitable desperation of undefeat . . . ; he could see it; he might even have been there. Then he thought *No. If I had been there I could not have seen it this plain.* (154–55)

Readers who discern in such a hypothetical recreation of the Sutpen narrative only the negative emphasis of man's inability to know and comprehend the past must discount Faulkner's stated preference for invention, even for "lies"—for imaginative "truth" over actual "facts."

In this connection Quentin's treatment of Sutpen may be meaningfully compared to Faulkner's observation concerning his legendary great-grandfather, Colonel W. C. Falkner:

> People at Ripley talk of him as if he were still alive, up in the hills some place, and might come in at any time. It's a strange thing; there are lots of people who knew him well, and yet no two of them remember him alike or describe him

the same way. One will say he was like me and another will swear he was six feet tall. There's nothing left in the old place, the house is gone and the plantation boundaries, nothing left of his work but a statue. But he rode through that country like a living force. I like it better that way.[15]

Faulkner "like[d] it better that way," presumably, because such ambiguities and uncertainties free the imagination for the creative process. An excessive reliance upon facts would stifle originality. "Research" and similar "documentary" approaches to fiction are thus to be eschewed. The imaginative faculty is indispensable to the creation of art.

Not surprisingly for a writer who expresses such faith in imaginative invention, Faulkner's work abounds in constructs that are, or border upon, pure fantasy. This aspect of his fiction has never been held in high regard by critics who insist on viewing Faulkner as a realist, yet it is crucial to an understanding of his art. Extreme examples are four of the stories that Faulkner included in the "Beyond" section of his *Collected Stories*. One of these, "Carcassonne," has been discussed earlier and lends its name to the focus of my present remarks. Another, the title story of the section, treats the death (actual or anticipated) of an elderly federal judge and his subsequent journey into the Hereafter. In this postmortal flight of consciousness he encounters a past acquaintance— an atheist named Mothershed—as well as his idol, agnostic Robert Ingersoll. The judge also views Christ as a baby but with crucifixion scars on his hands and feet. There is considerable conversation treating the questions of God and immortality, after which the judge is offered the opportunity to be reunited with his ten-year-old son who had been killed in a riding accident almost thirty years earlier. However, the judge declines, reluctant to sacrifice his long-held beliefs of agnosticism and humanism. In keeping with its exotic nature, Faulkner labeled "Beyond" "a tour de force in esoteria" (*FB* 809).

The subject matter of another of these stories, "Black Music, "is just as fabulous. This one treats the supernatural experience (again, whether real or imagined is left ambiguous) of Wilfred Midgleston, who for one day has been transformed into a faun and thus has "done and been something outside the lot and plan for mortal human man to do and be" (*CS* 821). Formerly an architect's draughtsman, "a small, snuffy, nondescript man whom neither man nor woman had ever turned to look at twice" (799), Midgleston believes himself to have been used by Pan to frighten away some rich Park Avenuers who threatened to alter an idyllic mountain retreat. The newspaper account of the incident had described a half-naked maniac who attacked Mrs. Carleton Van Dyming in her garden, but Midgleston is convinced that the newspaper account is erroneous. Now, twenty-five years later, he lives in self-exile in a foreign country, impoverished but contented with the knowledge that he has been "fortune's favorite, chosen of the gods" (799).

"The Leg" is a ghost story based on the idea of reincarnation.[16] The narrative opens with a flashback to 1914 when the narrator, Davy, a young American studying at Oxford, and his English friend woo a young lady named Everbe Corinthia. Then the scene shifts to 1915 and the battlefront in France, where George is killed and Davy loses his leg. In the hospital George's ghost appears to Davy, and Davy expresses the fear that his amputated leg is not dead. "I can feel it," he says. "It jeers at me" (*CS* 831). George promises to find the leg and make sure it is dead. Later, Davy is well enough to return to action as a flyer; the ghost no longer appears, but Davy is still haunted by vague fears regarding the leg. The story next shifts forward in time to reveal that Everbe Corinthia has died as the result of an unhappy love affair, that her father has followed her in death a week later, and that her brother Jotham, who has vowed to avenge himself upon his sister's lover, has attempted to murder Davy, who is astonished by all these developments and cannot understand Jotham's hatred toward him. Jotham also dies, but in his effects is found a recently inscribed photograph showing Everbe and her lover. When Davy sees this photograph, he is amazed to see his own face in the picture, since at the time the photograph was made, he was lying in the hospital talking to George's ghost. The implication is that the lost leg has worked its frightful purpose. "I told him to find it and kill it," Davy concludes. "I told him to. I told him" (842).

While fantasies such as "Carcassonne," "Beyond," "Black Music," and "The Leg" are infrequent in the Faulkner canon (one could add to the list the early play *Marionettes*, certain poems in *The Marble Faun*, and the child's story *The Wishing Tree*), these stories nevertheless serve to indicate the degree to which Faulkner associated creativity with fabrication. Such narratives also encourage readers to return to Faulkner's more "realistic" fiction with a heightened awareness of Faulkner's fondness for invented as opposed to representational art. In this context such experimentations as the use of clairvoyance in *As I Lay Dying*, the hypothetical exploration of a severely retarded person's consciousness in *The Sound and the Fury*, the surrealistic description of the wake in *Sanctuary*, and the startling adaptation of biblical myth in *A Fable* take on added significance. Many more instances of Faulkner's richly inventive originality might be cited; but I shall limit myself to only three additional examples. One examines Faulkner's handling of incident, another relates to style and characterization, and the third illustrates overall structure.

The initial example is the description of Ike McCaslin s first view of the giant bear, Old Ben, in *Go Down, Moses.*

> Then he saw the bear. It did not emerge, appear: it was just there, immobile, fixed in the green and windless noon's hot dappling, not as big as he had dreamed it but as big as he had expected, bigger, dimensionless against the dappled obscurity, looking at him. Then it moved. It crossed the glade without haste, walking for an instant into the sun's full glare and out of it, and stopped again and looked back at him across one shoulder. Then it was gone. It didn't walk into the woods. It faded, sank back into the wilderness without motion as he had watched a fish, a huge old bass, sink back into the dark depths of its pool and vanish without even any movement of its fins. (200–201)

As much as any passage in the story, this description captures the "fairy story" quality that Malcolm Cowley perceives in "The Bear."[17] Faulkner presents here not so much the objective, physical movements of an actual bear but rather a subjective dream-state that impresses the reader as a spiritual vision. The bear does not "emerge, appear"; it is "just there," all at once, come from nowhere, an epiphany like the mystic's view of God. Significantly, the bear is "dimensionless," and when it disappears, as suddenly and as mysteriously as it appears, it does not "walk" back into the woods but "fade[s], [sinks] back into the wilderness *without motion*" (emphasis added). Quite obviously Faulkner's interest is not in realistic, representational detail but in the subjective state of Ike's consciousness. The artistic intent is not to present a "real" bear but to communicate the idea of the bear as it exists in Ike's (and Faulkner's) imagination and as it can be recreated in the reader's imagination only through the vehicle of Faulkner's magical, evocative words. To appreciate the success of the technique, one has only to compare the film version of "The Bear" to Faulkner's marvelous prose. In the film version one sees a real bear, but it is not Old Ben; Faulkner's bear is larger than life, heroic, unreal, mythic. Faulkner clearly recognized the visionary quality of his narrative and linked the story to his overall concept of art. "There's a case," he said, "of the sorry, shabby world that don't quite please you, so you create one of your own, so . . . you make the bear a little more of a bear than he actually was" (*FIU* 59). Again, the world of fact has been infused and transformed by the creative imagination.

The next example is one of the most misunderstood and least appreciated passages in all of Faulkner's works: the description of the idiot Ike Snopes's love affair with the cow in *The Hamlet.* Many readers undoubtedly agree with

Phil Stone's judgment that this episode "ruined" the novel and typifies "the complete lack of aesthetic taste which Faulkner frequently shows."[18] More sympathetic critics manage to get past the shocking bestiality of the story but still tend to view the episode as scarcely important in its own right but only as an ironic counterpoint to the lust of Labove and McCarron and the selfish materialism of Flem. However, when viewed in terms of Faulkner's interest in language as the play of imagination on experience, this section becomes a centerpiece of the novel. Consider the following passage:

> then he would hear her, coming down the creekside in the mist. It would not be after one hour, two hours, three; the dawn would be empty, the moment and she would not be, then he would hear her and he would lie drenched in the wet grass, serene and one and indivisible in joy, listening to her approach. He would smell her; the whole mist reeked with her; the same malleate hands of mist which drew along his prone drenched flanks palped her pearled barrel too and shaped them both somewhere in immediate time, already married. He would not move. He would lie amid the waking instant of earth's teeming life, the motionless fronds of water-heavy grasses stooping into the mist before his face in black, fixed curves, along each parabola of which the marching drops held in minute magnification the dawn's rosy miniatures, smelling and even tasting the rich, slow, warm barn-reek milk-reek, the flowing immemorial female, hearing the slow planting and the plopping suck of each deliberate cloven mud-spreading hoof, invisible still in the mist loud with its hymeneal choristers. (165)

Surely this is language stretched to its physical limits. As Melvin Backman recognized decades ago, "The Keatsian poetry of the language evokes another world where reality has been suspended and the poet's imagination rules: the idiot and the cow might be lovers out of a storied past who, at one with nature and themselves, partake of a serene ineffable moment when time no longer exists."[19] At the realistic level, as other parts of the novel make clear, the idiot's story functions, literally, as an instance of "stock-diddling" (201) that provides a sordid entertainment for the debased and dehumanized inhabitants of Frenchman's Bend. Through the transforming power of the mythic imagination, however, the episode becomes, if only briefly, a joyous and moving account of a perfectly devoted lover who braves fire and beast to rescue his beloved. Burlesque though it may be, there is no better example in all of Faulkner's fiction of the power of imaginative wordplay to convert "the sorry, shabby world" into a place of heroism and beauty. Not coincidentally, it is Ratliff, one of Faulkner's great fabulists (and thus one who is sensitive to the opposition of actuality and invention), who defends Ike from the populace and refuses to pass moral judgment on his behavior.

The most impressive examples of the power of invention in Faulkner, though, are not to be found in his visionary handling of incident, style, and characterization but in his often brilliant and always daring experiments with form. Any one of a number of novels could be used to demonstrate this point: *The Sound and the Fury*, with its four overlapping viewpoints of the central action and its gradual unfolding of plot and meaning; *Light in August*, with its ascending and descending story lines and its frequent dislocations of chronology; *Absalom, Absalom!*, with its multiple viewpoints, its artistic interweaving of past and present, and its mythic parallels; *The Wild Palms/If I Forget Thee, Jerusalem*, with its startlingly original counterpointing of two distinct yet thematically related stories; or *Requiem for a Nun*, with its fusion of prose narrative and dramatic form. But the novel I have chosen for emphasis on this occasion is *As I Lay Dying*, principally because its simple plot (the simplest in all of Faulkner's major novels) allows the imaginative structure of the novel to stand forth in bold relief. What happens in *As I Lay Dying* can be summarized in one sentence: the Bundrens travel from their home below Frenchman's Bend to convey the corpse of Addie, the wife and mother, to Jefferson for burial. But the way Faulkner chose to narrate this basic story line placed him at the forefront of the modern experimental novelists. And even today, almost a century after its publication, the technique of the novel is still strikingly fresh and innovative. The kaleidoscopic shifting of viewpoint from one to another of the fifteen narrators, with their sometimes-collaborative and sometimes-contradictory perspectives, allows for a gradual, progressive illumination of both the external action and the inner thoughts and motivations of the characters. Moreover, the strategic placement of Addie's monologue two-thirds of the way through the novel, casting its light of revelation both backward and forward, further contributes to the suspensive design of the book. No novel better demonstrates the risk-taking that Faulkner expected of all writers who aspire to greatness, and no novel better illustrates the technical virtuosity that even negative critics like Clifton Fadiman[20] and Alfred Kazin must concede to Faulkner's credit. "Technically," Kazin wrote in 1942, "[Faulkner] soon proved himself almost inordinately subtle and ambitious, the one modern American novelist whose devotion to form has earned him a place among even the great experimentalists in modern poetry."[21] Where in Oxford (or in any actual place), one might ask, did Faulkner find the models for such radical experiments in form? The answer comes in Faulkner's own words. Once asked about his use of a specific historical prototype in his fiction, he replied, "I think that whenever my imagination and the bounds of that pattern conflicted, it was the pattern that bulged . . . that gave" (*FIU* 51–52). In matters of form, therefore, as in the areas of incident, style, and characterization, Faulkner resorted "to his own imagination, to create his own Carcassonne."

I have spent considerable time in documenting Faulkner's aversion to facts and "the sorry, shabby world" of actuality and his corresponding exaltation of the creative imagination because these points are crucial to understanding precisely what type of fictionist Faulkner is. It has become an accepted point of Faulkner criticism to identify his emergence as a major writer with the moment he discovered, upon the advice of Sherwood Anderson, the fictional possibilities contained within his native milieu. As he later told Jean Stein, "Beginning with *Sartoris* I discovered that my own little postage stamp of native soil was worth writing about and that I would never live long enough to exhaust it, and *by sublimating the actual into apocryphal* [emphasis added] I would have complete liberty to use whatever talent I might have to its absolute top" (*LIG* 255). A careful examination of this statement reveals that Faulkner's rediscovery of his native materials was just the initial step in his maturation as an artist. Even more crucial was his *handling* of those materials, his recognition that only "by sublimating the actual into apocryphal" could he develop his talent "to its absolute top." Those readers who view Faulkner as a realist, or, worse, a mere regionalist, make much of the first half of Faulkner's statement to Stein but usually ignore the second. Faulkner, of course, placed the emphasis exactly where it belongs. The "postage stamp of native soil," Oxford and its environs, may have supplied the raw materials he needed, but it was the imagination, Carcassonne, that produced the great art.

In studying Faulkner's fiction one quickly becomes aware that his art is quite removed from the photographic realism advocated by William Dean Howells or the scientific documentation of Frank Norris and other naturalists. Faulkner's approach to art may be more profitably compared to that of Nathaniel Hawthorne, whose *The Scarlet Letter* explores that "neutral territory, somewhere between the real world and fairy-land, where the Actual and the Imaginary may meet, and each imbue itself with the nature of the other,"[22] or of Henry James, who understood the limitations of mimetic theories of art and who celebrated in that remarkable short story "The Real Thing" "the alchemy of art"[23] whereby imaginative invention triumphs over mere copying. When compared to his successors rather than his predecessors, Faulkner seems to belong more in the company of, for example, John Barth or Robert Coover than of, say, John Updike or Norman Mailer. For Faulkner the actual world, Oxford, was never more than "somewhere to start from" (*ESPL* 8).

Like the surrealist painters with whom he has so much in common, Faulkner sought to capture a new realism—a super-realism—that combines elements of the everyday, outer world and the inner world of the artist's creative vision. In his curious geography of the imagination, both Oxford and Carcassonne are part of Yoknapatawpha. And the only map on which that fabulous land appears is the one the artist himself drew—the one signed by "William Faulkner, Sole Owner & Proprietor."[24]

NOTES

1. For Blotner s treatment of Faulkner's 1925 visit to Europe, see *FB*, 444–83. Collins's opinion is expressed in a letter to me, dated August 15, 1982.

2. Cleanth Brooks, *William Faulkner: Toward Yoknapatawpha and Beyond* (New Haven: Yale University Press, 1978), 61.

3. T. Graydon Montague, "Citadels of the Centuries," *Travel* 39 (May 1922): 6.

4. These arguments resurfaced when additional excavations were done in 1923 and 1927.

5. Although Faulkner elected to conclude both *These 13* (New York: Cape and Smith, 1931) and *Collected Stories* with "Carcassonne," for years the story received little critical attention. Recent treatments include Richard A. Milum, "Faulkner's 'Carcassonne': The Dream and the Reality," *Studies in Short Fiction* 15 (Spring 1978): 133–38; Robert W. Hamblin, "'Carcassonne': Faulkner's Allegory of Art and the Artist," *Southern Review* (Spring 1979): 355–65; M. E. Bradford, "The Knight and the Artist: Tasso and Faulkner's 'Carcassonne,'" *South Central Bulletin* 41 (Winter 1981): 88–90; Noel Polk, "William Faulkner's 'Carcassonne,'" *Studies in American Fiction* 12 (Spring 1984): 29–43; and James B. Carothers, *William Faulkner's Short Stories* (Ann Arbor: UMI Research Press, 1985), 81–83.

6. Dorothy Tuck, *Apollo Handbook of Faulkner* (New York: Thomas Y. Crowell, 1964), 163.

7. Brooks, *William Faulkner*, 60.

8. Willard Huntington Wright, *The Creative Will: Studies in the Philosophy and the Syntax of Aesthetics* (New York: John Lane, 1916).

9. See James W. Webb and A. Wigfall Green, eds., *William Faulkner of Oxford* (Baton Rouge: Louisiana State University Press, 1965), 228.

10. A detailed history of Faulkner's work on this project is recorded in Louis Daniel Brodsky and Robert W. Hamblin, eds., *Faulkner: A Comprehensive Guide to the Brodsky Collection, Volume III: The De Gaulle Story* (Jackson: University Press of Mississippi, 1984).

11. See Brodsky and Hamblin, eds., *De Gaulle Story*, 354–59.

12. See Brodsky and Hamblin, eds., *De Gaulle Story*, 376–95.

13. Brodsky and Hamblin, eds., *De Gaulle Story*, 395–96, 398.

14. See, for example, Michael Millgate, *The Achievement of William Faulkner* (New York: Random House, 1966), 154–55.

15. Quoted in Robert Cantwell, "The Faulkners: Recollections of a Gifted Family," in *William Faulkner: Three Decades of Criticism*, ed. Frederick J. Hoffman and Olga W. Vickery (New York: Harcourt, Brace and World, 1963), 56.

16. I have adopted the usual interpretation of the story. For an impressive argument that Faulkner's rendering of the events is highly ambiguous, and perhaps explicable in terms of

psychological realism, see James B. Carothers, "Faulkner's Short Stories: 'And Now What's to Do,'" in *New Directions in Faulkner Studies: Faulkner and Yoknapatawpha, 1983*, ed. Doreen Fowler and Ann J. Abadie (Jackson: University Press of Mississippi, 1984), 219–23.

17. See A. I. Bezzerides, *William Faulkner: A Life on Paper*, ed. Ann Abadie (Jackson: University Press of Mississippi, 1980), 97.

18. Louis Daniel Brodsky and Robert W. Hamblin, eds., *Faulkner: A Comprehensive Guide to the Brodsky Collection, Volume II: The Letters* (Jackson: University Press of Mississippi, 1984), 29.

19. Melvin Backman, *Faulkner: The Major Years* (Bloomington: Indiana University Press, 1966), 151–52.

20. See, for example, Fadiman's review of *Absalom, Absalom!*, "Faulkner, Extra-Special, Double-Distilled," *New Yorker*, October 31, 1936, 62–64. Though Fadiman ridicules Faulkner's style and content, he concedes that "as a technician [Faulkner] has Joyce and Proust punch-drunk" (63).

21. Alfred Kazin, *On Native Grounds: An Interpretation of Modern American Prose Literature* (New York: Harcourt, Brace, 1942), 457.

22. Nathaniel Hawthorne, *The Scarlet Letter* (New York: W. W. Norton, 1978), 31.

23. Henry James, *The Real Thing and Other Tales* (New York: Macmillan, 1893), 17.

24. The map appears as an insert at the back of *Absalom, Absalom!*

Beyond the Edge of the Map
Faulkner, Turner, and the Frontier Line

James Cowan's fascinating novel *A Mapmaker's Dream*, subtitled *The Meditations of Fra Mauro, Cartographer to the Court of Venice*,[1] records the lifelong efforts of a sixteenth-century monk to create an accurate and comprehensive map of the entire world. In his cloister of an island monastery, Fra Mauro interviews explorers, merchants, and visitors from distant lands; reads letters and books by world travelers; and pores over maps created by other cartographers. In the process of conducting his research and mapping his findings, Fra Mauro comes to understand, and accept, the paradoxical and mysterious relationship between the known and the unknown, civilization and barbarity, culture and nature, science and myth, reality and ideality, experience and art. Ultimately, his life's work, the map, becomes the text in which he records his impressions of life, nature, and self.

Unlike Cowan, William Faulkner never wrote a philosophical novel about a mapmaker's quest for understanding and order; yet he too was a mapmaker of sorts (both literally and figuratively) who seriously explored the intersection of geography and culture. As demonstrated by the maps he drew of his imaginary Yoknapatawpha County,[2] his survey of the history of that county in *Requiem for a Nun* and "Mississippi," and the political and historical essays and addresses he produced during the 1950s, Faulkner was keenly interested in charting life and experience at the edge of the map, the frontier line—that point in the evolution of culture where wilderness and settlement meet, where nature and landscape are engaged and domesticated. Indeed, the story of Yoknapatawpha is one long chronicle of the advance of civilization, the repetitive cycle, as Faulkner expresses it in "Mississippi," of "the obsolescent, dispossessed tomorrow by the already obsolete" (*ESPL* 13): first the Mound Builders, then the Native Americans, then the white hunters and settlers who found Jefferson and establish a seat of government, then those like Thomas Sutpen who bring slaves and develop the plantations, then, during the Civil War and Reconstruction, the Northern soldiers and abolitionists and carpetbaggers, and eventually the lumbermen and bankers and industrialists who, in Faulkner's own time, "push what remain[s] of the wilderness further and further southward into the V of the Big River and hills" (24). By 1945, when Faulkner drew the second of his maps of Yoknapatawpha, only a tiny part of the original wilderness yet remained, and that some two hundred miles to the southwest deep in the Mississippi Delta.

Beginning just to the west of Oxford and Lafayette County, the Delta played a significant role in William Faulkner's life and work. His lifelong friend and one-time literary agent and editor, Ben Wasson, came from Greenville, and Faulkner often visited him there. Another Greenvillian, Hodding Carter, the founding editor of the *Delta Democrat-Times*, strongly influenced Faulkner's views on race and sectionalism.[3] As a young man, in the company of another friend, Phil Stone, the Oxford lawyer, Faulkner frequently traveled to Clarksdale to visit Reno's Place, a popular nightclub and gambling spot of the 1920s. In 1952 Faulkner delivered the annual Delta Council address on the Delta State College campus in Cleveland. Sections of two of Faulkner's finest and most significant narratives are set in the Delta: *Go Down, Moses* and *The Wild Palms/If I Forget Thee, Jerusalem.*

In both Faulkner's personal life and his art, the Mississippi Delta functions as a frontier society geographically and psychologically removed from the restraining social order of Oxford and Jefferson. The Delta is a place to explore personal freedom, to escape the censorious judgments of family and neighbors back home; it is a place to return to the primitive conditions of the wilderness, where bears and deer and squirrels outnumber humans, before the advent of plantations and lumber companies and railroads that would deplete the big woods and the animals; it is a place where individuals can test their mettle, where the worth of the individual and one's place in the social order is based on integrity and personal skill and courage and effort and not on authoritative decree or aristocratic privilege. Significantly, Faulkner's Delta begins at the westernmost edge and continues beyond the border of the maps he drew of Yoknapatawpha County, thus representing unincorporated space, virgin land as yet unsettled, uncivilized, and unspoiled. In this regard, as I shall subsequently demonstrate, Faulkner's Delta stands as a microcosm of that larger and continually expanding American frontier that Frederick Jackson Turner, in his highly influential *The Frontier in American History* and *The Significance of Sections in American History*, argued was the single most important factor in the development of American character, values, and institutions.[4]

The heart of Faulkner's vision of the Delta as frontier, of course, is "The Bear." Here, Ike McCaslin serves his apprenticeship as hunter under the tutelage of Sam Fathers in "the wilderness, the big woods, bigger and older than any recorded document" (*GDM* 183), "the same solitude, the same loneliness through which frail and timorous man had merely passed without altering it, leaving no mark nor scar, which looked exactly as it must have looked when the first ancestor of Sam Fathers' Chickasaw predecessors crept into it and looked about him, club or some axe or bone arrow drawn and ready" (194). If Sam Fathers is the priest who guides Ike's novitiate in the ways of the wilderness, the god that Fathers serves is Old Ben, the bear that both rules and incarnates these woods. Modeled in part, it would appear, on the Sacred Bear of Frazer's *The Golden Bough*,[5] Old Ben (and to a lesser degree the other animals of the forest) is the totem god that offers himself in sacrifice for man's survival and renewal. Like Frazer's primitives, but with corn whiskey substituted for the animal blood employed in the religious rituals of precivilized men, Faulkner's hunters ingest "those fine fierce instants of heart and brain and courage and wiliness and speed [that] were concentrated and distilled into that brown liquor which not women, not boys and children, but only hunters drank, drinking not of the blood they spilled but some condensation of the wild immortal spirit, drinking it moderately, humbly even, not with the pagan's base and baseless hope of acquiring thereby the virtues of cunning and strength and speed but in salute to them" (184).

Ike's entry into this spiritual order occurs in his eleventh year when he is afforded his first view of the giant bear. The scene that records this event draws upon both primitive initiatory rites and ritual acts of Christian mystics in their quest for a vision of God. First Ike must purge himself of all the trappings of material culture—the gun, the compass, and the watch. Then, purified, lost to self, having given himself completely to the spirit of the wilderness, he is granted his vision. That Old Ben is more than mere bear, is mythic and divine, is suggested by the ghostly, almost supernatural, nature of his sudden appearance and disappearance.

> Then he saw the bear. *It did not emerge*, appear: *it was just there*, immobile, fixed in the green and windless noon's hot dappling, . . . *dimensionless* against the dappled *obscurity*, looking at him. Then it moved. It crossed the glade without haste, walking for an instant into the sun's full glare and out of it. . . . Then it was gone. *It didn't walk* into the woods. It *faded*, sank back into the wilderness *without motion*." (200, emphases added)

Ike's novitiate is over; he has been accepted into the order of a spiritual, transcendent ideal.

To emphasize the ideal, even divine, quality of the wilderness, Faulkner compares the world of the big woods to the biblical Eden. Thus, Ike links the existence of the Delta wilderness to the original creation story:

> He told in the Book how He created the earth, made it and looked at it and said it was all right, and then He made man. He made the earth first and peopled it with dumb creatures, and then He created man to be His overseer on the earth and to hold suzerainty over the earth and the animals on it in His name, not to hold for himself and his descendants inviolable title forever, generation after generation, to the oblongs and squares of the earth, but to hold the earth mutual and intact in the communal anonymity of brotherhood. (246)

In the idyllic wilderness, then, there is no concern for ownership. Neither is social caste or race a factor. In the big woods southern aristocrats, poor whites, Blacks, and Native Americans conjoin in mutual fellowship and brotherhood, and the worth of a man is determined by his own merits, not by artificial definitions society might impose. In the woods all men—white, black, and red—are literally and symbolically brothers.

In the dialogue with his cousin Cass in section 4 of "The Bear," Ike parallels this ideal wilderness ruled by Old Ben and Sam Fathers with the genesis of American civilization. The American continent, Ike points out, was settled in idealism and hope, a place where man could escape "the old world's worthless twilight" and create "a new world where a nation of people could be founded in humility and pity and sufferance and pride of one to another" (247). In this brave new world, human beings would throw off the shackles of the past and begin anew to carve out an ideal commonwealth which would shun the sins and errors of previous civilizations. The bountiful and open frontier of the wilderness that settlers found in this new world contributed to the vision of perfection: "this land . . . for which [God] had done so much with woods for game and streams for fish and deep rich soil for seed and lush springs to sprout it and long summers to mature it and serene falls to harvest it and short mild winters for men and animals." Thus was born the American Dream, the belief that the "whole hopeful continent [was] dedicated as a refuge and sanctuary of liberty and freedom from . . . the old world's worthless evening" (271).

This dream, however, had not materialized, and Ike McCaslin's survey of the history of both the South and the nation explores some of the reasons why. For one thing there was the matter of how the white man had taken the land from the Native Americans. For another there was the curse of chattel slavery. America, which had been founded in freedom, had been built only in part on the noble virtues of courage, industry, and sacrifice: it was also based upon man's inhumanity to his fellow man, and this inhumanity was the practice of the New England slaver and manufacturer as well as the southern planter. This violation of the original spirit of the dream had led to disappointment and suffering, to exile from Eden. America had ultimately proven to be not an escape from Europe but a repetition of Old World mistakes and atrocities: "not only that old world from which [God] had rescued them but this new one too which He had revealed and led them to as a sanctuary and refuge were become the same worthless tideless rock cooling in the last crimson evening" (272). For Ike the symbol of this failure—and indeed of the judgment that comes to any society which substitutes greed and inhumanity and injustice for human brotherhood—is war and its horrible aftermath. The tragedies of the Civil War and Reconstruction, both of which pitted brother against brother and race against race, are interpreted as a working out of the curse which not only white southerners but indeed all Americans have inherited because of their misdeeds.

In its broadest allegorical application, of course, "The Bear" becomes a commentary on the universal history of humankind. Ike McCaslin sees all history as a continual rise and fall of empires, each founded on romantic dreams of permanence and perfection and each in its turn falling prey to human folly and weakness. What has been said of the American Dream is here extended to embrace all human experience. This application accounts for the many historical and biblical allusions in "The Bear"—not only to the discovery of America and the fall of the antebellum South but also to the destruction of Noah's world by flood, to the rise and fall of the Roman Empire, to the quest of the Jews for Canaan, and, as already noted and most importantly, to the Fall narrative in Eden. "Dispossessed of Eden" (246, 247)—this refrain serves as the unifying theme that links together all of the various allusions. The history of humanity, "The Bear" implies, is a cyclical reenactment of the loss of Eden and the quest to repossess the Garden experience in some "Promised Land" of the future. Thus caught between a forfeited Eden and a dreamed-of yet never-to-be-possessed Canaan, between community and frontier, humans exist in a paradoxical state of stasis and motion, achievement and failure, gain and loss, memory and desire.

Readers must be cautious, however, of accepting Faulkner's (or is it merely Ike McCaslin's?) characterization of the wilderness in "The Bear" at face value. As Peter Froehlich has convincingly argued, "The Bear" presents a highly romanticized and humanized view of nature, one that still lies very near to the civilized world, a user-friendly universe ruled by a benevolent God sympathetic to the needs and concerns of humanity.[6] The characterization is decidedly Wordsworthian, a nature that with "One impulse from a vernal wood / May teach you more of man, / Of moral evil and of good, / Than all the sages can."[7] Yet Faulkner well knew there was another type of nature. Post-Darwinian and schooled in the literary naturalism of Theodore Dreiser and others, he knew of a nature that is indifferent, even hostile, to civilization: "nature red in tooth and claw,"[8] ruled by natural selection and chance and the survival of the fittest. This nature resides off the edge of the map; it is the ultimate frontier, beyond the known world, unexplored and terror-filled, the place where land and water's end falls away into chaos and darkness. Before he wrote "The Bear," Faulkner had already presented this frightful view of nature, in the story of the tall convict in the "Old Man" section of *The Wild Palms/If I Forget Thee, Jerusalem.*

"Old Man" is set during the raging Mississippi River flood of 1927. At the height of the crisis, a group of prisoners in Parchman penitentiary are commanded to assist in shoring up levees along the river and in locating and rescuing refugees who have had to abandon their homes. Two of the prisoners, the protagonist of the story identified only as "the tall convict" and a second called "the plump convict," are given a skiff and an oar and assigned the task of rescuing a woman clinging to a cypress snag and a man sitting on the ridgepole of a cottonhouse. Almost immediately the quest turns into a horror-filled struggle for survival pitting a frail, solitary human being against the malevolent and destructive power of the river, Old Man. On the rushing sweep of the flooding current, the tall convict is swept uncontrollably on an atavistic journey backward through time, back to precivilization when, seemingly, the whole universe was one untraveled frontier. As in "The Bear," here Faulkner employs a biblical myth from Genesis, though in this case it is not the archetype of an idyllic Eden in which humans commune with God, but rather the image of Noah's flood which threatens to destroy humanity and all its endeavors, converting nature back into chaos.

"Old Man" contains some of the most visually descriptive language in all of Faulkner's works, and even a small sampling of this magnificent prose will demonstrate what the tall convict is up against. Quickly separated from his companion, the tall convict is left to fend for himself, solitary and defenseless. As the plump convict later recounts the incident:

Just all of a sudden the boat whirled clean around and begun to run fast backward like it was hitched to a train and it whirled around again and I happened to look up and there was a limb right over my head and I grabbed it just in time and that boat was snatched out from under me like you'd snatch off a sock and I saw it one time more upside down and that fellow . . . holding to it with one hand and still holding the paddle in the other (*WP* 66).

Finally managing to right and reboard the skiff and then, quite accidentally, discovering the woman, who is eight months pregnant, the convict attempts to resume the search for the man on the cottonhouse, but the current is too strong and continues to sweep the skiff downstream.

During the next three or four hours after the thunder and lightning had spent itself the skiff ran in pitch streaming darkness upon a roiling expanse which, even if he could have seen, apparently had *no boundaries* [emphasis added]. Wild and invisible, it tossed and heaved about and beneath the boat, ridged with dirty phosphorescent foam and filled with a debris of destruction—objects nameless and enormous and invisible which struck and slashed at the skiff and whirled on. (134)

Now Faulkner presents the convict not only as Noah but also as Ulysses, lost on the vast water and seeking his way back home. When the woman inquires if he knows where they are, he says, "I dont even know where I used to be. Even if I knowed which way was north, I wouldn't know if that was where I wanted to go." "Which way you fixing to go?" she then asks. "Ask the boat [he replies]. I been in it since breakfast and I aint never knowed, where I aimed to go or where I was going either" (128–29).

Unable to deliver the woman to shore, unable even to surrender to the authorities, who mistake his circumstance as an attempted escape and fire upon him, the convict is eventually forced to serve as unwilling attendant for the birth of the child. Then, resuming the journey with a child as well as the woman, the convict is swept still farther beyond civilization and security, quite literally now beyond the boundaries marked by maps. Much later, when he tries to explain his experiences with the Louisiana Cajuns who speak no English, identifying them as "Not Americans," the plump convict responds in amazement: "Not Americans? You was clean out of *America* even?" (201). Symbolically, the region the convict has now entered is that populated by early cartographers with monsters and demons that waited to devour anyone who ventured too far and fell off the edge of the world.

The monsters here are snakes and alligators, the first of which he fights armed only with the broken boat paddle, and the second with a small knife.

It is in the hand-to-hand combats of the alligator hunts that Faulkner depicts the struggle of man versus nature in its most extreme and elemental form, a vivid description of what life is like at the farthest side of frontier:

> [The convict] stooped straddling, the knife driving even as he grasped the near foreleg, this all in the same instant when the lashing tail struck him a terrific blow upon the back. But the knife was home, he knew that even on his back in the mud, the weight of the thrashing beast longwise upon him, its ridged back clutched to his stomach, his arm about its throat, the hissing head clamped against his jaw, the furious tail lashing and flailing, the knife in his other hand probing for the life and finding it, the hot fierce gush. (216–17)[9]

As terrible and painfully exhausting as the convict's struggle with elemental forces throughout "Old Man" proves to be, paradoxically it is also the means by which he discovers and acts upon his own strengths of character: courage, integrity, honor, honesty, fidelity ("I aint going without my boat" [227]), willfulness of purpose, ultimately the capacity to suffer, endure, and prevail. As Faulkner writes, "[H]e who had never ceased to flail at the bland treacherous water with what he had believed to be the limit of his strength now from somewhere, some ultimate absolute reserve, produced a final measure of endurance, will to endure" (124). The crisis has also produced in him a curious though satisfying sense of freedom: "the being allowed to work and earn money, that right and privilege which he believed he had earned to himself unaided, asking no favor of anyone or anything save the right to be let alone to pit his will and strength against the sauric Protagonist of a land, a region" (226). Originally an obscure, anonymous prisoner without even a name, next a Noah looking for a place to land his ark, then Ulysses wandering in search of home, the convict is finally a legendary Greek hero, triumphing over insurmountable odds: "Do not concern yourself about food, O Hercules," the Cajun cries. "Catch alligators" (219). As I shall shortly seek to demonstrate, he has also become something of the type, if a reluctant one, of Frederick Jackson Turner's American pioneer and frontiersman, pushing the frontier line farther and farther and in the process discovering his tremendous capacity for courage, self-reliance, and responsibility. And the reader now understands that the word "tall" in the convict's description is a reference not merely to his height but also to his heroic character.

Readers should not be surprised that the tall convict, despite the gains of self-discovery and victory over external nature, readily forfeits his life beyond the edge of the map to return to the safety and security of the known world.

Faulkner well understood (as he would later dramatize so poignantly in *A Fable*) that the human masses are followers, not pioneers and trailblazers, and that the anxiety and sheer weight of total freedom and responsibility are so great as to cause most individuals to seek the security of the familiar and the comfortable, even in extreme cases choosing to become a ward of the bureaucratic state or live under the tyranny of despotic rule. In the final analysis, therefore, the convict is not a frontiersman, despite his initial appearance of being so. Ultimately he will travel not farther West (as, incidentally, Charlotte Rittenmeyer and Harry Wilbourne do in the companion story to "Old Man") but back East, recross the ocean (in this case a river), and gladly surrender his newfound freedom to regain the secure footing of land, home, conventionality, community. But, even conceding this, we must also acknowledge that Faulkner understood the value of pioneering heroes, the need to keep alive the frontier spirit, the willingness to retain something of the wilderness mentality, to expand the map of experience by pushing the frontier line farther and farther into the unknown. (This is exactly what he did in his artistic life, of course, as he explored new forms of narrative and characterization and made his way into that unexplored territory with only his own genius and willpower as companions and without the aid of guide, mentor, institution, or government.) As I shall now seek to demonstrate, his views in this regard are remarkably similar to those of Frederick Jackson Turner.

A native of Wisconsin who became the foremost historian and theorist of the American frontier, Turner (1861–1932) taught history at the University of Wisconsin from 1889 to 1910 and at Harvard from 1910 to 1924. In July 1893 he delivered a paper at the annual meeting of the American Historical Association in Chicago entitled "The Significance of the Frontier in American History," published the following year. In succeeding years Turner expanded the application of his "frontier thesis" to various regions and stages of American history, finally publishing his most significant and influential book, *The Frontier in American History*, in 1920. Thus, the rise to preeminence of Turner's ideas occurred during William Faulkner's formative years, and Faulkner is almost certain to have read or heard about Turner's thesis.

What Turner sought to do in the field of history was what Mark Twain had only recently accomplished in literature: to demonstrate that the American frontier was not a barren wasteland, greatly inferior to the more sophisticated and educated East, but a vital and viable part of American, even world, culture and thought. Turner opposed both the eighteenth-century historians, who focused almost entirely on the original colonies as an extension of European (primarily English) history and culture, and the nineteenth-century historians who interpreted American history primarily as the result as the North/South split over slavery. To really understand the uniqueness of the American experiment, Turner argued, one must examine the ongoing dialectic between the eastern establishment and the continually expanding western and southwestern frontiers. "The West," Turner argued, "was a migrating region, a stage of society rather than a place," providing both individuals and the nation the opportunity of "beginning over on its outer edge as it advanced into the wilderness."[10]

Turner's basic ideas can be easily summarized. He contended that "the existence of an area of free land, its continuous recession, and the advance of American settlement westward, explain American development."[11] This development, which Turner saw as a near-Darwinian evolutionary process, results from the periodic return to primitive conditions on the advancing frontier that create an ongoing opposition between savagery and civilization, sectionalism and federalism, growth and stasis, freedom and restraint, opportunity and closure, West and East. "The West," he wrote, "opened a refuge from the rule of established classes, from the subordination of youth to age, from the sway of established and revered institutions."[12] What Turner viewed as the essential traits of the American character—a fervent individualism that is antagonistic toward centralized government, an egalitarian spirit that accepted immigrants from various ethnic backgrounds (not merely Anglo-Saxon), a preference for an agrarian over an industrial economy, a materialism that resulted from the opportunity for all persons to start over again and seek their fortune on the frontier, a pragmatism that resulted from the physical necessity of having to contend daily with the challenges of enemies and nature, a general optimism that resulted from success in overcoming obstacles and expanding onward— all of these evolve from the presence of a geographical frontier throughout the developing history of the American nation.

Turner, of course, was advancing these ideas at the time when the physical presence of an American frontier was coming to an end. He cited the report of the superintendent of the 1890 census, which stated: "Up to and including 1880 the country had a frontier of settlement, but at present the unsettled area has been so broken into by isolated bodies of settlement that there can hardly be said to be a frontier line. In the discussion of its extent, its westward movement, etc., it cannot, therefore, any longer have a place in the census reports."[13] Turner predicted that, just as the presence of the frontier had had profound effects on the American character, so now would its absence. While he never developed in great detail his theory of future development, his implications are quite clear, and quite logical. The loss of the frontier would reverse the

effects of its presence: there would be, in twentieth-century America, an ero-
sion of personal freedom and individuality; a rise in conformity and collectivism; an increase in federalism, urbanization, and socialism; a displacement
of the agrarian lifestyle by industrialization; and a general tendency toward
national conformity rather than regional distinctiveness. As Turner wrote as
early as 1907:

> The nationalizing tendencies are at the present time clearly in evidence. The
> control of great industries has passed to a striking extent into the hands of
> corporations or trusts, operating on a national basis and centered in a few
> hands. Banking and transportation systems show the same tendency to
> consolidation. Cities are growing at a rate disproportioned to the increase
> of general population, and their numerical growth is only a partial index of
> their influence upon the thought as well as the economic life of the country.
> On the whole, in spite of rivalry, the business world of these cities tends to
> act nationally and to promote national homogeneity. The labor organizations
> are national in their scope and purposes. Newspapers, telegraph, post-office—
> all the agencies of intercourse and the formation of thought—tend toward
> national uniformity and national consciousness. The cooperative publication of
> news furnished by national agencies, the existence of common ownership and
> editorial conduct of chains of newspapers, all tend to produce simultaneous
> formation of a national public opinion. In general the forces of civilization are
> working toward uniformity.[14]

The final, convincing evidence of both the geographical and psychological
closing of the frontier, Turner pointed out, could be seen in the region of
the frontier itself, where the policy of free land that had once promoted "old
individualistic principles and the *laissez faire* conception of government" has
now been replaced, through the actions of the federal Reclamation Service, by
government ownership and management of land and resources (310).

It is these consequences of the disappearing frontier that seem most relevant to a reading of Faulkner, since Faulkner was writing at the time when
the changes Turner predicted had already occurred and become entrenched
in the national agenda.

Turner's ideas find echo throughout Faulkner's works, but most explicitly
in the political essays and speeches like the one Faulkner presented at Delta
State College in Cleveland, Mississippi, in 1952. When Faulkner visited Delta
State to speak to the Delta Council, an organization of planters, farmers, and
businessmen, he was an internationally renowned figure who was being asked

to express his views on any number of subjects, not only writing but also race relations, politics, religion, psychology, and international relations. Significantly, though, Faulkner chose to travel to Cleveland not under the persona of the world figure but under that of the common, ordinary citizen. Joseph Blotner records an interesting anecdote about Faulkner's dress for the occasion. When Bob and Alice Farley arrived at Rowan Oak to drive Faulkner to Cleveland, they found him dressed in wrinkled cotton seersucker trousers, a shirt with a badly frayed collar, an old, belted jacket that was now much too small for him, and a felt hat that Farley dated from about 1915. (Faulkner's attire, by the way, would prove especially fortuitous for Bern Keating, the photographer from Greenville, who was destined to shoot on this day some of the most impressive photographs of Faulkner ever made.) Blotner continues the story: "You ready to go to Cleveland," [Farley] asked. "Oh, is this the day?" Faulkner replied, his eyes glinting. "It sure is." "Can I go like this?" "You can if you want to." "Let's go" (*FB* 1415). This makes for an amusing story, but it is extremely hard to believe that anyone, even an absent-minded author, would forget the date scheduled for him to make a significant speech on an issue of grave concern at the invitation of an important organization and before a large audience that would include the governor of the state and other important dignitaries. More likely, Faulkner deliberately chose his attire to identify with the hard-working, self-reliant Americans who were the subject of his remarks.

The speech Faulkner delivered that day, May 15, 1952, in Whitfield Gymnasium contains the essence of his views on the proper relationship between the individual and government. Drawing upon ideas expressed in his fiction all the way back to the 1930s and early '40s,[15] as well as upon the book that he was completing at the time of his visit to Cleveland, *A Fable*, Faulkner delivered, to a standing ovation, a scathing attack upon a federal welfare system that, he argued, devalued challenge and initiative and thus encouraged personal laziness and irresponsibility. Claiming that the contemporary American had forgotten that "the premise of the rights of man" (*ESPL* 127) carried with it a willingness "to be responsible for the consequences of his own acts, to pay his own score, owing nothing to any man" (129), Faulkner reviewed the historical accomplishments of "the old tough, durable, uncompromising men" (130) who "left [their] homes, the lands and graves of [their] fathers and all familiar things" (128) to secure their independence from the Old World and then successively conquer wildernesses from the Atlantic seaboard to the Pacific Ocean, in the process creating "a land of opportunity, in which all a man needed were two legs to move to a new place on, and two hands to grasp and hold with, in order to amass to himself enough material substance to last him the rest of his days and, who knew? even something over for his and his wife's children" (130). In words that could have been written by Frederick Jackson Turner, Faulkner celebrated these heroic actions:

> Even while we were still battling the wilderness with one hand, with the other we fended and beat off the power which would have followed us even into the wilderness we had conquered, to compel and hold us to the old way. But we did it. We founded a land, and founded in it not just our right to be free and independent and responsible, but the inalienable duty of man to be free and independent and responsible. (128-29)

Then "something happened to us" (129), Faulkner continued, offering his version of the nation that Turner had predicted at the turn of the century. Americans had discarded and forgotten the understanding that the word "rights" also implies duties and responsibilities and, as a result, had relinquished their freedom in order "to hold [their] individual place on a public relief roll or at a bureaucratic or political or any other organization's gravy-trough" (130). What made this development even more tragic and grievous, Faulkner claimed, was that the principal enemy of American freedom no longer was a foreign power across an ocean but rather

> faces us now from beneath the eagle-perched domes of our capitols and from behind the alphabetical splatters on the doors of welfare and other bureaus of economic or industrial regimentation, dressed not in martial brass but in the habiliments of what the enemy himself has taught us to call peace and progress, a civilization and plenty where we never before had it as good, let alone better; his artillery is a debased and respectless currency which has emasculated the initiative for independence by robbing initiative of the only mutual scale it knew to measure independence by. (132)

So seductive has been the beguiling power of this enemy to convert its subjects to "the right not to earn, but to be given" that "at last, by simple compound usage, we have made respectable and even elevated to a national system, that which the old tough fathers would have scorned and condemned: charity" (131).

Not all of Faulkner's remarks to the Delta Council, however, constituted a jeremiad of woe. In fact, he ended his speech with a glimmer of hope. Three times echoing a celebrated phrase from his Nobel Prize Acceptance Address, he emphasized that he "decline[d] to believe" that Americans were incapable of relearning and restoring the principle of self-reliant, responsible freedom. Americans could once again, with sufficient courage and fidelity and resolve, rediscover a social order based on the old frontier values, "where those who would stand on their own feet, could, and those who won't, might have to" (133). Only then, Faulkner concluded, could an appropriate type of welfare find its place in the republic. "Then the welfare, the relief, the compensation, instead of being nationally sponsored cash prizes for idleness and ineptitude, could go where the old independent uncompromising fathers themselves would have intended it and blessed it: to those who still cannot, until the day when even the last of them except the sick and the old, would also be among them who not only can, but will" (133–34).

Faulkner's appearance at Delta State, his dress for the occasion, and the speech he delivered there together form a symbolic representation of Faulkner's views of geography and culture. He had traveled beyond the edge of his map of Yoknapatawpha, to the area that still contained a remnant of the old lost wilderness, to express his continuing belief in frontier values in a nation that was becoming increasingly standardized and collectivist. He had traveled, as readers of his fiction would know, to the region he had described in "Delta Autumn."

"Delta Autumn" is the next-to-last story in *Go Down, Moses*, and the one immediately following "The Bear." The present-tense action of "The Bear" occurs in the 1880s, exactly contemporaneous with the period in which the superintendent of the census noted that the American frontier had closed. Thus, the simultaneous deaths of Old Ben, Lion, and Sam Fathers, which in Faulkner's chronology occur in 1883, may be taken as a symbolic representation of the larger event. And section 5 of the story, in which Major de Spain closes down the hunting camp but gives Ike permission to visit the site for one last time, stands as an elegy to the end of the wilderness not only in Yoknapatawpha County but in all of America.[16]

As the allusions to Hitler and war make clear, "Delta Autumn" is set in the early 1940s. It opens with a contrast of then and now, of how the annual hunts were conducted years ago and how they are conducted now. Ike McCaslin, now "Uncle Ike" to all of Yoknapatawpha County, is approaching eighty years old. Then they had entered the woods in wagons; now they go in cars. Then there had been bears and deer and wild turkey in the country; now there is left only a rapidly diminishing number of deer. Then one could hear the scream of panther in the wild; now one hears the long hoot of the locomotive. Then they had to travel only thirty miles from Jefferson to find big game; now they have to drive two hundred miles (roughly, as I calculate the actual distance, to what is today the Sharkey Delta National Forest located just north of Vicksburg) to find enough remaining woods to give habitat to deer. As Faulkner notes,

> Now the land lay open from the cradling hills on the East to the rampart of levee on the West, standing horseman-tall with cotton for the world's looms— the rich black land, imponderable and vast, fecund up to the very doorsteps of the negroes who worked it and of the white men who owned it; which exhausted the hunting life of a dog in one year, the working life of a mule in five, and of a man in twenty—the land in which neon flashed past them from the little countless towns and countless shining this-year's automobiles sped past them on the broad plumb-ruled highways. (*GDM* 324)

Nothing is left of the old time, Faulkner continues, but "the Indian names on the little towns and usually pertaining to water—Aluschaskuna, Tillatoba, Homochitto, Yazoo" (325).

A corresponding change has taken place in the character and behavior of the hunters. Paralleling the changes that Turner predicted would occur with the closing of the frontier, Faulkner presents the descendants of the old hunters as moral and physical lilliputians intruding into the former land of giants.[17] One of the hunters, in fact, Ike's cousin Roth Edmonds, the reader learns, has been coming to the woods not primarily to hunt but to engage in a love affair (thus all the inside jokes in the story about hunting does); and he has returned to the woods this time determined to end what has become a bothersome relationship. In Faulkner's characterization of Roth it quickly becomes clear that none of the lessons of the woods that Sam Fathers taught the young Ike McCaslin—courage, honor, responsibility—have been learned and assimilated by Roth. A hunter who indiscriminately shoots does as readily as bucks, and with a shotgun instead of a rifle, Roth refuses to meet his mistress face-to-face but instead leaves money and a one-word message, "No," for Ike to give to her when she comes to the camp seeking Roth. "What did you promise her that you haven't the courage to face her and retract?" Ike asks (339).

When the woman shows up at the camp, Uncle Ike discovers not only that she has her and Roth's child with her but also that she is part-Black and a cousin of him and Roth, being the granddaughter of Tennie's Jim, one of the biracial descendants of old L. Q. C. McCaslin. Now it is Uncle Ike who says no. "He cried, not loud, in a voice of amazement, pity, and outrage: 'You're a n——r!'" (344). Sadly, it would appear, even Uncle Ike in his old age has forgotten the lesson of universal brotherhood he learned under the tutelage of Sam Fathers,

in whose veins ran the blood of three races. "Go back North," Uncle Ike advises
the woman. "Marry: a man in your own race. That's the only salvation for you—
for a while yet, maybe a long while yet. We will have to wait. Marry a black man"
(346). Earlier he had thought: "*Maybe in a thousand years or two thousand years
in America. . . . But not now! Not now!*" (344, Faulkner's italics). The hunting
horn that Uncle Ike subsequently gives to the woman for the boy, in lineage the
last known descendant of old Lucius Quintus Carothers McCaslin in Faulkner's
work, seems nothing more than a hollow gesture. The meek may have inherited
in this case, if not the earth at least some symbol of familial rights, but the
legacy seems merely a sop to salve an old man's guilty conscience.

In terms of the map and frontier images that I have employed from time
to time, "Delta Autumn" suggests how far modern America has fallen from
the rugged individualism of the old West/Southwest. In the post-frontier
America, apparently, even old pioneers who had stood strong in the wilderness in support of their convictions now grow soft and conform to the will
of the timid majority. The setting of "Delta Autumn" is far west of Faulkner's
Yoknapatawpha, almost as far west as the tall convict's harrowing experiences
in "Old Man." But there is something of the character of the old frontier still
operative in "Old Man," whereas the frontier of "Delta Autumn" is a diminished, tamed one, in terms of both the woods and the men who frequent
them. As Turner had predicted, with the closure of an authentic frontier, the
West has been assimilated into the pattern of the East, both now standing in
uniformed and unified defense of the status quo.

I have sought to demonstrate that there are considerable parallels between
Faulkner's depiction of the western frontier of Yoknapatawpha County and
Frederick Jackson Turner's characterization of the broader American frontier.
In conclusion, however, I would like to emphasize a couple of key distinctions
in the respective treatments.

Turner's theory of the influence of the presence and now absence of the
frontier in America, as indeed his overall emphasis on the importance of
geography upon a national consciousness, is highly deterministic in nature.
Living and writing under the growing influence of Darwinian evolution,
particularly as Darwin's ideas had been filtered and recycled by the British
philosopher and sociologist Herbert Spencer, Turner allowed little room for
human free will and choice in the development of a civilization and its values.
His metaphors and ideas are drawn primarily from the sciences, particularly
geography and geology, not from the traditional humanities and certainly not
from the Bible. Humankind, along with its governments and institutions and
values, is principally the result of environmental conditions. Logically and

predictably, when those conditions change, the individuals and governments and institutions and values will likewise inevitably change. While Turner occasionally acknowledged that there were forces in human affairs other than climate and landscape, by and large he continued to advocate geographical determinism as the major factor in the development and decline of civilizations. In the final analysis, while brilliant in its conception, design, and application, it is nevertheless, as many later historians and cultural theorists have argued, a greatly oversimplified and reductionist approach to human history.[18]

Faulkner's views of history, civilization, and government, it seems to me, are both more moral and more complex than Turner's. Faulkner, too, was influenced by deterministic thought, Sherwood Anderson and Theodore Dreiser being two of his early influences, but Faulkner never became a convert to a wholly deterministic view of life. The Snopeses, Compsons, Sartorises, and McCaslins in his fiction are all products of a particular time and place, and of identifiable and influential economic and social conditions, but they are also possessed of a high degree of free will and alternative choice. For Faulkner the question of human history and destiny always remained a problem of "the heart's driving complexity" (*GDM* 249), of "the human heart in conflict with itself" (*ESPL* 119). Human beings are not primarily the product of biological or environmental forces, but free moral agents who make choices either for good or for bad. Thus, the Bible, with its insistence on a moral agency that produces salvation or damnation, would be, from beginning to end, a dominant influence upon Faulkner's work.

Still, despite their differences, it is helpful to place Faulkner's work alongside Turner's. They share a mutual love and respect for the land, for the men and women who live close to it, and for freedom and individuality; and they are both skeptical about the growing conformity and standardization that they see in the modern world. If nothing else, examining these two writers together serves at least partially to position Faulkner in the mainstream of American literature and history, as opposed to the tributaries of southern regionalism or European modernism. Over the years Faulkner's works have been extensively analyzed in relation to the peculiar history and culture of the American South and to the literary values and methods of modernism as exemplified by Joyce and Eliot. Just as Turner quarreled with those who interpreted American history altogether in terms of European or North-South elements, perhaps it is now time to look beyond similar international and regional affinities and position Faulkner more centrally in the American literary tradition—as a writer far more concerned than is generally acknowledged with significant issues of national policy and import.[19]

NOTES

1. James Cowan, *A Mapmaker's Dream: The Meditations of Fra Mauro, Cartographer to the Court of Venice* (Boston: Shambhala, 1996).

2. Faulkner's first published map of Yoknapatawpha County was printed at the end of *Absalom, Absalom!* in 1936. He revised the map in 1945 for inclusion in Malcolm Cowley's *The Portable Faulkner*.

3. See Robert W. Hamblin, "Teaching *Intruder in the Dust* through Its Political and Historical Context," included in this volume.

4. Frederick Jackson Turner, *The Frontier in American History* (New York: Henry Holt, 1950); Frederick Jackson Turner, *The Significance of Sections in American History* (New York: Henry Holt, 1932).

5. See Sir James George Frazer, "Killing the Sacred Bear," in *The Golden Bough: A Study in Magic and Religion*, abbr. ed. (New York: Macmillan, 1963), 585–600.

6. See Peter Alan Froehlich, "Teaching 'The Bear' as an Artifact of Frontier Mythology," in *Teaching Faulkner: Approaches and Methods*, ed. Stephen Hahn and Robert W. Hamblin (Westport, CT: Greenwood Press, 2000), 137–49. Froehlich astutely argues that "the actual frontier experience, the settlement of Jefferson, occurs in Ike's grandfather's generation," and thus "[t]he main action of ["The Bear"] does not concern this primary frontier experience, but rather the situation of a young man of a later generation negotiating his relationship to the myth, struggling to come to terms with the legacy of the frontier and to revise the myth into something that will be practically and ethically useful in his life" (146).

7. William Wordsworth, "The Tables Turned," in *Selected Poems* (New York: Gramercy Books, 1993), 77–78.

8. Now commonly viewed as a description of Darwin's view of nature, the phrase is from Tennyson's *In Memoriam*. See Alfred Lord Tennyson, *In Memoriam*, ed. Susan Shatto and Marion Shaw (Oxford: Clarendon Press, 1982), section 56.

9. Compare the elemental savagery of this incident with Boon Hogganbeck's killing of the bear in *Go Down, Moses* and Thomas Sutpen's hand-to-hand combats with his slaves in *Absalom, Absalom!*

10. Turner, *Sections*, 23.

11. Turner, *Frontier*, 1.

12. Turner, *Sections*, 25.

13. Turner, *Frontier*, 1.

14. Turner, *Sections*, 311–12.

15. Consider, for example, the antifederalist views expressed in "Lo!" and "The Tall Men," both of which appear in *Collected Stories*.

16. Froehlich calls the setting of "The Bear" "the McCaslin-DeSpain-Compson hunt club" (141) and argues that it "functions in Faulkner's imagination the way Teddy Roosevelt envisioned the national parks would: as a space that would allow the residents of a modern, industrialized, fully settled culture access to the ethical and cultural lessons that can only be learned in contact with wild nature" (146–47).

17. John Steinbeck employs the same theme in his short story "The Leader of the People."

18. For a good critique of both the positive and negative aspects of Turner's views, see Richard Hofstadter, *The Progressive Historians: Turner, Beard, Parrington* (New York: Alfred A. Knopf, 1968), 118–64.

19. As indicated by the title of his biography, *William Faulkner: American Writer*, Frederick Karl has attempted to do precisely what I call for here. But to date few critics have followed his lead in this matter.

"No Such Thing as Was"
Faulkner and Southern History

A dominant theme in twentieth-century American literature is the search for meaningful values in a rapidly changing and often-confusing world. One after another of our modern poets, playwrights, and fictionists has treated the perilous quest of the individual who seeks to find purpose and meaning in a society and universe which seem at times to lack either purpose or meaning—which, indeed, seem to be enigmatic, chaotic, even absurd. In such a Humpty Dumpty (or Catch-22) world, we hear many voices calling out for our attention, our allegiance; and we must carefully weigh the claims of all these voices in arriving at our own beliefs and values. Though this quest to find truths to live by is no easy task, it is imperative. As Wallace Stevens, one of our great modern poets, has observed, human beings are driven by a "blessed rage for order"; and the more disordered and divided the world becomes, the more crucial and obsessive becomes that "rage for order."[1]

Like their counterparts in other sections of the country, southern writers also perceive the modern world as synonymous with change, mutability, loss, confusion, and uncertainty; and they are no less desirous for order, purpose, and meaning. However, as historian C. Vann Woodward has noted in his classic work *The Burden of Southern History*, there is a key distinction between southern writers and most other modern American authors. That distinction may be summed up by the phrase "historical consciousness." As Woodward points out, "The characters in the novels of Dreiser, Anderson, and Lewis appear on the scene from nowhere, trailing no clouds of history, dissociated from the past." Woodward continues: "A Hemingway hero with a grandfather is inconceivable," and the characters of Dos Passos "are haunted by no ghosts of the past."[2] Southern writers, by contrast, have been preoccupied, even obsessed, by the continuance of the past into the present. As a result, the southerner (reader as well as writer) is bombarded with all the voices that other Americans hear, plus some more: the voices of history. Like the voices of the present, these voices from the past are both negative and positive.

No American writer surpasses William Faulkner in dramatizing the cacophony of voices, both past and present, that impinge upon the modern consciousness. No American writer better dramatizes the individual's search for order and values among these multitudinous voices. And no writer more than Faulkner recognizes the insistent demand that this quest be successfully resolved.

A genuine respect for the individual and for self-reliance is one of Faulkner's strongest convictions. One of the frightening things about the modern world, according to Faulkner, is the emergence of totalitarian and bureaucratic and conformist states that would rob people of their uniqueness. There is, Faulkner warned, the widespread contemporary belief that "individual man can no longer exist," that "man himself can hope to continue only by relinquishing and denying his individuality into a regimented group" (*ESPL* 161). But it is not groups or organizations that will save humanity, Faulkner insisted; it is individual men and women. As he told his daughter's graduating class at Pine Manor Junior College, "It is us, we, not as groups or classes but as individuals, simple men and women individually free and capable of freedom and decision, who must decide, affirm simply and firmly and forever never to be led like sheep" (*ESPL* 138–39).

Many of Faulkner's fabled eccentricities—his unorthodox lifestyle, his unusual habits of dress, his obsessive desire for privacy, his distrust of crowds and large cities—derive from his code of individualism. So, too, do his opinions about writers and writing. Faulkner believed that writers, at least the good ones, must be self-dependent, free and courageous enough to experiment, even to the point of making mistakes and risking failure. "Only an individualist can be a first-rate writer," Faulkner once said (*FIU* 33); and he frequently criticized Hemingway for his tendency to do the same thing over and over rather than "splashing around to try to experiment" (*FIU* 206). Neither, Faulkner believed, should the good writer be overly concerned with mentors, critics, and censors. As he told one interviewer, "The young writer would be a fool to follow a theory. Teach yourself by your own mistakes; people learn only by error. The good artist believes that nobody is good enough to give him advice" (*LIG* 244). Faulkner himself, of course, benefited from advice from various associates throughout his career, among them Phil Stone, Sherwood Anderson, Ben Wasson, and Saxe Commins; but he never allowed himself to become slavishly dependent upon any of these persons. He always insisted on marching to his own tune. Undoubtedly it was this strong bent toward individualism which limited Faulkner's success as a screenwriter in Hollywood. Scriptwriting, according to Faulkner, was too much "a matter of compromise, a compromise with the actor, with the director, and mainly with the people that put up the money" (*FIU* 149). In producing a movie, Faulkner said, "There's no chance for the individual to make something as he himself thinks it should be made. . . . It's made by too many people, too many forces" (*LIG* 153).

As much as Faulkner celebrated individualism, however, both in his manner of living and in his artistic principles, he never advocated a rampant or licentious individualism that operates independently from social awareness and responsibility. Every individual, Faulkner insisted, is a product of an inherited tradition and must define himself or herself in relation to that tradition. As Faulkner observed in one of his class conferences at the University of Virginia, "To me, no man is himself, he is the sum of his past. There is no such thing really as was because the past is. It is a part of every man, every woman, and every moment." Since the present is ever an extension of the past, Faulkner went on to say, "a character in a story at any moment of action is not just himself as he is then, he is all that made him" (*FIU* 84).

Just as individuals cannot be divorced from their past, their tradition, neither can they be isolated from fellow human beings. Faulkner frequently spoke of "the family of mankind" (*LIG* 200) or "the human family" (*FIU* 80; *LIG* 202), and he stressed that man is "responsible, terribly responsible" (*LIG* 70). Freedom, Faulkner cautioned, is never to be confused with ruthlessness and license. A person "must be free within a pattern of responsibility always" (*LIG* 206). One of the privileges of the writer, as Faulkner makes clear in his Nobel Prize Acceptance Speech, is to promote human solidarity by "reminding [man] of the courage and honor and hope and pride and compassion and pity and sacrifice which have been the glory of his past" (*ESPL* 120). Faulkner, of course, was wise enough to know, and honest enough to tell us, that not every person possesses a moral sense. Some, like his characters Flem Snopes and Jason Compson, are selfish, ruthless materialists; and others, like Popeye Vitelli, are amoral nihilists. But Faulkner's villains are always presented in relation to standards of morality and decency.

The individual and society, then, both of which Faulkner understood to be products of a historical past, are the two poles of Faulkner's fictional creation, and I want to examine the interrelationship of these poles in one of Faulkner's most undervalued novels, *The Unvanquished*. Before I do that, however, I need to emphasize once again Faulkner's acute historical sense. As he clearly demonstrates in work after work, society is never in stasis; it is always in a state of flux, of becoming. Hence, Faulkner's subject is not merely humanity but, as he once said, humanity "as a part of a living literature, [in which] 'living' is motion and 'motion' is change."[3] To read Faulkner's books is to become immersed in a world that has undergone, and continues to undergo, tremendous change. In this regard the broad outlines of Yoknapatawpha correspond to the history of the American South. The displacement of the Native American tribes, the establishment of a planter aristocracy and the introduction of chattel slavery, the ravages of the Civil War and Reconstruction, the emancipation and the subsequent rise of the Black freedman, the replacement of the aristocracy by the yeoman farmers of the middle and lower classes, the encroachment of industrialization and mercantilism upon an agrarian culture, the conflicts and changes ushered in by desegregation and the civil rights movement—these are some of the principal elements that contribute to Faulkner's recognition of history as an evolving, developing process. Added to the regional disruptions cited above are other crises which Faulkner's South has shared with other parts of the nation and globe: two world wars, the Great Depression, the Cold War, to name only a few. Given such unsettling shocks to human beings' demonstrated preference for stability and order, one can well understand why Faulkner metaphorically characterizes humanity, as he does in the person of the tall convict in *The Wild Palms/If I Forget Thee, Jerusalem*, as adrift in a small and fragile skiff, at times completely out of control, upon the surging waters of a huge flood. The problem, as the convict well perceives, is to restore order, or at least get terra firma under his feet again and wait out the raging storm.

This desperate need to establish order in the midst of uncertainty and threatening chaos is mirrored in the dominant characteristics of Faulkner's literary technique. Unlike the typical well-made novel of the nineteenth century—with its chronological ordering of a discernible beginning, middle, and end, and its frequent editorial glosses from the omniscient author to assist the reader in following and interpreting the story (a novel form, by the way, which clearly exhibits the confidence and absolutism of the age that produced it)—Faulkner's works utilize radical disruptions of standard chronology, numerous plot intersections, multiple narrators, and countless ambiguities and unresolved situations and themes. Like a cubistic painting by Pablo Picasso, the Faulkner novel images a world that has become, or at least is perceived as, disjointed and fragmented. In such a world, obviously, participants can hardly be expected to speak in a single voice. Crises, whether they be of short duration or, as in Faulkner's chronicle, stretch over a hundred years, beget loss of confidence, confusion of purpose, conflict of values, and a multitude of voices offering, sometimes screaming, solutions.

Thus we have Faulkner's characteristic employment of multiple narrators, each viewing a central situation from a uniquely particular vantage
point or bias. In *The Sound and the Fury*, for example, four narrators (five,
if one counts the appendix) tell somewhat the same story, but with all the
incompleteness and contradiction one expects from disparate treatments.
In that remarkable tour de force of technique, *As I Lay Dying*, fifteen different narrators recount the story, and the reader, much in the manner of a
courtroom juror, must sort through the various testimonies and assemble
and interpret the narrative as best one can. In *Absalom, Absalom!*, in many
respects the most complicated of all Faulkner's novels, Quentin Compson seeks to reconstruct, "out of the rag-tag and bob-ends of old tales and
talking" (243), the principal events in the history of Thomas Sutpen's family—events that occurred some fifty years earlier. Since no one of Quentin's sources knows the complete Sutpen story, and since, moreover, each
of the individual narrators exhibits a particular attitude or bias, Quentin
(and the reader) must infer the actual story from the multiple and contradictory treatments. The result is a Chinese box arrangement in which
what appears to be true on one page of the novel is opposed or refuted on
another. This technique makes *Absalom, Absalom!* simultaneously one of
the greatest detective stories in the English language and a grand metaphor of the circuitous and problematical ways in which one assimilates
and interprets past and present experience. Faulkner described the method
of *Absalom, Absalom!* as "thirteen ways of looking at a blackbird." "But the
truth," Faulkner continued, "comes out, that when the reader has read all
these thirteen different ways of looking at the blackbird, the reader has his
own fourteenth image of that blackbird which I would like to think is the
truth" (*FIU* 273–74). With the exception of *As I Lay Dying*, Faulkner does
not actually present to the reader as many as thirteen different perspectives
of a subject, but he almost always pairs off, or "counterpoints," conflicting
views, usually without resolving the question and thus leaving individual
readers to arrive at their own approximation of truth.

What I have sought to demonstrate thus far is Faulkner's abiding interest
in the individual and his relationship to society, and the problematical way in
which individuals must proceed to discover for themselves what their relationship to that society will be. I have also noted Faulkner's recognition that
society is ever in a state of uncertainty and flux, a fact which further com-
plicates the individual's task of defining values, much in the manner that a
moving target is harder to hit than a stationary one. Now, having said all this,
I propose to relate the theme I have just elaborated to *The Unvanquished*, a

novel which, not coincidentally, Faulkner published (in 1938) near the end of a decade in which American civilization seemed to many writers and thinkers to be on the verge of collapse.

The Unvanquished, an episodic novel in the pattern of *Huckleberry Finn*, traces the coming of age of Bayard Sartoris, the son of Colonel John Sartoris, a legendary Yoknapatawpha hero. The heart and climax of the novel is the final chapter, "An Odor of Verbena," which is frequently printed as a separate story and is hence all too often treated out of its context in the novel. Set in 1875, "An Odor of Verbena" dramatizes the inner conflict of Bayard, a twenty-four-year-old law student, as he contemplates his response to the murder of his father by a former business partner named Redmond. As Bayard well knows, one part of the historical tradition that has nurtured him requires that he avenge his father's death. In fact, Bayard himself has previously participated in a revenge killing—that of Grumby for the murder of Granny Millard. However, another part of his tradition, based on the biblical assertions "Thou shalt not kill" and "Who lives by the sword shall die by it," argues against revenge. In deciding which part of his tradition he will obey, which voice he will heed, Bayard must not only examine his own heart and motives but also scrutinize the character of his father.

In order to experience the full impact of Bayard's moral dilemma, the reader must recall the relationship developed between Bayard and his father in the earlier sections of *The Unvanquished*. At the opening of the novel, Bayard remembers the time when he was twelve years old and his father was away fighting Yankees. Bayard describes the moment when he and his Black companion, Ringo, had stood in front of the house and watched his father returning home from battle:

> He was not big; it was just the things he did, that we knew he was doing, had been doing in Virginia and Tennessee, that made him seem big to us. . . . He stopped two steps below [Granny], with his head bared and his forehead held for her to touch her lips to, and the fact that Granny had to stoop a little now took nothing from the illusion of height and size which he wore for us at least. (9–10)

From his adult perspective Bayard realizes that this larger-than-life view of his father is an "illusion." But, as he constantly reminds the reader in this section of the novel, "I was just twelve then" (5).

Bayard's romanticized view of his father is reinforced by the opinions of others. Once, in Jefferson, Bayard is observed by Uncle Buck McCaslin. "By Godfrey, there he is! There's John Sartoris' boy!" When a captain of

Confederates bivouacked nearby notes that he has heard of Colonel Sartoris, Uncle Buck retorts: "Heard of him? . . . Who ain't heard about him in
this country? Get the Yankees to tell you about him sometime. By Godfrey,
he raised the first damn regiment in Mississippi out of his own pocket, and
took 'em to Ferginny and whipped Yankees right and left with 'em." Recognizing that Bayard, Granny, and Ringo are on their way to Memphis to escape
the advancing Yankee army, Uncle Buck offers this benediction: "I won't say
God take care of you and your grandma on the road, boy, because by Godfrey you don't need God's help nor nobody else's help; all you got to say is
'I'm John Sartoris' boy; rabbits, hunt the canebrake' and then watch the blue-
bellied sons of bitches fly" (51–52). This heroic view of Colonel Sartoris is
further confirmed in Bayard's innocent eyes when the colonel almost single-
handedly ambushes and captures a group of Yankee soldiers. As *The Unvanquished* progresses, however, and as Bayard grows older, another, less heroic
view of Colonel Sartoris emerges.

This shift of characterization is quite evident in the chapter entitled "Skir-
mish at Sartoris." In this section, set during the Reconstruction era, Colonel
Sartoris opposes the African Americans and carpetbaggers who now threaten
the old order of southern society. His methods are highly arbitrary, though
hardly surprising during the unsettled period that Bayard calls "strange times"
(194, 198). On election day, when a freed slave, Cassius Q. Benbow, is a candidate for the office of marshal in Jefferson, Colonel Sartoris shoots two Mis-
sourians who are organizing the Blacks to vote, confiscates the ballot box, and
conducts the election at his own house. As Bayard recalls:

> They set the box on the sawchunk where Louvinia washed, and Ringo got the
> pokeberry juice and an old piece of window shade, and they cut it into ballots.
> "Let all who want the Honorable Cassius Q. Benbow to be Marshal of Jefferson
> write Yes on his ballot; opposed, No," Father said.
>
> "And I'll do the writing and save some more time," George Wyatt said. So
> he made a pack of the ballots and wrote them against his saddle and fast as he
> would write them the men would take them and drop them into the box. . . .
> It didn't take long. "You needn't bother to count them," George said. "They all
> voted No." (210)

Colonel Sartoris's violent and dictatorial actions are scarcely ameliorated by
his remark that he let the carpetbaggers shoot first and by his insistence that
he post bond following the killings. "Don't you see we are working for peace
through law and order?" he says (208). The irony of this statement may have
escaped Colonel Sartoris, but it is obvious to most readers.

What Bayard, who was fifteen years old at the time, comes to think of his father's actions on that election day is not disclosed until the next, and final, chapter of the book, "An Odor of Verbena." Nine years have passed, and Bayard, now a law student at the University of Mississippi, has received word of his father's death at the hand of Redmond. As suggested earlier, Bayard's decision as to what he will do in response to his father's murder forces him to examine contradictory impulses in his native tradition.

Drusilla, Bayard's stepmother, becomes the dominant voice advocating the code of vengeance. Riding the forty miles to Jefferson, Bayard foresees Drusilla waiting for him, wearing a sprig of verbena, her symbol of courage, and offering in her outstretched hands the two dueling pistols. To Bayard she seems "the Greek amphora priestess of a succinct and formal violence" (219). However, as the reader soon learns, Bayard has already determined that he will refuse the weapons. He will face his father's enemy as the revenge code, and his own integrity, demand, but he will go unarmed. There are two primary reasons for Bayard's startling decision.

For one thing, Bayard as a twenty-four-year-old has long since outgrown the hero worship which characterized his youthful attitude toward his father. Faulkner employs several details to demonstrate how Bayard's perception of his father has altered significantly since boyhood. For example, there are Bayard's feelings about his father's killing of three men. Drusilla argues that the shootings were motivated by the colonel's dream of a rebuilt and unified South. "He is thinking of this whole country," Drusilla says, "which he is trying to raise by its bootstraps." The end justifies the means, Drusilla implies, since all people—Black and white, rich and poor—stand ultimately to benefit from the colonel's actions. Bayard, unconvinced, responds:

> "But how can they get any good from what he wants to do for them if they are—after he has—"
> "Killed some of them? I suppose you include those two carpetbaggers he had to kill to hold that first election, don't you?"
> "They were men. Human beings."

Drusilla goes on to observe that all dreams are dangerous and usually cause somebody to get hurt.

> "But if it's a good dream, it's worth it. There are not many dreams in the world, but there are a lot of human lives. And one life or two dozen—"
> "Are not worth anything?"
> "No. Not anything." (223–24)

Even if Bayard could manage, as Drusilla does, to rationalize the killing of the carpetbaggers, he would still be left with the question of his father's killing of the third man. Of this latter incident Bayard recollects, "The dead man was almost a neighbor, a hill man who had been in the first infantry regiment when it voted Father out of command: and we never to know if the man actually intended to rob Father or not because Father had shot too quick" (221). Bayard's recognition that this victim had been a member of the regiment that voted Colonel Sartoris out as commander and that "Father had shot too quick" obviously suggests that a desire for personal revenge, and not some idealistic scheme for saving the South, may have led to the death of the hill man. Beyond these nagging questions about the three killings, there is also Bayard's knowledge that his father had frequently and mercilessly taunted Redmond, his eventual assassin, for not fighting in the war, for losing control of his railroad, and for futilely opposing the colonel's election to the state legislature. Concerning this abuse of Redmond, Bayard acknowledges that his father was wrong and believes that his father, too, had realized his mistake but, "just as a drunkard reaches a point where it is too late for him to stop" (225), was unable to quit badgering Redmond.

But it is not merely realistic and honest assessment of his father's errors that leads Bayard to resist the demands of the revenge code. Perhaps more importantly, he has drumming in his mind voices other than Drusilla's, these others advocating the principle of nonviolence. One such voice is the generalized New Testament tradition admonishing him to turn the other cheek. Another is that of his iconoclastic Aunt Jenny Du Pre, with her admonition, "No bloody moon, Bayard" (245). Still another voice advising nonviolence, surprisingly and ironically, is none other than his father's, remembered by Bayard from their last meeting together, just two months before his father's death. In that conversation Colonel Sartoris had said it was time for "a little moral housecleaning" in his life. "I am tired of killing men," the colonel said, "no matter what the necessity nor the end. Tomorrow, when I go to town and meet Ben Redmond, I shall be unarmed" (231–32).

Like so many of Faulkner's plots, the ending of "An Odor of Verbena" turns on a series of paradoxes. We recognize, for instance, the ambivalence of Bayard's feelings for his father. While he acknowledges that his father's character was tragically flawed, Bayard still loves his father very much, as his actions beside the casket clearly demonstrate. We are also made aware that Bayard, by facing Redmond unarmed, has rejected the violence of the revenge code, but he has retained and acted upon that part of the same code which insists upon personal courage and family honor. Moreover, in adopting the stance of nonviolence, he is following in part the advice of a man whose hands, Bayard believes, are stained with "needless blood" (236).

Such paradoxes serve to underscore what Faulkner perceives to be the complex relationship of every individual to his or her inherited tradition. Bayard does not—indeed, cannot—divorce himself from that tradition; instead, he immerses himself in it, judges it, and adopts as his own those parts of the tradition that best serve his own personal code.

Initiation stories such as that of Bayard Sartoris appear repeatedly in Faulkner's novels and stories. Quentin Compson, Ike McCaslin, Chick Mallison, Temple Drake, Horace Benbow, Gail Hightower, Thomas Sutpen, Harry Wilbourne, Linda Snopes, and Lucius Priest are other prominent Faulkner characters who struggle to define themselves in the context of their society and its traditions and practices. Some of these characters resolve their quests quite happily; others experience pathos and tragedy; but all are individuals wrestling with tough decisions about themselves and their world. The predominance of the initiation motif in his fiction helps to explain what Faulkner meant when he wrote Malcolm Cowley, "I am telling the same story over and over, which is myself and the world" (FCF 14). Faulkner amplified this notion in a comment at the University of Virginia, when he said of one of his first-person narrators: "Every time any character gets into a book, no matter how minor, he's actually telling his own biography—that's all anyone ever does, he tells his own biography, talking about himself, in a thousand different terms, but himself" (FIU 275). Anyone familiar with Faulkner's biography can identify numerous instances in which Faulkner, like so many of his characters, was forced to examine the prevailing values of his society, judge those values, and arrive at his own independent conclusions. One such example is found in Faulkner's commitment to a high standard of art in a materialistic culture. Another is his opposition to the exploitation of nature and the agrarian ideal in the name of "progress." Still another—the focus of my concluding remarks—relates to Faulkner's involvement in the desegregation conflict.

Faulkner came of age in a South dominated by a belief in white supremacy and committed to a regional, as opposed to a national, agenda. It is hardly surprising that the young Billy Falkner did not totally escape the biases of this tradition. For example, a cartoon that Faulkner drew for a proposed high school yearbook in 1913 shows Miss Ella Wright, Faulkner's history teacher, preparing to grind out punishment from a "demerit mill" for a fierce, bearded figure standing beside her. The culprit is identified as Abraham Lincoln. At Lincoln's feet, and with Lincoln's obvious approval, a bully holding aloft a Union flag and brandishing a knife is attacking a much smaller, unarmed figure holding a Confederate flag. The caption, printed in Faulkner's juvenile hand, reads: "Them's my sentiments."[4] While the caption is doubtless intended as a commentary on the way Miss Wright taught American history, that is, from a Confederate point of view, there is a good likelihood that the caption also expresses Faulkner's own personal bias.

Another Faulkner drawing, this one produced in the 1920–21 Ole Miss yearbook, shows a graceful white couple dancing in front of a jazz band, possibly W. C. Handy's. The Blacks in this drawing appear as grotesque caricatures; the profiled head of one musician is strikingly ape-like. Even in his first Yoknapatawpha novel, *Sartoris*, published in 1929, Faulkner shows little disposition to view Blacks as anything more than comic buffoons or crafty, shiftless servants who plot to deceive their white "betters." While it would be a gross distortion, I think, ever to identify Faulkner, at any stage of his life, with "racist" attitudes and beliefs, there can be little doubt that in his early work he fell victim to the false and stereotypical impressions that many whites of that period held regarding Blacks.

Fortunately, all of that changed. In his characterization of Dilsey in *The Sound and the Fury*, also in 1929, Faulkner demonstrated that he was capable of treating a Black character with remarkable admiration and sensitivity. Throughout the 1930s, in such works as "Dry September," *Light in August*, *Absalom, Absalom!*, and *The Unvanquished*, Faulkner expanded his sympathetic treatment of African Americans, effectively dramatizing their exploitation and even murder at the hands of white supremacists and movingly depicting Blacks' yearnings for dignity and equality. With *Go Down, Moses* in 1942 and *Intruder in the Dust* in 1948, Faulkner moved beyond mere dramatization of the racial problem to offer broad principles of social reform. (In *Intruder*, in fact, he predicted school desegregation six years before the Supreme Court's historic ruling in *Brown v. Board of Education*.) After winning the Nobel Prize in 1950, Faulkner utilized the public attention that accompanied his worldwide fame to speak out against injustice and archaic racial patterns and to champion the cause of integration. In one of his strongest public statements, he vehemently condemned the 1955 lynch-style murder of Emmett Till, a fourteen-year-old Black youth, near Greenwood, Mississippi, concluding that "if we in America have reached that point in our desperate culture when we must murder children, no matter for what reason or what color, we don't deserve to survive, and probably won't" (*FB* 1571). In addition to such public pronouncements, Faulkner collaborated behind the scenes with Mississippi reformers James W. Silver and P. D. East to discredit segregationists and effect changes in attitudes and laws. It was during this period that Melvin B. Tolson, a Black author keenly concerned about civil rights issues, mailed a book of his own poems to Faulkner with the inscription, "To William Faulkner—a rock in a weary land."[5]

It is extremely important to note that although Faulkner was highly critical of Mississippi for its abuses of Black citizens, he never ceased to love his native state. One of the best evidences of that love is the fact that Faulkner, unlike certain other southerners of this period, never identified with any tendency toward a self-imposed exile from his native home. Though he traveled extensively and lived and worked briefly in other parts of the country, Faulkner always called Oxford home and never absented himself from there for any extended period of time.[6] Moreover, Faulkner passionately shared the common southern skepticism about outside intervention in southern affairs. He sincerely believed that the positive aspects of the southern tradition provided a far greater hope for meaningful change and progress than any force the federal government or any other outside agency might bring to bear on the situation. This latter conviction led to considerable misunderstanding of Faulkner's position. Torn between his sincere love for his homeland and genuine desire to see the elimination of an abominable social condition, Faulkner seemed at times, both in his books and in his public statements, to straddle the fence, to defend the South at the same time he condemned it. Thus, in one ill-advised statement which caused him to be identified with reactionary Dixiecratic Party politics, Faulkner said: "I will go on saying that the Southerners are wrong and that their position is untenable, but if I have to make the same choice Robert E. Lee made then I'll make it" (*LIG* 262). What Faulkner actually preferred was a middle-of-the-road position, though, as suggested earlier, this stance led to attacks from extremists in both liberal and conservative camps. But Faulkner held his ground, offering no sympathy for the alternatives expressed in the "love it or leave it" attitudes of his day. Instead, he chose to show his love for his native state by remaining in it and seeking to change it for the better. His choice was based on his understanding of the meaning of the word *love*. As he explained in his semi-autobiographical essay titled "Mississippi," "you dont love because: you love despite; not for the virtues, but despite the faults" (*ESPL* 43).

I have attempted to demonstrate that William Faulkner, both in his books and in his personal life, sought to explore, honestly and faithfully, the ambivalent and delicate relationship that exists between every individual and society. Although Faulkner recognized that the specific issues and questions will change from one generation or culture to the next, he believed there are certain general principles that apply to all situations. The overriding principle is that all such issues must be considered in the context of a genuine concern for ethical, moral values, for what he called "the old verities and truths of the heart," specifically, "love and honor and pity and pride and compassion and sacrifice" (*ESPL* 120). In order to be faithful to such truths, the individual must never allow allegiance to society to blind one to its failings and shortcomings. At the same time, a hatred for those things which are contemptible in one's society should never seduce the individual into betraying those elements in personal and cultural history that are positive and good. As the content and form of Faulkner's fiction imply, only the individual can decide which aspects of any tradition are worth preserving; it is left to each person to discover, even to fashion, as best one can, one's own voice out of the many voices that float through one's mind and experience. As Faulkner recognized, this process of discovery and growth is a difficult and sometimes painful one; yet to engage in that quest is to realize the very essence of what it means to be human.

NOTES

1. Wallace Stevens, "The Idea of Order at Key West," *The Collected Poems of Wallace Stevens* (New York: Alfred A. Knopf, 1955), 130.

2. C. Vann Woodward, *The Burden of Southern History*, 3rd ed. (Baton Rouge: Louisiana State University Press, 1993), 30–32.

3. See the prefatory note to *The Mansion*.

4. The Lincoln cartoon is part of the Brodsky Collection, Center for Faulkner Studies, Southeast Missouri State University. It is reproduced in Robert W. Hamblin and Louis Daniel Brodsky, *Selections from the William Faulkner Collection of Louis Daniel Brodsky: A Descriptive Catalogue* (Charlottesville: University Press of Virginia, 1979), 19.

5. This copy of Tolson's book *Rendezvous with America* is in the Brodsky Collection.

6. The lone exception to this rule was near the very end of his life when, as a result of harsh criticism and even physical threats directed against him because of his public support of desegregation, he considered moving permanently to Virginia. He died before the move could be executed.

The Artistic Design of
The Sound and the Fury

Over the course of his remarkable career, William Faulkner produced a number of outstanding novels that are now generally ranked among the greatest of the twentieth century—novels that are so impressive in the aggregate that critics can hardly agree on which should be considered Faulkner's masterpiece. Some readers, myself included, would argue for *Absalom, Absalom!*; others prefer *The Sound and the Fury* or *As I Lay Dying* or *Light in August*; still others, though fewer in number, would vote for *The Hamlet* or *Go Down, Moses* or *Sanctuary*. Faulkner also had difficulty in identifying his single greatest work. He told a fellow screenwriter in Hollywood that he thought *Absalom, Absalom!* was "the best novel yet written by an American" (*FB* 927), and he continually referred to *A Fable* over the long ten years of its composition as his "big book."[1] But if Faulkner, like his admirers, never could quite settle on which of his novels is his finest, there was never any question in his mind about which was his favorite. From the time he handed the completed manuscript to his friend and literary agent Ben Wasson with the comment, "Read this, Bud. It's a real son-of-a-bitch" (*FB* 590), until his class conferences at the University of Virginia late in his life, Faulkner consistently maintained that his favorite book was *The Sound and the Fury*.

In an introductory essay that he wrote in the summer of 1933 for a proposed reissue of the novel (an essay that remained unpublished until after his death), Faulkner offers some of the reasons why *The Sound and the Fury* would always hold the preeminent place among his writings. For one thing, Faulkner explains, for the first and only time in his writing career, he had experienced in creating *The Sound and the Fury* something approaching the divine inspiration that the Romantic poets had believed in and celebrated: as Faulkner expressed it, "that emotion definite and physical and yet nebulous to describe: that ecstasy, that eager and joyous faith and anticipation of surprise which the yet unmarred sheet beneath my hand held inviolate and unfailing, waiting for release." Such elation, if I read the remainder of Faulkner's essay rightly, derives from the sense of a near-perfect balance of form and subject, of artistic design and realistic content, of art as art and art as life. In seeking to clarify this point, Faulkner alludes to a scene in Henryk Sienkiewicz's popular historical novel *Quo Vadis* (1895) in which an old Roman keeps at his bedside a lovely Tyrrhenian vase, the rim of which he slowly wears away by continually kissing it. Faulkner continues the analogy: "I had made myself a vase, but I suppose I knew all the time that I could not live forever inside of it. Much better the muddy bottom of a doomed little girl climbing a blooming pear tree in April to look in the window at the funeral." [2] In other words, Faulkner appears to be saying, while it is always an attractive alternative for any artist to seek to escape the realities of life and "live forever inside" an urn, that is, his perfected art, it is "much better" to leave the enclosure of the urn and contemplate a realistic and tragic story such as that "of a doomed little girl" caught in the paradox of the blooming springtime and the death of her grandmother. From this comment we can infer Faulkner's belief that an ideal work of art would be one that possesses both the artistic qualities of an urn and the realistic qualities of actual experience.

Following what I understand to be Faulkner's advice here on how to read his favorite—and perhaps his greatest—novel, I propose to examine three ways in which the artistic design of *The Sound and the Fury* supports and enhances its realistic purpose. The three technical aspects I will examine are viewpoint, style as characterization, and the use of counterpoint.

VIEWPOINT

Much of Faulkner's 1933 introduction to *The Sound and the Fury* is devoted to the degree to which the shifting perspectives of the successive chapters are central to the narrative technique of the novel. Faulkner was asked about this aspect of the novel many times throughout his career. A typical response is the one he made to an interviewer in 1955:

> I had already begun to tell [the story] through the eyes of the idiot child since I felt that it would be more effective as told by someone capable only of knowing what happened, but not why. I saw that I had not told the story that time. I tried to tell it again, the same story through the eyes of another brother. That

was still not it. I told it for the third time through the eyes of the third brother. That was still not it. I tried to gather the pieces together and fill in the gaps by making myself the spokesman. It was still not complete, not until 15 years after the book was published when I wrote as an appendix to another book the final effort to get the story told and off my mind, so that I myself could have some peace from it. (*LIG* 245)

Faulkner further clarified the technique in his comment about the three separate narrators of *The Town*, published in 1957.

It was used deliberately to look at the object from three points of view. Just as when you examine a monument you will walk around it, you are not satisfied to look at it from just one side. Also, it was to look at it from three different mentalities.... That seemed to me to give a more complete picture of the specific incidents as they occurred if they could be [viewed] three times. (*FIU* 139–40)

These statements reflect that Faulkner's use of shifting viewpoints is both conscious and deliberate, and the latter quotation suggests something of the purpose of the technique. For one thing, treatment of a subject from varying perspectives is linked to a pleasurable aesthetic experience: one is more "satisfied" to view a monument from different angles. Secondly, for Faulkner as for Henry James, the use of multiple narrators is associated with the perception of truth: such treatment provides "a more complete picture" of a character or an event. Thus, Faulkner's choice of perspective is a matter of both aesthetics and epistemology, beauty and truth.

That Faulkner relates viewpoint to aesthetic strategy is supported by his observations on the characterization of Caddy. Once asked why he did not let Caddy, his "heart's darling" (*FIU* 6), tell her own story to supplement the accounts by her brothers, Faulkner replied, "Because Caddy was still to me too beautiful and too moving to reduce her to telling what was going on, that it would be more passionate to see her through someone else's eyes" (*FIU* 1). But further clarification is needed. Why is it that indirect treatment of Caddy is "more passionate" than self-characterization? A partial answer is found in the reply Faulkner made when once asked to describe his ideal woman:

Well, I couldn't describe her by color of hair, color of eyes, because once she is described, then somehow she vanishes. That the ideal woman which is in every man's mind is evoked by a word or phrase or the shape of her wrist, her hand. Just like the most beautiful description of anyone . . . is by understatement.

Remember, all Tolstoy said about Anna Karenina was that she was beautiful and could see in the dark like a cat . . . And every man has a different idea of what's beautiful. And it's best to take the gesture, the shadow of the branch, and let the mind create the tree. (*LIG* 127–28)

Here, Faulkner expresses the desire to engage the reader in the aesthetic process. The writer, through the use of understatement and implication, invites the reader to create the subject, in a sense, for herself. In this regard, of course, Faulkner may be identified with the impressionist painters of the late nineteenth century and, beyond them, with the prevailing tendency among most modern artists—painters, sculptors, musicians, and poets, as well as novelists. In modern art the artist renders and evokes; the respondent engages, interprets, and applies. This is as true of a Faulkner novel as of a Monet or Picasso painting. Faulkner's narrative technique allows—indeed, requires—the reader to become a partner in the act of creativity. This intent, expressed in Faulkner's contention that "it's best to take the gesture, the shadow of the branch, and let the mind create the tree," explains not only Faulkner's inclination toward understatement and indirection (as in the plot structure of "Dry September" or *Absalom, Absalom!* and the handling of the horror element in "A Rose for Emily") but also his habit of looking at a central character or incident from multiple points of view. Confronted with different and even contradictory narratives, the Faulkner reader must assemble, order, and interpret the story for himself. That this task is a pleasurable, if difficult, aesthetic experience is attested by the great number of Faulkner's admirers.

But Faulkner's use of multiple narrators, it was noted, is a matter of truth as well as beauty. As Faulkner said in his observation about the ideal woman, "Every man has a different idea of what's beautiful." This notion of a relative perception of truth runs throughout Faulkner's fiction—and, indeed, might well be its most distinguishing characteristic. The narrator of the short story "Black Music" says, "Nothing ever looks the same to two different people. Never looks the same to one person, depending on which side of it he looks at it from" (*CS* 814). In *The Mansion* Linda Snopes observes that "the Paris of Hemingway and the Paris of Scott Fitzgerald . . . were not the same ones; they merely used the same room" (209). And in what is perhaps the greatest tour de force of viewpoint among all modern novels, *As I Lay Dying*, Faulkner employs no less than fifteen different narrators, each with a different set of facts, prejudices, and desires, to present the story of the Bundrens' journey to Jefferson to bury Addie. Perhaps the clearest statement by Faulkner concerning the relationship between truth and perception is the following observation on the multiple narrators of *Absalom, Absalom!*:

> I think that no one individual can look at truth. It blinds you. You look at it and you see one phase of it. Someone else looks at it and sees a slightly awry phase of it. But taken all together, the truth is in what they saw though nobody saw the truth intact. . . . It was, as you say, thirteen ways of looking at a blackbird. But the truth, I would like to think, comes out, that when the reader has read all these thirteen different ways of looking at the blackbird, the reader has his own fourteenth image of that blackbird which I would like to think is the truth. (*FIU* 273–74)

The Sound and the Fury clearly demonstrates the principles delineated here. The novel consists of four sections (five, if one counts the "Appendix"), each recounted by a different narrator. The first three parts are presented in turn by three brothers, members of the once aristocratic but now declining Compson family: Benjy, the thirty-three-year-old with the mind of a child; Quentin, the distraught college student who commits suicide; and Jason, the selfish and ruthless materialist. These three sections employ the Joycean technique of interior monologue, but each unit possesses a unique style and method determined by the intelligence, outlook, and emotional state of the respective narrator. In the fourth chapter of the novel, Faulkner discards the private and personal viewpoint to relate the story in an objective, third-person narration. Even in this section, however, the point of view remains restricted, since the author seldom intervenes to explain or interpret the action.

The manner in which each of the successive narratives presents only one perspective on a multifaceted and ambiguous truth is most apparent in the implied characterization of Caddy. To Benjy (or, more accurately, to the reader, who must draw inferences from Benjy's camera-track recordings), Caddy is the one member of the family who loves him. She exhibits concern for his physical welfare, soothes him in his mental and emotional anguish, and frequently pacifies him by sleeping with him. In one key passage demonstrating Caddy's compassion and concern, Benjy and Caddy are sitting together by the fire when Mrs. Compson calls Benjy to her. Caddy begs her mother to wait until Benjy is through looking at the fire, but Mrs. Compson is insistent, and Caddy reluctantly carries Benjy to his mother's side. Concerned at this point about Benjy's crying, Caddy asks her mother to hold the boy in her lap, but Mrs. Compson refuses: "A five year old child. No, no. Not in my lap. Let him stand up." When Caddy then tries to placate Benjy with his favorite cushion,

Mrs. Compson orders it taken away: "He must learn to mind." A few minutes later, after Benjy's continued wailing has upset Mrs. Compson to the point that she must retire to her bed, Caddy leads Benjy back to the fire, where he can content himself with "the bright, smooth shapes" (*SF* 62–64).

There is a suggestion, of course, even in the Benjy section, of a quite different Caddy. As she grows into adolescence, Caddy begins to wear perfume and date boys. Later (as one subsequently learns from the Quentin narrative) she has an affair with Dalton Ames, becomes pregnant, and marries Herbert Head to legitimize her child. During this period of her life, her interest in Benjy naturally diminishes, despite his protests; and she eventually leaves Benjy to the care of his successive keepers. By the time of the present-tense action, 1928, Caddy exists for Benjy only as the sound of the golfer's call to his "caddie" and as a vaguely recollected parallel to Miss Quentin, who presumably bears a strong physical resemblance to her mother. The astute reader can hardly escape notice of the manner in which Caddy's desertion of Benjy and her subsequent absence are ironically juxtaposed with those scenes in which Caddy expresses concern for her brother and promises not to leave him, as well as those scenes in which Benjy is subjected to abuse at the hands of Luster. Still, from Benjy's point of view, Caddy represents essentially feelings of comfort and security.

To Quentin, on the other hand, Caddy comes to symbolize the lost honor of the once-proud Compson family. Quentin's genuine love for his sister is complicated by his judgments upon her sexual promiscuity; thus, Quentin's attitude is an ambivalent one. Like Benjy, Quentin would like to preserve the idyllic innocence of childhood, symbolized by brother-sister love, but he recognizes that such is impossible in a postlapsarian world of time and change. As Robert Slabey has pointed out, "In Quentin there is a Manichean revulsion against the physical, the sexual, the limited, the temporal, a romantic repudiation of the immediate realities of human life, and a direction toward the infinite and the timeless."[3] In Quentin's mind the loss of innocence has become associated with Caddy's promiscuity and with sexuality in general. As Mr. Compson explains, "It's nature is hurting you not Caddy" (116); but Quentin is unable, or unwilling, to make any such distinction.

Because of his obsession with ideality and purity (Head refers to him as Galahad [136]), and thus with virginity, Quentin views Caddy as the embodiment of sin and evil. He frequently thinks of her in conjunction with phrases like "little dirty sluts" (78) and "bitches" (92) and on one occasion calls her "whore" (159). He berates her for her adolescent kissing games with boys and for her teenage involvement with Dalton Ames: "*Why wont you bring him to the house, Caddy? Why must you do like n——r women do in the pasture the ditches the dark woods*" (92). Whereas in Benjy's narrative Caddy is associated primarily with the symbol of trees (though occasionally with that of perfume), here she is linked to roses—"Not virgins like dogwood, milkweed" (77)—and with honeysuckle and cedars, reminders of Caddy's meetings with her lovers in the swing. Other associational symbols are brought forward with a similar shift in meaning: in the Benjy section the pasture, fire, and sleep are connected with feelings of peace and security; in the Quentin section the pasture (as evidenced by the earlier quotation) is the place where Caddy fornicates, fire is the Hell in which Quentin desires to isolate Caddy and himself, and sleep is identified with death. Such changes in the meaning of recurring symbols reflect the degree to which truth in the novel is in part subjective, altering with the angle of perception.

In the Jason section Caddy is again the center of focus. But once more her characterization has altered with the viewpoint. To Benjy, Caddy is the child who tenders him compassion and tenderness; to Quentin, Caddy is the wayward adolescent who stains the Compson family honor; to Jason, Caddy is the woman who cheated him of his chance for a position in a bank and who dumped her child on her family to rear. "Once a bitch always a bitch" (180), Jason says at the opening of his narrative, and his remark is directed as much toward Caddy as it is the niece. Indeed, like Benjy, Jason scarcely distinguishes between the two: Miss Quentin, as the physical embodiment of the shame which cost Caddy her husband and Jason his job in the bank, becomes a scapegoat, recipient of the contempt and abuse which Jason continually directs at Caddy.

As in the narratives of the other brothers, however, there are actually two Caddys presented in the Jason section: the one which the character-narrator describes and the one which the reader infers from Faulkner's arrangement of incident and employment of irony. If Caddy is not as "good" as Benjy's limited intelligence infers, then neither is she as bad as Jason implies. The Jason narrative reveals that Caddy sends money to support her daughter and returns to Jefferson to attend her father's funeral and to see her child. These details, which serve to move the reader toward sympathy for Caddy, ironically counterpoint Jason's harsh judgments upon his sister and provide the reader with another dimension to the already fragmented, paradoxical view of Caddy.

In the concluding section of the novel, Faulkner abandons the personal viewpoint to present the story objectively. In the 1933 introduction to *The Sound and the Fury* that I cited earlier, Faulkner notes that he had reached an impasse after completing the first three sections of the novel, that there would need to be a more objective rendering of the characters and events.

I saw that I was merely temporizing: That I should have to get completely out of the book. I realized that there would be compensations, that in a sense I could then give a final turn to the screw and extract some ultimate distillation. Yet it took me better than a month to take pen and write *The day dawned bleak and chill* before I did so. (224)

The result of this ultimate strategy, of course, is the Dilsey section, in which for the first time the Compsons are viewed from the outside, in a treatment not prejudiced by the limitations and biases of first-person narrators. Here, Benjy is presented not in terms of his stream-of-consciousness impressions but externally, as

a big man who appeared to have been shaped of some substance whose particles would not or did not cohere to one another or to the frame which supported it. His skin was dead looking and hairless; dropsical too, he moved with a shambling gait like a trained bear. His hair was pale and fine. It had been brushed smoothly down upon his brow like that of children in daguerreotypes. His eyes were clear, of the pale sweet blue of cornflowers, his thick mouth hung open, drooling a little. (274)

Likewise, Jason is described objectively: "cold and shrewd, with close-thatched brown hair curled into two stubborn hooks, one on either side of his forehead like a bartender in caricature, and hazel eyes with black-ringed irises like marbles" (279). One finds in this section also the photographic rendering of "the square, paintless [Compson] house with its rotting portico" (298). Similarly, and even more importantly, the myopic, self-centered perspectives of the Compson brothers are now displaced by the selfless and communal attitudes and actions of Dilsey. In both viewpoint and characterization, therefore, in the Dilsey section subjective rendering has given way to objective presentation.

The detachment created by this objectivity provides the reader, as Faulkner acknowledged, with a needed counterpoint to the distorted views of the previous sections. Shockingly, Caddy, the central focus in the other narratives, barely appears in the final chapter, except as the pattern of her life is recycled in the experiences of her daughter Quentin. This absence stands as the greatest irony in the entire book. The single character with whom each of the narrators has been so obsessed plays no part in the denouement of the family history (Faulkner altered this original design of the novel with the later "Appendix"). It is as if Faulkner used Caddy's absence to call into question the egocentricity of the Compson brothers and to place their family story into the context of the world at large. As Olga Vickery has noted, it would appear that "in this larger context the sound and fury of the family signifies very little if anything."[4] Whether that be true or not, it is true that yet again, this time in viewing the Compson story in relation to the outside world, the reader is forced to shift perspectives and to reevaluate all that has been previously presented. If one feels that one has arrived at truth in the process, such realization comes only after the recognition of the interplay of subjective and objective reality and with a heightened awareness of the difficulty of the quest.

STYLE AS CHARACTERIZATION

Faulkner not only utilizes a shifting viewpoint to suggest something of both the relativity and complexity of truth but also employs radically different styles as means of individualized characterizations. Such is not always the case with Faulkner. For example, in *As I Lay Dying, Absalom, Absalom!*, or the Snopes trilogy, his other novels that make the most extensive use of shifting viewpoints, scarcely any distinction is made in the syntax, vocabulary, or imagery employed by the separate narrators—the result being that all of the characters, regardless of age, gender, class, or race, speak in a kind of general "Faulknerese" that lends itself so readily to the burlesque found in entries to the Faux Faulkner contests. In *The Sound and the Fury*, however, Faulkner perfectly matches the style of narration to the characterization of the respective speaker. Let me demonstrate by briefly calling attention to the openings of each of the four sections of the novel.

In the first section Faulkner depicts the consciousness of the mentally challenged Benjy through the use of an extremely simplistic style characterized by a limited vocabulary and elementary sentence structure. The opening paragraph establishes the pattern of the whole:

> Through the fence, between the curling flower spaces, I could see them hitting. They were coming toward where the flag was and I went along the fence. Luster was hunting in the grass by the flower tree. They took the flag out, and they were hitting. Then they put the flag back and they went to the table, and he hit and the other hit. Then they went on, and I went along the fence. Luster came away from the flower tree and we went along the fence and they stopped and we stopped and I looked through the fence while Luster was hunting in the grass. (3)

This passage of seven sentences contains only two subordinate clauses. By contrast the conjunction *and* appears ten times linking simple coordinate clauses. Moreover, of the seventeen independent elements, only three contain ten words or more, while eleven contain five words or less. The average number of words per independent unit is 5.7. A further indication of the simplicity of the passage is the degree to which nouns and verbs predominate: if one excludes articles and accepts *flower spaces* and *flower tree* as compound nouns, then only one adjective (*curling*) appears in the entire paragraph. The restricted vocabulary, limited to concrete terms such as *fence, flag, flower,* and *tree* (the closest approximation of an abstraction is the word *hunting*), provides an additional means of avoiding complexity. Surprisingly, in view of Faulkner's general fondness for figurative language, the passage contains not a single simile or metaphor. (Technically, it could be argued, the words *table* and *flower tree* take the form of metaphor—but for the reader, not for Benjy. In his mind such forms, including the widely quoted "Caddy smelled like trees," represent literal associations and substitutions, not abstract comparisons of metaphoric thought.) All of the above factors contribute to the convincing illusion that the reader readily accepts as an accurate documentation of Benjy's limited thought processes.

How different is the Quentin section. Just as the style of the Benjy section is designed to approximate the mental processes of a person of limited intelligence, that of the Quentin section is adapted to suggest the consciousness of a bright, sensitive, but highly troubled college student. Instead of a restricted vocabulary and simplified sentence structure, Quentin's monologue displays an expanded word choice and an extended use of subordination and abstraction. Again, the opening sentences establish the pattern for the entire section.

When the shadow of the sash appeared on the curtains it was between seven and eight oclock and then I was in time again, hearing the watch. It was Grandfather's and when Father gave it to me he said I give you the mausoleum of all hope and desire; it's rather excruciating-ly apt that you will use it to gain the reducto absurdum of all human experience which can fit your individual needs no better than it fitted his or his father's. I give it to you not that you may remember time, but that you might forget it now and then for a moment and not spend all your breath trying to conquer it. Because no battle is ever won he said. They are not even fought. The field only reveals to man his own folly and despair, and victory is an illusion of philosophers and fools.

It was propped against the collar box and I lay listening to it. Hearing it, that is. I dont suppose anybody ever deliberately listens to a watch or a clock.

You dont have to. You can be oblivious to the sound for a long while, then in a second of ticking it can create in the mind unbroken the long diminishing parade of time you didn't hear. Like Father said down the long and lonely light-rays you might see Jesus walking, like. And the good Saint Francis that said Little Sister Death, that never had a sister. (76)

This passage opens with a complex sentence that expresses a somewhat sophisticated deduction concerning the relationship between the positioning of shadows and the time of day—a deduction that Benjy's limited mind could never make. One is impressed with the percentage of abstract terms (for example, *hope, desire, folly, despair, victory*), with the use of metaphoric structure ("the mausoleum of all hope and desire" and "the long diminishing parade of time"), and with the allusions to Jesus and Saint Francis. All such elements contribute to the highly cerebral nature of the style, one that is perfectly suited to the intelligent, introspective, troubled Quentin.

The Jason section presents still another character type and yet another style. His chapter opens as follows:

Once a bitch always a bitch, what I say. I says you're lucky if her playing out of school is all that worries you. I says she ought to be down there in that kitchen right now, instead of up there in her room, gobbing paint on her face and waiting for six n——s that cant even stand up out of a chair unless they've got a pan full of bread and meat to balance them, to fix breakfast for her. (180)

The vocabulary and sentence structure of this passage fit neither the overly simplified pattern of the Benjy section nor the elaborately complex form of the Quentin chapter. Here the words are more conventional, though highly colloquial, with just the degree of vulgarity one expects from the embittered, pragmatic Jason. What makes the style of the Jason section unique, however, and so perfectly suited to the character portrayed, is the pervasive tone: the narrative is a masterpiece of verbal irony and sarcasm. One might consider, for example, the following excerpt:

"Well, then," I says, "I reckon that conscience of yours is a more valuable clerk than I am; it dont have to go home at noon to eat. Only dont let it interfere with my appetite," I says, because how the hell can I do anything right, with that dam family and her not making any effort to control her nor any of them like that time when she happened to see one of them kissing Caddy and all next day she went around the house in a black dress and a veil and even Father couldn't get her to say a word except crying and saying her little daughter was dead and Caddy about fifteen then only in three years she'd been wearing haircloth or probably sandpaper at that rate. Do you think I can afford to have her running about the streets with every drummer that comes in town, I says, and them telling the new ones up and down the road where to pick up a hot one when they made Jefferson. I haven't got much pride, I can't afford it with a kitchen full of n——s to feed and robbing the state asylum of its star freshman. Blood, I says, governors and generals. It's a dam good thing we never had any kings and presidents; we'd all be down there at Jackson chasing butterflies. (229–30)

This passage evidences a remarkable wit, but one which fails to ameliorate a deep-seated intolerance, even hatred, for others. Jason's family, of course, receives the bulk of this ire. As he says in another place, "Like a man would naturally think, one of them is crazy and another one drowned himself and the other one was turned out into the street by her husband, what's the reason the rest of them are not crazy too" (233). Jason's values have become so perverted by his paranoia and his desire for revenge that his humor has become merely the tool of a savage, denunciatory cynicism. But the writing is some of Faulkner's finest, and, as Cleanth Brooks has noted, "Faulkner does more in these eighty pages to indict the shabby small-town businessman's view of life than Sinclair Lewis was able to achieve in several novels on the subject."[5]

In the final chapter of the novel, as noted previously, Faulkner abandons the first-person characterizations of the previous sections to present the story in neutral omniscience. The style shifts accordingly, as the opening paragraph demonstrates:

The day dawned bleak and chill, a moving wall of gray light out of the northeast which, instead of dissolving into moisture, seemed to disintegrate into minute and venomous particles, like dust that, when Dilsey opened the door of the cabin and emerged, needled laterally into her flesh, precipitating not so much a moisture as a substance partaking of the quality of thin, not quite congealed oil. She wore a stiff black straw hat perched upon her turban, and a maroon velvet cape with a border of mangy and anonymous fur above a dress of purple silk, and she stood in the door for a while with her myriad and sunken face lifted to the weather, and one gaunt hand flac-soled as the belly of a fish, then she moved the cape aside and examined the bosom of her gown. (265)

While the style of the novel has once again shifted radically, its function here, identical to that of the previous sections, is to serve the purpose of characterization. A number of readers have noted how the description of Dilsey here establishes her superiority to the weak and decaying Compsons: regal in dress and bearing, seemingly impervious to both time and the weather, identified with the Christian symbol of the fish, she is presented as the one heroic character in the entire novel, the only one deserving of praise, emulation, and honor. Some critics have questioned why Faulkner chose not to allow Dilsey to speak in her own voice in this section, some even suggesting that because he is white and male he dared not seek to enter the consciousness of a Black female. But I would argue that the objective treatment Faulkner employs is required to elevate Dilsey to the saintly role that Faulkner wants her to occupy in the novel. Dilsey's goodness, no less than Caddy's tragic fall, is best perceived from a distance, its definition and portrayal not approached too directly or too closely, its mystery allowed to remain intact. Whether that be an accurate assessment or not, the incontrovertible fact remains that Faulkner has once again brilliantly shifted the style and viewpoint of the novel, and that shift seems closely tied, as in the previous sections, with the characterization of the focal character.

THE USE OF COUNTERPOINT

Counterpoint is a narrative technique that modernist authors have adapted from the field of music composition. In music the technique involves the combination of two or more independent melodies into a single harmonic texture in which each retains its linear character. Writers use counterpoint to juxtapose separate incidents, images, symbols, voices, or characters to create a unity out of diversity. One of the most famous examples, one that Faulkner was quite familiar with, is Aldous Huxley's novel, *Point Counter Point.* Writers of stream-of-consciousness prose find counterpoint especially useful as a means of imposing an order and unity on the seemingly random and disorganized thought process. As Faulkner expressed it, counterpoint enables the writer to take "a mass of stuff" (*LIG* 56) and use judgment and taste "to arrange the different pieces in the most effective place in juxtaposition to one another" (*FIU* 45).

Faulkner frequently used the terms "counterpoint" and "contrapuntal" to describe his method of narration, applying them specifically to such novels as *The Wild Palms, Requiem for a Nun, Absalom, Absalom!,* the Snopes trilogy, and *The Sound and the Fury.*[6] To my mind Faulkner's most pervasive and artistic use of counterpoint is found in *The Sound and the Fury.*

Mention has already been made of the manner in which Faulkner plays off one narrative perspective against another in the structure of *The Sound and the Fury*. But the use of counterpoint in the novel extends far beyond the shifting of viewpoint. Incidents, symbolic motifs, and themes are likewise juxtaposed in an intricate design employing extensive allusion and repetition. No reader of *The Sound and the Fury* can fail to recognize the degree to which Faulkner repeats or parallels key incidents as the novel progresses. Caddy's wedding, Quentin's suicide, Jason's materialistic schemings, Benjy's wailings, Dilsey's protective gestures—these matters, central concerns of the novel, predictably appear again and again. But the pattern of reiteration and scene paralleling is applied to other, even minor, concerns as well. Indeed, there is hardly an incident in the entire novel which does not have its counterpart elsewhere in the book. The experiences of Miss Quentin, for example, are made to parallel those of her mother, even to the point of employing the same swing as a trysting place. "Im bad anyway you cant help it" (158), Caddy says to Quentin; "I'm bad and I'm going to hell, and I dont care" (189), the daughter says in her time. Benjy's chasing the young schoolgirl has its counterpart in Quentin's involvement with the little Italian girl: in each instance the young girl is mistaken for Caddy, and an innocent act is misinterpreted as perversion. And these scenes have their ironic reversal in Jason's chase of Miss Quentin; again the young girl becomes a surrogate for Caddy. Quentin's plaintive "sister" (125ff.) finds its echo in Uncle Maury's "poor little sister" (197) on the occasion of Mr. Compson's funeral. The castration of Benjy is linked to the story Quentin recalls of the man who mutilated himself with a razor—and through this story Quentin's desire to emasculate himself. The promises of Caddy and Quentin to take care of Benjy are ironically juxtaposed with the abuses heaped upon the idiot by Luster and by Jason. Caddy's wedding, for obvious symbolic connotations, is set beside Damuddy's funeral. Benjy's birthday is paralleled with Quentin's reference to his own "birthday" celebration at Harvard. Quentin's encounter with Dalton Ames is fused with his fight with Gerald Bland. Dilsey's simple and sincere worship on Easter morning is contrasted with Jason's satanic desecration of the Sabbath and his open cursing of God. Many of these repetitions and parallels go beyond the demands of stream-of- consciousness association technique. Carried over from one section of the novel to another, they become a principal means by which Faulkner expresses the central ironies and dominant themes of the work.

In addition to counterpointing specific incidents, Faulkner also utilizes recurring symbolic motifs to unify the various sections of the novel. As Melvin Backman demonstrates in his excellent analysis of the work,

Certain themes—love, time, and the world's destruction of innocence—are part of each section. Certain symbols—honeysuckle, water, the stain, trees, flowers, the mirror, fire, and light—run light musical motifs through the novel; they fuse, intensify, heighten, and enrich the novel's emotion and meaning.[7]

Perhaps the most successful of these various motifs is that of time. Each section of the novel dramatizes a different concept of time. For Benjy, of course, there is no such thing as time. Fixed in time, but unable to distinguish between present and past, Benjy lives in a timeless order beyond an awareness of the interconnectedness of events. Quentin desires a world, like Benjy's mind state, of permanence and timelessness, but he is painfully aware of the reality of mutability and transience. Quentin's fruitless quest to escape the ravages of time finds expression in various symbolic acts. He twists the hands off his watch, but the watch continues to tick. He attempts to play tricks on his shadow but finds that he cannot halt the relentless progression of the sun or escape the shadows cast thereby. He contemplates his rendezvous with death and, as the moment approaches, counts down the minutes: "A quarter hour yet. And then I'll not be. The peacefullest words. Peacefullest words" (174). Jason is likewise obsessed with time, though not in the manner of Quentin. To Jason time (like everything else) is money. He carries out his monetary scheming under the large face and loud striking of the courthouse clock, and he is constantly observing this clock or looking at his pocket watch to ascertain the exact time. Throughout his narrative Jason frantically dashes from place to place, and always—as in his pursuit of Miss Quentin and his trip to the Western Union office to check on the stock market report—he arrives late. In his struggle against time, therefore, Jason is no more successful than Quentin.

It is Dilsey who represents the ideal relationship of humans to time, a standard against which the inadequacies and failures of the Compson brothers may be measured. As Perrin Lowrey has noted,

> Dilsey is aware of time, and aware of it in what might be called the "correct way." She is neither obsessed with time, as Jason and Quentin are, nor is she insensible of it, as Ben is. Whereas Jason tends to think of time only as something concrete, something to be used, and Quentin tends to think of time as an abstraction, Dilsey thinks of time in both senses.[8]

Dilsey's "correct" relationship to time is symbolized by her ability to compensate for the inaccuracies of the kitchen clock:

> On the wall above a cupboard, invisible save at night, by lamp light and even
> then evincing an enigmatic profundity because it had but one hand, a cabinet
> clock ticked, then with a preliminary sound as if it had cleared its throat,
> struck five times.
>
> "Eight oclock," Dilsey said. (274)

Dilsey's age and experience support, much in the manner of the traditional
Greek chorus, her authoritative position with regard to time. In this novel of
kaleidoscopic shifting of scene and viewpoint, Dilsey is the one constant and
absolute: Benjy's keepers change faces with the passing of time, and Damuddy
and Caddy and Quentin and Mr. Compson drop successively from the pages
of the novel, but Dilsey is omnipresent, from the beginning to the end. "I've
seed de first en de last. . . . I seed de beginning, en now I sees de endin" (297),
she says, in a statement which reflects both her longevity and her insight.
Because of her superior perspective, Dilsey views the Compson story with
an understanding lacking in the brothers' limited and egocentric treatments.
Identifying with the simple and timeless verities vocalized in the Easter
church service, Dilsey stands in sharp contrast to the chaos and disintegration
within the Compson household. Patient, experienced in the ways of the world,
but understanding and accepting the relationship of time to eternity, Dilsey
is not victimized by time as the Compsons are. She is the one character in the
novel who is capable both of living within time and of transcending time to
perceive eternity. By developing this and other contrasts, Faulkner employs
counterpoint as a means of fusing the separate elements of *The Sound and the
Fury* into a unified whole.

In conclusion, I have sought in these remarks to suggest something of
the technical brilliance, the virtuosity, of *The Sound and the Fury*. If *Absalom, Absalom!* or *Light in August* or *Go Down, Moses* seem to be more ambitious novels, utilizing broader canvases to treat more crucial issues affecting
the whole of society; if *As I Lay Dying* appears to be, in some respects, more
imaginative and creative; if *The Hamlet* strikes one as a better blending of the
tragic and comic elements of life, the fact remains that none of Faulkner's
other novels, as great as they are, approach the near-perfect form of technique
and content found in *The Sound and the Fury*. Faulkner was right when he
told Ben Wasson this book was "a real son-of-a-bitch." It is the closest he ever
came to producing the perfect urn that all artists dream about.

NOTES

1. Louis Daniel Brodsky and Robert W. Hamblin, eds., *Faulkner: A Comprehensive Guide to the Brodsky Collection, Volume II: The Letters* (Jackson: University Press of Mississippi, 1984), 82ff.

2. David Minter, ed., *The Sound and the Fury: A Norton Critical Edition*, 2nd ed. (New York: W. W. Norton, 1994), 219, 224.

3. Robert M. Slabey, "Quentin Compson's 'Lost Childhood,'" in *Twentieth Century Interpretations of* The Sound and the Fury, ed. Michael H. Cowan (Englewood Cliffs, NJ: Prentice-Hall, 1968), 81–82.

4. Olga W. Vickery, *The Novels of William Faulkner*, rev. ed. (Baton Rouge: Louisiana State University Press, 1964), 46.

5. Cleanth Brooks, *William Faulkner: The Yoknapatawpha Country* (New Haven: Yale University Press, 1963), 339.

6. See, for example, *FIU*, 8, 122, 171, 176, 178.

7. Melvin Backman, *Faulkner: The Major Years: A Critical Study* (Bloomington: Indiana University Press, 1966), 14.

8. Perrin Lowrey, "Concepts of Time in *The Sound and the Fury*," in *Twentieth Century Interpretations of* The Sound and the Fury, 9.

Contextual Readings of
The Sound and the Fury

Like all great literature, *The Sound and the Fury* invites and rewards a variety of reading approaches. At its most literal level, the novel presents the tragic disintegration of the once proud and prestigious Compson family. But the novel also incorporates broader levels of meaning that may be suggested by the various contexts of the novel. I will examine five of the most significant of these contexts: personal, regional, national, international, and universal (or mythic).

PERSONAL

Paul Valery once remarked that every creative work or theory is "a fragment, carefully prepared, of some autobiography."[1] And Faulkner, commenting on Quentin Compson's "authorship" of the Sutpen story in *Absalom, Absalom!*, said: "He's actually telling his biography—that's all anyone ever does, he tells his own biography, talking about himself, in a thousand different terms, but himself" (*FIU* 275). Faulkner's legendary insistence on personal privacy, as well as his calculated efforts to hide behind various public personae (for example, vagabond, wounded soldier, farmer), tended to veil from his contemporary readers the highly autobiographical nature of his fiction. However, with the publication of a series of Faulkner biographies, from Joseph Blotner's pioneering one in 1974 to the latest one by Carl Rollyson in 2020–21,[2] readers can now discern the strong personal and familial elements that Faulkner drew upon in creating *The Sound and the Fury*.

The surface parallels between the Falkners and the Compsons are easy to identify. The Falkners had been a highly notable Mississippi family since the

1850s when their progenitor, William C. Falkner, had risen to prominence as a lawyer, soldier, landholder, slave owner, and author. A lieutenant during the Mexican War and a Confederate colonel in the Civil War, Falkner was later the leading figure in the construction and operation of the Ripley Railroad, a line that originally ran from Ripley, Mississippi, to Middleton, Tennessee, and was eventually extended to the Gulf Coast. Falkner also authored a number of books, including one frequently reprinted novel, *The White Rose of Memphis.* In 1889, on the day he was elected to serve in the Mississippi legislature, he was assassinated by a former business partner on the Ripley town square. This legendary figure, who becomes Colonel John Sartoris in his great-grandson's novels and stories, looms over William Faulkner's life and fiction as his marble statue still stands high above the other monuments in the Ripley cemetery.[3] Succeeding generations of the Falkner family produced a successful banker and an influential judge.

Like the Compsons in *The Sound and the Fury*, however, the Falkners, by the time of William's birth, had lost most of their wealth and much of their social and political eminence. For William this decline came to be symbolized in the person of his father, Murry, who moved the family from New Albany, where William was born in 1897, first to Ripley and then to Oxford, where he initially operated a livery stable (quite a comedown from the family railroad) and later a hardware store (much like the one in which Jason works in *The Sound and the Fury*) before landing a steady but largely unrewarding job in the business office of the University of Mississippi. Unlike the fictional Compsons, the Falkners could claim no governor in their family line, but they did have the legendary Colonel Falkner, and since his day the family had experienced a severe financial and social decline.

In addition to the broad similarity of family histories, Faulkner worked other details drawn from personal knowledge and experience into the text of *The Sound and the Fury*. The setting of the novel is Jefferson, a small town much like Faulkner's hometown of Oxford, with its town square, courthouse, Confederate monument, and cemetery. Faulkner's paternal grandparents' home, the "Big Place," just south of the square, provided the model for the Compson house and grounds, including the branch where the children play. Moreover, Faulkner had three brothers, and, though he had no sister, a first cousin, Sallie Murry Wilkins, came with her mother to live at the Big Place following the death of her father, and she became a constant playmate of the Falkner boys. A neighbor family, the Chandlers, included a mentally challenged son, Edwin, who became Faulkner's Benjy Compson. Finally, the circumstances of the death of "Damuddy" in the novel are based upon the death of Faulkner's own "Damuddy," his maternal grandmother, Lelia Swift Butler, which occurred when he was ten years old.

More important, however, than these numerous concrete parallels is Faulkner's psychological and emotional state at the time he conceived and wrote *The Sound and the Fury*. As a number of critics have argued, the general pessimism of the novel and particularly the suicidal despair of Quentin Compson seem to derive in part from Faulkner's lingering heartache over the successive losses of two women whom he loved and sought to marry— Estelle Oldham and Helen Baird—both of whom rejected him to marry someone else.

Billy Falkner and Estelle Oldham fell in love during their early teens. They attended school together, played together, read together, dreamed together. In 1913, when Billy was sixteen, Estelle, several months older, was sent by her parents to Mary Baldwin College, a girls' school in Virginia. The ensuing separation served to convince both sweethearts how truly they loved one another, so when Estelle returned to Oxford in 1915 to attend Ole Miss, it was understood and accepted by both (as well as by many in the community) that they would eventually be married. Billy, at this time a fledgling poet, not yet a novelist, was writing Swinburnian verse about fauns in pursuit of nymphs who are characterized as beautiful, ideal, ethereal, divine. The actual Estelle, however, proved far less heavenly than her poetic counterparts. At Ole Miss she developed the reputation for being something of a flirt and coquette, attending dances and parties with numerous beaus and even entertaining proposals of marriage from more than one of them. Her parents, meanwhile, had voiced objections to her proposed match with Billy Falkner, whom they viewed as an irresponsible young man with little prospect of future success. They greatly preferred well-to-do Cornell Franklin of Columbus, who was seven years older than Estelle and, already in possession of a law degree from Ole Miss, a far likelier prospect for a son-in-law than poor, unpromising Billy Falkner.

At the urgings of Mr. and Mrs. Oldham, Estelle accepted a proposal of marriage from Cornell, but immediately began to have doubts about the relationship. She desperately turned to Billy for help, even offering to elope with him. But he gallantly declined, refusing to marry her without her parents' consent. Seeing no other way to escape her dilemma, Estelle married Franklin on April 18, 1918. Shortly thereafter Faulkner enlisted in the Royal Flying Corps and began his flight training in Toronto. By the end of the year, however, the war having ended before he had completed his training, Faulkner was back in Oxford, where he worked at odd jobs, enrolled for a few classes at the university, wrote verse as well as a play for a local drama group, and, from some acute need to be perceived as manly and heroic, passed himself off as a wounded war veteran.

Following their marriage Estelle and Franklin lived first in Honolulu and then in Shanghai, and the couple had two children. But the union seemed doomed from the start: based more on social arrangement than love, undermined by Cornell's infidelity, and plagued by the heavy drinking of both husband and wife. Within a couple of years, Estelle was making frequent return visits to her home in Oxford, amid rumors that her marriage was in jeopardy. After her visit in 1921, she took back with her a gift from Billy Falkner—a handcrafted book of fourteen poems entitled *Vision in Spring*.

During the next five years, Faulkner published his first book, a collection of poems entitled *The Marble Faun* (1924); lived briefly in New Orleans, where he wrote prose sketches for the *Times-Picayune* and discussed writing with Sherwood Anderson; took a walking tour of Europe with an artist friend, William Spratling; and published his first novel, *Soldiers' Pay* (1926). He also became romantically involved with Helen Baird, who lived in Pascagoula but spent a lot of time in New Orleans. Faulkner wrote for her a fairy tale called "Mayday" and a sonnet sequence, "Helen: A Courtship"; he also dedicated to her his second novel, *Mosquitoes* (1927)—and years later incorporated her personality and artistic talent into the characterization of Charlotte Rittenmeyer in *The Wild Palms* (1939). But Helen was not nearly as serious about their relationship as Faulkner was, and when Faulkner proposed marriage, she, just as Estelle had done before her, rejected him to marry another man. Once again Faulkner returned to Oxford to nurse his psychic wounds.

Even while he was courting Helen, Faulkner continued to see Estelle occasionally when they both happened to be back in Oxford; and when Estelle and her two children returned to Oxford in 1927, living with her parents while she awaited her decree of divorce, Faulkner renewed his intense courtship of his childhood sweetheart. Estelle's divorce was not finalized until April 29, 1929; but, if town gossip had it correct, by then the two had already become lovers. In fact, Faulkner was spending so much time with Estelle that neighbors jokingly referred to him as the "Oldhams' yard boy"; and, according to one family source, Estelle's sister Dorothy was so upset that she confronted Faulkner, demanding that he marry Estelle because their relationship was becoming a local scandal.

Faulkner and Estelle were married on June 20, 1929 (four months before the publication of *The Sound and the Fury*); but a letter Faulkner wrote to his publisher Harrison Smith less than a month previously reveals how anxious and ambivalent he was about the match. "I am going to get married," he wrote. "Both want to and have to, for my honor and the sanity—I believe life—of a woman." Faulkner went on to comment on Estelle's "mental condition, her nerves" and admitted that he was partly responsible for the problem (perhaps Dot had persuaded Faulkner that he was scandalizing her family): "It's a situation that I engendered and permitted to ripen which has become unbearable, and I am tired from running from the devilment I bring about."[4] Faulkner's reservations about the marriage, and particularly the state of Estelle's emotional health, were proven accurate when, during their honeymoon on the Gulf Coast, Estelle, apparently drunk, tried to drown herself in the Gulf of Mexico.

Although Faulkner reportedly told an acquaintance in Paris in 1925 that he was writing a novel about a declining family with three brothers, one an idiot, and a sister, the work that we now know as *The Sound and the Fury*—that is, a novel largely about childhood innocence, loss of virginity, promiscuity, incestuous desires, guilt, regret, and a strong dose of cynicism—was begun in early 1928. It hardly seems mere coincidence that this was precisely the time when Faulkner, reeling from the disappointment of his rejection by Helen Baird, was redirecting his romantic gaze back toward his childhood sweetheart who had also been, in their early years together, almost a sister to him. But the woman Faulkner turned to when he was nearly thirty years old was not Estelle Oldham, the girl he had known and loved in their teen years; she was Estelle Franklin—the woman who had betrayed him, and who, her purity and innocence stained, was now a divorcée with two children by another man, an alcoholic, and an emotional and psychological wreck. Did Faulkner believe that by marrying Estelle they could turn back the clock to recapture the idyllic relationship they had known in their childhood and youth? Or was he acting out of a sense of personal honor because he indeed felt that he had partly created her present crisis? Or was he responding to a deep-seated and possibly even unconscious guilt because he had refused to elope with Estelle in 1918 and thus by that refusal had brought about her shame, dishonor, and unhappiness with Franklin? Did he love her, or hate her, or both? Whatever the answers to these complicated questions, it seems almost beyond dispute that the distance between Caddy Compson's childhood innocence and her promiscuous adulthood, Quentin's despair, and Jason's vengeful anger may be measured as the distance between the Estelle Oldham that Faulkner loved and idealized and the Estelle Franklin whom he married. More than a decade later, in one of the screenplays Faulkner wrote in Hollywood, he has a character say, "The best way . . . to change the idea of a woman in a man's mind from a dream to a nightmare is for the man to marry her."[5] It is little wonder that Faulkner invested so much emotion and significance in a little girl's muddy panties.

REGIONAL

In *Absalom, Absalom!* Shreve McCannon, a Harvard student from Canada, pleads with Quentin Compson, "Tell about the South" (142). While *Absalom, Absalom!* represents Faulkner's most sustained—and agonizing—attempt to explore the meaning of what it means to be "southern" ("You cant understand it," Quentin says to Shreve; "you would have to be born there" [289]), *The Sound and the Fury* also draws upon Faulkner's ambivalent feelings for his homeland.

Because Faulkner is viewed by many readers and critics as primarily a "southern" writer—indeed, he is unquestionably the leading figure in the early twentieth-century literary resurgence known as the "Southern Renaissance"—it is understandable that *The Sound and the Fury* is often interpreted as a symbolic dramatization of the effects of the collapse of the agricultural and aristocratic Old South and the emergence of a New South characterized by industrialization, mercantilism, and urbanization. While this dramatic shift came to be identified in the popular imagination with the South's defeat in the Civil War, in actuality the change was far more gradual, beginning with Lee's surrender to Grant at Appomattox but continuing through the years of Reconstruction, Jim Crow, the rise of mercantile capitalism, and the initial phases of the Great Migration—and continuing on into the Newer South of the Great Depression, the civil rights movement, and the alterations in landscape that C. Vann Woodward has called the "Bulldozer Revolution."[6] It is this long panorama of southern history that fuels Faulkner's imagination and sentiment and serves as the backdrop for all of his fiction, including *The Sound and the Fury.*

A highly useful avenue to an understanding of the pervasive "southernness" of Faulkner's novel is provided by *I'll Take My Stand*, a symposium published in 1930, the approximate time of the appearance of *The Sound and the Fury.* Drawing its title and defiant, almost militant mood from the song lyrics of the (white) southern anthem, "Dixie," *I'll Take My Stand* presents the rejoinder of twelve prominent southerners, including such well-known literary figures as John Crowe Ransom, Donald Davidson, Allen Tate, Andrew Nelson Lytle, Robert Penn Warren, and Stark Young, to the historical and cultural pressures that were bearing down upon the modern South.[7]

The overall purpose of *I'll Take My Stand* is explained in an introductory "Statement of Principles" that was written by Ransom but (probably accurately) attributed to all the contributors. All dozen of the essays, Ransom wrote, "tend to support a Southern way of life against what may be called the American or prevailing way; and all as much as agree that the best terms in which to represent the distinction are contained in the phrase, Agrarian *versus* Industrial" (ix). The American or industrial way of life, the introduction continues, is characterized by a greatly exaggerated optimism regarding the benefits of industrialization and its means of implementation, the applied sciences and the machine. Rather than representing progress, however, as is generally thought, these have "enslaved our human energies to a degree now clearly felt to be burdensome" (xi).

The negative effects of industrialization, Ransom contends, may be traced in the economic, religious, and cultural life of the South. The machine culture, mistakenly assuming "that labor is an evil, that only the end of labor or the material product is good" (xii), displaces "the act of labor as one of the happy functions of human life" and results in "overproduction, unemployment, and a growing inequality in the distribution of wealth" (xiii). To counter these problems, the industrial state relies on advertising and consumerism, which provide no solutions but merely perpetuate and enlarge the problem. Religion, too, suffers under the impact of industrialism, since authentic religion stresses man's creaturely role within a mysterious and inscrutable universe, whereas industrialism posits man as superior to and manipulator of nature, his own god and ruler rather than a steward of a higher being. Neither can art and culture, both dependent on a certain degree of leisure, flourish in an industrial state. "Neither the creation nor the understanding of works of art is possible in an industrial age except by some local and unlikely suspension of the industrial drive," Ransom writes (xv). Likewise, "the amenities of life," which he lists as "manners, conversation, hospitality, sympathy, family life, romantic love" (xv), are undervalued and thus greatly diminished in an industrial society. And all of these negative results, if left unchecked, will only get worse. "The tempo of the industrial life is fast," Ransom notes, "but that is not the worst of it; it is accelerating" (xvi), leading to "an increasing disadjustment and instability" (xvii).

While overly simplistic in its defense of the South and overly aggressive in its attack on the North, *I'll Take My Stand* is altogether understandable when considered in the context of its time and place. The book was intended as an intellectual response to national critics such as H. L. Mencken, whose savagely satirical "Sahara of the Bozart" (1929) and other essays characterized the South as an uncultured, backward, uncivilized wasteland. Such a negative view of the South had been given added impetus by the derogatory and often hysterical treatment of the South by the national media (including Mencken) during the coverage of the Scopes "monkey" trial in Dayton, Tennessee, in 1925.

Faulkner agreed and disagreed with both the agrarians and Mencken. Like the former, he resented northern intrusion and influence upon southern life; but he was not as willing as they to ignore the negative side of his culture. Attacking industrialization during the onset of the Great Depression and ignoring the evil aspects of the southern tradition—especially slavery and Jim Crow—must have seemed to Faulkner not merely wrongheaded but downright silly. At the same time, like Mencken, Faulkner was acutely aware of the shortcomings and failures of the South, but his criticisms of his native region were always tempered by a great deal of love and respect. The tensions generated by these paradoxes—rural versus urban, South versus North, past versus present—contributed to some of Faulkner's finest creations. In *The Sound and the Fury* these oppositions can be traced by contrasting the Benjy and Quentin sections with Jason's.

Benjy's section equates the childhood innocence of the Compson children with pastoral images. Benjy's favorite place to play is the pasture, and he is frequently associated with flowers, trees, and water. Like eventually his beloved sister and his testicles, these natural elements will come to symbolize Benjy's lost world of childhood and innocence; but they also suggest the South's agrarian past. The fate of that old world is suggested by the macabre irony of having Benjy, a mentally retarded descendant of the old aristocratic Compsons, tended by Luster, a descendant of Black enslaved people.

If Benjy's section can be linked through its nature imagery to the Old South agrarian ideal, Quentin's section may be linked to another aspect of the Old South—the idealization of women. All readers note Quentin's obsession with Caddy's purity—and his desire to stop time in order to keep her frozen in a prepubescent state of childhood innocence. Numerous critics have noted the chivalric nature of Quentin's attitude and behavior. Herbert Head refers to him as a "half-baked Galahad" (110), and Quentin remarks that he and his father, like all southern gentlemen, "protect women" (96). Quentin's confrontation with Dalton Ames is the modern-day equivalent of an Old South duel in defense of a woman's honor.

In the Jason section, however, the reader is planted in quite another world. Significantly, as John Matthews has noted, the date assigned by historian C. Vann Woodward to the collapse of the Old South and the emergence of the New South is 1910—the date of Quentin Compson's suicide in *The Sound and the Fury*.[8] And, as if to heighten the parallel, Faulkner assigns the death to June 2, the eve of Confederate Memorial Day, Jefferson Davis's birthday.

In contrast to Benjy's and Quentin's identification with a South that is, no less for Faulkner than for Margaret Mitchell, "gone with the wind," Jason may be taken as a representative of the New South. In fact, Jason's characterization reads like a litany of the defects of the New South listed by Ransom in the preface to *I'll Take My Stand*. A merchant rather than a planter, Jason finds no joy in his work, seeing it only as a means to make money. Except for money, the love of his life is his automobile, a machine. He has no respect for women, family, neighbors, or God. A townsman, he is clearly out of his element when he chases his niece into the countryside.

> I kept thinking that when I got across the field at least I'd have something level to walk on, that wouldn't jolt me every step, but when I got into the woods it was full of underbrush and I had to twist around through it, and then I came to a ditch full of briers. . . . I had gotten beggar lice and twigs and stuff all over me, inside my clothes and shoes and all, and then I happened to look around and I had my hand right on a bunch of poison oak. (240–41)

This passage represents more than the old ploy of a trickster tricked: it shows a man out of harmony with the natural world, one who, in Ransom's words, evidences "an increasing disadjustment and instability" (xvii). In short, Jason is an embodiment of the very worst features of the New South.

Let me hasten to add, however, that in treating *The Sound and the Fury* as a contrast of Old South/New South attitudes and values, I am not suggesting that Faulkner should be linked to the "Lost Cause" literature that idealized and sentimentalized the southern past. In this connection Faulkner belongs more in the camp of Ellen Glasgow than in that of Thomas Nelson Page. Like Glasgow, Faulkner saw the failings in both the Old and the New South. For him truth was always complex, somewhere in between the polarities, both-and rather than either-or. While Jason is a villain, one of the worst in all of Faulkner, readers must not forget that Benjy is mentally challenged and Quentin a hopeless suicide. The reader will search in vain for anything approaching an ideal, past or present, in any of the Compsons. For that one must turn to Dilsey, who represents neither the Old South nor the New South but a timeless realm that transcends any historical epoch, southern or otherwise.

NATIONAL

While *The Sound and the Fury* is indisputably one of the most "southern" novels ever written, it would be a serious mistake to see it as merely southern: it is simultaneously one of the great American novels. This point can best be made by placing Faulkner's novel alongside some of the works by his contemporaries.

American authors in the decade immediately following World War I produced a number of fictional works that still rank among the nation's finest. The consequences of the war for both individuals and the nation provided rich material for E. E. Cummings's *The Enormous Room* (1922), Willa Cather's *One of Ours* (1922), John Dos Passos's *Three Soldiers* (1923), and Ernest Hemingway's *In Our Time* (1924), *The Sun Also Rises* (1926), and *A Farewell to Arms* (1929), as well as Faulkner's own *Soldiers' Pay* (1926). James Branch Cabell utilized mythic materials in his epic series of Poictesme novels, most notably *Jurgen* (1919). Cather dramatized the oppositions of past versus present and tradition versus change in *My Antonia* (1918), *A Lost Lady* (1923), *The Professor's House* (1925), and *Death Comes for the Archbishop* (1927). Sherwood Anderson, who became something of a mentor to Faulkner in New Orleans in 1925–26, applied Freudian principles of psychology to an exploration of character and behavior in *Winesburg, Ohio* (1919), *Poor White* (1920), *The Triumph of the Egg* (1921), and *Dark Laughter* (1925). Sinclair Lewis, in *Main Street* (1920) and *Babbitt* (1922), examined the stultifying effects of small-town provincialism and business values on American life, as also did Thomas Wolfe in his masterful and influential *Look Homeward, Angel* (1929).

The year 1925 was truly an *annus mirabilis* for American literature. In addition to Cather's *The Professor's House* and Anderson's *Dark Laughter*, previously mentioned, that year saw the publication of F. Scott Fitzgerald's *The Great Gatsby*, Theodore Dreiser's *An American Tragedy*, and Ellen Glasgow's *Barren Ground*.

All of these books from the 1920's share with *The Sound and the Fury* a general sense of something sadly gone wrong in human affairs, of an idealism and hope that had been shattered into skepticism and doubt. How *The Sound and the Fury* fits into this pattern can readily be seen by its many comparisons with perhaps the best known and most representative novel of the period, Fitzgerald's *The Great Gatsby*. The two novels are remarkably similar in characterization, theme, tone, and even technique.

For example, each novel features a lost woman: Daisy Buchanan and Caddy Compson. While Caddy's overt sexuality is emphasized more than Daisy's, both women are presented as objects of physical desire by more than one male character. Moreover, both women, in the manner of the socially liberated women of the twenties, are headstrong, spirited, independent, and indifferent to public opinion. And both are great disappointments to the men who obsess over them.

Jay Gatsby and Quentin Compson, of course, are those men. While Gatsby's fixation on Daisy is romantic in nature and Quentin's on Caddy is brotherly (and incestuous), both men elevate their beloveds to a state of purity, grace, and beauty that becomes unearthly, ethereal. When reality obtrudes upon their dream worlds, they both go into denial and seek to return to the Edenic idyll from which they have been forcibly exiled. "You can't repeat the past," Nick Carraway says to Gatsby; and he replies, "Why of course you can," adding, "I'm going to fix everything just the way it was before."[9] A similar attempt to recapture the past and "fix everything" may be observed in Quentin Compson's thoughts and actions, as, for example, his befriending and protecting the little lost Italian girl (whom he calls "sister" [125ff.], thus identifying her with his lost sister, Caddy) and his seeking to persuade his father that he and not someone else is Caddy's lover. The obsession and disillusionment of both Quentin and Gatsby drive them to their deaths: Quentin's in suicide and Gatsby's in what appears to be almost a willed death, since he offers no resistance to the figure moving toward him on the lawn.

Jay Gatsby and Quentin Compson are viewed as quixotic, anachronistically romantic lovers because they live by a chivalric ideal in a world governed by crass materialists, respectively Tom Buchanan and Jason Compson. Buchanan and Jason are alike in their greed for money and possessions, their degrading treatment of women, and their cynical view of life and experience. "Civilization's going to pieces," Tom says. "I've gotten to be a terrible pessimist about things" (13). Jason says: "Blood, . . , governors and generals. It's a dam good thing we never had any kings and presidents; we'd all be down there at Jackson chasing butterflies" (230). Fitzgerald's portrayal of Buchanan is absent the sardonic humor of Jason, but the general views and behavior of the two characters are quite similar.

Although Fitzgerald's novel lacks the multiple stream-of-consciousness monologues that are the hallmark of *The Sound and the Fury*, *The Great Gatsby* does employ the disruption of standard chronology that one finds in *The Sound and the Fury*, as well as other modernist fiction. Fitzgerald's novel begins at the end and uses flashbacks throughout the narrative. And the aesthetic distance on the Gatsby-Daisy story that is created by the first-person narration of Nick Carraway is similar to the outsider's view of the Compsons that is provided in the fourth section, the so-called Dilsey section, of Faulkner's novel. While not as experimental as *The Sound and the Fury*, *The Great Gatsby* is still a brilliantly managed plot and perspective. Even the deservedly famous endings of the novels bear a strong resemblance. Fitzgerald's novel closes with the image of boats moving against a strong current;

Faulkner's ends with a horse and carriage moving down the street. In both cases, however, the sense of progress is illusionary. Fitzgerald's boat is actually in retrograde, being "borne back ceaselessly into the past" (182), and the scene culminating in the final words of Faulkner's ending, "each in its ordered place" (321), has been violently imposed by the satanic Jason. Thus, both novels, like so many of that era, end in irony and pathos.

INTERNATIONAL

Viewed from a still wider perspective, *The Sound and the Fury* may be identified with that influential group of literary works associated with the post–World War I "Lost Generation." Taking its name from Gertrude Stein's reported remark to Ernest Hemingway in Paris in 1925, "You are all a lost generation" (immortalized as the epigraph to Hemingway's *The Sun Also Rises*), the term refers to the intellectuals, writers, and artists who came out of World War I disillusioned by the loss of traditional values and the escalating problems of the twentieth century. While the horrors of modern war—trench warfare, mechanized weaponry such as airplanes and tanks, chemical agents, the unbelievable number of casualties—came to symbolize the disillusion, the generation's alienation and estrangement from the past actually resulted from broader cultural forces that had been set in motion even before the war. As Malcolm Cowley, the foremost historian of the generation, has noted:

> It was lost, first of all, because it was uprooted, schooled away and almost wrenched away from its attachment to any region or tradition. It was lost because its training had prepared it for another world than existed after the war (and because the war prepared it only for travel and excitement). It was lost because it tried to live in exile. It was lost because it accepted no older guides to conduct and because it had formed a false picture of society and the writer's place in it. The generation belonged to a period of transition from values already fixed to values that had to be created.[10]

While it was an American, Stein, who named the group, and another American, Hemingway, who wrote its definitive story, the Lost Generation was actually an international phenomenon. Writers as diverse as William Butler Yeats, Wilfred Owen, Siegfried Sassoon, Ezra Pound, T. S. Eliot, Ford Madox Ford, Hemingway, Willa Cather, Virginia Woolf, John Dos Passos, E. E. Cummings, Erich Maria Remarque, and Faulkner all shared to a degree the cynicism and disillusionment that came to be characteristic of the Lost Generation. And it was a German philosopher, Oswald Spengler, who provided the philosophical and historical argument for the attitudes of the group.

Spengler's *The Decline of the West*, published in two volumes in 1918 and 1923 (the revised first volume was published in an English translation in 1922), challenges the prominent nineteenth-century view of history as an ever-advancing progression toward higher and better forms of knowledge, culture, and civilization. Instead, Spengler argues, history is characterized by a deterministic rise and fall of civilizations—all imitating the natural-life cycle of birth, youth, maturity, decline, and death, as well as the cyclical movements of the seasons: spring, summer, autumn, and winter. According to Spengler's calculations, the zenith, or summer, of Western civilization was the period of the Renaissance: since that time the West has been declining, and its ultimate demise is only a matter of time. Evidence of this decline and impending death Spengler finds in such developments as the rise of democracy, socialism, pacifism, and liberalism and the loss of significance for blood and instinct. Modernist writers who were strongly influenced by Spengler's ideas were not so much persuaded by his specific agenda as by his overarching assertion that Western civilization had passed its apex and was inevitably doomed to decline and die.

Among major authors and works, T. S. Eliot's *The Waste Land* (1922) is perhaps the closest literary parallel to Spengler's notion of decline. Drawing upon the legend of the wounded Fisher King and his sterile, dying land (as Hemingway later did in *The Sun Also Rises*), Eliot dramatizes a sick and decaying modern culture. In this sterile wasteland spring brings no rebirth, the rich heritage of the past has been diluted or lost, people wander about lost and confused, life is dull and mechanical, love has given way to lust, heroes or saviors are nonexistent, and skepticism and doubt outweigh hope and faith. "London Bridge is falling down falling down falling down" (1. 426): this line symbolizes a general collapse, and there appears to be no reversal of the downward spiral.

Faulkner, in all likelihood, never read Spengler; but he was heavily influenced by Eliot, especially "The Love Song of J. Alfred Prufrock" and *The Waste Land*. There are allusions to both works in Faulkner's early poems and novels, and the tragic tone of those works is consistent with both Spengler and the literary representatives of the Lost Generation.

The character in *The Sound and the Fury* who most clearly expresses the pessimism and cynicism associated with the Lost Generation is Mr. Compson. "No battle is ever won," he tells Quentin. "They are not even fought. The field only reveals to man his own folly and despair, and victory is an illusion of philosophers and fools" (76). "One day you'd think misfortune would get tired," he says on another occasion, "but then time is your misfortune" (104). Human beings, he says, are "impure properties carried tediously to an unvarying nil: stalemate of dust and desire" (124), "just accumulations dolls stuffed with sawdust swept up from the trash heaps where all previous dolls had been thrown away" (175). He defines women as "delicate equilibrium of periodical filth between two moons balanced" (128) and claims they possess "an affinity for evil" (96). He is even cynical about Harvard: "dead ivy vines upon old dead brick" (95).

All of the quotations from Mr. Compson just cited come from the Quentin section of the novel, and such ideas and attitudes contribute significantly to Quentin's own despair and eventual suicide. Most critics relate Quentin's motive for suicide to his obsessive desire for, and his disillusion with, his sister, Caddy. However, it can be argued that it is the influence of his father that pushes Quentin over the edge of his despair. The phrase "Father said," which appears some twenty times in the section, demonstrates how dependent Quentin is on the opinions of his father. Significantly, his last reflections before he drowns himself are of the conversation in which he had sought to persuade his father that he had committed incest with Caddy, and he is saddened and, I think, stunned that his father takes the entire matter—Caddy's behavior, Quentin's obsession with it, Quentin's thoughts of suicide—so lightly. Quentin's stance throughout the dialogue is that things such as purity and honor and integrity matter tremendously, while his father basically argues that nothing really matters. "You cannot bear to think that someday it will no longer hurt you like this," Mr. Compson says (177). All of Mr. Compson's pessimistic musings funnel down to a belief in *nada* (nothing), a phrase made famous by Hemingway but representative of a widespread philosophical and artistic attitude during the 1920s. And it would appear that it is his father's *nada* as much as his sister's promiscuity and disgrace that pushes Quentin off the Charles River bridge.

In a well-known essay Mark Spilka identifies the theme of Hemingway's *The Sun Also Rises*—a sourcebook of Hemingway's *nada*—as the death of romantic love.[11] But Hemingway's is not the only book of this period with that theme. A few years later, in *The Wild Palms*, Faulkner would have Harry Wilbourne say: "There is no place for [love] in the world today. . . . We have eliminated it. It took us a long time, but man is resourceful and limitless in inventing too, and so we have got rid of love at last just as we have got rid of Christ" (115). But Faulkner had already demonstrated that point in the lives of the Compsons in *The Sound and the Fury*. And it is that loss, and the sadness that results, that places Faulkner's great novel solidly in the mainstream of Lost Generation literature.

UNIVERSAL

At its broadest level of interpretation *The Sound and the Fury* is concerned not with personal, regional, national, or international issues so much as with the nature of the human condition, what Faulkner referred to in his Nobel Prize Acceptance Speech as "the old verities and truths of the heart, the old universal truths lacking which any story is ephemeral and doomed" (*ESPL* 120). At the University of Virginia, he said: "I feel that the verities which these [characters] suffer are universal verities—that is, that man, whether he's black or white or red or yellow still suffers the same anguishes, he has the same aspirations, his follies are the same follies, his triumphs are the same triumphs" (*FIU* 197). At West Point, just weeks before he died, Faulkner reiterated this point: "The writer is simply trying to use the best method he possibly can find to tell you a true and moving and familiar old, old story of the human heart in conflict with itself for the old, old human verities and truth, which are love, hope, fear, compassion, greed, lust" (*FWP* 59).

To communicate these universal truths through the use of particulars, Faulkner, like other modernist writers of his generation, employed "the mythical method." The term is T. S. Eliot's, used in his now-famous review of James Joyce's *Ulysses* in 1923. Eliot asserts that in using Homer's narrative of the epic journey of Ulysses in the *Odyssey* as the framework for the twentieth-century story of Leopold Bloom, "Mr. Joyce is pursuing a method which others must pursue after him. Instead of narrative method, we may now use the mythical method."[12] While authors like Joyce and Eugene O'Neill frequently incorporated Greek myths into their narratives, others, including Faulkner, demonstrated a greater fondness for biblical archetypes. Thomas Mann's *Joseph and His Brothers*, Robinson Jeffers's *Tamar*, Nathanael West's *Miss Lonelyhearts*, Archibald MacLeish's *J. B.*, Thornton Wilder's *The Skin of Our Teeth*, and John Steinbeck's *The Grapes of Wrath* and *East of Eden*, as well as Faulkner's *Absalom, Absalom!*, *Go Down, Moses*, and *A Fable*, in addition to *The Sound and the Fury*, all demonstrate a contemporary application and relevance of biblical myth.

The two principal myths that Faulkner employs in *The Sound and the Fury* are the most universally recognized stories in the Bible—the Eden story from the Old Testament and the passion of Christ from the New. The only direct allusion to the Eden story appears in Quentin's several recollections of the hymn sung at Caddy's wedding, "The Voice That Breathed o'er Eden" (81). This song, which celebrates "the pure espousal" of Adam and Eve, serves as an ironic and painful reminder to Quentin of his sister's dishonor and arranged marriage with Herbert Head, in Quentin's view a cheat and "blackguard" (111). But Quentin's remembrance of the wedding hymn is only one of several Eden parallels within the novel.

The key incident in the Benjy section, one that epitomizes childhood innocence but at the same time foreshadows the fall into awareness that will occur as the children grow older, is the scene in which Caddy climbs a pear tree to look through the parlor window to view her grandmother's wake. This tree equates with the tree of knowledge in the Eden story. In this connection, one is struck by the serpent imagery of the passage: "A snake crawled out from under the house. Jason said he wasn't afraid of snakes and Caddy said he was but she wasn't" (37). Then, displaying the curiosity and courage of Eve in the garden, and ignoring Versh's reminder that her father had warned her to avoid "that tree," Caddy climbs the tree while the other children watch "the muddy bottom of her drawers" (39). Caddy's soiled panties, of course, foreshadow her later sexual promiscuity; but the stain also symbolizes original sin, which Faulkner, like Hawthorne and indeed a host of writers since St. Augustine, identifies with carnal knowledge. As though to underscore this association, Faulkner has Dilsey chase Caddy out of the tree with the reprimand, "You, Satan" (45). Later, after trying unsuccessfully to clean the mud from Caddy's clothes, Dilsey comments, "It done soaked clean through onto you" (74). It is hardly surprising that this episode, fusing a child's discovery of death with a foreshadowing of the loss of virginity, contained for Faulkner the very essence of the novel. In its widest application of meaning, *The Sound and the Fury* is a retelling of the loss of Eden, of humanity's recurring initiation into the tragic realities of life.

Faulkner's use of the Christ story in the novel is more direct than his use of the Eden story. Faulkner alerts the reader to the centrality of the Christ myth by means of the chapter headings for the present-tense sections of the novel: April 6, 7, and 8, 1928, as the reader eventually discovers, fall on Good Friday, Holy Saturday, and Easter Sunday. While the reader might not become aware of this fact until the Dilsey section, and while many of the Christian allusions and parallels might escape notice on a first reading of the book, reexamination of Faulkner's text reveals a plethora of Christian elements distributed through each of the four sections.

Benjy's section contains numerous references to Christmas, and Benjy, thirty-three years of age, may be viewed as an innocent though impotent Christ figure, scourged and victimized in a fallen world. Quentin—who frequently alludes to Christ, partakes of a Last Supper (June 2, 1910, fell on a Thursday, the day of the week commonly associated with Christ's last meal with his disciples), is captured by a mob and taken before a magistrate, and pours out his anguished soul to his father—is also an impotent Christ, distinguished like Benjy by his suffering but incapable of transforming his experiences into any redemptive results. His death effects no resurrection. Jason, from his own point of view, is also something of a Christ figure, a scapegoat persecuted by Jews and others, and misunderstood and "crucified" by the world. Jason's distresses on Good Friday—his headache, the flat tire, his failure to catch Miss Quentin with the carnival showman—take place at the same time of day as Christ's execution. In reality, though, Jason is an anti-Christ. Dilsey, the moral and ethical center of the novel, says of him, "I dont put no devilment beyond you" (185); and the description of his "close-thatched brown hair curled into two stubborn hooks, one on either side of his forehead" (279) suggests popular caricatures of Satan. Moreover, Jason sarcastically ridicules Easter, spitefully saying to his mother, "You never resurrected Christ, did you?" (279); and he openly curses and defies God, imagining himself as "dragging Omnipotence down from his throne" (306).

In depicting the Compson brothers as various types of pseudo-Christ figures, Faulkner is inverting the older heroic myth for ironic purposes, as Joyce does with the Homeric materials in *Ulysses*. That such is Faulkner's intent becomes evident in the description of the Easter worship service in section four. In a church tackily adorned with shabby ornaments, the Reverend Shegog, an "undersized" and "insignificant looking" man (293), preaches a sermon that ironically counterpoints the tragedy of the Compsons. The preacher opens with a grim reminder of the endless human pilgrimage toward death, already depicted in the novel by the deaths of Damuddy, Roskus, Quentin, and Mr. Compson: "Dey passed away in Egypt, de swingin chariots; de generations passed away" (295). Shegog goes on to describe Jesus as the innocent child victimized by the world—and to identify his fate with the children in this congregation: "Look at dem little chillen settin dar. Jesus wus like dat once. . . . I sees de closing eyes; sees Mary jump up, sees de sojer face. . . . We gwine to kill yo little Jesus!" (296).

Both of these themes—the passing away of the generations and the Slaughter of the Innocents (that is, innocence)—are embodied in the experience of the Compsons. Dilsey, appearing to recognize the parallel, reacts with compassion and grief: weeping, she observes, "I seed de beginning, en now I sees de endin" (297). This remark, repeated several times as a choral refrain, applies Jesus's claim to be to be "Alpha and Omega, the beginning and the ending" (Revelation 1:8) to a human situation of failure and loss. So obsessed seems Dilsey with the final Compson disintegration, one wonders if she even hears the Reverend Shegog's concluding remarks, stressing the traditional Easter message of resurrection and joy. If she has heard, the testament of faith and hope has brought her little consolation in her distress. Preoccupied as she is with the dissolution of the Compson family, Dilsey finds little cause to celebrate on this particular Easter day.

That Shegog's final affirmation is intended ironically is further under-scored by the hateful actions of Jason on this day. Just as Caddy's wedding is juxtaposed with Damuddy's funeral in the Benjy section, the Easter church service is undercut by Jason's vengeful pursuit of his niece and the money she has taken in her flight. While Shegog preaches of Christ's resurrection, Jason is cursing God and the churches he passes. The preacher's references to the soldiers seeking to kill the infant Jesus are counterpointed with Jason's vision of himself leading a troop of soldiers against the Almighty. While Dilsey sits in church with the rejected and suffering Benjy, Jason is violently attacking a stranger in a neighboring town.

The contrast between Jason's satanic behavior and Dilsey's genuine faith and compassion suggests that Dilsey is the authentic Christ figure in the novel. Significantly, she possesses a keen awareness of evil, recognizing its existence not only in Jason but also in others, even in her own family. "Lemme tell you somethin, n——r boy," she says to Luster, "you got jes es much Comp-son devilment in you es any of em" (276). However, unlike Benjy, who is inca-pable of coping with the evil of the world, or Quentin, who seeks to escape it, or Jason, who embraces it, Dilsey actively combats evil. "Git on back to hell, whar you belong at," she commands the jaybirds (269); and she rebukes Frony for objecting to Benjy's being brought into the Negro church (290). Her role as intermediary "savior" is evident not only in her protection of Benjy but also in her intervention in the feud between Jason and Miss Quentin—"She came hobbling between us, trying to hold me again," Jason narrates. "'Hit me, den,' she says, 'ef nothing else but hittin somebody wont do you. Hit me,' she says" (185). Dilsey is, quite literally, the suffering servant; but unlike the pseudo-Christs of the novel, she is able to transcend her suffering to embrace the Christian virtues of love, compassion, and forgiveness.

Nevertheless, sadly, one must recognize that such virtues seem to have little practical effect upon the world that Dilsey inhabits. The Compson family unit is past saving (though some readers find some small consolation—and even hints of an empty tomb—in the escape of Miss Quentin from Jason's greedy clutches), and Jason's final act of venting his rage and frustration on the helpless Benjy and the youthful Luster adds a disturbing note to the ending of the novel. The reader cannot fail to notice that it is Jason, and not Dilsey—Satan, not Christ—who controls the final scene by physically attacking Luster and Queenie. From the final perspective of the novel, that of Benjy, the violently enforced order described in the final phrases—"as cornice and façade flowed smoothly once more from left to right, post and tree, window and doorway and signboard each in its ordered place" (321)—ends the novel on a highly problematic note. Jason's actions mock the poetry of these lines, just as he has earlier mocked God.

CONCLUSION

By looking at the varying contexts of *The Sound and the Fury*, I have sought to demonstrate that the novel is not one book but several. The book is unquestionably one of the masterpieces of world literature. It presents a moving, tragic story with a dazzling virtuosity of technique. But its greatness is enhanced by its openness to a variety of interpretations and approaches. Terry Eagleton has observed that a literary classic does not become such because it expresses a single universal meaning that all readers throughout the ages can find and agree upon, but rather because it allows and invites multiple and changing interpretations and responses over time.[13] *The Sound and the Fury* is that type of classic. Its greatness is evidenced by the host of readers who continue to find new and varied meanings in its pages.

NOTES

1. Qtd. in Richard Ellman and Charles Feidelson, Jr., *The Modern Tradition: Backgrounds of Modern Literature* (New York: Oxford University Press, 1965), 75.

2. The several Faulkner biographies include Joseph Blotner, *Faulkner: A Biography*, 2 vols. (New York: Random House, 1974); one-volume edition, 1984; David Minter, *William Faulkner: His Life and Work* (Baltimore: Johns Hopkins University Press, 1980); Stephen B. Oates, *William Faulkner: The Man and the Artist* (New York: Harper and Row, 1987); Frederick R. Karl, *William Faulkner: American Writer* (New York: Weidenfeld and Nicolson, 1989); Joel Williamson, *William Faulkner and Southern History* (New York: Oxford University Press, 1993); Richard Gray, *The Life of William Faulkner: A Critical Biography* (Oxford: Blackwell, 1994); Jay Parini, *One Matchless Time: A Life of William Faulkner* (New York: Harper-Collins, 2004);

M. Thomas Inge, *William Faulkner: Overlook Illustrated Lives* (New York: Abrams Press, 2006); Philip Weinstein, *Becoming Faulkner: The Art and Life of William Faulkner* (New York: Oxford University Press, 2010); Robert W. Hamblin, *Myself and the World: A Biography of William Faulkner* (Jackson: University Press of Mississippi, 2016); and Carl Rollyson, *The Life of William Faulkner*, 2 vols. (Charlottesville: University Press of Virginia, 2020, 2021).

3. I treat Faulkner's extensive use of Colonel Falkner's life and death in "The Old Colonel: W. C. Falkner as the Prototype for Yoknapatawpha," in *Papers Presented at the Faulkner Heritage Festival, 2007–2010*, ed. Renelda Owen (Ripley, MS: Ripley Main Street Association, 2011): 7–26.

4. Quoted in Williamson, *William Faulkner and Southern History*, 222. There were rumors that Estelle's emotional state perhaps related to an abortion that Faulkner allegedly arranged for her. I treat this issue in "Biographical Fact or Fiction? Faulkner, Estelle Oldham Franklin, and Abortion," *Mississippi Quarterly* 60 (Summer 2007): 579–87.

5. Louis Daniel Brodsky and Robert W. Hamblin, eds., *Faulkner: A Comprehensive Guide to the Brodsky Collection, Volume III: The De Gaulle Story* (Jackson: University Press of Mississippi, 1984), 49.

6. C. Vann Woodward, *The Burden of Southern History*, 3rd ed. (Baton Rouge: Louisiana State University Press, 1993), 10.

7. Twelve Southerners, *I'll Take My Stand: The South and the Agrarian Tradition* (New York: Peter Smith, 1951).

8. John T. Matthews, *"The Sound and the Fury": Faulkner and the Lost Cause* (Boston: Twayne, 1991), 97.

9. F. Scott Fitzgerald, *The Great Gatsby* (New York: Charles Scribner's Sons, 1953), 111.

10. Malcolm Cowley, *Exile's Return: A Literary Odyssey of the 1920s* (New York: Viking Press, 1956), 9.

11. Mark Spilka, "The Death of Love in *The Sun Also Rises*," in *Hemingway and His Critics*, ed. Carlos Baker (New York: Hill and Wang, 1961), 80–92.

12. T. S. Eliot, "Ulysses, Order and Myth," *Dial* 75 (November 1923): 483.

13. See, for example, *Literary Theory: An Introduction* (Oxford, UK: Blackwell, 2008), 10–11.

As I Lay Dying
The Oprah Book Club Lectures

In 2005 I led the Oprah Book Club's online discussions of As I Lay Dying *for Oprah Winfrey's "Summer of Faulkner." Those discussions included a number of videotaped mini-lectures on my introduction to the book as well as the characters, themes, structure, and context of the novel.*

INTRODUCTION

I first read Faulkner many years ago in a class at Delta State University taught by T. D. Young, one of the pioneer scholars in the field of southern literature. Interestingly, the first Faulkner book I read was *As I Lay Dying*, which partly explains why it has remained one of my favorite Faulkner books. Later, in graduate school, I continued my study of Faulkner at the University of Mississippi under the expert guidance of John Pilkington, an outstanding teacher and scholar and author of an excellent book on Faulkner's major novels. For the past several years, I've had the good fortune to work with a renowned Faulkner collector, L. D. Brodsky, of St. Louis, collaborating with him on books, articles, lectures, and exhibits based on the materials in his fabulous collection. In 1988 my university acquired the Brodsky Collection, created its Center for Faulkner Studies, and appointed me the director.—All of that simply to say that I've been hanging out with Faulkner for quite a long time now, and I still enjoy reading and reflecting upon his work.

Even these many years later, I distinctly remember my first impression of *As I Lay Dying*, and it had nothing at all to do with the story being told. I was simply amazed at the unusual way Faulkner chose to tell the story. All those characters, jumping around in time, each telling his or her own version of the events, sometimes collaborating, sometimes contradicting each other. It was like Faulkner had scattered a deck of cards on the floor and left me to pick them up and reassemble them: 52-pickup—or in this case, 59-pickup. I found the technique daring, innovative, provocative, awesome. And I was so taken with Faulkner's technical virtuosity that it hardly mattered that I was having trouble holding all the cards in my hand and arranging them into some kind of coherent and comprehensible order.

As I continued to read Faulkner I discovered that this shifting of narration from one character to another and these violent disruptions of standard chronology were hallmarks of his technique, along with some of the most luxuriant, poetic prose I had ever read. And I also soon discovered that he did indeed have a story to tell—dozens of them, involving all kinds of people: old and young, male and female, white, Black, and red, good and evil, noble and ignoble, tragic and comic—in short, a variety and range of personalities that made his "little postage stamp of native soil" (*LIG* 255), which he named Yoknapatawpha for the first time in *As I Lay Dying*, representative of the entire human race.

As I Lay Dying, as Dan Young taught me years ago, is a good place to begin reading Faulkner. Although the narrative technique and the characterization are quite complex, the story line is actually quite simple and relatively easy to follow. The tone of the story is both tragic and comic, the characters funny and pathetic. The language is fresh, lively, startling, memorable. And the subjects treated are as huge as subjects can get: life and death, love and hate, success and failure, wealth and poverty, faith and doubt, sanity and madness, individual and family, family and community. Significant stuff.

So, let's join the Bundrens on their journey to Jefferson. You may be surprised to learn, as I did years ago, that your journey with Mr. Bill won't stop there.

VIEWPOINT IN *AS I LAY DYING*

The first thing that almost all readers notice about *As I Lay Dying* is that the narration of the story is tossed around like a football on a playground. First, Darl speaks, and then Cora, and then Darl again, and then Jewel. Eventually we learn, if we bother to keep count, that there are fifteen different narrators and fifty-nine separate chapters in the novel. Fortunately the story line being presented is a fairly simple one: about a rural Mississippi family, the Bundrens, who are taking the corpse of Addie, the mother, back to her hometown, Jefferson, to be buried with her family. So it's not the plot, which is actually quite simple, but the way Faulkner chooses to unravel the plot, that makes this a complicated novel. And why would anyone choose to tell a story in this fashion?

Like all truly original artists, Faulkner prized uniqueness, creativity, experimentation. He seldom tells a story the same way twice. He once criticized Hemingway because he felt that Hemingway had perfected a single style that he employed over and over again, without "splashing around to try to experiment" (*FIU* 206). Faulkner, by contrast, is one of the most experimental of all novelists, and *As I Lay Dying* is one of his finest experiments, a tour de force of technique.

The principal result of Faulkner's shifting the storytelling from one character to another is fairly easy to identify, and quite compelling. We know from our own experience that if two or more people observe the same event, they will see it, and later tell it, somewhat differently. Anyone who has ever served on a jury knows how a parade of witnesses, some friendly, some hostile, present varying and often contradictory versions of the same event. And the juror must decide what actually happened and who's telling the truth and who isn't. It's the same with this novel, with the reader playing the role of the juror. Is Cora right about which of the sons is Addie's favorite? What is Anse's real reason for wanting to go to Jefferson? Why is Jewel so angry and spiteful? What is Darl's problem? Answers to such questions depend on who's talking. Clearly, what Faulkner is conveying here is not absolute Truth (with a capital T) but a truth (little t) that depends in large measure on viewpoint.

Scholars have pointed out that Faulkner may have been influenced by the impressionist and cubist painters such as Monet and Cézanne in his depiction of a truth that is very subjective and almost constantly evolving. Faulkner viewed, and wrote home about, the works of these artists on his visit to Paris in 1925. Certainly one can easily see the similarity of *As I Lay Dying* to Monet's series of paintings of the same object—for example, haystacks or the cathedral of Rouen. In both these paintings and Faulkner's novel, truth is always, to a great degree, personal, relative, and ever changing.

AUTOBIOGRAPHICAL ELEMENTS IN *AS I LAY DYING*

Almost all writers incorporate their own personal experiences into their work, though it would be a huge mistake ever to argue for a direct correlation between an author and a character. The Hemingway hero is not Ernest Hemingway, though Hemingway's protagonists clearly have a great deal in common with their creator. Faulkner frequently noted that he used "experience, observation, and imagination" (*LIG* 248; *FIU* 78, 103) in creating his characters and plots; and though he always insisted that the imagination was the key component, he also acknowledged the personal element in his work.

It's highly doubtful that Faulkner (or any other Mississippian) ever saw a family transporting an unembalmed, decaying corpse on a weeklong trek through the north Mississippi countryside, shooing away the buzzards along the way. But there are elements in *As I Lay Dying* that are almost certainly drawn from Faulkner's personal experience. In fact, the characterization of Addie Bundren may be modeled in part on two individuals whom Faulkner knew very well: his mother and himself.

As Joseph Blotner and other Faulkner biographers have told us, Maud Falkner was an intelligent, well-educated, talented, and strong-willed woman who was married to a husband who was never much of a success in anything he attempted. To make matters worse, Murry Falkner was an alcoholic who frequently withdrew into long periods of apathy and self-pity. In her final illness, at age eighty-eight, Maud asked her son if she would have to see her husband in heaven. "No, not if you don't want to," Faulkner told her. "That's good," she replied; "I never did like him" (*FB* 679). This is quite similar to what Vernon Tull says of Addie: "Wherever she went, she has her reward in being free of Anse Bundren" (92).

But Faulkner didn't have to be reminded of his mother and father when writing about an unhappy marriage: he was living one himself. Faulkner and Estelle Oldham had been childhood sweethearts and planned to be married, but when Estelle's parents objected to the match, Estelle jilted Faulkner and married a wealthy lawyer, Cornell Franklin, instead. That marriage, however, lasted only a few years; and when Estelle and her two children returned to Oxford in 1927, she and Faulkner resumed their relationship. This time it was Faulkner who was reluctant, but the couple was married in 1929. From the very start, however, it became obvious that this would be a troubled marriage: Estelle, drinking heavily and still emotionally wounded from her previous marriage and divorce, attempted to drown herself in the Gulf of Mexico on the honeymoon. Faulkner's correspondence of this period clearly reflects his feeling that he had made a mistake in marrying Estelle, and his ambivalence toward her and the marriage seems reflected in the portrayals of Caddy Compson in *The Sound and the Fury* and Temple Drake in *Sanctuary*. And Addie Bundren's disillusionment and despair in *As I Lay Dying*, set down just five months after Faulkner's marriage to Estelle, may well be Faulkner's own.

Addie may also be speaking for Faulkner in other ways. Her views on religion and her doubts about an afterlife find parallels in Faulkner's life and comments. Moreover, he seems to share her skepticism about words and deeds. For example, he called *The Sound and the Fury*, almost universally acknowledged as one of the greatest novels ever written, his "magnificent failure" (*FIU* 61). None of his books, Faulkner said, ever matched the "dream of perfection" (*LIG* 238) he had in his head. Something was always lost when that dream was reduced to "cold words on the paper" (*FWP* 112).

While there may be significant parallels between Addie Bundren and William Faulkner, there is one monumental difference: she took her attitudes, thoughts, and emotions with her to the grave, while Faulkner transmuted his into some of the most remarkable prose ever written—including the dying thoughts of Addie Bundren.

THE JOURNEY MOTIF IN *AS I LAY DYING*

Many of the world's great stories center on a journey of some type—Ulysses's struggle to get back home after the Trojan War; the Hebrews' exodus and search for the Promised Land; Dante's tour of Hell, Purgatory, and Heaven in *The Divine Comedy*; the medieval knightly quest for the Holy Grail; Chaucer's pilgrims on the road to Canterbury; Tom Jones's trip to London; Ishmael's voyage aboard a whaleship in *Moby Dick*; Huck Finn's float trip down the Mississippi.

As Joseph Campbell, the famous comparative mythologist, has reminded us, epic journeys in myth and literature are typically long and quite dangerous, requiring great skill and courage and sacrifice, and thus are undertaken only by gods or godlike heroes. Usually, too, these stories dramatize not only the growth and maturation of the hero but also some benefit to the community that derives from the hero's struggle, sacrifice, and triumph.

Faulkner reprises this legendary motif, or pattern, in his description of the Bundrens' trip through the north Mississippi countryside on the way to Jefferson, and his use of this old, familiar story involves many of the traditional elements. Certainly there can be no question of the Bundrens' resolve and courage in the face of difficulty and danger; one can accurately apply to them the statement Faulkner wrote about another group of characters in another book: "They endured" (*PF* 721). And what the Bundrens endure are the age-old, elemental threats of flood and fire.

Nevertheless, Faulkner's depiction of the Bundrens' journey, when compared to the older stories, seems largely ironic. While the Bundrens exhibit an impressive degree of tenacity and even courage, and while their quest eventuates in a successful conclusion (at least in terms of its stated intention of burying Addie), their heroism and triumph are undercut and diminished in a significant number of ways. For example, Faulkner's travelers are neither gods nor larger-than-life heroes: they are poor hill farmers whose outlandish attitudes and behavior flout common morality and decency and lead to their social estrangement. The heart of the story—the conveyance of a decaying corpse from one end of the county to the other—strikes most readers as not merely unconventional and bizarre but even slightly insane. Additionally, whatever nobility may be found in keeping a promise, even a foolish one, to a dead wife and mother is mocked by the selfish motives of each of the travelers. Anse's remark is typical: "Now I can get them teeth" (111). And finally, there seems to be no redemptive communal effect to the trials of the Bundrens—no baptismal cleansing by water or spiritual purification by fire or epiphany of awareness or insight. On the contrary, the trip leads to the disintegration of the family (not at all ameliorated by the introduction of a new Mrs. Bundren) and a sharp division of neighbors.

Of course, this is only one possible reading of the novel. Like much else in this novel, as indeed in all of Faulkner's works, it's left to the reader to decide whether the Bundrens' journey is heroic or comic, noble or ludicrous, genuine or ironic. Then again, maybe it's something of all of these—and maybe Faulkner's intent is to mirror the mysterious and contradictory nature of all human motives and endeavors.

ADDIE'S DEATH AND BURIAL

It's highly doubtful that William Faulkner (or any other Mississippian) ever witnessed a funeral procession like the one described in *As I Lay Dying*. But there is a historical precedent for such an action.

In 1290 King Edward I of England commanded that the corpse of his beloved wife, Eleanor of Castile, be transported from Harby, in Nottinghamshire, back to London to be buried in Westminster Abbey. As a further tribute Edward later ordered that memorial crosses be erected at each of the twelve places where the funeral procession made overnight stops. Three of these original crosses still stand today; a fourth (and the best known), Charing Cross in London, was restored during the Victorian period.

Was Faulkner perhaps aware of this historical event, and did he wish for Addie's death, funeral procession, and burial to be compared with that of a royal queen? Whether intentional or not, several inferences can be drawn from noting the parallel.

One of the books that Faulkner, and other writers of his generation, greatly admired was James Joyce's *Ulysses*. In this famous novel Joyce parallels the legendary exploits of the hero of Homer's great epic the *Odyssey* with the ordinary, everyday experiences of Leopold Bloom, an advertising agent for a Dublin newspaper, in 1904. Critics debate whether Joyce's intent is to satirize the modern age, showing how far short it falls from a classical ideal of courage and chivalry, or to uplift the role of the ordinary citizen, showing that modern-day life and citizens can be just as dramatic and meaningful as those of the fabled past.

In Shakespeare's day, to cite a further example, heroes must be from the nobility; so the Bard's great tragedies and comedies focus on kings and princes, like Lear and Hamlet. In those plays the "somebodies" even speak an exalted, poetic language—blank verse—as opposed to the prose spoken by the "nobodies"—that is, the servant class. With the coming of democracy, however, literary heroes could now be drawn from the middle and lower classes. Thus, in American literature we have such heroes as a frontiersman in Cooper's Leatherstocking Saga, or a semiliterate young boy in Twain's *Adventures of Huckleberry Finn*, or an immigrant farm girl like Willa Cather's Antonia, or a young African American seeking equality in Ralph Ellison's *Invisible Man*.

As is the case with Joyce and Bloom, one cannot quite be sure what Faulkner's personal attitude toward the Bundrens may be. But in general, throughout his novels and stories, Faulkner seems to view the high and the mighty, the rich and the powerful, with a great degree of skepticism and sometimes even loathing. Conversely, he typically exhibits a good deal of sympathy with the less advantaged: the enslaved, sharecroppers, the poor, the oppressed, and simple, ordinary folks. Addie Bundren is no aristocrat and certainly no queen, but Faulkner clearly feels great compassion for her; and one shouldn't be surprised that he affords her the same respect and treatment once given to a legendary British queen.

AS I LAY DYING AND STREAM OF CONSCIOUSNESS

As I Lay Dying is an outstanding example of what is called stream-of-consciousness narration. The term is borrowed from psychology and is used to identify any literary narrative that focuses upon the unspoken thoughts of a character. While there are some technical distinctions that need not concern us here, the term is often used interchangeably with another literary device, the "interior monologue." In both forms the focus is upon the random, disordered, fragmented, and momentary flow of thought (hence, "stream") before it has become conscious speech. Novelists who have become noted for their extensive use of stream of consciousness include Marcel Proust, James Joyce, Virginia Woolf, Dorothy Richardson, and Faulkner.

Authors are drawn to stream of consciousness as an excellent means of dramatizing the subjective, private, and often unconscious thoughts and motives of their characters. In such narratives the interior workings of a character's mind are given precedence over external actions and events. Indeed, many stream-of-consciousness narratives, like Joyce's *Finnegans Wake*, seek to present pure consciousness largely divorced from any significant external action or plot. But it should be noted that Faulkner is something of an exception in this regard, since even in his most extended stream-of-consciousness narrations, there is always a substantial action being referenced. In fact, one way to view Faulkner's place in the history of the novel is to recognize how effectively he combines the traditional emphasis upon action or plot with the modern concern for mental processes and the psychological motives for human behavior. A typical Faulkner novel is concerned with both *what* happens and *why* it happens.

Consider how this definition applies to *As I Lay Dying*. Certainly there is an unfolding external action that the reader follows with interest and suspense. Addie Bundren is dying, and her husband, Anse, has promised her that he will bury her in town. Their oldest son, Cash, is making her a coffin, and the entire family is preparing to transport the body by mule-drawn wagon to town. Much of the novel deals with this trip and the obstacles the Bundrens face along the way, and a considerable part of the reader's interest is to find out what the next obstacle might be and whether they will ever arrive at their destination.

But this simple surface action is not at all what Faulkner's great novel is really about. The real journey a reader takes in this book is not to Jefferson but deep inside the complex, conflicted, and often nightmarish thoughts of the characters. Darl's brooding questions about identity and reality, Jewel's pent-up anger and desire for revenge, Cash's obsession with neatness and order, Dewey Dell's anxiety over her personal circumstance, Vardaman's innocent confusion over death and grief, Anse's inner struggle between inertia and honor, Addie's frustrations, regrets, and secrets—these are the dark, hidden places explored and exposed by Faulkner's marvelous stream-of-consciousness prose. And while to neighbors like Tull and Samson the Bundrens may appear to be a devoted family unified by a common, if quite absurd and even slightly crazy, cause, the reader knows the other, secret Bundrens: selfish, divided, frightened, dysfunctional, lonely, and, worst of all, unloving and unloved.

AS I LAY DYING AND THE PROBLEM OF LANGUAGE

One of the dominant themes of *As I Lay Dying* is the difficulty of human communication, caused not only by the problem of finding the right word but also by the discrepancy between words and deeds. Addie Bundren expresses this theme most distinctly when she says that "words are no good; that words don't ever fit even what they are trying to say at" (171). We quickly discover that Addie is not the only character in the novel who feels this way. Others—particularly Vardaman, Darl, Cash, and Dewey Dell—also have difficulty in communicating their innermost thoughts and relating words to deeds.

It might seem surprising that any writer, whose medium of expression is words, and particularly a writer like Faulkner, one possessed with such an immense vocabulary, would have characters voice such skepticism about the adequacy of language. But it is not so surprising when we recognize that this is an attitude shared by many of the writers of Faulkner's generation—Ernest Hemingway, E. E. Cummings, John Dos Passos, and Willa Cather, to name only a few. We must recall that this was the so-called Lost Generation that felt betrayed by the abstractions and inflated rhetoric of the nineteenth century—a century whose ideas and values had crumbled in the wake of the colossal tragedy of World War I. To Hemingway's Frederic Henry of *A Farewell to Arms*, words like *sacred*, *glorious*, and *sacrifice* have become, in the context of the folly of the war, meaningless and obscene. It's a theme that would reverberate throughout the literature of the twentieth century.

This problem of communication, of using language to create accurate representations of reality and meaningful, fulfilling relationships, is everywhere present in *As I Lay Dying*. We see it in the multiple and fragmented viewpoints, each character imprisoned in his or her own little box of stream-of-consciousness thought, side by side on the pages of the book, sometimes overlapping in content but never quite merging into an overall unity. We see it in the disparity of styles within these individual sections, which are sometimes presented in the colloquial folk language appropriate for the characters but at other times in words and concepts that seem quite beyond these characters' situation and circumstances. We see it in the characterization of Darl, who disdains speech yet often knows things about other characters that have never been expressed in words. We see it perhaps best of all in Vardaman, who surely has the highest intellect and largest vocabulary of any schoolboy in Mississippi yet finds that all that thought and language ultimately fail him, leaving him only with the metaphoric riddle "My mother is a fish" (84).

Regarding the issue of language and its relationship to reality and truth, this sentence, perhaps the most enigmatic statement in American literature, may well represent the very essence of the novel. As we have known since Plato, a word is not the thing; it is only a symbol or an approximation of the thing (hence, the need for metaphors); and ultimate meanings about life and reality—or ourselves and other human beings—are extremely difficult to reduce to words and thus always remain something of a mystery.

ANSE BUNDREN

Anse Bundren is one of the most fascinating characters in American literature. Poor, lazy, shiftless, self-centered, and basically irresponsible, he is, in many respects, a caricature of the ignorant country bumpkin, the legendary hillbilly/redneck. Even his physical description fits the stereotype: tall, hump-backed, toothless, wearing patched overalls and a hangdog expression, unshaven, lower lip filled with snuff. But this is only the surface appearance, a first impression. Faulkner, as he typically does with most of his characters, probes far beneath the surface, revealing a character of immense complexity and paradox, one who if not heroic certainly is not villainous, one who if not deserving of the reader's sympathy may at least be afforded an ounce of pity.

The past is always crucial in the life of any Faulkner character, and it's important to recognize that Anse was not always the person he is in the present tense of the story. Though he is now afraid of work, believing that he will die if he sweats, he has not always been averse to hard labor: "[His] feet are badly splayed, his toes cramped and bent and warped, with no toenail at all on his little toes, from working so hard in the wet in homemade shoes when he was a boy" (11). This is where many people must begin: poor but with a strong work ethic. Eventually, Anse was industrious and successful enough to own his own farm—no small feat for a Mississippi hill farmer in the 1920s. And his wooing and winning of Addie was no less an achievement. A townswoman, a schoolteacher (and thus very likely the best-educated person in Anse's part of Yoknapatawpha County), Addie represents quite a catch for a young farmer. And while Anse's courtship of Addie is anything but romantic, it is sincere, and persistent, and successful.

But all of that was before the rich storekeepers in town (who cheat the country folk) and the politicians (who build the roads) and the lawyers and sheriffs (who would take Darl away, leaving Anse short-handed in the fields) and the bad weather and hard times have made it so very tough for hardworking farmers. It may be that Anse hasn't become lazy so much as he just got tired, beaten down and worn out by his long, losing struggle with what Faulkner calls in another book the "implacable earth" (*CS* 705).

And, say what one will about the unconventional actions he takes to prove his point, he does have a sense of honor. He made a promise to Addie, and come (literally) hellfire and high water, he intends to keep it. Yes, it's true that the promise gets all mixed up with his desire for some false teeth (the new wife seems to be a bonus, not premeditated), but it's the promise and not the teeth that impels the journey to Jefferson. He didn't lose his teeth just last week.

Once, in response to a question about *As I Lay Dying*, Faulkner commented that all of the characters in the book were victims of their environment, "of land in which there wasn't much relief from the arduous hard work for very little of the time, [where] there was nothing to please the spirit—no music, no pictures, most of them couldn't read and when they could, the books were not available, and so they took what relief they could" (*FIU* 114). In such circumstances, Faulkner said, people just do the best they can do.

By the time we meet him, Anse Bundren has been robbed of his youth, his health, his material well-being, his desire, and, now, his wife. Perhaps the trip to Jefferson is one last attempt to regain his manhood and dignity. Perhaps he's just doing the best he can do.

ADDIE BUNDREN

Addie Bundren is one of the great tragic heroines in all of literature. A number of critics have associated her story with that of Hester Prynne in Hawthorne's *The Scarlet Letter*. But there are other famous heroines with whom she can be equally compared—Flaubert's Emma Bovary, for example, or Tolstoy's Anna Karenina, or Lawrence's Lady Chatterley. All of these women are strong characters who feel trapped in unfortunate personal and social circumstances and long for some means of escape.

Faulkner presents Addie as a fiercely independent, strong-willed woman who is driven to bitterness and despair by the discrepancy between the reality of her situation and the expectancy of her dreams. In actuality she is an idealist who longs for, but never finds, fulfillment of her hopes and aspirations. Hers is the agony of all romantics who feel betrayed by life.

Her father told her it would be this way. "The reason for living," he said, "was to get ready to stay dead a long time" (169). But Addie resists this thinking for as long as she can. Unlike Cora and other religionists, she has no faith in an afterlife, and this disbelief adds to her urgency to find meaning and happiness on this side of the grave. She searches for what existentialists call "authentic existence," stripped of all props and illusions. She whips her students, attempting through such violence to force herself into their "secret and selfish" lives (170). Then she marries Anse, hoping that marriage and motherhood might supply relief from her angst. Those failing, she takes Whitfield for a lover, but that relationship too cools and ends unhappily. Finally she is left only with her distrust of all relationships and ideals—and, of course, her precious Jewel, a symbolic reminder, like his horse, of the wild and free and energetic life that she desperately longed for but never found.

Her disillusionment is best expressed in her skepticism about language: "how words go straight up in a thin line, quick and harmless, and how terribly doing goes along the earth, clinging to it, so that after a while the two lines are too far apart for the same person to straddle from one to the other; and that sin and love and fear are just sounds that people who never sinned nor loved nor feared have for what they never had and cannot have until they forget the words" (173–74). Addie's despair is worse, she says, in early spring, when she realizes, with the narrator of T. S. Eliot's *The Waste Land*, that "April is the cruelest month," since it ironically brings a false promise of life and vitality to the land of the dead.

Addie may be ready to die, but Faulkner is unwilling to let her do so. He compounds the irony of her situation by allowing her, like the characters in Edgar Lee Masters's *Spoon River Anthology*, to speak, as it were, from the grave. Addie may not believe in a spiritual life after death, but clearly she continues to have tremendous power and influence over her family and neighbors even after her death. Though she is given only one monologue, she is the center of the story, after her death as much as before. Even when she is in her coffin, her children still vie for her attention and favor; neighbors still recollect and gossip about her; and, most significantly, almost miraculously, her lethargic husband gets off his haunches and begins to move, albeit slowly and indecisively, with some degree of ambition and purpose. It is as though something of the passion and vitality and will of Addie has escaped the coffin (as Vardaman had hoped) to infuse and empower all who have known her. It is a distinctly ironic and secular form of resurrection, but a resurrection nonetheless. And through it Faulkner dramatizes the indisputable force and appeal of this truly remarkable character.

JEWEL VERSUS DARL

Early in the novel the reader becomes aware that there exists a strong sibling rivalry among all the Bundren children, but this conflict is most intense in the relationship between Jewel and Darl. Jewel fantasizes about being alone with his mother, "just . . . me and her on a high hill and me rolling the rocks down the hill at their faces" (15). Darl knows that Jewel is Addie's favorite, and he further knows, somehow, that Jewel is not Anse's son. This knowledge leads Darl to taunt Jewel mercilessly. "Jewel, do you know that Addie Bundren is going to die?" "Who was your father, Jewel?" (40, 212).

Though we are not aware of it on a first reading, this rivalry between the brothers for the affection of the mother is symbolized in the opening chapter of the novel, when we first meet Darl and Jewel. They are coming from the field, and Darl is walking ahead of Jewel. But when they come to the cotton-house, Jewel takes a shortcut by stepping through the windows and moves ahead of Darl on the path. One of the first things we learn in graduate school is that any object that is longer than it is wide is a phallic symbol, and any object that contains openings is a female symbol. So the windows here may be associated with the female principle, in this case, Addie. Jewel is embraced by his mother, Darl is not: so Darl must walk around the cottonhouse. And Jewel has now moved ahead of his brother on the path just as he has in the favor of their mother. The alienation that Darl feels from being displaced in Addie's affection is further symbolized in the scene in which Darl, drifting off to sleep in a stranger's room, reflects, "I don't know what I am. I don't know if I am or not," and concludes: "How often have I lain beneath rain on a strange roof, thinking of home" (80, 81).

But Darl has no home and, he feels, no mother. "I cannot love my mother," he says, "because I have no mother" (95). And for this reason he hates and avenges himself upon his brother Jewel.

AS I LAY DYING: WHAT DRIVES DARL MAD?

Almost any character in this book would provide an interesting case study for a psychoanalyst. But Darl presents a special case, since at the end of the book he is presumed insane and committed to the asylum. What is it that drives Darl mad, if indeed he is actually so?

The most intelligent and thoughtful, even philosophical, of the Bundrens, and certainly the most widely traveled (he has been to France during World War I), he is also possessed of a clairvoyance (or maybe it's just a heightened imagination and intuition) that enables him to see and know things that appear to be beyond the normal powers of perception. He knows without being told, for example, that Jewel is not Anse's son and that Dewey Dell is pregnant. And he knows that, of all the Bundrens, he is the most alienated, the most troubled, the most lost.

Everyone, Bundren or not, recognizes that Darl is different, weird, even abnormal. Dewey Dell, who represents the body, physicality, fears his preternatural powers, noting that he knows and says things "without the words" and sits at the table "with his eyes gone further than the food and the lamp" (27). Cash says of him at the end of the novel, "This world is not his world; this life his life" (261), confirming at that point what the reader has already suspected for quite some time. According to Vernon Tull, Darl's problem is that "he just thinks by himself too much" (71); and as Tull goes on to say, too much thinking divorced from action is not healthy.

And what is it that Darl thinks about in these nineteen interior monologues that are among the most brilliant passages that Faulkner ever wrote? The most obvious answer to the question is the obsessive sibling rivalry that leads him to taunt Jewel with reminders of his paternity and the death of his mother. But Darl's struggle with identity and meaning seems to involve much more than a simple, if extreme, case of sibling rivalry. A careful reading of the text suggests that a deeper source of his problem might be a conflicted sexuality. Though he is very curious about Jewel's suspected all-night trysts with a mysterious lover, and though he is acutely conscious of Dewey Dell's "leg coming long from beneath her tightening dress" (104), as well as her "mammalian ludicrosities" (164), and though he brings home from France a spyglass in which he could see "a woman and a pig with two backs and no face" (254), the only sex act he confesses in the novel is his childhood practice of "[lying] with my shirt-tail up, . . . feeling myself without touching myself, feeling the cool silence blowing upon my parts" (11). His neighbors, especially Cora and Eula Tull, think he should get married, but, although he is in his late twenties or early thirties, he gives no indication of desiring to do so.

And what is the source of Darl's apparent aversion to sexuality? Could it be the adulterous behavior of his mother and her subsequent rejection of him in favor of Jewel? If so, then the characterization of Darl begs comparison with that of Shakespeare's Hamlet, another character who thinks too much and whose mother's act of infidelity leads to the son's rejection of both women and sexuality. "I have no mother," Darl says (95); that woman is now just "Addie Bundren." So, is it really Jewel whom Darl hates, or is Jewel just a scapegoat on which Darl heaps his hatred of his mother? And is Darl's attempted burning of Addie's corpse an act of mercy intended to stop an insane journey or an act of vengeance in which he avenges himself upon the mother who has abandoned him by seeking to deny her wish to be buried in Jefferson? Typically,

Faulkner leaves such questions to the reader. And, it must be added, he offers yet another possibility: as Cash points out, maybe Darl isn't mad after all. "Sometimes," Cash says, "I think it aint none of us pure crazy and aint none of us pure sane until the balance of us talks him that-a-way" (233).

CASH BUNDREN: UNLIKELY HERO

As I Lay Dying is, according to most readers, a book without a hero, at least in the traditional sense of the term; but the character who probably comes closest to that role is Cash.

Silent as a narrator for the first third of the novel, Cash speaks through his work. "Chuck. Chuck. Chuck," goes his adze as he builds the coffin, day and night, in sunshine or rain; and Darl says of him, "A good carpenter, Cash is. . . . Addie Bundren could not want a better one, a better box to lie in" (4–5). When he does first speak in his own voice, Cash explains, in a thirteen-point outline, why he made the casket on the bevel: it is a voice not only of reason and pragmatism but also of adjustment and accommodation, of doing the best one can with the tools available. And if you have a barn to build and a funeral to attend, take your tools with you to the funeral so you won't have to make a second trip.

Cash knows there are dreamers and idealists who want more from life than life can deliver: "It aint always the safe things in this world that a fellow . . . ," he says of Jewel's night prowling (132); but he leaves the sentence unfinished, perhaps not wanting his mind to go where his life has no way to follow. It's best to accept one's limitations, don't let them defeat you, in fact, turn them to your advantage and benefit. If you don't have the lumber to build a courthouse, Cash says, then build a chicken coop, because "it's better to build a tight chicken coop than a shoddy court-house." Whatever you build, "drive the nails down and trim the edges well" (234).

(A parenthetical note: Faulkner frequently compared the work of the writer to that of a carpenter. For example, he said of one of his early books: "That was the chips, the badly sawn planks that the carpenter produces while he's learning to be a first-rate carpenter" [*FIU* 257]. Such statements lead some critics to view Cash as one of Faulkner's several portrayals of the artist. This parallel adds one more reason for possibly viewing Cash's role in the novel as heroic.)

All of the Bundrens suffer on the way to Jefferson, but none of the others undergoes the physical pain that Cash endures. Only recently recovered from a broken leg, he breaks the same leg again in the river fording. And then, when the pain from riding in a bumpy wagon becomes increasingly severe, the family places the leg in a concrete cast. Through it all, as his leg and foot turn black and then red from bleeding when the concrete is hammered off, Cash never complains. "It feels fine," he says (208). In town Darl asks Cash if he wants to go see Dr. Peabody, but Cash refuses until after Addie is buried.

Cash's tremendous capacity to endure, even deny, great physical pain seems symbolic of his handling of psychological pain as well. The oldest son, he surely must have experienced something of the same rivalry and jealousy for the love of the mother that we see in Darl and Jewel (his building the casket seems one last effort to purchase her love), yet he is not as troubled and mentally unbalanced by the situation as his brothers. And unlike Jewel, who says to those who subdue Darl at the end, "Kill him. Kill the son of a bitch" (238), Cash expresses sincere grief and regret that his brother is being carried to Whitfield. He may be the one Bundren capable of love.

We should not overlook the fact that, in this novel of multiple voices, Cash is given the last word—and a future vision of the Bundrens: back home, sitting in the house on a winter evening, listening to another mail order record on the gramophone. For most readers this seems to be so little for the Bundrens to have to look forward to, but for Cash, apparently, it is enough.

HOW OLD ARE THE BUNDRENS?

Many readers of this novel ask, How old are the Bundrens? It's a good question. And searching for its answer reveals something of both the challenge and the joy of reading a Faulkner novel.

Here are the most relevant textual details that help us in arriving at an answer.

1. Vernon Tull tells us that Addie kept Anse "at work" (in the loosest possible sense of the phrase, I presume) for "thirty-odd years" (33).
2. Addie lists the birth order of the children as Cash, Darl, Jewel, Dewey Dell, and Vardaman (171–76).
3. Darl explains that Jewel was fifteen years old when he acquired his horse (128).
4. Cash notes that he and Darl were "born close together" and "nigh ten years before Jewel and Dewey Dell and Vardaman begun to come along" (234).
5. Darl informs us that he was in France during World War I (254).
6. Dewey Dell tells Moseley she is "seventeen" (200), and Anse later confirms the fact (256).

If we date the present tense of the action in the year of the composition of the novel (1929) and assume that Darl entered military service in, say, 1918 (the same year that Faulkner did) at the age of eighteen, then Darl was born around 1900 and would now be twenty-nine years old.

Since the births of Cash and Darl occurred close together, probably within a year or two of each other, then Cash would be about thirty years old.

Both of these ages would be consistent with Tull's statement that Anse and Addie had been married for "thirty-odd years." Given that bit of information and the calculated ages of the two oldest boys, we can place the marriage somewhere around 1898 or 1899. In all likelihood Cash and Darl were born very early in the marriage, another argument in support of the approximate ages listed above.

If Cash's "nigh ten years" is interpreted as more than nine but not quite ten, then Jewel would be about twenty years old. That would mean that he has been unable to tame his wild horse in five years; but, as we know from other Faulkner stories, particularly "Spotted Horses," those Snopes ponies were incorrigible.

Dewey Dell, the only character whose precise age is stated in the novel, is seventeen.

Judging from his physical size and his immature behavior and thought, Vardaman, the youngest child, appears to be no more than seven or eight years old. However, it should be noted that some critics surmise that Vardaman may be mentally challenged: if such is the case, then he might be an undersized ten- to twelve-year-old (there is no indication in the novel that he has reached puberty).

How old are Addie and Anse? Addie could have taught school in those days on a temporary certificate as early as her late teens; and given her hatred of the children, she probably didn't stick with teaching for more than a year or two. Thus, she could have been as young as twenty when she married Anse, although, since her union with Anse is presented somewhat as a desperate, last chance at marriage, it is possible that she was in her mid-twenties. According to this last surmise, she would be in her mid-fifties when she dies. Note, however, that the older we make Addie, the older Vardaman must be. If Addie is fifty-five when she dies and Vardaman is twelve, then Addie would have been forty-three when Vardaman was born, a rather advanced age for childbearing. If Vardaman is eight, then Addie is probably no more than fifty. Since Anse was already established as a farm owner when he meets Addie, he was probably no younger than his mid to late twenties when they married. That would make his present age around fifty-five to sixty.

The process of informed guesswork that has led to the above conclusions says a great deal about how we must read Faulkner and what the final results of that reading will and will not be. First of all, note that there is far more information provided on this matter than one might be aware of on a first reading. Note, too, that this information is scattered throughout the text and thus comes to the reader gradually and incrementally (and perhaps only after multiple readings and diligent searching). Finally, note that any conclusions based on the information provided must remain, to a highly significant degree, tentative, approximate, and speculative. This is true of Faulkner's presentation of specific facts but even truer of such larger matters as character motivation, symbolism, and theme. Faulkner supplies the reader with clues, large and small, but he leaves it to the reader to locate, assemble, and interpret them. Little wonder that Faulkner has been called a writer of detective fiction—with his reader playing the role of Auguste Dupin or Sherlock Holmes.

There is another point I would like to make about the suspenseful patterns of Faulkner's novels and stories: they provide a strong argument in support of collaborative reading. Few, if any, individuals can read a complex author like Faulkner on our own: we need to draw upon the intelligence and critical abilities and insights of others. Certainly reading can be, as it always has been and will be for many people, a private, individual activity; but it can produce additional, and surprisingly pleasant, rewards when conducted in group and communal settings—like book clubs and Faulkner conferences and the Oprah Book Club website. That's one of the best lessons that writers like Faulkner teach us.

AS I LAY DYING AND HUMOR

"Dark comedy" is the label applied to Shakespearean plays that are considered too tragic to be comedies yet too comic to be tragedies. It's a term that may also be used to describe Faulkner's *As I Lay Dying*, a novel that is essentially tragic but at the same time is also one of the most humorous books Faulkner ever wrote.

A list of the funniest lines in this novel would certainly include the following:

1. Jewel: "because if there is a God what the hell is He for" (15).
2. Anse: "God's will be done. Now I can get them teeth" (52).
3. Tull: "I think that if nothing but being married will help a man, he's durn nigh hopeless" (71).

4. Vardaman: "My mother is a fish" (84).
5. Cash, explaining how far he fell off the church: "Twenty-eight foot, four and a half inches, about" (90).
6. Darl, on Jewel's suspected lover: "She's sure a stayer. I used to admire her, but I downright respect her now" (133).
7. Addie, on Cora's self-righteous arrogance: "Like Cora, who could never even cook" (174).
8. Armstid: "A man aint so different from a horse or a mule, come long come short, except a mule or a horse has got a little more sense" (185).
9. MacGowan, to his fellow clerk when Dewey Dell enters the store: "I'm going into conference" (243).

Consider also the following descriptions:

1. Of Jewel, exhausted from working around the clock, falling asleep while milking the cow, "his hands up to his wrists in the milk and his head against the cow's flank" (129); and at the table, "going to sleep in his plate, with a piece of bread halfway to his mouth and his jaws still chewing" (130).
2. Of Anse, who "looks like a figure carved clumsily from tough wood by a drunken caricaturist" (163).
3. Of Cash, after he has fainted from the pain of his broken leg: "with big balls of sweat standing on his face like they had started to roll down and then stopped to wait for him" (186).
4. Of the young Mack Gillespie: "his eyes and mouth three round holes in his face on which the freckles look like English peas on a plate" (220).
5. Of the new Mrs. Bundren: "a kind of duck-shaped woman . . . , with them kind of hard-looking pop eyes like she was daring ere a man to say nothing" (260).

Even quite a few of the major plot details strike a reader as comic, though in a macabre sort of way: a decaying corpse kept above ground for nine days before burial; a child boring holes in the casket so his mother can breathe; setting a broken leg in cement and then, when that has clearly done more harm than good, breaking the cement apart with a hammer and a flat iron; the seduction of a naïve, ignorant country girl by a town knave; a grieving husband using his wife's funeral as the occasion to get himself some new teeth and a new wife.

Many readers find in *As I Lay Dying*—its absurd actions, its grotesque characters and imagery, its disjointed style—the influence of surrealist painters. But there is another influence that is equally as important: the yarn-spinning tradition of the Old Southwest. Begun by frontier humorists such as Augustus B. Longstreet, made famous by Mark Twain, and perpetuated by southern writers as different as Erskine Caldwell, Eudora Welty, Flannery O'Connor, and Faulkner, these comic tall tales feature unsophisticated and often grotesque frontier or hillbilly characters who are involved in exaggerated, outlandish, and often outrageous behavior.

Faulkner clearly belongs in the southwestern yarn-spinning tradition, but, like O'Connor's, his humor is typically more bleak and pessimistic than his predecessors'. *As I Lay Dying* is an extremely funny book, but its humor often serves cruelty, hypocrisy, stupidity, misogyny, class prejudice, even misanthropy. In this novel laughter is never very far from tears—and in the case of Darl, who laughs more than anyone at the end, the laughter teeters on insanity.

THE HORSE AND THE FISH

Among the most frequently asked questions by readers of this novel are: Why does Jewel call his mother a horse, and Why does Vardaman call her a fish? To attempt to answer those questions, we must begin with a consideration of what's involved in any act of literary interpretation.

There are three fundamental questions at issue here: What do these statements/symbols mean to the characters who speak or hear them? What do they mean to the readers who read them? And what did they mean—if such can be ascertained—to the author who wrote them? All of these are valid questions; however, although they are intertwined and interrelated, they will not yield the same answers. But then, a literary text is not an algebraic equation for which everyone is expected to arrive at the same, correct answer. Literature (like issues in politics and economics and religion and, indeed, life itself) is more ambiguous and multifaceted than that.

So, in that context, let's begin. I'll deal first with what I take to be the easier question of the two: why is Jewel's mother said to be a horse?

On one level, the horse represents a displacement of Addie in Jewel's life. At the same time, the horse, associated as it is throughout the text with energy, passion, and wildness, symbolizes the affair that Addie has had with Whitfield. Jewel is like the horse, which is like Addie. But these are conclusions that I draw as a reader: what more might the statement mean to Darl?

Darl's labeling his mother "a horse" seems clearly an insult, in fact, very nearly an obscenity. Significantly, he first utters the statement immediately after he says, "I have no mother" (95). Like Hamlet, Darl has come to view his mother as a vile and loathsome adulteress who has upset the natural order of things—if not (as in Hamlet's view) the order of the universe, at least the order of this family. Jewel is the embodiment of his mother's misdeed. This, I take it, is why Darl says in another place, "*Are* is too many for one woman to foal" (101). While this statement foreshadows the split into *he* and *I* that Darl will suffer by the end of the book, it also alludes to the unwanted intrusion of Jewel into the Bundren circle, an intrusion that has come between Darl and his mother. Before Jewel was born, Darl was *is*; but now that Jewel is *are* (the mistaken grammar symbolizes the error that Addie has committed), Darl is now *was*. Note also Darl's use of the word "foal" in the passage. In Darl's eyes Addie Bundren has become less than human—animalistic; worse than immoral—amoral. Hamlet compares his mother to "a beast that wants [that is, lacks] discourse of reason." To Faulkner's Hamlet, the beast is a horse. But both Hamlet and Darl agree on the meaning of the symbol: "Frailty, thy name is woman."

Now to the fish. To Vardaman's confused and grieving (and, some readers think, mentally challenged) mind, his mother has been displaced into the fish he has caught. The fish was once alive, and now it is dead, just like his mother. Vardaman, in all the ways he knows how, vehemently and violently protests this tragedy, this immense loss, this cosmic injustice. He clings to the fish, dragging it about the house and yard. Associating his mother's lying in the coffin with the claustrophobic fear he once experienced when he was locked inside a windowless corn crib (65), he bores holes in the coffin and opens the windows so Addie can breathe (73). He beats and stampedes Peabody's horses because he thinks that somehow the doctor is involved in his mother's death (54). And later, he imagines that Addie, as a fish, escapes the coffin and swims away in the river (151).

But still, why a fish—instead of, say, some farm animal such as a horse or cow or dog or cat? A number of critics point out that the fish may be intended as a Christian symbol. In the early days of Christianity, because the letters of the Greek word for "fish," *ichthys*, form an acrostic that can be read as *Iesous Christos theou huios soter* ("Jesus Christ, Son of God, Savior"), persecuted and closet Christians used a picture of a fish as a coded message to identify themselves to each other. The word takes on additional Christian associations because the New Testament gospels contain many stories and metaphors of fish and fishermen. If one accepts the parallel between Vardaman's fish and Christ, then the reference to the eating of the fish, "Cooked and et. Cooked and et" (57), becomes an allusion to the Last Supper and the Christian church's celebration of the mass/communion.

Vardaman's fish is not the only Christian allusion in *As I Lay Dying*. The log that crashes into the wagon during the river crossing "*surged up out of the water and stood for an instant upright upon that surging and heaving desolation like Christ*" (148). In addition, Cora reports that Addie spoke of Jewel as her savior (thus, a Christ figure): "He is my cross and he will be my salvation. He will save me from the water and from the fire. Even though I have laid down my life, he will save me" (168). Life, death, and resurrection—clearly *As I Lay Dying* deals with these matters, though readers disagree about the nature of the resurrection that is presented here (and in other Faulkner works).

It's impossible to say, of course, what Faulkner intended, either consciously or subconsciously, with all of this horse and fish business. To my knowledge he never explained the meaning of the two metaphoric statements—and even if he had, we should be cautioned to beware of the "intentional fallacy" (that is, the mistaken notion that the only legitimate meaning a literary work can have is the one intended by its author). But we do know certain things. For example, Faulkner loved horses, and, as Terrell Tebbetts explains in his excellent article on the topic in *A William Faulkner Encyclopedia*, all of the many horses in Faulkner's fiction are associated with power, virility, and masculinity. I would add that Faulkner was undoubtedly familiar with the classical tradition that associated the horse with art and immortality (the story of Bellerophon and Pegasus, for example, which Faulkner seems to allude to in his short story "Carcassonne"). In this regard the horse represents qualities similar to those represented by the fish in the Christian tradition: indeed, many Christian thinkers and artists from the Middle Ages onward have associated Pegasus with Christ.

Regarding Faulkner's use of Christian elements in his stories, we are on surer ground. Of that Faulkner said: "The Christian legend is part of any Christian's background, especially the background of a country boy, a Southern country boy. . . . I grew up with that. I assimilated that, took that in without even knowing it" (*FIU* 86). Given the preponderance of Christian and biblical allusions scattered throughout Faulkner's works, it would be quite startling not to find some in *As I Lay Dying*.

I would emphasize, however, that the presence of Christian allusions in *As I Lay Dying* does not necessarily make the novel a Christian novel, any more than Faulkner's many allusions to mythological horses make him a Greek. In fact, I would argue that all mythic references in this novel are highly ironic. Jewel is a Christ figure of sorts in the book, but an extremely human and fallible one—one who may be able to rescue a casket from a burning barn but not one who can save anyone's agonizing soul, including his own; and the only resurrection and immortality that Addie Bundren achieves (or so it seems to me) are natural ones, not supernatural (I view her monologue as a flashback to her deathbed, not as a voice speaking from beyond the grave). Sadly, the heroic world of greatness and significance represented by the mythological horse and fish seems to be a world impossibly beyond the Bundrens' scope and compass—an ideal to be dreamed of and yearned for, but never attained.

AS I LAY DYING: IS IT HOPEFUL OR PESSIMISTIC?

Readers who have read Faulkner find it difficult to square his tragic and, on the surface at least, pessimistic works—especially those of his early to middle career like *As I Lay Dying*—with the optimistic remarks of the Nobel Prize speech. "I decline to accept the end of man," Faulkner said. "I believe that man will not merely endure: he will prevail" (*ESPL* 120). The statement is often taken as a supreme profession of hope and optimism. It's a message that resonates with great force in American society, where winning is our national creed.

Some argue that the speech is mere rhetoric (the kind that Addie Bundren would deplore), a public posturing that has little relevance to the great fiction. Others accept the sentiments of the speech as genuine and sincere. The truth may lie somewhere in between, as *I Lay Dying* seems to demonstrate.

There can be no question that the Bundrens (whose name is suggestive of "burdens") endure a natural catastrophe, public scorn, and violent conflict within their own family to succeed in their endeavor to return Addie home to Jefferson for burial. And, at least in a legalistic sense, the family unit is restored at the end with the acquisition of a new wife and mother.

But the Bundrens' victory is considerably compromised by the tragic consequences of their trip. Anse may have a new wife and a set of false teeth, but the rest of the family seems to have lost more than a mother: Darl is declared insane and is forcibly delivered to the asylum in Jackson; Dewey Dell has failed to secure her abortion and, in the attempt, has been sexually victimized once more; Cash has been crippled, possibly for life; Jewel has lost his horse; and Vardaman has failed to even see, much less acquire, the toy train that he covets. These may have endured, but it can hardly be said that they have prevailed.

Or maybe they have, in Faulkner's sense of the word. Faulkner is essentially a tragic writer, and the Nobel Prize speech may not be as optimistic a statement as it is generally taken to be. For one thing, the speech is more about the role of art than it is a commentary on the human condition, and for Faulkner the artist, art is always superior to actuality. Secondly, his statement about prevailing is in response to a specific question he raises: will human-kind destroy itself with the atomic bomb? No, Faulkner says, humans will not destroy themselves; they will go on and on and on. But the downside to that future, as he makes clear in all of his books and numerous interview statements, is that human nature and behavior will not likely change for the better. Human history will continue, but it will be characterized by the same old struggles between good and evil that have marked the past. Human beings can be brave and tenacious and kind and idealistic and good, but we are also selfish and hateful and greedy and lustful and evil. Just like the Bundrens.

Teaching *Intruder in the Dust* through Its Political and Historical Context

Intruder in the Dust not only is one of Faulkner's most enjoyable and accessible texts but also provides one of the few instances in which Faulkner's fiction comments directly upon a contemporary political situation. This latter point is not insignificant, since many of today's students know very little about the history of racial segregation in the South and the degree to which that tradition became a divisive issue in the 1948 presidential campaign. Examining the political and historical context of *Intruder in the Dust* enables students to reflect on the manner in which a great modern writer blends fiction and fact to create a work of literature that, in keeping with the classical definition of art, both "delights" and "instructs."

I begin the study of *Intruder in the Dust* by leading a class discussion based on a close reading of chapters 1 and 2, which I believe represent one of the most discerning treatments of race in all of Faulkner. There we note how a twelve-year-old white boy (whom we subsequently learn is named Charles "Chick" Mallison[1]) has incurred a debt of obligation to Lucas Beauchamp, an African American. This indebtedness has resulted from Lucas's charitable acts of rescuing the boy from an icy creek, taking the boy home with him, drying his clothes, and feeding him dinner. With a quick reference to the deconstructionist notion of binary oppositions, in this case the *privileged* and *unprivileged* terms of *white* and *Black*, I ask the class to identify the ways Faulkner inverts the traditional racial hierarchy and to analyze how and why this inversion creates such profound embarrassment and shame in the young boy.

Students quickly note that at the start of the rabbit hunt, Chick and his two Black companions assume for that time and place the expected roles of their respective races: Chick leads the way and carries a gun, while the Blacks follow, armed with tapsticks. But Chick's fall into the creek upsets (both literally and symbolically) this traditional order, as the image of Chick lying helpless at the feet of the towering Lucas makes clear. From this point on the white boy is subjected to a series of commands by a Black man. "Come on to my house," Lucas says (7), and now Chick follows rather than leads. Chick would prefer to go to his white relative's house, but he finds "that he could no more imagine himself contradicting the man striding on ahead of him than he could his grandfather . . . because like his grandfather the man striding ahead of him was simply incapable of conceiving himself by a child contradicted and defied" (8). In other words, Chick recognizes that Lucas requires their relationship to be that of man and boy, not Black and white. Inside Lucas's house Chick is ordered to strip naked and, while his clothes are being dried, to wrap himself in a quilt belonging to the Beauchamps. These actions, too, are symbolic, as Chick is stripped of his "whiteness" and made to take on the "Blackness" that he has been taught all his life to scorn. Sometimes an alert reader will comment on the death and rebirth imagery that Faulkner employs in the description of Chick's being "enveloped in the quilt like a cocoon, enclosed completely now in that unmistakable odor of Negroes" (11). The reversal of roles is completed when Chick is required to eat the "n——r food" (13) that Lucas's wife Molly has prepared for him.[2]

Now floundering in a strange and confusing environment (for which a near-drowning is a very appropriate symbol), Chick seeks to reclaim the advantage he has lost. Thus, he attempts to relegate Lucas to the traditional role of subservience by attempting to pay him for his trouble. When Lucas, recognizing and declining the gambit, refuses payment, Chick drops the money to the floor. After Chick has refused to pick up the coins, Lucas orders Chick's Black companions to return the money to the white youngster. Finally outside the house again, Chick seeks to rid himself of the symbol of his shame by throwing the coins into the creek, though he recognizes that "Lucas had beat him" (17).

For the next four years, unable to shake the feeling that his defeat at the hands of Lucas has "debased not merely his manhood but his whole race too" (21), Chick struggles to free himself from his obligation to Lucas, hoping by so doing, of course, to reassert the canceled order of his old familiar world. A comical game of one-upmanship now ensues. Chick sends Lucas and Molly a Christmas present of cigars and snuff, and he mails Molly a new dress—only to have Lucas reciprocate by sending a white boy on a mule to deliver a gallon of molasses to Chick. Now Chick is more frustrated than ever, "because this time Lucas had commanded a white hand to pick up his money and give it back to him" (23). Recognizing that Lucas will never allow him to repay the debt, Chick can only hope that in time Lucas will forget him. Until such time, the youngster reasons, his shame, and that of his race, will continue. Thus, Chick plots to meet Lucas on the street, anxiously awaiting the day when he can pass his benefactor and encounter no sign of recognition. Finally, three years after the creek episode, Chick is persuaded that his hope of escape has finally been realized: "Lucas looked up and once more looked straight into his eyes for perhaps a quarter of a minute and then away.... *It's over. That was all* because he was free, the man who for three years had obsessed his life waking and sleeping too had walked out of it" (25–26). Chick's freedom, however, is an illusion. Lucas has not forgotten, and he still controls the game, as the boy learns a year later. When Lucas is brought to the Jefferson jail accused of murdering a white man, he turns immediately to Chick for help, commanding him in the same manner he had on the day of the mishap at the creek: "You, young man," Lucas says. "Tell your uncle I wants to see him" (45).

Most students have no difficulty in defining the basic conflict between Chick and Lucas. While generally not agreeing with Chick's attitude, students understand the powerful social forces that require a young white southerner immersed in the racist traditions of his society to feel compelled, with other white Jeffersonians, "to make a n——r out of [Lucas] once in his life anyway" (32). And today's students, who are well informed of civil rights issues concerning racial minorities, women, and gays, can certainly identify with Lucas's insistence upon equality and dignity. But I want students to see that Faulkner depicts, from the very beginning, the conflict between Chick and Lucas as a very complex issue. I ask them to identify ways that Chick and Lucas defy the respective stereotypes of white racist and Black confrontationist.

Several significant points surface during this part of the discussion. Concerning Chick, students note, for example, the close friendship that exists between the white boy and his Black playmate Aleck Sander—a friendship that is symbolized, in ironic contrast to Chick's behavior in Lucas's house, by the meals they have shared together, "the food tasting the same to each" (12). Students also notice that Chick, observing Lucas, is reminded of his own grandfather, and that, after watching Lucas's response to the death of Molly, he realizes that "you don't have to not be a n——r in order to grieve" (25). Occasionally a student may even call attention to Chick's precocious observation that the smell that he has typically associated with Blacks might not be, after all, "the odor of a race nor even actually of poverty but perhaps of a condition: an idea: a belief" (11).

Similar contradictions exist in the characterization of Lucas. While Lucas is initially perceived as a militant Black victim of white racism, the students quickly realize that Lucas, a descendant of old Carothers McCaslin, is part white. What are the implications, I ask, of the fact that Lucas insists on thinking of himself as "white," while the community is determined to define him as "Black"?[3] And what are readers to make of Lucas's pomposity, arrogance, and self-pride? These are qualities that are generally held to be defects, whatever the race of the individual who exhibits them. What I want students to see is that in his initial presentations of both Chick and Lucas, Faulkner has refused to oversimplify the issue of race or character. Through the reversal of roles, by making Chick partly "Black" and Lucas partly "white," and by simultaneously showing both with serious character flaws, Faulkner has inverted the binary oppositions and, in so doing, has blurred the standard assumptions that will be challenged even more strongly as the novel progresses.

At this point I interrupt the discussion of the novel for a side excursion into the political and historical context of the work. I initiate this part of our study by citing an incident from Faulkner's life recorded by Ben Wasson in *Count No 'Count: Flashbacks to Faulkner*. As Wasson recalls, in late February 1948, when Faulkner was engaged in the composition of *Intruder in the Dust*, he entertained at Rowan Oak an individual whom he greatly admired and respected—Hodding Carter, the publisher-editor of the influential Greenville *Delta Democrat-Times*. The outspoken Carter, who had been awarded a Pulitzer Prize in 1946 for his editorials condemning racial injustice and inequality, was one of the most controversial Mississippians of his day.[4]

Carter had traveled to Oxford in the company of Wasson, another Greenville resident who was Faulkner's friend from college days and for a time thereafter his literary agent. According to Wasson, the three men spent most of their day together drinking toddies, but they also talked about politics and Faulkner's novel in progress. Specifically, Wasson notes, Faulkner and Carter discussed "the burning question of the moment: 'Shall the South integrate or remain segregated?'" (162–63). Wasson does not record Faulkner and Carter's actual conversation that February day at Rowan Oak on "the burning question" of desegregation, but, as my students quickly discover, it is relatively easy to reconstruct the political context—and perhaps even something of the substance—of their remarks. It is even easier to document Faulkner's support of Carter's position. Shortly after Carter's visit to Rowan Oak, Faulkner included the following characterization of the newspaperman in a letter to Robert Haas, one of Faulkner's Random House editors: "[Carter's] name is familiar to you, probably: lecturer, liberal, champion of Negro injustice though no radical, no communist despite Bilbo and Rankin" (*SL* 264). Then, just days before the 1948 presidential election, Faulkner told an interviewer: "I'd be a Dixiecrat myself if they hadn't hollered 'n——r.' I'm a States' Rights man. Hodding Carter's a good man, and he's right when he says the solution of the Negro problem belongs to the South" (*LIG* 60).

With Wasson's question of integration versus segregation and Faulkner's stated preference for Carter and states' rights over Bilbo and the Dixiecrats before us, the students and I head for the library, where I challenge them to reconstruct, as best they can, the various attitudes that were being expressed for and against desegregation, particularly in the South, at the time Faulkner was writing *Intruder in the Dust*. The more knowledgeable students quickly lead the others through a search of the periodicals section, where they scan newspaper and magazine articles of the period. Their out-of-class assignment for the next class session is to continue this general search, adding book searches to their perusal of the periodical literature.

Back in the library for the next class meeting, I organize the students into small research groups and assign each group a specific topic that ideally has already surfaced in their previous search: President Truman's stand on civil rights, the reactions of the Dixiecrats to the president's proposals, and the contrasting opinions of Hodding Carter and Theodore G. Bilbo. At the next class meeting, each group is asked to present the results of its research to the entire class. Following are brief summaries of the type of information that they present—information that I want the students to know before we resume our discussion of *Intruder in the Dust*.

1. President Truman's stand on civil rights

Just days before Wasson and Carter drove from Greenville to Oxford to visit with Faulkner, Truman had become the first American president in history to send to Congress a legislative package dealing solely with the issue of civil rights.[5] Truman's proposals were based on the recommendations of the President's Committee on Civil Rights, published as *To Secure These Rights* the previous October. This report, which examined the hardships experienced by a number of minority groups but particularly southern Blacks, blamed segregation for the conditions of poverty, violence, and discrimination that continued to deny African Americans both freedom and socioeconomic advancement. While the report did not go so far as to recommend that segregation be made illegal, it did identify Jim Crow laws as the principal cause for the plight of Blacks and argued that so long as the "separate but equal" concept prevailed, inequality and injustice would remain. The report called upon the federal government to pursue a course of active intervention to ensure the civil rights of Black citizens.

Specifically, the President's Committee endorsed such measures as the passage of anti–poll tax and anti-lynching legislation, the immediate desegregation of the armed forces and other government agencies, the creation of a Fair Employment Practices Committee (FEPC) and a permanent commission on civil rights, and the prohibition of Jim Crow in interstate transportation. The committee even recommended that federal aid be denied to states that did not comply with the proposed measures.

2. The Dixiecrat response to the president's proposals

The southern, states' rights wing of the Democratic Party, popularly known as Dixiecrats, recognized, rightly, that the president's general position on civil rights, if enacted into legislation, would change the racial, social, and political character of the South forever.[6] Such anxiety was especially acute in states that had the largest Black populations. Disgruntled Democrats in those states, under the direction of Governor Fielding Wright of Mississippi, Governor Strom Thurmond of South Carolina, Governor Frank Dixon of Alabama, and political boss Leander Perez of Louisiana, sought to organize a grassroots opposition to the liberal leadership of the national party and, if necessary, pursue an independent course.

Shortly after President Truman sent his historic civil rights package to Congress, the Southern Governors' Conference convened in Wakulla Springs, Florida. The pressing item on the agenda was what should be the South's response to the president's and the nation's reforming zeal. Most of the governors present, believing that Truman could not win his party's nomination—and certainly not the election—without the support of the South, favored lobbying the national Democratic Party to defeat or modify the civil rights package. Such was the view of the influential Thurmond. But Wright argued for a more radical approach: he wanted the southern states to disassociate themselves from the Democratic Party.

In early May, Wright hosted a conference for the dissident southerners in Jackson. At that meeting the Dixiecrats agreed to meet again in Birmingham in July if the Truman wing of the Democratic Party prevailed at the Philadelphia convention. Truman, of course, did secure the Democratic nomination in Philadelphia; and two days later, at the rump convention in Birmingham, some six thousand disaffected southerners unanimously selected an alternate ticket of Governor Thurmond for president and Wright for vice-president. In the November election this ticket would carry four states—South Carolina, Mississippi, Alabama, and Louisiana. The remaining southern states, holding to their longtime tradition, voted for the national party's ticket of Truman and Alben Barkley. Further demonstrating that from the beginning race had been the chief factor in the southern revolt, predictably the strongest Dixiecrat showing in the election came in the states that had the largest Black populations: in Faulkner's Mississippi with 87 percent of the vote, in Alabama with 80 percent, and in South Carolina with 72 percent.

3. Hodding Carter's views

Carter's views on all these matters—and thus presumably the opinions he shared with Faulkner at Rowan Oak—are easy to ascertain. Carter's prizewinning first novel, *The Winds of Fear* (1944), had dramatized the rising fears and the violent reactions of southern whites to the increasingly militant demands of southern Blacks and their northern supporters.[7] In the characterization of Alan Mabry, however, Carter demonstrated that some southerners supported racial tolerance and a break with Jim Crow tradition. If *The Winds of Fear* was Carter's attempt to help northern readers understand the thoughts and feelings of both the reactionary and moderate white southerners, the editorials he wrote for the *Delta Democrat-Times* were attempts to get his fellow southerners to look at their traditions and institutions in relation to broader issues of national policy and constitutional law.

As coincidence would have it, at the time of his visit with Faulkner, Carter was probably already at work on an essay expressing his personal views for the *New York Times Magazine*. That essay, entitled "The Civil Rights Issue as Seen in the South," would be published less than a month later, on March 21, 1948.[8]

In that essay Carter presented the views of both "the average white southerner" and the "southern liberals" toward President Truman's civil rights proposal. To the first of these, the president's program was nothing less than "a politically motivated and all-out offensive against the conglomerate of laws, customs and attitudes which gives expression to the doctrine of white supremacy" (15), which, according to Carter, was "the most persistent concept that has come down to us from our Western European predecessor" (54). To this group of southerners, by far the majority of the white population, the proposed reform program represented "an attempt by a coalition of Communists, Northern Negroes, and self-seeking Northern Democrats to end abruptly segregation of any kind in the South and to replace local and state self-government with Federal domination" (15).

Carter acknowledged that the opposition of the reactionary southerners to federal legislative and judicial mandates was both illogical and futile; but in the present political climate of the South, Carter argued, emotion was a far stronger motivation than reason. "The truth is," Carter explained, "that the South is afraid that its old racial pattern is going, and going too fast" (15). From such fear came the southerner's anger, frustration, and "an undeniable desire to hit back somehow" (52). The political counteraction of the Dixiecrats, despite the heavy odds against its success, seemed to offer the only available weapon to use in the struggle.

The liberal white southerners, whom Carter characterized as "a small and relatively voiceless minority" (15), were highly suspicious of the political motivations of the Dixiecrats; but they shared with their reactionary kinsmen a distrust of federal intervention. Moreover, while these individuals had rejected the political and economic tenets of the doctrine of white supremacy, most of them were still unwilling to accept the "social equality" (52) that would come with integration. Even the most liberal of the liberals, Carter pointed out, tended to be "gradualists" (53) who believed that any meaningful and lasting reform must come over an extended period of time and must be the result of southern initiative rather than outside compulsion.

Carter concluded his essay with an alarmingly pessimistic view of the situation. The voices of the moderates and pragmatists (among whom Carter counted a significant number of southern Blacks) were being drowned out by extremists represented, on the one hand, by the Grand Dragon of the Ku Klux Klan, who predicted bloodshed if the proposed civil rights legislation was enacted, and, on the other, by northern Black revolutionaries like P. L. Praddis, editor of the *Pittsburgh Courier*, who equated Winston Churchill (because of Great Britain's policy in South Africa) with Hitler and Mussolini. Such incendiary positions, added to the long-standing (and, Carter feared, possibly ineradicable) antipathy between the white and Black races, created a complex problem that defied easy and immediate solution. When and if a solution did come, Carter argued, it would be "unrelated and largely impervious to legislation" and would be effected by the South itself, "gradually and with the consent and participation of the white Southerners" (55).

4. Theodore G. Bilbo's views

How liberal in his day was Hodding Carter can best be understood by placing his views beside those espoused by the white supremacist Theodore G. Bilbo. One of the most popular politicians Mississippi has ever produced, Bilbo was elected to one term as lieutenant governor, two terms as governor, and three terms as US senator. His book, *Take Your Choice: Separation or Mongrelization*,[9] was published just ten months before Faulkner began work on *Intruder in the Dust*. Originally presented as a patriotic effort to save American civilization from destruction, Bilbo's book today impresses most readers as clearly and irrefutably one of the most racist statements in all of American history.

Bilbo begins by claiming that "the Negro problem" (5), as he calls it, represents as huge a threat to the survival of white America as the recently concluded war with Germany and Japan. Recalling the end of that war, Bilbo notes: "Personally, the writer of this book would rather see his race and his civilization blotted out with the atomic bomb than to see it slowly but surely destroyed in the maelstrom of miscegenation, interbreeding, intermarriage, and mongrelization" ("Preface"). According to Bilbo, there is only one alternative to such interrelationships: the complete and permanent separation of the two races. Bilbo argues that the ideal way to achieve this goal would be to return all American Blacks to Africa, which he had sought to implement by introducing his Greater Liberia Act in the US Senate in 1939; but, that effort having failed, the responsibility now falls to the white southerner to resist the demands of reformers and maintain all patterns of social segregation.

Bilbo's harshest words are for those who would remove the traditional social barriers that have been erected between the two races. He pillories Eleanor Roosevelt and the Fair Employment Practices Committee for promoting integration in the nation's capital.

> By orders issued at the top, all partitions have been torn out in order to compel the whites and blacks to eat together in the same rooms and at the same tables. Negro wash basins and toilets have been wrecked or removed in order to compel whites and Negroes to use the same wash basins, the same towels, and the same toilet facilities. Hundreds of complaints have come to my office from white girls who are now forced to stand and wait patiently until the odoriferous females of the Negro race have finished their toilets in closets formerly used and occupied by white girls only. (124)

Other individuals and organizations whom Bilbo lambasts for supporting social equality between the races include A. Philip Randolph, W. E. B. Du Bois, Richard Wright, Lillian Smith, Wendell Wilkie, Henry A. Wallace, the National Association for the Advancement of Colored People, the Southern Conference for Human Welfare, the United Council of Church Women, and the Communist Party of America.

Predictably some of Bilbo's most vitriolic attacks are hurled at individuals who promote school integration. He devotes an entire chapter of his book to lambasting "The Springfield Plan," an early experiment with desegregation implemented by John Granrud, superintendent of schools in Springfield, Massachusetts. Bilbo vehemently disagrees with Granrud's contention that segregation in American schools is "destructive of our concepts of democracy and our theory of the equality of all peoples and all races" (187). Bilbo also castigates A. Ritchie Low, a Vermont minister, for sponsoring summer visitations of Black children from Harlem with white families in New England.

> Hundreds of Negro children from Harlem who had been exposed to life in this slum section with all the vices connected therewith have been placed in white homes throughout New England to "live, eat, and sleep" with white children. What possible good could come from such an experiment? . . . Any white man, minister or layman, who would promote such a program certainly is either totally misinformed or has no regard for the integrity of his race. (189–90)

In Bilbo's view, there can be no compromise on the issue of race:

> If we sit with Negroes at our tables, if we attend social functions with them as our social equals, if we disregard segregation in all other relations, is it then possible that we maintain it fixedly in the marriage of the South's Saxon sons and daughters? The answer must be "No." By the absolute denial of social equality to the Negro, the barriers between the races are firm and strong. But if the middle wall of the social partition should be broken down, then the mingling of the tides of life would surely begin. (55)

Despite the pressures exerted from both without and within, Bilbo argues, the white South will never surrender its position on this matter.

> The South stands for blood, for the preservation of the blood of the white race. We shall not relax in any way whatsoever the social barriers which have been erected to maintain the purity of that blood. There is not enough power in all the world, not in all the mechanized armies of the Allies and the Axis, including the atomic bomb, which could now force white Southerners to abandon the policy of the social segregation of the white and black races. (58–59)

As students quickly discover, such views as the ones cited here clearly demonstrate just how entrenched and rabid were the prejudices with which southern moderates like Hodding Carter, and Faulkner, had to contend.

Supplied with this background information, the class is asked to turn its attention again to the text of *Intruder in the Dust*. I begin this phase of our discussion by first telling the students that Faulkner described the novel as "a mystery story plus a little sociology and psychology" (*SL* 267) and then asking them to align the major characters of the novel with the various attitudes toward race that have surfaced in their investigation of the cultural and political context of the novel. Some of these links are fairly obvious: the students have no doubt that the Gowries and their Beat Four cohorts voted for Bilbo, and they recognize Gavin Stevens's preachments on politics and race in chapters 7, 9, and 10 as remarkably similar to the views of Hodding Carter.[10] Students find frequent allusions to President Truman's civil rights proposals in Stevens's speeches (for example, the references to "lynch-rope," "legislation," and "the simple ratification by votes of a printed paragraph" [155] are probably allusions to *To Secure These Rights*), but they note that most such references are negative in tone, and they find no character who can be said clearly to identify with the position of a "Northern liberal." Some try to force Miss Habersham into this role; others, more persuasively, argue that Lucas's confrontational behavior best conveys the "Northern" stance; still others point to the Chick at the end of the book, as opposed to the Chick of the beginning. But the final consensus is that Faulkner has intentionally devalued this viewpoint in his text. "What are readers to make of this fact?" I ask. The students eventually conclude (correctly, I believe) that Faulkner's implied position is one marked by a strong degree of defensiveness and rationalization. A moderate, not a liberal, and a gradualist, Faulkner, like Stevens/Carter, impresses students as a constitutional states'-righter, one who is deeply distrustful of northern intervention and genuinely persuaded that "the Negro question" is the South's problem and one that can be solved only over a long period of time. Noninterference, expiation, and gradualism—these are essentially Faulkner's views on the race question.[11] Some of my students (not all white, by the way) agree with Faulkner on the issue, while others (not all Black) strongly disagree.

Only now am I ready to lead the class in a close examination of the initiation of Chick Mallison, whom I take to be the protagonist of the novel. The class has already noted, in its discussion of the opening chapters of the book, how Chick initially shares many of the racial attitudes and prejudices of his society. At this stage of the narrative, significantly, Chick is closely identified with his mother, who in her overly protective behavior and unwillingness to grant him freedom and independence is associated with "that nightraddled dragonregion of fears and terrors in which women—mothers anyway—seemed from choice almost to dwell" (32). As the novel progresses, however, Chick gradually but steadily moves beyond her reach and control, entering a strange and forbidden world in which he allows his actions to be directed by a Black man. This latter behavior is so radical (at least for a white Mississippi boy in 1948) that it can only be described as a type of rebirth:

> It would be some time yet before he would realise how far he had come: a provincial Mississippian, a child who when the sun set this same day had appeared to be . . . still a swaddled unwitting infant in the long tradition of his native land—or for that matter a witless foetus itself struggling . . . blind and insentient and not even yet awaked in the simple painless convulsion of emergence. (96–97)

It does not escape the students' notice that this emergence culminates in an act of social rebellion—an act that is even more startling because of the young age of the perpetrator. "So, by the end of the novel, where are we to place Chick on the political spectrum we identified earlier?" I ask the students. All place him somewhere left of center; some are even inclined to see in him the making of a "liberal." "If he were old enough to vote," I inquire, "would he vote for Truman?"[12] The students are always uncertain of the answer to this hypothetical question, although recently a student with a keen sense of southern history responded, "Probably not, but when he's in his twenties he might vote for John Kennedy and support Martin Luther King." I agree, partly because I know a sizable number of actual Mississippians of Chick's generation whose political views evolved precisely in such a direction.

I conclude the study of *Intruder in the Dust* by asking the class to discuss the meaning of the title. Students immediately associate the title with the act of gravedigging by Chick, Aleck, and Miss Habersham; as Gavin says, "You violated a white grave to save a n——r" (242). But I want students to move beyond this literal level of the story to see that what Chick, Alex, and Miss Habersham unearth and expose in this novel is not merely a corpse but the outworn and outdated stereotypes perpetuated by the Jim Crow South. In this regard they are "intruders" in a far greater realm than a rural cemetery; what they violate is the "dust" of southern tradition.[13] And in the Mississippi of 1948, a Mississippi still largely under the control of the Bilbos and the Dixiecrats, rather than moderates like Hodding Carter and William Faulkner, this violation of tradition was a far greater crime than digging up a grave.

NOTES

1. The fact that Chick is nameless in the early pages of the novel reinforces his lack of individual identity and his dependence upon his culture's mores and traditions.

2. The act of eating is a dominant motif in this work, serving, as the extended passage on page 207 reveals, as a symbol of the rite of initiation. If time permits, the instructor might discuss Faulkner's use of this symbol in relation to the sacrament of the Holy Communion.

3. Here a brief discussion of miscegenation and the "one-drop rule" may be required, but hopefully the end result will be a recognition that Lucas's color—white, black, or mixed—is immaterial: that ultimately, as both Lucas and (I think) Faulkner's text make clear, in a lawful and democratic society all individuals are equal and justice must be color-blind.

4. Ben Wasson, *Count No 'Count: Flashbacks to Faulkner* (Jackson: University Press of Mississippi, 1983), 162–63.

5. For a detailed discussion of President Truman's position, see William C. Berman, *The Politics of Civil Rights in the Truman Administration* (Columbus: Ohio State University Press, 1970), 79–135.

6. See Robert Garson, *The Democratic Party and the Politics of Sectionalism, 1941–1948* (Baton Rouge: Louisiana State University Press, 1974), 281–314.

7. Hodding Carter, *The Winds of Fear* (New York: Farrar and Rinehart, 1944).

8. Hodding Carter, "The Civil Rights Issue as Seen in the South," *New York Times Magazine* March 21, 1948: 15ff. For a broader treatment of Carter's views on civil rights, see John T. Kneebone, "Liberal on the Levee: Hodding Carter, 1944–1954," *Journal of Mississippi History* 49 (1987): 153–62.

9. Theodore G. Bilbo, *Take Your Choice: Separation or Mongrelization* (Poplarville, MS.: Dream House, 1947). The conflict between Bilbo and Carter is treated in Garry Boulard, "'The Man' versus 'The Quisling': Theodore Bilbo, Hodding Carter, and the 1946 Democratic Party," *Journal of Mississippi History* 51 (1989): 201–17.

10. Richard Gray's *The Life of William Faulkner: A Critical Biography* (Oxford: Blackwell, 1994) perpetuates the mistaken notion that the Gavin Stevens of *Intruder* is modeled on Phil Stone (23). Stevens, like Stone, is a lawyer; but Stone's ideas on race were closer to Bilbo's than to Carter's and Faulkner's.

11. If students want to pursue this matter, I point them to Faulkner's later essays, such as "On Fear: The South in Labor" and "If I Were a Negro," both printed in *ESPL*.

12. I once commented to Jimmy Faulkner, Faulkner's nephew, "I would dearly like to know how Faulkner voted in the 1948 presidential election." Jimmy replied, "He probably didn't even vote."

13. Occasionally a student will quarrel with this interpretation by pointing out that Faulkner's title employs the singular rather than the plural form of "Intruder." If one wants to make much of this fact, then, as some classes conclude, the "intruder in the dust" may well be Lucas Beauchamp, since his behavior is the catalyst for all the actions of the novel.

"A Fine Loud Grabble and Snatch of AAA and WPA"

Faulkner, Government, and the Individual

In this essay I want to suggest something about the way Faulkner's long-held and cherished belief in personal freedom and self-reliance found expression during the 1930s and early 1940s, a time of course when the nation as a whole felt compelled, because of the successive threats of economic depression and international war, to adopt a style of government increasingly characterized by a centralized bureaucracy, a planned economy, and a consensual collectivism—in short, a New Deal socialism that would evolve into what would eventually be termed a "welfare state." In this connection I will examine two short stories, "Lo!" published in 1934, and "The Tall Men," published in 1941.[1] But first I need to establish a context for my remarks.

William Faulkner, both man and writer, was always an individualist. In his desire for personal privacy, his preference for small-town Oxford over the literary centers of the nation, his often-eccentric dress and behavior, and his unique writing style, Faulkner celebrated nonconformity. In his second novel, *Mosquitoes*, published in 1927, Faulkner has one character pronounce the following judgment on another, a Rotarian: "That's what you'll come to by joining things, by getting the habit of it. As soon as a man begins to join clubs and lodges, his spiritual fiber begins to disintegrate" (36). "Only an individualist can be a first-rate writer," Faulkner once said. "He can't belong to a group or a school and be a first-rate writer" (*FIU* 33).

Ironically and paradoxically, in the years following his winning the Nobel Prize for Literature in 1950, Faulkner became, for the first time in his life, something of a public figure, granting interviews, giving commencement addresses, traveling as a goodwill ambassador for the US State Department to Greece, South America, Japan, and other places, and even on one occasion chairing, at the request of President Dwight D. Eisenhower, a writers' committee for the People-to-People Program. But Faulkner was never very comfortable or adept in such public roles; and even as he increasingly took on added social and political responsibilities, he frequently reverted to the staunch individualist that he had been for most of his life. Indeed, Faulkner generally used the public forum granted him by his international fame to speak out against groups and organizations and governments and to defend individual rights and freedoms.

For example, in 1951 he warned his daughter's high school graduating class that among the greatest threats in modern society are "the forces . . . which are trying to use man's fear to rob him of his individuality, his soul, trying to reduce him to an unthinking mass" (*ESPL* 123). That same year one of his interviewers concluded, "He is a staunch individualist, a lone and seemingly lonely holdout against the 20th century's passion for joining and wearing badges and uniforms" (*LIG* 67). In religion, in government, in protest movements, in literary groups, Faulkner believed, the individual is in danger of being submerged in faceless anonymity. There is the widespread belief, Faulkner told a group of young writers at the University of Virginia, that "individual man can no longer exist," that "man himself can hope to continue only by relinquishing and denying his individuality into a regimented group" (*ESPL* 161). But Faulkner insisted that such a view is mistaken. "People accomplish things by individual protest," he said (*FIU* 80). Faulkner occasionally applied this principle specifically to writers. He was predictably very skeptical toward various types of governmental support for writers and other artists. "I don't think," he once said, "that an artist should be subsidized too much by anyone. I think that he has got to be free, and even a little hardship may be good for him" (*FIU* 169). On another occasion, Faulkner stated that "the writer's freedom has been abrogated when he must accept money from a governmental source" (*LIG* 211).

Keeping in mind Faulkner's near-obsession with individualism and self-reliance, let's now look briefly at the stories "Lo!" and "The Tall Men," neither of which is considered among Faulkner's greatest stories, but both of which are extremely relevant to the political situation not only of the 1930s but also of today.

"Lo!" describes a political encounter between an American president who, although not named, closely resembles Andrew Jackson, and a group of Chickasaw Indians who have traveled to Washington to protest their treatment by white men back home in Mississippi. A member of the Indian tribe has been indicted for the murder of a white man who had attempted to cheat the Indians out of a valuable piece of property, a ford crossing a river. The Indians want the President to acquit the murderer, who is the nephew of a chief, in a ceremony required by the traditions of their tribe. To dramatize their dilemma, the Indians have camped out in tents on the White House lawn, and two of their number have managed to infiltrate the White House itself, sleeping in the hallway just outside the President's bedroom. They all insist they will not leave Washington and return home until the President accedes to their demands.

While "Lo!" purports to be a historical narrative set a hundred years previously, it may also be considered a veiled treatment of the US government in the early years of the Great Depression—a satire directed against the ineffectiveness of a remote and indifferent federal government in dealing with problems that are primarily local or provincial in nature. As a number of readers have surmised, the story may have been suggested by the protest march on Washington, during the summer of 1932, by the Bonus Expeditionary Force, comprised of 60,000 unemployed veterans of World War I who were demanding an early payment of a military service bonus that was not actually due to be paid until 1945. Unlike Faulkner's comic story, the real-life incident ended tragically, with President Hoover's mobilization of federal troops under the command of Major General Douglas MacArthur, who ignored the president's order against excessive force and commanded his troops to overrun the protesters' encampment and push the marchers out of the city. Two of the protesting veterans were killed in the melee, and the consequent animosity toward the federal government by the general public was so pronounced that Franklin D. Roosevelt, the Democratic presidential candidate, is said to have told a close friend after the debacle, "Well, this elects me president."[2]

In Faulkner's story the government is a blundering, ill-informed bureaucracy that is defensive, paranoid, and fundamentally incompetent. The opening paragraphs set the tenor for the entire narrative. The president of the United States, one of the political leaders of the entire world, who has just risen from his night's sleep, surreptitiously cracks his dressing-room door and, slyly using a hand mirror so as not to reveal his own presence, peeps down the corridor to see if the two Indians camped outside his door are still there. They are, along with the residue of bones left from their latest meal. "Damn. Damn. Damn," the President exclaims, then retreats, "on tiptoe, carrying [his] boots in [his] hands," to a back stairway which will allow him to escape his own house, "[a] cloak about his face," unrecognized by his antagonists (CS 384–85).

Following his escape from the White House, the President meets a high-ranking government official who is identified merely as the Secretary and, after first demanding some breakfast ("Give us some breakfast. . . . We don't dare go home" [386]), discusses with him what to do about the Indian problem. When the Secretary suggests that the Indians are the President's responsibility, the President angrily retorts:

> Aren't they subject to your Department? I'm just the President. Confound it, it's got to where my wife no longer dares leave her bedroom, let alone receive lady guests. How am I to explain to the French Ambassador, for instance, why his wife no longer dares call upon my wife because the corridors and the very entrance to the House are blocked by half-naked Chickasaw Indians asleep on the floor or gnawing at half-raw ribs of meat? And I, myself, having to hide away from my own table and beg breakfast. (388)

Eventually, finding no other convenient way to end the siege of the nation's capital by the Chickasaws, and warned that more Indian reinforcements are on the way, the President relents, gives the Indians their ceremony, acquits the chief's nephew, and restores the river ford to the tribe. In a coda to the story, when the same Indian murderer kills another white man and the absurd scenario threatens to repeat itself, the President deeds the land being disputed to the Indians "from now on in perpetuity" (402)—provided they never again leave the property to enter the white man's domain.

"Lo!" obviously belongs to the yarn-spinning tradition of the tall tale, marked as it is by grotesque humor and exaggeration, but it also reflects the seriousness of the problem when a powerful government is reduced to helplessness in the face of an antagonist whom it can neither understand nor control. Perhaps the greatest joke in the entire story, expressed in typical Faulkner ambiguity, appears at the very end, as a "happy" President prides himself upon the "shrewd cunning" (403) that has enabled him to outwit a group of uncivilized and uncouth primitives, not knowing that it is the Indians who have won the encounter, having duped the American government into giving them back their land and setting a permanent boundary between the two nations. As Frederick Karl has noted, Faulkner has here retold the story of secession, with the Indians standing in for the rebellious Confederates.[3] But there is one important difference: this time the secessionists win. Like the writings of John Dos Passos, John Steinbeck, and other antiestablishment writers of the Great Depression, "Lo!" is hardly a story designed to inspire confidence in a wise and efficient federal government.

"The Tall Men," set just before the outbreak of World War II, also dramatizes the conflict between a misguided, uninformed, and blundering federal government and an independent, self-reliant group of citizens. In this instance the protesters are the McCallums, a Yoknapatawpha farm family that places individual responsibility and family pride above a collective loyalty to a distant, impersonal, and abstract federal government.

At the opening of the story, a government official, a military draft investigator, shows up at the McCallum farm to serve a warrant for the arrest of Rafe McCallum's twin sons, who have refused to obey the law requiring all male adults to register for the draft. "You mean we have declared war?" Rafe asks. "That's not the question," explains the government official. Then, completely misunderstanding the twins' motives, he continues: "All required of them was to register. Their numbers might not even be drawn this time; under the law of averages they probably would not be. But they refused—failed anyway—to register" (CS 47–48).

As the story unfolds, the investigator, who has tended to stereotype all rural southerners as worthless, shiftless draft dodgers and lazy welfare recipients, learns to his great surprise about the courage, honor, and fierce individualism of the McCallum family. He learns, for example, that the McCallums had previously refused to grow cotton according to the new government regulations that set allotments for tillable acreage and controlled the sale price of the harvested crop. Neither would they accept the cash payments offered to farmers who would agree to let their land lie fallow. The local marshal, who has been forced against his will to accompany the draft investigator to enforce the warrant, recounts the history of the McCallums' quarrel with the government:

> It was when the Government first began to interfere with how a man farmed his own land, raised his cotton. . . . So they wouldn't sign no papers nor no cards nor nothing. They just went on and made the cotton like old Anse had taught them to; it was like they just couldn't believe that the Government aimed to help a man whether he wanted help or not, aimed to interfere with how much of anything he could make by hard work on his own land, making the crop and ginning it right here in their own gin, like they had always done, and hauling it to town to sell, hauling it all the way into Jefferson before they found out they couldn't sell it because, in the first place, they had made too much of it and, in the second place, they never had no card to sell what they would have been allowed. So they hauled it back. (55–56)

As the marshal goes on to explain, the McCallums' experience with their cotton crop represents the fate of private enterprise and individual freedom in a world ruled by government regulations and bureaucratic controls—by, as he puts it, the "fine loud grabble and snatch of AAA and WPA and a dozen other three-letter reasons for a man not to work" (58). Continuing this attack against New Deal relief programs, the marshal says that the trouble with America is that "we done invented ourselves so many alphabets and rules and recipes that we can't see anything else; if what we see can't be fitted to an alphabet or a rule, we are lost" (59).

The draft investigator is even more surprised to learn that the McCallum twins, instead of being the cowardly draft dodgers he thought them to be, are actually proud descendants of a family whose members had voluntarily and courageously served in both the Civil War and World War I. Believers in an old-fashioned tradition of personal honor and patriotic duty, the McCallums, who are "tall men" not because of their physical stature but because they "stand tall" in crisis, will be among the first to volunteer for military service when actual warfare breaks out and the country needs them, but they will not be coerced into service against their will. Honor and virtue and patriotism, according to the McCallums (and Faulkner), are qualities that must be freely willed; they cannot and should not be forced upon people by governmental conscription.

As in "Lo!" the characterization of the federal government in "The Tall Men" is extremely negative. Not at all a government "of the people, by the people, for the people," the government Faulkner presents in these stories is out of touch with the common citizen, controlled by bureaucrats more concerned with legalistic rules and requirements than with justice, and obsessed with protecting and perpetuating its own power base.

As critical as Faulkner is of centralized power, however, it would be a mistake to see him as a defender of unlicensed freedom and individualism. While Faulkner almost certainly agreed with the long-popular premise that "that government is best which governs least," he was not willing to follow Henry David Thoreau's extension of that logic to the position of "that government is best which governs not at all."[4] We must not forget that in Thomas Sutpen of *Absalom, Absalom!*, published in 1936, and in Flem Snopes of *The Hamlet*, published in 1940 (two more Great Depression works), Faulkner presents a character type that might be considered a representative of an entrepreneurial, laissez-faire capitalist. With the advent of the Great Depression, however, such character types, as indeed all the business practices of capitalism, were being called into question. The characterizations of Thomas Sutpen and Flem Snopes, no less than that of Jay Gatsby, offer a serious critique of the American Dream.

Nevertheless, I think it is accurate to say that Faulkner would never assign to government the solution of the problems of crass materialism and rampant individualism. Faulkner believed the economic and political problems of the 1930s, like all problems through the ages, resulted from "the human heart in conflict with itself' (*ESPL* 119); and the solutions to those problems must also be sought in the human heart, not in governmental power or edict. Ultimately, in his view of the relationship of citizens to their government, Faulkner was a Jeffersonian, not a Hamiltonian—believing, with Jefferson, in limited government, an agrarian as opposed to an industrial lifestyle, and a noblesse oblige that championed moral responsibility and the common good. We see this most clearly in Faulkner's opposition in the 1950s to federally enforced integration, even as he simultaneously (and perhaps illogically) championed racial justice and equality. But Faulkner's notion that the South should be allowed to work out its own problems without northern intervention was not an idea he discovered late in life: he was already expressing that notion in the 1930s and early 1940s in such stories as "Lo!" and "The Tall Men."

NOTES

1. "Lo!" first appeared in the November 1934 issue of *Story*; "The Tall Men," in the May 31, 1941, issue of *Saturday Evening Post*. Both are included in *CS*.

2. For a detailed discussion of the eviction of the Bonus Expeditionary Force from Washington, see Donald J. Lisio, *The President and Protest: Hoover, Conspiracy, and the Bonus Riot* (Columbia: University of Missouri Press, 1974), 166–225.

3. Frederick R. Karl, *William Faulkner: American Writer* (New York: Weidenfeld and Nicolson, 1989), 419.

4. While the statement "That government is best which governs least" is often attributed to Thomas Jefferson, historians have pointed out that the phrase does not appear in any of his writings. Thoreau's revision of the statement appears in his essay "On the Duty of Civil Disobedience."

Faulkner and Hollywood

A Call for Reassessment

For L. D. Brodsky, collaborator and friend

Today people say that Faulkner hated Hollywood. I don't think he actually did hate Hollywood. It was fashionable among writers at the time to say they hated the place. But most of them didn't mean it, as evidenced by how long they stayed and how often they came back for jobs.

—BEN WASSON[1]

I begin with a few quotations.[2] You'll easily recognize the source.

- "I was born of a Negro slave and an alligator, both named Gladys Rock. I had two brothers, one Dr. Walter E. Traprock and the other Eagle Rock, an airplane."
- "I would have liked for you to have had my dog-tag, R.A.F., but I lost it in Europe, in Germany. I think the Gestapo has it. I am very likely on their records right now as a dead British flying officer-spy."
- "But if it came to fighting I'd fight for Mississippi against the United States even if it meant going out into the streets and shooting Negroes."
- "I have never read *Ulysses.*"
- "I think of myself as a farmer, not a writer."

And these on Hollywood:

- "I am at the salt mines again."
- "Hollywood is the only place on earth where you can get stabbed in the back while you're climbing a ladder."

- "I would just keep saying under my breath, 'They're gonna pay me Saturday, they gonna pay me Saturday, they gonna pay me Saturday.'"
- "I don't like the climate, the people, their way of life. Nothing ever happens and then one morning you wake up and find that you are sixty-five. I prefer Florida."

By now we all know that when William Faulkner speaks and writes, we had better pay close attention—not merely to the words but to the situational context: the time and place, the audience, the tone, the intended purpose, and, in some cases, whether he's drunk or sober. We've learned that sometimes Faulkner tells the truth; sometimes he expresses a half-truth; sometimes he slightly misrepresents facts; sometimes he out-and-out lies. We know all this; thus, we know always to be on guard and even a bit skeptical when Faulkner addresses such topics as his biography, his military experience, his reading habits, his vocation, his politics, or his views on race, gender, and socioeconomic class.

The only Faulkner statements, it would appear, concerning which most Faulknerians never voice even the slightest degree of skepticism or doubt are those portraying a negative characterization of the time he spent in Hollywood. Typically, and for way too long, when Faulkner says nasty things about Hollywood and the film industry, we accept his words at face value, nod in agreement, laugh if the remark is funny, and then go back to reading *The Sound and the Fury*. But I submit that it is time to reassess Faulkner's Hollywood career, not only in and of itself, but also with regard to the impact it had on his fiction.

All told, Faulkner spent almost four years in Hollywood (and was under contract with movie studios for more than seven years)—far more time than he spent in the military, in New Orleans, in Paris, or (probably) even in Memphis or the Big Woods. Yet, while the influence of these other experiences and places is extensively cited and analyzed by critics, most Faulkner biographers and scholars are dismissive of the Hollywood years, often ignoring them altogether. Apart from Joseph Blotner's monumental biography of Faulkner, the most detailed record of Faulkner in Hollywood is Meta Carpenter Wilde's memoir, *A Loving Gentleman: The Love Story of William Faulkner and Meta Carpenter*; additionally, a number of books on writers in Hollywood include chapters on Faulkner.[3] But with the exception of Tom Dardis's *Some Time in the Sun*, all of these books, including Blotner's and Wilde's, deal more with Faulkner the man than with Faulkner the screenwriter.

As I shall demonstrate, Faulkner's work in Hollywood was considerable. Yet the critical attention devoted to that work can fit into a single shopping bag. The first extended analysis of Faulkner's screen career was George Sidney's doctoral dissertation, "Faulkner in Hollywood: A Study of His Career as a Scenarist," completed at the University of New Mexico in 1959. The fact that Sidney's study has never been published speaks volumes about the lack of critical interest in Faulkner's screenwriting. The first book-length study of the topic was Bruce F. Kawin's *Faulkner and Film*, which appeared in 1977. Kawin was also a featured presenter at the 1978 Faulkner and Yoknapatawpha Conference, which incorporated the subject of film into its program, and the proceedings of which were subsequently published as *Faulkner, Modernism, and Film*. Kawin extended his study by editing *To Have and Have Not*, which Faulkner coscripted, in 1980 and *Faulkner's MGM Screenplays* in 1982. From 1984 until 1989 L. D. Brodsky and I coedited four volumes of Faulkner's Warner Bros. scripts, focusing on *The De Gaulle Story, Battle Cry, Country Lawyer*, and *Stallion Road*. Gene D. Phillips published *Fiction, Film, and Faulkner: The Art of Adaptation* in 1988, although only two of his eight chapters deal with Faulkner's own screenplays.[4] John Matthews's 1995 essay "Faulkner and the Culture Industry," analyzes Faulkner's script of "Turn About" (filmed as *Today We Live*) as a meeting point of modernism and mass culture. The 2000–2001 issue of the *Faulkner Journal* is a special number devoted to "Faulkner and Film." Peter Lurie published *Vision's Immanence: Faulkner, Film, and the Popular Imagination* in 2004. A search in the MLA International Bibliography yields only two dozen or so journal articles on Faulkner's film work. In sum, then, the critical attention to Faulkner's film work is minuscule when compared to the huge amount of criticism devoted to his novels and stories.[5]

Given the relative paucity of scholarship on the subject, perhaps it will be useful to provide an overview of Faulkner's Hollywood work. Faulkner's on-again, off-again relationship with Hollywood began in 1932 when, following the popular success of *Sanctuary*, Faulkner signed a contract with MGM, reporting to work on May 7, 1932. Within hours, though, he walked off the job and disappeared. He later explained, "I was scared by the hullabaloo over my arrival, and when they took me into a projection room to see a picture and kept assuring me it was all going to be very easy, I got flustered" (*FB* 773). By May 16, however, he had conquered his anxieties and returned to the studio, and over the next four weeks he worked diligently, producing four story treatments for the studio's consideration.[6] For the first, "Manservant," Faulkner reworked his minor short story, "Love," into the story of a Malayan servant, Das, who sacrifices his own life to save the life and ensure the happiness of the British officer who had saved Das's life during World War I. Faulkner's second effort, "The College Widow" (initially "Night Bird"), features a party-loving, sexually aggressive protagonist who reminds one of Temple Drake in *Sanctuary*. Faulkner next wrote a treatment entitled "Absolution," which depicts two boyhood friends whose estrangement and eventual deaths are the result of their attentions to the same girl/woman. The story line in Faulkner's fourth MGM treatment, "Flying the Mail," was not original with him but an adaptation and integration of previous treatments based on a magazine series about the early air-mail pilots.

Even though, as Kawin points out, these initial efforts show some understanding of the types of movies Hollywood was producing at that time (for example, sentimental love stories, "buddy films" celebrating male bonding, narratives of wanton females, and aviation stories), as well as an ability to adapt the work of other writers, the studio found nothing usable in these treatments and allowed Faulkner's contract to lapse after two and a half months. Coincidentally, however, Howard Hawks had just purchased the movie rights to Faulkner's recently published short story "Turn About," and he asked Faulkner to write the script. According to Hawks, within five days Faulkner delivered a full-length screenplay (this version has not survived), and Hawks used that script to sell MGM on the film idea and to persuade the studio to put Faulkner back under contract. Very quickly, though, a major problem surfaced: Faulkner's short story and script included no female character, and Irving Thalberg, the head of MGM, instructed Hawks to add a starring role for Joan Crawford. Faulkner willingly complied by rewriting the script to give one of his protagonists a sister, completing this work back home in Oxford, where he had returned because of the death of his father. By early October, though, he was back in Hollywood, collaborating with Hawks and scriptwriter Dwight Taylor to polish the revised version. The movie was released as *Today We Live* on April 21, 1933, with Gary Cooper, Joan Crawford, Franchot Tone, and Robert Young in the leading roles. Even though the script had been revised even further by other writers (and by Hawks during the filming), Faulkner was given screen credit, his first, for the story and dialogue. More importantly, he had established a close friendship and working relationship with Hawks that would extend over the next two decades.

At home in Oxford in late 1932 and early 1933, awaiting the appearance of *Today We Live* and anticipating future projects with Hawks, Faulkner wrote two additional full-length screenplays, "War Birds" (also called "A Ghost Story") and "Mythical Latin-American Kingdom Story." In the first of these, an adaptation of a *Liberty* magazine serial based on the actual diary of a World War I aviator who died in battle, Faulkner incorporated, and in some places rewrote, his own story of the Sartoris brothers, Bayard and John, as it had been told previously in *Flags in the Dust/Sartoris* and two short stories, "Ad Astra" and "All the Dead Pilots." George Sidney considers "War Birds" to be "perhaps the best thing Faulkner wrote for Hollywood" (203). In the other screenplay, the last that he wrote for MGM, Faulkner drew upon the contemporary political unrest in Cuba, as well as Joseph Conrad's *Nostromo*, a novel he greatly admired, to create an original story of love, intrigue, and revolution centered in a populist uprising against a dictator in an unnamed Latin-America country. While neither of these screenplays was ever filmed, they both, combined with the work he did on *Today We Live*, offer evidence that Faulkner made steady and significant progress in his skill as a scriptwriter during the year he was employed by MGM.

In December 1935 Hawks arranged for Faulkner to be invited to return to Hollywood to collaborate with Joel Sayre on the script of *The Road to Glory*,[7] a war movie directed by Hawks and produced by Darryl F. Zanuck for Twentieth Century–Fox. Faulkner remained under contract with that studio until August 15, 1937. Although he was assigned to eight properties during this period (including one project for which he was on loan to RKO Studios), he received screen credit only for *The Road to Glory* (1936) and *Slave Ship* (1937), an adaptation of a novel by George S. King.[8] Toward the end of this tenure, he was paid the highest salary he would ever earn as a scenarist ($1,000–$1,250 per month); however, in terms of scriptwriting this second sojourn in Hollywood was less productive than his first, in large measure because of the emotional and psychological instability brought on by his heavy drinking, his deteriorating marriage, and complications resulting from his love affair with Meta Carpenter. Many of the famous stories about Faulkner's marathon drinking bouts and his professional unreliability—the type of stories that fueled the stereotypical characterization of the Faulkner-based character in the 1991 movie *Barton Fink*—date from this period.

Faulkner and Carpenter first met in 1935 when Faulkner was working on the script of *The Road to Glory* and Carpenter was secretary to Howard Hawks. They soon became lovers, that relationship continuing until Carpenter's marriage to Wolfgang Rebner, a concert pianist, in 1937. Following the Rebners' divorce in 1942, and upon Faulkner's return to Hollywood that same year, Faulkner and Carpenter resumed their affair. The liaison essentially ended when Carpenter remarried Rebner in 1945, although the two lovers rendezvoused one last time in Hollywood in 1951 and continued to correspond until Faulkner's death in 1962. Elements of Faulkner's romance with Carpenter appear in the Harry Wilbourne-Charlotte Rittenmeyer relationship in *The Wild Palms*, as well as some of the Linda Snopes story in *The Town* and *The Mansion*.

Faulkner's third and longest sojourn in Hollywood, interrupted only by two extended leaves to return home to Oxford, lasted from July 1942 to September 1945, when he worked for Warner Bros. Studio at a salary ranging from $300 to $500 a week, a figure far below the usual amount paid to a writer of Faulkner's stature, and less than half of what Faulkner had been paid during his previous stints in Hollywood. This contract, negotiated by agent William Herndon and agreed to by Faulkner only because he desperately needed money, included, without Faulkner's full knowledge, a series of options that obligated him to Warner Bros. for seven years. More than anything else, it was this contract, which Faulkner came eventually to view as both unfair and servile, that left Faulkner with such a negative, even hostile, feeling toward Hollywood. Disenchanted with the studio's refusal to renegotiate his salary and desirous of turning his full attention to his "big book,"[9] A Fable, Faulkner walked out on Warner Bros. in September 1945. Two years later the studio abandoned its efforts to persuade him to fulfill the remainder of his contract.

Despite his unhappiness in his business dealings with Herndon and Jack Warner, the Warner Bros. years were Faulkner's most productive and successful years in Hollywood. His previous work in Hollywood, in the 1930s, represented his apprenticeship to the trade; but when he came back in the 1940s he returned as a competent, experienced scriptwriter. His first assignment, beginning on July 27, 1942, was to author an original screenplay on the career of General Charles de Gaulle, the leader of the Free French forces and an American ally in World War II. Given his patriotic feelings and his recent attempts to secure a commission in the US Navy, Faulkner found this project quite compatible; and he threw himself into it with energy and enthusiasm. Over a four-month period, incorporating advice from Free French consultants representing General de Gaulle, Faulkner produced a story outline, initial and expanded story treatments, and two different versions of a completed screenplay. These and related materials, which total more than 1,000 pages and are now a part of the Brodsky Collection at Southeast Missouri State University, present the most comprehensive start-to-finish record of Faulkner's work on any single film project and offer compelling evidence that, at this stage of his Hollywood career, he was a skilled, professional screenwriter.[10]

There were several reasons that "The De Gaulle Story" never made it to the screen,[11] none of which seems to have had much to do with the quality of Faulkner's script. Most importantly, there was the ongoing conflict between Faulkner and the Free French consultants regarding the focus of the script. The Gaullists wanted the film to be primarily a biography of Charles de Gaulle, whereas Faulkner wanted to focus on ordinary French citizens (in the script, two brothers) caught up in the conflict between the Free French and the Vichy French. In addition to the recalcitrance of the Gaullists, shifting wartime politics also contributed to the demise of the project. Increasingly, de Gaulle had become more troublesome to the Allied cause, and President Roosevelt and Prime Minister Churchill had begun to exclude the Frenchman from their military strategies. As a result, by mid-November 1942, the date of Faulkner's last work on the project, a movie about the leader of the French underground had ceased being a major priority, first for the US government and subsequently for Warner Bros., the movie studio most closely aligned with the national defense effort.[12]

While Faulkner was greatly disappointed over the cancellation of the de Gaulle project, and rather indifferent about his next few assignments,[13] his hopes were renewed just four months later with the invitation to work on Howard Hawks's proposed epic film celebrating the combined war efforts of the Allied forces. Faulkner expressed his enthusiasm for this assignment in a letter home to his daughter Jill:

> I am writing a big picture now, for Mr Howard Hawks, an old friend, a director. It is to be a big one. It will last about 3 hours, and the studio has allowed Mr Hawks 3 and ½ million dollars to make it, with 3 or 4 directors and about all the big stars. It will probably be named "Battle Cry." (*SL*, 173–74)

Unlike "The De Gaulle Story," with its relatively simple plot line and Faulkner as the sole author, the work on "Battle Cry" involved the adaptation of separate properties by multiple authors depicting American, British, French, Russian, Chinese, and Greek resistance to the Axis powers on various fronts.[14]

During the early and intermediate stages of the project, Faulkner worked with Hawks and screenwriters William Bacher and Steve Fisher to adapt and fashion these various materials—previously published short stories, film story treatments, even a musical cantata about Abraham Lincoln—into a unified script. Ultimately, however, the task of crafting the final version of the screenplay fell to Faulkner, and he proved more than equal to the challenge. In interweaving the various narrative components, shifting the viewpoint and focus, and disrupting standard chronology, Faulkner was employing signature narrative techniques that he had used in *The Sound and the Fury*, *Absalom, Absalom!*, and other novels. Indeed, Meta Carpenter records that Faulkner's enthusiasm for *Battle Cry* was in large measure because of its experimental nature: "It was something new in form, cycloramic, with jumps in time and place, and with the camera utilized beyond any previous attempt."[15] Thus, *Battle Cry* possibly represents Faulkner's most ambitious attempt to adapt the high modernist techniques of his early novels to cinematic purposes.

Understandably, Faulkner thought that his work on *Battle Cry* would earn him a renegotiated contract with Warner Bros. and thus allow him to escape his precarious financial situation. His confidence is reflected in one letter he wrote Estelle:

> [Hawks] is going to establish his own unit, as an independent: himself, his writer, etc., to write pictures, then sell them to any studio who makes highest bid. I am to be his writer. He says he and I together as a team will always be worth two million dollars at least. That means, we can count on getting at least two million from any studio with which to make any picture we cook up, we to make the picture with the two million dollars, and divide the profits from it. When I come home, I intend to have Hawks completely satisfied with this job, as well as the studio. If I can do that, I wont have to worry again about going broke temporarily. (*SL* 177)

Faulkner went on to describe *Battle Cry* as "something I believe in" and to note that "now that [he had] written a good picture," he should be able to negate the onerous contract to which Herndon had committed him.

Once again, however, Faulkner's hopes were dashed. When the Warner Bros. budget office concluded that it would cost at least $4,000,000 to produce the epic film, the studio closed the project down. Thus for the second time in twelve months, a project for which Faulkner held high hopes—both financially and artistically—was terminated, and all the writing he had done for both projects was buried in the studio's vaults.

Faulkner's disappointment over the cancellations of *The De Gaulle Story* and *Battle Cry* was immense, but his Hollywood luck was about to change for the better; and, as was the case a decade earlier, Howard Hawks was the catalyst. In early 1944 Hawks persuaded Warner Bros. to produce a film based on Ernest Hemingway's novel *To Have and Have Not*. Hawks first enlisted a well-known screenwriter, Jules Furthman, to write the screen adaptation, but when Furthman left the project to work on another film, Hawks secured Faulkner to revise Furthman's script.

To Have and Have Not, in both Hemingway's novel and Furthman's adaptation, recounts the story of Harry Morgan, a down-and-nearly-out fishing boat captain who survives the Great Depression by using his charter boat to smuggle liquor, illegal immigrants, and revolutionaries between Cuba and Key West. Faulkner, however, apprised of the US government's sensitivity to political developments in Cuba and coming fresh from the French material he had used in *The De Gaulle Story* and *Battle Cry*, persuaded Hawks to recast Hemingway's story as a World War II drama depicting the conflict of the Free French and Vichy French.[16] To support this reinterpretation, Hawks shifted the setting from Cuba to the island of Martinique, a French province under the control of the Vichy government. This reshaping of Hemingway's novel provided Morgan with a means of moral redemption and also allowed Humphrey Bogart, who played Morgan, to reprise the Free French role that had been such a great success in the recent Warner Bros. film *Casablanca* (1942).

Faulkner shared with Furthman the screen credit for the script of *To Have and Have Not*, and his success on that project led to his assignment to work on the film adaptation of Raymond Chandler's mystery thriller *The Big Sleep*, which starred Bogart and Lauren Bacall, as had *To Have and Have Not*. Leigh Brackett, a young, relatively inexperienced screenwriter, was assigned to work with Faulkner, and Hawks directed them to deliver a script with lots of action and witty dialogue. The two writers succeeded admirably on both counts, but their ending was both overlong and unacceptable to the censors, who took issue with the hero of the story deliberately allowing another character—even if she is a murderess, a nymphomaniac, and a drug addict—to walk into a trap and be shot to death. So Hawks called in Jules Furthman to rewrite the ending, the result being that all three writers received a film credit for the screenplay. *The Big Sleep* remains Faulkner's most successful and best-known film; in 1997 the United States National Film Preservation Board deemed the movie "culturally, historically, or aesthetically significant" and listed it for inclusion in the National Film Registry at the Library of Congress.[17]

Faulkner's next principal assignment involved reworking a previous adaptation of *Mildred Pierce*, James M. Cain's hard-boiled novel about a strong-willed, unconventional divorcée who struggles in both her newfound business career and her relationships with a succession of lovers and a wayward daughter.[18] Faulkner was the fifth of seven screenwriters to be asked to script Cain's novel, and while little of Faulkner's work made it into the filmed version, Faulkner's screenplay deserves to be studied in its own right and published. Albert J. LaValley, who has closely examined all of the various scripts, notes that Faulkner's is highly original and at times "veers off into the Gothic," especially in the characterization of Veda.[19] Among the most interesting of Faulkner's changes to the plot line is his decision to cast Lottie, Mildred's maid, as a Black woman much like Dilsey of *The Sound and the Fury*. Faulkner was especially pleased with the scene in which Lottie comforts Mildred following her lover's death, holding the white woman in her arms and singing "Steal

Away." In one copy of the script that LaValley examined, Faulkner has written in the margin, "God damn! How's that for a scene?"[20]

Faulkner's screen adaptation of Stephen Longstreet's novel *Stallion Road*, his last work for Warner Bros. before he walked out on his contract, is instructive in his acquired competence as a scenarist, as well as some of the obstacles to his ultimate success in that medium.[21] Faulkner's compatibility with the themes of Longstreet's novel—love of horses, preference for a rural and small-town way of life, a skeptical attitude toward modern "progress," an admiration of common, ordinary citizens, a celebration of individual rather than collective values,[22] a contempt for rampant materialism and greed—undoubtedly contributed to Faulkner's success in authoring the screenplay. But in converting the novel to a script, Faulkner also faced a number of challenging issues.

First and foremost, of course, was the necessity to compress the three-hundred-page novel into a seventy-five-minute movie script. Faulkner accomplished this task primarily by eliminating characters, deleting or combining scenes, and, crucially, ignoring the lengthy editorial passages in Longstreet's pages. The result was a streamlined plot centered on one main character, Larry Hanrahan, and the two women in love with him (as opposed to the novel's presentation of two main characters with multiple sex/love interests), as well as an altered communication of theme by indirection and implication instead of direct preachments.

While Faulkner's compression of Longstreet's novel into a unified, artistic script was successful, his handling of the realistic details of his plot failed to get past Hays Act censors. In his evaluation of Faulkner's initial version of the screenplay, Joseph I. Breen, the director of the Production Code Administration of the Motion Picture Producers and Distributors of America, informed Warner Bros. that several changes would be required. For one thing, all of the scenes involving animals would have to conform to the standards of the American Humane Society. A more serious concern related to the adulterous affair between Hanrahan and Daisy Otis. Breen advised, "Kindly keep down to a minimum all scenes of kissing or embracing between Mrs. Otis and Larry."[23]

Despite Breen's expressions of concern, Faulkner did not abridge the sexual elements of the story. In his final version of the script, Daisy is still the aggressive, uninhibited nymphomaniac, and she and Larry continue to flaunt their adulterous relationship in public. In addition, Daisy and Fleece, the rival for Hanrahan's affection, engage in a relentless and often prurient repartee of sexual innuendoes and double entendres. It was primarily these aspects of the plot that Stephen Longstreet had in mind when he said that Faulkner's script was "a little strong for then."[24] Predictably, the unconventional sexual details are missing from the next version of the screenplay, written by Emmet Lavery, and from the film version scripted by Longstreet. While Faulkner's version of *Stallion Road* represents one of his most artful movie scripts, it also provides evidence that, in the Hollywood of 1945, Faulkner was considerably ahead of his time.

When Faulkner walked out on Warner Bros. in September 1945, he thought he was done with Hollywood for good, but such proved not quite to be the case. In February–March 1951, he returned to Hollywood for one final time to assist Hawks on a script based on William E. Barrett's novel *The Left Hand of God*; and in 1953–54 he joined Hawks, first in Paris and Switzerland, and finally in Egypt, to collaborate on the script of *Land of the Pharaohs*, an epic film depicting the building of the pyramids. Although Faulkner received the lead credit for the screenplay of *Land of the Pharaohs* (1955), the movie today is memorable primarily as the inspiration for one of Faulkner's most comical remarks regarding his movie work. Commenting on the collaboration of Faulkner and Harry Kurnitz on the script, Hawks later recalled that the biggest challenge they faced was how to depict the speech of the Egyptian pharaohs. Faulkner suggested the solution: to make them sound like Confederate generals.[25]

I turn now to a discussion of the intersections that occur between Faulkner's film work and his fiction. Faulkner wrote to Malcolm Cowley that he kept his "movie work locked off into another room" from his fiction (*FCF* 16). But such an observation contradicts not only what is known about human psychology but also what Faulkner repeatedly stated about the writing process. Faulkner variously referred to a writer's memory bank of experience as "a filing cabinet," "a lumber room," and "a storehouse," all of which terms identify the subliminal repository of, in Faulkner's words, "what [the writer] has read, what he has seen and smelled and heard and remembered."[26] At West Point Faulkner commented,

> I think that every experience of the author affects his writing. That he is amoral or thief, he will rob and steal from any and every source; he will use everything; everything is grist to his mill from the telephone book up or down, and naturally all his own experience is stored away. He has a sort of a lumber room in his subconscious that all this goes into, and none of it is ever lost. Some day he may need some experience that he experienced or saw, observed or read about, and so he digs it out and uses it. (*FWP* 96)

Such is no less true of Faulkner's Hollywood experience than of his time in Oxford or Toronto or New Orleans or Paris. Thus, no one should be surprised that Faulkner's time in Hollywood and his work as a screenwriter significantly correlate with his fiction. Some of these connections have been noted by scholars, but few of them, to my mind, have received anything approximating the critical attention they deserve.

One obvious product of Faulkner's Hollywood experience is the intriguing and too-much-neglected short story "Golden Land." This story, published in *American Mercury* in May 1935 and included in Faulkner's *Collected Stories*, recounts the experiences of Ira Ewing, a forty-eight-year-old, highly success-ful real estate agent in Beverly Hills. It is only in his accumulation of wealth, however, that Ewing might be considered a success: his emotional life is in shambles. An alcoholic and adulterer, he lives with his embittered, judgmental wife and transvestite son, and his daughter is a small-time actress presently on trial for a sex orgy that apparently has involved the granting of sexual favors in exchange for a bit part in a movie. The most shocking element of the story is the revelation that Ewing seeks to profit commercially from his daughter's scandal by selling the story to a tabloid journalist. The only positive charac-ter in the story is Ewing's elderly mother, who longs to return to the family's Nebraska farm and who regrets that her son has not embraced the values that she and her husband "had learned through hardship and endurance of honor and courage and pride" (*CS* 722).

On its surface "Golden Land" is clearly an indictment of the culture of Hollywood—its corruption, emptiness, sensationalism, greed, shallowness, and rootlessness.[27] Like Nathanael West's *Day of the Locust* (1939), for which Faulkner's story serves as a precursor, Hollywood is a cultural wasteland where dreams and morality come to die. As Faulkner describes it,

> Hollywood is . . . the city in the bright soft vague hazy sunlight, random, scattered about the arid earth like so many gay scraps of paper blown without order, with its curious air of being rootless—of houses bright beautiful and gay, without basements or foundations, lightly attached to a few inches of light penetrable earth, lighter even than dust and laid lightly in turn upon the profound and primeval lava, which one good hard rain would wash forever from the sight and memory of man as a firehose flushes down a gutter (*CS* 719).

Faulkner even anticipates the apocalyptic conflagration with which West con-cludes his novel:

> . . . that city of almost incalculable wealth whose queerly appropriate fate is to be erected upon a few spools of a substance whose value is computed in billions and which may be completely destroyed in that second's instant of a careless match between the moment of striking and the moment when the striker might have sprung and stamped it out. (719)

As H. R. Stoneback observes, "Golden Land" is Faulkner's "definitive land-scape study of California as anti-Edenic cacotope—the epitome of displace-ment, rootlessness, and corruption."[28]

But it is a mistake to limit Faulkner's critique in "Golden Land" to the cul-ture of Hollywood. As West will do later, Faulkner presents Hollywood as a microcosm of the larger American culture—the American Dream become nightmare. It is not a new theme for Faulkner. He had been treating it in one form or another since *The Sound and the Fury*, but especially in *Sanctuary* and more recently in *Pylon*. Indeed, in *Pylon* he specifically links Hollywood to the broader American landscape: the Shumann house in Ohio is "a bungalow, a tight flimsy mass of stoops and porte-cochères and flat gables and bays not five years old and built in that colored mud-and-chickenwire tradition which Cali-fornia moving picture films have scattered across North America as if the cellu-loid carried germs" (270). Whether in Beverly Hills, or Ohio, or New Valois, or Memphis, or Jefferson, Americans are becoming, in Faulkner's view, displaced, rootless, soulless: "a new race not yet seen on the earth" (*CS* 721), who "aint human . . . ; you can't anymore imagine two of them making love than you can two of them aeroplanes back in the corner of the hangar, coupled" (*P* 204).

There are numerous other intersections between Faulkner's Hollywood experiences and his fiction. The barnstorming pilots Faulkner wrote about in "Flying the Mail" are carried forward under different names in *Pylon*. In his story treatment "The Damned Don't Cry,"[29] Faulkner's characterization of the protagonist, the strong-willed and resilient Zelda O'Brien, is remarkably similar to that of Temple Drake in *Requiem for a Nun*. Moreover, the play sec-tions of that novel, employing a scenic viewpoint that advances the story pri-marily through dialogue, have more affinity with the movie genre than with a typical Faulkner novel. In the "Appendix" to the Compson family history that Faulkner wrote for Malcolm Cowley to use in *The Portable Faulkner*, Caddy Compson, after divorcing "a minor movingpicture magnate," disappears "in Paris with the German occupation, 1940," and reappears in a photograph with "a handsome lean man of middleage in the ribbons and tabs of a German staff-general" (711, 713)—the same milieu Faulkner had written about in "The De Gaulle Story" and "Battle Cry." *A Fable* had its genesis in discussions in Hollywood among Faulkner, William Bacher, and Henry Hathaway about a potential movie based on the idea that the unknown French soldier buried in the tomb under the Arc de Triomphe is a reincarnated Jesus Christ, and the depiction of Charles de Gaulle in "The De Gaulle Story" as something of a Christ figure anticipates the fuller use of the Christ analogy in the novel. Even the plot outline of *A Fable* that Faulkner wrote on the wall of his office in Rowan Oak owes something to the charts that screenwriters and directors used to block out scenes during story conferences in Hollywood. Additionally, one speech by a priest in "The De Gaulle Story" adumbrates ideas and phrasing of Faulkner's Nobel Prize Acceptance Speech.[30]

Similarly, "Battle Cry" contains material and ideas on race relations that will be developed more fully in *Intruder in the Dust* and essays and speeches Faulkner wrote in the 1950s. In the American unit fighting in North Africa, Faulkner includes a white southerner, Akers, and a Black soldier symbolically named America, who is paralyzed as a result of a battle wound. While Akers exhibits an impressive sensitivity toward his wounded comrade, he simultaneously expresses a strong regional and even racial bias. When an Italian taken prisoner by the unit describes the United States as a place "where all men have a vote in what all are or are not to do," one of the American soldiers, Battson, replies: "All of them except America's folks. There are parts of it where America's folks don't have any say. Ask Akers." However, it is not Akers but the Italian who rallies to the South's defense. The South will change, he insists, "just as soon as the people outside that part of the country, whose concern it is not, stop trying to force them to give America's people a vote" (102).[31]

It is patently ludicrous, of course, for an Italian prisoner to lecture American soldiers in the North African desert about racial discrimination in the United States; and Faulkner wisely eliminated the passage when he revised the script. Nevertheless, it is revealing to note that Faulkner was already, in 1943, thinking about themes and issues that would eventually find expression through the voice of Gavin Stevens in *Intruder in the Dust*, as well as in Faulkner's own voice in such essays as "A Letter to the North" and "If I Were a Negro."

The intersections of Faulkner's film work and his fiction work both forward and backward: not only does some of his scriptwriting subsequently find its way into his fiction, but also material from his fiction is occasionally woven into his movie treatments and scripts. For example, in his script of "Turn About," in addition to the use of the short story's plot and characters, there is a near-incestuous relationship between brother and sister, a scene of children playing in a brook (in Faulkner's script but deleted from the film version), and mention of the wedding hymn "The Voice That Breathed o'er Eden"—all details drawn from the text of *The Sound and the Fury*. As noted previously, "Manservant" is a reworking of an earlier short story, "Love"; "The College Widow" draws upon *Sanctuary*; and "War Birds" recycles characters and incidents from *Sartoris/Flags in the Dust*, "Ad Astra," and "All the Dead Pilots." *Revolt in the Earth* is a loose adaptation (and, in Kawin's view, a poor one) of *Absalom, Absalom!*[32]

Faulkner's most thoroughgoing attempt to transpose Yoknapatawpha into a Hollywood format can be found in his story treatment based on Bellamy Partridge's novel *Country Lawyer*. Faulkner transferred Partridge's setting from Phelps, New York, to Jefferson, Mississippi, and traced the histories of the Galloway and Hoyt families through four generations and two wars, much like his handling of the Yoknapatawpha families named Sartoris, Compson, Sutpen, McCaslin, and Snopes. The close relationship of Sam Galloway, Jr., and his Black companion, Spoot Moxey, reprises the biracial friendships in *The Unvanquished* and *Go Down, Moses* (as it anticipates the one in *Intruder in the Dust*). Rachel, Spoot's grandmother, reminds one of Dilsey from *The Sound and the Fury* and (as Faulkner makes clear in his reference to the funeral oration and the nighttime errands for ice cream) is similarly based on the actual Caroline Barr, "Mammy Callie." Such Yoknapatawpha names as Tobe ("A Rose for Emily"), Mitchell (*Flags in the Dust*), Coldfield (*Absalom, Absalom!*), and "Spoot" ("Pantaloon in Black") are repeated in *Country Lawyer*, and the epitaph on the tombstone of Edith Bellamy Galloway is remarkably similar to the one that Faulkner will later place on the monument erected for Eula Varner Snopes in *The Town*.

Thus far I have sought to demonstrate that Faulkner's time and work in Hollywood and the characters, plots, and themes of his fiction are more closely intertwined than is generally recognized—and, in fact, so much so that it is really quite untenable to maintain that the two are altogether separate, unrelated categories. Now, in conclusion, I would like to explore some ways that Faulkner's Hollywood years possibly impacted, perhaps even changed, the stylistics of his fiction. Here one moves into nebulous and uncertain territory, since it is much easier to recognize similarities in characters' names, types, and actions than to identify commonalities involving the deeper, less explicit elements of form and style.

It has long been commonly accepted by most Faulkner critics that there is a significant difference in the fiction of Faulkner's early, middle, and late years. Typically the first period is associated with apprenticeship, the second with monumental achievement, and the third with decline. According to this classification, and paraphrasing what was once said of Henry James, there is Faulkner the First, Faulkner the Second, and Faulkner the Great Pretender. As reflected in such phrases as "the major years," "the heart of Yoknapatawpha," and "one matchless time,"[33] the distinction between the Faulkner of the middle and late periods is typically accompanied by—indeed, propelled by—the judgment that Faulkner's great run of creative genius ends with *Go Down, Moses* in 1942 and that everything written thereafter exhibits a decline of his literary prowess. Despite the persuasive arguments of Noel Polk, James B. Carothers, Joseph Urgo, Theresa Towner, and others for recognizing the artistic worth of such novels as *Intruder in the Dust*, *Requiem for a Nun*, *A Fable*, the later volumes of the Snopes trilogy, and *The Reivers*, there remains a general consensus among Faulkner readers that his literary greatness rests almost exclusively on the works he produced between 1929 and 1942.

I wish to propose a different way of viewing Faulkner's fictional output during his middle and late career, with the years in Hollywood signaling the transition and the influence from those years producing a major shift. Before Hollywood, I submit, Faulkner wrote fiction primarily in the "high modernist" style as represented by Conrad, Joyce, and Eliot; after Hollywood he principally wrote in what might be termed a "filmic" style. Modernist fictional techniques involve such features as interior monologues, radical disruptions of chronology, plot juxtapositions, shifting points of view, classical allusions, a questioning of absolute truth, and a high degree of ambiguity. Filmic fiction, as Faulkner learned and practiced it in the 1930s and '40s, typically employs not only a heightened sense of photographic effects but also a simpler plot, a single focus, standard chronology, a greater reliance upon dialogue, and a lessening, if not a complete avoidance, of classical analogues, multiple perspectives, and ambiguity.

Before I make the case for my argument, I need to offer a couple of clarifications. First, by using the term "filmic fiction," I have deliberately avoided the term "cinematic fiction" that is employed, for example, by Kawin, Phillips, Doug Baldwin, and Peter Lurie, among the principal critics who apply that term to Faulkner's fiction. All of these scholars find cinematic elements in Faulkner's novels and stories even before he worked in Hollywood, and all except Lurie view such elements as altogether consistent with, sometimes virtually synonymous with, Faulkner's high modernism.[34] Phillips even contends that "Faulkner's fiction was no more cinematic in style and construction after he went to Hollywood than before" (56). Perhaps it is no more "cinematic," as that term is defined by the critics I have just mentioned; but, as I shall seek to demonstrate, it is more "filmic" and in many respects stands in opposition to, not synonymous with, the earlier "high modernist" style.

Still, I want to emphasize that I am not proposing an absolute dichotomy between Faulkner's high modernist and his filmic fiction. Few things in Faulkner are matters of *either/or*; his mode of thought and practice is nearly always *both/and*. Certainly there are cinematic, and even filmic, elements in Faulkner's pre-Hollywood work, as there are high-modernist elements in the post-Hollywood fiction. The differences to be found in the fiction of the two periods are differences in degree, not of kind. Nonetheless, there are significant differences; and some of these, I contend, are at least partly attributable to Hollywood.

The oppositions in the two styles as I am employing the terms can be found in the startling contrast between *Absalom, Absalom!*, arguably the last of Faulkner's great high modernist novels, and *Pylon*, which I would call the first of his filmic novels. Faulkner started writing what became *Absalom, Absalom!* in 1931, with the completion of the short story "Evangeline," shortly before his first trip to Hollywood the following year; and he continued to work on the novel both in Oxford and in Hollywood over the next four years, finally finishing it in Hollywood in January 1936. There are several identifiable reasons for Faulkner's delays in completing *Absalom, Absalom!*: for example, his lingering grief over his brother Dean's death, his marital and financial difficulties, the demands of the Hollywood screenwriting assignments, his drinking problem. But I would add to that list the challenge of continuing to write in a high modernist style at a time when he was being required to retrain, retool, himself to write in a filmic mode. It is as though there were two writers named Faulkner: one writing straightforward movie treatments and scripts for MGM and the other writing a dense, complex novel of southern history with biblical and classical overtones.

One result of this divided focus is *Pylon*, written in late 1934 following his year of work for MGM. Faulkner said that he wrote *Pylon* "because I'd got in trouble with *Absalom, Absalom!* and I had to get away from it for a while so I thought a good way to get away from it was to write another book, so I wrote *Pylon*" (*FIU* 36). It seems significant that the novel Faulkner wrote "to get away from" the high modernist *Absalom, Absalom!* is a book patterned to a degree after Hollywood criteria. Daniel Singal calls *Pylon* "a serious work of Modernist fiction,"[35] and certainly it has modernist (and even postmodernist) characteristics: the Joycean portmanteau words, the explicit references to "The Love Song of J. Alfred Prufrock," the wasteland imagery and themes, the displacements and ambiguities, the double ending. But in several other respects the novel is pure Hollywood. Not only does it reprise material and character types from Faulkner's story treatment "Flying the Mail," but it also exhibits a number of characteristics that replicate movies of the 1930s: an action-packed story of adventurous, larger-than-life characters; an exploitative interest in love and sex; a simple and linear story line; strong, realistic dialogue; and, in the description of Shumann's death, a heroic, redemptive ending. It is not at all surprising that *Pylon* translated quite easily, and successfully, to the screen as *The Tarnished Angels* in 1957. The surprising thing is that the movie did not appear sooner.

Although neither Faulkner nor his readers could have known it at the time, *Pylon* would be more predictive of the novels to come than *Absalom, Absalom!* While Faulkner would never totally abandon his high-modernist tendencies, as evidenced by the stream-of-consciousness section of "The Bear," the time shifts in *Intruder in the Dust*, the multiple viewpoints in *The Town* and *The Mansion*, and the convoluted style and structure of *A Fable*, his post-Hollywood fiction became typically more accessible, more linear, more focused in form and structure, less interior-oriented—in other words, more like the movie scripts he had authored than like *The Sound and the Fury* and *As I Lay Dying.*[36]

As *Pylon* may be viewed as the filmic novel most immediately derivative of Faulkner's Hollywood experience of the 1930s, so *Intruder in the Dust* may be considered a novel resulting from the 1940s Hollywood experience. Here again there is a mixture of high modernist and filmic techniques, but it is the filmic qualities that predominate: the use of the popular "murder mystery" formula; the simple plot structure (disrupted only by the political editorializing of Gavin Stevens); the effective blocking of scenes, especially in the early sections treating the young Chick's successive encounters with Lucas; the advancement of the story through spoken dialogue; the impressive visual effects, as, for example, in the depiction of the creek episode at the opening of the book. Once again, as in the case of *Pylon* (and later with *The Reivers*), the novel proved to be readily adaptable to the screen format.

Even in *A Fable*, his most modernist novel from the late period, there are strong evidences of the filmic style, particularly in the handling of the "big" (sometimes melodramatic) scenes. For example, the opening chapter, one of the most effective narrative passages in all of the late Faulkner works, reads like a detailed story treatment, with clearly implied uses of camera angles. The scene opens with an aerial or "bird's-eye" view of city streets and tenements, as hordes of citizens begin to move toward the location where the treasonous soldiers are being brought.[37] Faulkner establishes the overhead perspective by noting, "A French or British or American aviator . . . could have watched it best: hovel and tenement voiding into lane and alley and nameless *cul-de-sac*, . . . as the trickles became streams and the streams became rivers, until the whole city seemed to be pouring down the broad boulevards converging like wheel spokes into the *Place de Ville*" (F 4). Progressively, Faulkner's camera-eye technique zooms in on the scene, employing the equivalent of dolly and trucking shots to capture a sense of the frantic but relentless movement of the crowd: in the words of the text, "the motion, the friction, the body, the momentum, speed" (15).

As the chapter unfolds, the camera-eye narration cuts and pans from one to another of the principal figures in the scene: the sergeant, the young woman, the tall man, the corporal, the old general. There are long and medium shots of the infantry, "a whole battalion, armed except for packs, emerging from the *Place de Ville* in close route column, led by a light tank with its visor closed for action, which, as it advanced, parted the crowd like a snowplow" (6), and similar shots of the cavalry and the lorries transporting the disgraced regiment. With the appearance of the regiment, the camera zooms in initially on the thirteen soldiers who are isolated from the rest, and then on the four, and finally on the single individual toward whom the ire of the crowd is directed, first in a close-up shot of him "[standing] near the front, his hands resting quietly on the top rail, so that the loop of chain between his wrists and the corporal's stripes on his sleeve were both visible," and then in an extreme close-up of his face—"a face merely interested, attentive, and calm, with something else in it which none of the others had: a comprehension, understanding, utterly free of compassion" (17). There are other extreme close-ups in the chapter: of the sergeant's uniform, of the young woman who has fainted, of the hand that offers her bread, of the exchange of gazes between the corporal and the old general.[38]

In manipulating the perspectives of the narrator-as-camera, Faulkner strategically places individual characters within the larger context of the sweeping movements of both the anonymous crowd and the historical and military forces that threaten to overwhelm them. As importantly, Faulkner uses the shifting camera angles to establish mystery and suspense designed to lead the reader (as viewer) into the rest of the story. There are few better examples in all of Faulkner of how he adapted the filmic techniques he learned in Hollywood to his own fictional purposes.

In summary, then, what can be said of Faulkner's Hollywood career and its impact on his literary works? Certainly, it would appear, any screenwriter who worked on more than forty film projects, authored or co-authored a dozen screenplays, and received six screen credits, two of those (three, if one adds *The Road to Glory* to *The Big Sleep* and *To Have and Have Not*) for movies that are now considered classics, is deserving of serious consideration of his work. Moreover, if that writer happens to be a Nobel Prize–winning fictionist, and there are clear linkages between much of that fiction and his screenwriting, then the case for study is even stronger. Such a study might result in a heightened appreciation not only for Faulkner's screenplays but also for his later fiction, breaking it out of the straitjacket of high-modernist comparison and viewing it, therefore, not as a decline or failure but merely as a different mode of writing fiction—a shift, by the way, that is altogether consistent with an author who puts a premium on experimentation and uniqueness.

Fifty years ago, in his pioneering study of Faulkner's Hollywood career, George Sidney observed:

> The scholars and critics—the modern apostles of totality, unity, and the complete frame of reference—appear to have treated Faulkner's film career as irrelevant to and, presumably, as detracting from, his career as a writer of serious fiction. Without doubt they are correct in relegating Faulkner's screen writing to a position of secondary importance in the body of his work. But I do think that such writing as Faulkner did in Hollywood should be analyzed and interpreted before being so relegated. (ii)

That observation is still valid today.[39]

NOTES

1. Qtd. in Ann J. Abadie, ed., *William Faulkner: A Life on Paper: A Transcription from the Film Produced by the Mississippi Center for Educational Television* (Jackson: University Press of Mississippi, 1980), 78.

2. The listed quotations may be found in *LIG*, 9, 30, 59, 261; *SL*, 170; *FCF*, 7; Joseph Blotner, *Faulkner: A Biography*, rev. ed. (New York: Random House, 1984), 320; Abadie, ed., *William Faulkner: A Life on Paper*, 92; and Lavon Rascoe, "An Interview with William Faulkner," *Western Review* 15 (Summer 1951), 303.

3. Joseph Blotner, *Faulkner: A Biography* (New York: Random House, 1974); Meta Carpenter Wilde and Orin Borsten, *A Loving Gentleman: The Love Story of William Faulkner and Meta Carpenter* (New York: Simon and Schuster, 1976); Tom Dardis, *Some Time in the Sun* (New York: Scribner's, 1976). See also Ian Hamilton, *Writers in Hollywood, 1915–1951* (New York: Harper & Row, 1990).

4. As Phillips demonstrates, the adaptations of Faulkner's novels and stories for film treatment are a significant part of Faulkner's relationship to Hollywood, but that topic lies beyond the scope of the present essay.

5. George Sidney, "Faulkner in Hollywood: A Study of His Career as a Scenarist" (unpublished doctoral dissertation, University of New Mexico, 1959); Bruce F. Kawin, *Faulkner and Film* (New York: Frederick Ungar, 1977); Evans Harrington and Ann J. Abadie, eds., *Faulkner, Modernism, and Film: Faulkner and Yoknapatawpha, 1978* (Jackson: University Press of Mississippi, 1979); Bruce F. Kawin, ed., *To Have and Have Not* (Madison: University of Wisconsin Press, 1980); Bruce F. Kawin, ed., *Faulkner's MGM Screenplays* (Knoxville: University of Tennessee Press, 1982); Louis Daniel Brodsky and Robert W. Hamblin, eds., *A Comprehensive Guide to the Brodsky Collection, Volume III: The De Gaulle Story; Volume IV: Battle Cry* (Jackson: University Press of Mississippi, 1984, 1985); William Faulkner, *Country Lawyer and Other Stories for the Screen*, ed. Louis Daniel Brodsky and Robert W. Hamblin

(Jackson: University Press of Mississippi, 1987); Gene D. Phillips, *Fiction, Film, and Faulkner* (Knoxville: University of Tennessee Press, 1988); William Faulkner, *Stallion Road: A Screenplay*, ed. Louis Daniel Brodsky and Robert W. Hamblin (Jackson: University Press of Mississippi, 1989); John Matthews, "Faulkner and the Culture Industry," in *The Cambridge Companion to William Faulkner*, ed. Philip M. Weinstein (Cambridge: Cambridge University Press, 1995), 51–74. Peter Lurie, *Vision's Immanence: Faulkner, Film, and the Popular Imagination* (Baltimore: Johns Hopkins University Press, 2004); Stefan Solomon, *William Faulkner in Hollywood: Screenwriting for the Studios* (Athens: University of Georgia Press, 2017).

6. For an analysis of these and the other scripts Faulkner produced for MGM, see Kawin, ed., *Faulkner's MGM Screenplays*.

7. A partial version of this script, in Faulkner's handwriting, is among the Faulkner manuscripts housed in the John Williams Library at the University of Mississippi.

8. The other projects were *Banjo on My Knee*, *Gunga Din* (RKO), *Four Men and a Prayer*, *Splinter Fleet*, *The Giant Swing*, and *Drums along the Mohawk*.

9. See *SL*, 314, 316, 328, 338, and elsewhere.

10. See "Introduction," in Brodsky and Hamblin, eds., *Comprehensive Guide to the Brodsky Collection, Volume III: The De Gaulle Story*, ix–xxxiii.

11. In Hollywood, that is. In November 1990 an adaptation of Faulkner's script titled *Moi, General DeGaulle* was shown on French television as part of the celebration of de Gaulle's hundredth birthday and the fiftieth anniversary of the beginning of de Gaulle's resistance movement from London. See Robert W. Hamblin, "The Curious Case of Faulkner's 'The De Gaulle Story,'" included in this volume.

12. Given his weeks of fruitless labor on "The De Gaulle Story," Faulkner must have found it ironical that two brief scenes that he wrote during a recess in the de Gaulle project for another movie, *Air Force*, did make it to the screen, although he received no screen credit for that work. "See Air Force," Faulkner wrote to his family back home in Oxford. "I wrote Quincannon's death scene, and the scene where the men in the aeroplane heard Roosevelt's speech after Pearl Harbor" (*FB* 1143). Ian Hamilton notes a further irony in the fact that the *Air Force* script won an Academy Award nomination for writer Dudley Nichols, an achievement for which Faulkner, it would appear, deserved some small part of the credit (205).

13. During this period Faulkner wrote a story treatment loosely based on Bellamy Partridge's novel *Country Lawyer*, and another story treatment entitled *Life and Death of a Bomber*, which dramatizes how selfish interests delay the production of a bomber and thus threaten national security (see Faulkner, *Country Lawyer and Other Stories for the Screen*, ed. Brodsky and Hamblin); he also worked briefly on *Background to Danger*, *Northern Pursuit*, and *Deep Valley*.

14. See Brodsky and Hamblin, eds., *Comprehensive Guide to the Brodsky Collection, Volume IV: Battle Cry*.

15. Brodsky and Hamblin, eds., *Comprehensive Guide to the Brodsky Collection, Volume IV: Battle Cry*: ix.

16. See Kawin's introduction to his edition of *To Have and Have Not*.

17. See https://www.loc.gov/programs/national-film-preservation-board/film-registry.

18. In addition to those already mentioned, other Warner Bros. projects on which Faulkner worked include *God Is My Co-Pilot*, *The Adventures of Don Juan*, *Fog over London*, *Strangers*

in Our Midst, and *The Southerner*. Sometime during this period Faulkner also wrote a full-length, unproduced screenplay, *Dreadful Hollow*, for Howard Hawks (see Kawin, *Faulkner and Film*, 136–43).

19. *Mildred Pierce*, ed. with introduction by Albert J. LaValley (Madison: University of Wisconsin Press, 1980), 35.

20. *Mildred Pierce*, 36. For a further discussion of Faulkner's portrayal of Black women who offer succor to besieged white charges, see Deborah Barker's essay "Demystifying the Modern Mammy in *Requiem for a Nun*," in *Faulkner and Film: Faulkner and Yoknapatawpha, 2010*, ed. Peter Lurie and Ann J. Abadie, 71–97 (Jackson: University Press of Mississippi, 2014).

21. See Faulkner, *Stallion Road: A Screenplay*, ed. Brodsky and Hamblin.

22. For a discussion of Faulkner's developing treatment of this theme, see Stefan Solomon, "Faulkner and the Masses: A Hollywood Fable," in *Faulkner and Film: Faulkner and Yoknapatawpha, 2010*, ed. Peter Lurie and Ann J. Abadie, 98–119 (Jackson: University Press of Mississippi, 2014).

23. Qtd. in "Introduction," Faulkner, *Stallion Road*, xv.

24. Louis Daniel Brodsky, "Glimpses of William Faulkner: An Interview with Stephen Longstreet," in Faulkner, *Stallion Road*, xxvi. Longstreet continues: "It was quite powerful, didn't pay too much attention to my novel. What Bill had done was to write a purely Faulknerian narrative, a beaut, all shadow and highlights and with the smell of the best horses."

25. See Dardis, *Some Time in the Sun*, 149.

26. See *FIU*, 116, 117, 258.

27. For a helpful discussion of the story along these lines, see Robert Jackson, *Seeking the Region in American Literature and Culture: Modernity, Dissidence, Innovation* (Baton Rouge: Louisiana State University Press, 2005), 50–59.

28. "Golden Land," in Robert W. Hamblin and Charles A. Peek, eds., *A William Faulkner Encyclopedia* (Westport, CT: Greenwood Press, 1999), 155.

29. In Faulkner, *Country Lawyer and Other Stories for the Screen*, ed. Brodsky and Hamblin, 85–101.

30. See Brodsky and Hamblin, eds., *Comprehensive Guide to the Brodsky Collection, Volume III: The De Gaulle Story*, 110.

31. One cannot fail to notice that this view is similar to some of Faulkner's statements in his public letters and essays. Critics have long observed that Faulkner's personal views on race seem more conservative than the position inferred from his novels and stories.

32. See Kawin, *Faulkner and Film*, 126–35.

33. Melvin Backman, *Faulkner: The Major Years* (Bloomington: Indiana University Press, 1966); John Pilkington, *The Heart of Yoknapatawpha* (Jackson: University Press of Mississippi, 1981); Jay Parini, *One Matchless Time: A Life of William Faulkner* (New York: Harper-Collins, 2004).

34. In his influential *Faulkner and Film*, Kawin examines Faulkner's use of montage, demonstrating the technique primarily with *The Sound and the Fury*. Phillips agrees with Kawin's assessment, similarly finding parallels in Faulkner's modernist works with cinematic techniques. Baldwin ("Putting Images into Words: Elements of the 'Cinematic' in William Faulkner's Prose," *Faulkner Journal* 16 [2000–2001]: 35–64) expands Kawin's definition of "cinematic" beyond the use of montage but, like the others, makes "cinematic" and "modernist"

virtually synonymous. Peter Lurie is closer to my position, treating "modernist" and "filmic" techniques as distinctive categories; but whereas, for point of emphasis, I stress their oppositional nature, he focuses on Faulkner's use of them as "dialogical."

35. Daniel J. Singal, *William Faulkner: The Making of a Modernist* (Chapel Hill: University of North Carolina Press, 1997), 192. Other discussions of *Pylon* as a modernist novel include Donald Torchiana, "*Pylon* and the Structure of Modernity," *Modern Fiction Studies* 3 (1957–58): 291–308; Karl F. Zender, *The Crossing of the Ways: William Faulkner, the South, and the Modern World* (New Brunswick, NJ: Rutgers University Press, 1989), 44–52; and Michael Zeitlin, "*Pylon*, Joyce, and Faulkner's Imagination," in Donald M. Kartiganer and Ann J. Abadie, eds., *Faulkner and the Artist: Faulkner and Yoknapatawpha, 1993* (Jackson: University Press of Mississippi, 1996), 181–207. Postmodern treatments of the novel include Joshua Gaylord, "The Radiance of the Fake: *Pylon*'s Postmodern Narrative of Disease," *Faulkner Journal* 20 (2005–2006): 177–95, and Taylor Hagood, "Media, Ideology, and the Role of Literature in *Pylon*," *Faulkner Journal* 21 (2005–2006): 107–19. By contrast, the Hollywood aspects of the novel have received almost no attention.

36. A similar pattern is observable in the short stories, although, as Lurie points out in *Vision's Immanence*, Faulkner's later short stories are also heavily influenced by his involvement in writing for mass market publications like the *Saturday Evening Post*. Compare, for example, the stories in *These Thirteen* (1931) and *Doctor Martino and Other Stories* (1934) with those in *The Unvanquished* (1939), *Go Down, Moses* (1942), excepting section four of "The Bear," and *Knight's Gambit* (1949). John T. Matthews also examines the impact of the mass market magazines on Faulkner's short stories: see his essay, "Shortened Stories: Faulkner and the Market," in Evans Harrington and Ann J. Abadie, eds., *Faulkner and the Short Story: Faulkner and Yoknapatawpha, 1990* (Jackson: University Press of Mississippi, 1992), 3–37.

37. Cf. the Solomon essay cited previously.

38. Faulkner's narrative devices here and elsewhere may be usefully compared to "suture theory" in film studies: that is, the shot-reverse technique used by filmmakers to make the viewing audience forget that the camera is actually doing the looking. See, for example, Jacques-Alain Miller, Jean-Pierre Oudart, and Stephen Heath, "Suture," *Screen* 18, no. 4 (1977–78): 24–34.

39. This essay was first published in 2014, before the appearance of Volume II of Carl Rollyson's biography of Faulkner (2021), which offers precisely the kind of analysis of Faulkner's film work that Sidney called for—and also before the publication of Sarah Gleeson-White's *William Faulkner at Twentieth Century-Fox: The Annotated Screenplays* (New York: Oxford University Press, 2017).

The Curious Case of Faulkner's
"The De Gaulle Story"

In 1942, in dire financial need and unable to secure a desired military appointment, William Faulkner turned to Hollywood for employment. He began work on July 27 as a screenwriter for Warner Bros. Pictures at a salary of $300 per week. His first assignment was to write a screenplay based on the career of General Charles de Gaulle, the leader of the Free French/Fighting French resistance against Germany's invasion and continuing occupation of France. Over the next five months, under the supervision of producer Robert Buckner, Faulkner wrote, in rapid succession, a story outline, a treatment, a revised treatment, a full-length screenplay, and a revised screenplay of a story first called "Journey to Dawn" or "Journey to Hope," then "Free France," and eventually "The De Gaulle Story."[1] Thus began, in Hollywood in the early years of World War II, the curious history of a movie script that would not conclude until nearly fifty years later in Paris.

Faulkner labored diligently on "The De Gaulle Story," initially believing that the film would secure his place as a successful and well-paid scriptwriter (*SL* 162). However, even though he produced some 1,000 pages of manuscript on the several versions, "The De Gaulle Story" never went into production. There were a number of reasons why the script was never filmed, one of the major factors being the conflict that developed between Faulkner and the de Gaulle representatives who served as consultants on the project. Principal among these were Adrien Tixier, a Free French lobbyist in Washington, DC, and Henri Diamant-Berger, a French film director and producer who was the Gaullist representative in Hollywood. To retrace the exchanges between Faulkner and these French advisors as the project unfolded is to follow a debate on a topic that engaged Faulkner's interest throughout his career—the fundamental conflict between fact and fiction.

In the early stages of his work on "The De Gaulle Story" Faulkner drew heavily upon Philippe Barres's book *Charles De Gaulle* (1941), as well as upon various chronologies of events provided by both the Warner Bros. Research Department and the French Research Foundation, a Gaullist front organization located in West Hollywood. Demonstrating his typical disdain for facts, however, Faulkner quickly began to substitute fictional characters and events for the historical details. Given the Free French representatives' loyalty to de Gaulle and their deep commitment to the liberation of France, in addition to their excessive literal-mindedness, the results of Faulkner's alterations were predictable. When Tixier read Faulkner's story treatment, he responded with a long list of "Observations on Inexact Details," challenging Faulkner's accuracy and verisimilitude (*DGS* 354–59). For example, Tixier noted that the French army had been on alert in May 1940 and would not have been granting furloughs to soldiers as Faulkner had allowed in his narrative. Moreover, Tixier pointed out, Faulkner further erred in assigning a Breton peasant family a cook; in having the French play dominoes in cafes; in claiming the general French public had knowledge of de Gaulle's book on tank warfare; and in characterizing de Gaulle's first followers as desperate crowds of beggars and refugees.

Later, when Diamant-Berger evaluated Faulkner's completed script, he reiterated Tixier's demand for closer adherence to the historical record (*DGS* 376–95). According to Diamant-Berger, Faulkner had grossly misrepresented de Gaulle's military strategy, and he had placed the general in Syria at a time when he was in France. In addition, noted Diamant-Berger, Faulkner was wrong in characterizing Bretons as more loyal to their region than to their nation; in describing the roles and behavior of French mayors, constables, and maids; in creating a situation involving forced labor when in fact there had been none; and in anachronistically alluding to announcements over loudspeakers in public places. What bothered Diamant-Berger most, however, was that de Gaulle's role in the script was being steadily diminished as Faulkner focused more and more on the political opposition of two fictional brothers: Georges, a de Gaulle sympathizer, and Jean, a Vichy collaborator. As Diamant-Berger rightly noted, "General De Gaulle disappears practically from the story after the first third, and the Fighting French movement with him" (378).

For a time Faulkner sought to placate the French consultants by making many of the changes in the script they requested. But finally, exasperated by the unbending facticity of the Free Frenchmen and recognizing the impasse as having become insurmountable, Faulkner petitioned Buckner for a free hand in structuring the screenplay. In an interoffice memorandum dated November 19, 1942, Faulkner suggested to Buckner: "Let's dispense with

General De Gaulle as a living character in the story." The problem, as Faulkner stated it, was that the Frenchmen wanted to produce "a document" rather than "a story." As a consequence, they would continue to "insist upon an absolute adherence to time and fact, no matter how trivial the incident nor imaginary the characters acting it, and regardless of the sacrifice of dramatic values and construction or the poetic implications or overtones." Only by overruling the Frenchmen's demands, Faulkner insisted, could the filmmakers "gain the freedom to make a picture which the American audience whose money will pay for it will understand and not find dull" (*DGS* 395–98).

Faulkner's pleas, however, were to no avail, and shortly thereafter the studio abandoned its plan to produce a movie about General de Gaulle and the Free French movement. But, as future events would demonstrate, Faulkner's involvement with the materials he had developed in the rejected script was only just beginning.

One of the most interesting discoveries that results from studying Faulkner's Hollywood career is the extent to which his scriptwriting parallels many aspects of his novelistic work. For example, in the scripts one finds the typical Faulkner sympathy for the underdog, his distrust of power, his genuine concern for both personal integrity and corporate justice, and his abiding faith in humankind's ability to endure and prevail. Moreover, one finds, as in the fiction, a tendency to recycle material, to retell earlier stories in altered contexts. In connection with this last point, it is not at all surprising that Faulkner found a subsequent use for the material and themes that had failed as "The De Gaulle Story."

Less than a year after Warner Bros. abandoned "The De Gaulle Story," director/producer Howard Hawks persuaded the studio to produce a movie version of Ernest Hemingway's 1937 novel *To Have and Have Not*. Hawks secured a well-known scriptwriter, Jules Furthman, to write the initial draft of the proposed screenplay; but when Furthman left the project to work on another film, Hawks enlisted Faulkner to revise Furthman's work.[2] Hawks had held Faulkner in high esteem, both as a writer and as a person, since the two men had collaborated on *Today We Live* (1933), the film adaptation of Faulkner's World War I short story, "Turn About." Faulkner received his first screen credit for his work on the script of *Today We Live*, and ever after he and Hawks were close personal friends. It is worth noting that all of Faulkner's best Hollywood work, in the 1940s as in the 1930s, was done under the direction of Hawks.

To Have and Have Not, both in Hemingway's novel and Furthman's initial script, presents the story of Harry Morgan, a ne'er-do-well who survives during the Great Depression by using his charter boat to smuggle liquor, illegal immigrants, and Cuban revolutionaries between Cuba and Key West. What Faulkner brought to the project, as a result of his recent work on "The De Gaulle Story," was the notion to recast Hemingway's story as a World War II drama depicting the conflict between the Free French and the Vichy French,[3] the same conflict that had divided the two brothers Georges and Jean in "The De Gaulle Story." To support this reinterpretation, Hawks shifted the setting of *To Have and Have Not* from Cuba to the island of Martinique, a French province under the control of the Vichy government. This recasting of Hemingway's novel produced two significant effects, one dramatic and one practical. In Faulkner's handling of the story, Morgan, by giving his life in support of the Free French, is presented with a means of moral redemption. In addition, the shift of focus enabled Humphrey Bogart, who played the part of Harry Morgan, to reprise the Free French role that had been such a success in the recent Warner Bros. production of *Casablanca* (1942).

As it turned out, his work on the script of *To Have and Have Not* was not the only instance in which Faulkner reused and reshaped the materials of "The De Gaulle Story" for other purposes. An even more significant example is the Pulitzer Prize–winning novel *A Fable*, which though not published until 1954 was actually conceived and initiated during Faulkner's tenure at Warner Bros. from 1942 to 1945. *A Fable* recasts the Passion Week of Christ in the story of a World War I French corporal who is martyred because of his attempts to stop the war.

"The De Gaulle Story" similarly employs the Christ myth as a controlling motif, as Faulkner draws numerous parallels between De Gaulle and Christ. For example, in one scene De Gaulle says to a soldier, "I thought you were dead. What brought you back to life?" "France, General," the soldier replies. A comrade adds, "Someone whispered De Gaulle in his ear." "Does that raise the dead in France?" De Gaulle inquires. "It will do better than that now," the soldier answers. "It will raise the living" (*DGS* 276). Later, a De Gaulle disciple offers a Free French version of Christ's Great Commission (Matthew 28:19–20): "There are many more like me, that he has sent, to go among the villages and towns as I have come here, to bring his message" (*DGS* 299). Christ references like these recur repeatedly throughout Faulkner's script.[4]

Admittedly, Faulkner's use of the Christ story undergoes a distinct metamorphosis from "The De Gaulle Story" to *A Fable*. The technique of the screenplay is allusive; the method of the novel tends toward allegory. Moreover, in *A Fable* the Christ figure is an obscure corporal who opposes a war rather than a famous general who seeks to promote one. Nevertheless, the fact remains that the narrative designs of both script and novel depend heavily upon the biblical pattern, and it seems altogether plausible that Faulkner might never have developed the gospel structure of his novel without having previously employed that structure in his screenplay.

What I have presented here about Faulkner's writing of "The De Gaulle Story" in 1942 and the influence of the screenplay on subsequent Faulkner works is clearly evident in retrospect and is now fairly common knowledge among Faulkner scholars. But this information was not available to readers and scholars in the 1940s, or at the time of Faulkner's death in 1962, or even when Joseph Blotner published the first full-length biography of Faulkner in 1974. The complete account of Faulkner's involvement with "The De Gaulle Story" was not made public until 1984, and the individual primarily responsible for uncovering that story was Faulkner collector Louis Daniel Brodsky.

A native of St. Louis, Brodsky first became fascinated with Faulkner in 1959 when, as an undergraduate student at Yale University, he studied Faulkner's work in R. W. B. Lewis's course in American Studies. Shortly thereafter, with the help of New Haven bookdealer Henry Wenning, he began to acquire first editions and inscribed copies of Faulkner's books. Over the next three decades, Brodsky gradually but persistently built his collection to a "world class" status, adding manuscripts, letters, photographs, movie scripts, wills, and other memorabilia to his outstanding collection of Faulkner books. In 1988 Brodsky transferred ownership of his collection to Southeast Missouri State University, which has since established a Center for Faulkner Studies to enable students and scholars to take full advantage of the voluminous resources of the Brodsky Collection.

In 1982 Brodsky acquired the Warner Bros. copies of "The De Gaulle Story," along with a number of other scripts Faulkner had written for the studio. Warner Bros., having decided to divest itself of a large number of its vault properties, had placed the Faulkner scripts with San Francisco bookdealer Warren Howell for sale to a research institution or an individual collector. The studio had selected the Faulkner materials from its vast archive both to test the market and to determine the potential value of its remaining scripts. Howell knew of Brodsky's reputation as a big-time Faulkner collector, and he offered him the Warner scripts. Brodsky quickly accepted. The acquisition of a number of Faulkner's movie scripts encouraged Brodsky to investigate Faulkner's Hollywood connections in the hope of discovering additional materials. One of the individuals Brodsky contacted was A. E. "Buzz" Bezzerides, a scriptwriter with whom Faulkner boarded for several months in 1942. In 1983 Brodsky visited Bezzerides in his Los Angeles home and while there negotiated the purchase of a number of books Faulkner had inscribed to Bezzerides. On the last day of his visit Brodsky was given permission to search the house for any additional Faulkner materials that might be there; and just hours before he was scheduled to catch his return flight to St. Louis, he found, in Bezzerides's basement, in a box stored in the typewriter compartment of an old desk, a blue folder that was immediately recognizable as the cover of a Warner Bros. script. On the front was typed "The De Gaulle Story by William Faulkner." It was a complete early draft—perhaps the original—of the screenplay, typed by Faulkner in his characteristic amateurish fashion and corrected in his small, sometimes nearly illegible handwriting. A companion folder contained numerous memos, research files, and chronologies that Faulkner utilized in writing the script.

At the time Brodsky acquired "The De Gaulle Story," he and I were busily at work on a multivolume series entitled *Faulkner: A Comprehensive Guide to the Brodsky Collection*, being issued by the University Press of Mississippi. Two volumes, *The Biobibliography* and *The Letters*, had already been completed, and Brodsky and I were deep into our work on *The Manuscripts*, which would eventually become Volume V of the series. The acquisition of the film scripts, however, led us to suspend our work on *The Manuscripts* in order to hasten into print two of Faulkner's previously unpublished World War II screenplays, "The De Gaulle Story" and "Battle Cry."

"The De Gaulle Story" was published in 1984 by the University Press of Mississippi as Volume III of *Faulkner: A Comprehensive Guide to the Brodsky Collection*. Since we included not only the completed screenplay but also the progressive versions from original story treatment to the revised script, as well as the Warner Bros. file materials relating to the project, the volume provided for the first time a fairly complete record, from beginning to end, of Faulkner's work on a single movie project. Brodsky and I coauthored an introduction to the volume which traces the history of Faulkner's work on the project and offers some conclusions about the merits of the script and the reasons it was never filmed. Brodsky and I believed then, and still believe, that "The De Gaulle Story" clearly dispels the popular myth (frequently advanced by Faulkner himself) that Faulkner never really took screenwriting seriously and engaged in the work solely for the money. The truth is that Faulkner worked extremely hard in Hollywood and eventually became a more than competent, if not outstanding, scriptwriter.

The positive critical response to the publication of "The De Gaulle Story" indicated that most scholars and readers were pleased that a Faulkner work, even one that is definitely inferior to the great fiction, had finally been published after lying dormant for so many years. But one individual took great offense to the appearance of the book. Catherine Gavin, a British historian, wrote me a personal letter, claiming that much of the new material that Brodsky and I presented in our introduction was "rubbish" and questioning whether the publication of Faulkner's script was a late attempt to revive and defend Gaullist politics. She concluded as follows:

> Owing no doubt to some oversight of the editors, your name does not appear in *Who's Who in America*, so I have no idea of your age. Are you one of the new breed of academics, eager for publicity, in your case by climbing on the Gaullist bandwagon even at this late date? Or were you an adult in 1940? I was, and on June 18, 1940, I listened to de Gaulle's first mendacious broadcast on the BBC. I have been his enemy, through life and death, from that hour onwards.[5]

Fortunately, other critics and reviewers were less emotionally involved, less hostile, and more grateful.

For the final segment of the curious history of "The De Gaulle Story," the setting shifts from the United States to France. In 1989 Faulkner's French publisher, Editions Gallimard, issued a French translation of the Mississippi Press volume Brodsky and I had prepared.[6] Yannick Guillou, a representative of Gallimard, had initially contacted Brodsky about a possible French translation shortly after learning of the pending publication of the American edition; and Gallimard's interest was significantly heightened after a five-page feature story about Faulkner's rediscovered script appeared in *L'Express*, the French news weekly.[7] François Forestier, the author of that story, had traveled to the United States to interview not only Brodsky and me but also Buzz Bezzerides and other of Faulkner's 1940s Hollywood acquaintances.

The interest of both Gallimard and *L'Express* in Faulkner's script about the former French general and president was undoubtedly governed more by political and historical than by literary motives, since the appearance of both the book and the article coincided with the plans of the French nation to celebrate, in 1990, the hundredth anniversary of de Gaulle's birth and the fiftieth anniversary of the beginning of de Gaulle's resistance movement from London. In conjunction with this nationwide celebration, TF1, a French television network, announced plans to produce a 20-million-franc television movie based on Faulkner's script.[8] Bertrand Poirot-Delpech, a well-known literary columnist, was employed to adapt Faulkner's script for the screen; and Henri Serre, a noted French actor, was enlisted to play the role of de Gaulle. The film was released under the title *Moi, Général de Gaulle* and telecast in November

1990. Most reviewers concluded that the movie was not very good; moreover, it varied significantly from Faulkner's original script. Still, although in an altered state, Faulkner's story of de Gaulle and the Free French had finally made its way to the screen. Thus concluded, in France, a curious story that had had its beginning nearly fifty years earlier in Hollywood.

NOTES

1. For the texts of these different versions, as well as a detailed history of the entire project, see Louis Daniel Brodsky and Robert W. Hamblin, eds., *Faulkner: A Comprehensive Guide to the Brodsky Collection, Volume III: The De Gaulle Story.* Jackson: University Press of Mississippi, 1984 (cited internally in this essay as *DGS*).

2. This version of the script is a part of the Brodsky Collection, Center for Faulkner Studies, Southeast Missouri State University.

3. For the most detailed history of this film project, see Bruce Kawin, "Introduction: No Man Alone," *To Have and Have Not*, ed. Kawin (Madison: University of Wisconsin Press, 1980), 9–53.

4. For a more comprehensive list of the parallels between de Gaulle and Christ, see Brodsky and Hamblin, *DGS*, xxxi–xxxii.

5. Letter from Catherine Gavin to Robert Hamblin, dated August 25, 1989, Center for Faulkner Studies, Southeast Missouri State University.

6. William Faulkner, *De Gaulle: Scénario*, ed. Louis Daniel Brodsky and Robert W. Hamblin, trans. Didier Coupaye, Michel Gresset, and Philippe Mikriammos (Paris: Gallimard, 1989).

7. François Forestier, "Quand Faulkner inventait De Gaulle," *L'Express*, October 11, 1985, 57–61.

8. See Michel Gresset, "The De Gaulle Story Comes Full Circle," *Faulkner Newsletter and Yoknapatawpha Review* 12, no. 2 (1992): 1f.

Homo Agonistes, or,
Faulkner as Sportswriter

Selections by William Faulkner are seldom found in anthologies of sport literature,[1] yet, as readers of his novels and stories well know, his works manifest a keen and abiding interest in a variety of sports and competitive games. Indeed, so pervasive are Faulkner's allusions to sport and play that there is scarcely a fictional work of his, whether tragic or comic, that does not contain some reference to competitive sports or gamesmanship. Such a preponderance of sporting images suggests that for Faulkner the very essence of the human condition is conflict, struggle, competition. Man, Faulkner seems to imply, may be defined as *homo agonistes,* man the athlete or competitor.[2]

A representative sampling of sporting activities in Faulkner's work should begin, of course, with Faulkner's favorites: hunting, horse racing, and flying. "The Bear" is universally acknowledged as one of the greatest hunting stories in the English language. *The Reivers* is, among other things, a celebration of the challenges and excitement of horse racing. *Pylon* provides an inside view of the hazardous competition among the barnstorming aviators of the 1930s.

While hunting, horse racing, and flying represent Faulkner's principal sporting interests—what might be termed his "major sports"—references to additional sports and games are scattered throughout his novels and stories. A list of Faulkner's "minor sports" would include football, basketball, baseball, golf, boxing, wrestling, rowing, gambling, chess, and such folk amusements as swapping horses, tall tales, and pranks. Whatever the particular sport, however, and whether it be "major" or "minor," Faulkner treats the sporting spirit as a key aspect of human experience. It is also one of the most revealing: as Faulkner has Gavin Stevens say in *Knight's Gambit* (he is speaking of chess, but his comment applies to all games), "Nothing by which all human passion and hope and folly can be mirrored and then proved, ever was just a game" (192).

Without wishing to argue for any derivative influence, I would suggest that Faulkner's view of the sporting spirit is remarkably similar to Johan Huizinga's. In the classic *Homo Ludens: A Study of the Play Element in Culture,* Huizinga traces the various historical associations between the concepts of play and competition and notions of culture, religion, and art.[3] Pointing out that the word "athlete" derives from the Greek word for "prize" (*aethlon*), he notes, "Here the ideas of contest, struggle, exercise, exertion, endurance and suffering are united" (51). Similarly, Huizinga adds, the English word "play" has evolved from an Indo-European term that meant "to take a risk, to expose oneself to danger for someone or something" (39). Thus, in Huizinga's mind, play and sport are closely related, and both are quite serious pursuits. Indeed, Huizinga argues, in early cultures play and sport were ritual acts linked to the sacred, though by the Middle Ages this association had been largely lost: "Mediaeval life was brimful of play: the joyous and unbuttoned play of the people, full of pagan elements that had lost their sacred significance and been transformed into jesting and buffoonery, or the solemn and pompous play of chivalry" (179). Although in modern times its profane elements have displaced the sacred, sport and play continue, according to Huizinga, to occupy a crucial place in modern culture and art and therefore are deserving of serious attention.

Faulkner, too, understood the sports and games we play—indeed, all human creativity—as an elaborate, multifaceted myth treating existence as a struggle, a cosmic athletic contest, an *agon*—in Faulkner's case, between imagination and fact, dream and reality, individualization and anonymity, survival and annihilation, victory and defeat, the sacred and the profane. Both athletes in their sport and artists in their craft symbolize this struggle, and together they embody the struggle inherent in the human condition.

Given his fondness for sport and games, it is not surprising that, on two separate occasions, both in 1955, Faulkner signed on as a sportswriter of sorts for *Sports Illustrated.*[4] The first time was in January of that year when he agreed to supply the magazine with his impressions of a hockey match (the first, and probably only, one he ever saw) between the New York Rangers and the Montreal Canadiens. The second time was in May, when he traveled to Louisville as an *SI* correspondent to cover the 1955 Kentucky Derby. The essays that resulted, entitled "An Innocent at Rinkside" and "Kentucky: May: Saturday," were published, respectively, in the January 24 and May 16, 1955, issues.[5]

As even a cursory reading of these essays will reveal, the term "sportswriter" can be applied to Faulkner only in the loosest possible sense. What is one to think, for example, of a treatment of a hockey match in which neither the opposing teams nor the final score is recorded, or the account of a horse race in which the winner is never identified? Yet it is the absence of this type of factual information that makes Faulkner's sports essays so revealing. "I don't care much for facts, am not much interested in them," Faulkner once wrote to Malcolm Cowley; his greater concern, as he went on to make clear, was "truth" (*FCF* 89). And this is precisely the principle that one observes Faulkner pursuing in his *SI* pieces: not so much the factual details of a sporting event, but rather what Faulkner perceived as the truth, the essence, of the sporting experience.

Consider, for example, Faulkner's treatment of the hockey match (*ESPL* 48–51). He begins with a description of "the vacant ice," which, for reasons that will become clear only in retrospect, "looked tired." In contrast to the innocent and excited spectator who is viewing his first hockey match, the playing surface seems "not expectant but resigned." In terms of the metaphor of life that Faulkner will subsequently develop, the skating rink is the arena of history, a bare, impersonal stage on which the age-old drama of human existence—what Faulkner called in another place "the problems of the human heart in conflict with itself" (*ESPL* 119)—will unfold. Faulkner moves quickly to the action of the play:

> Then [the rink] was filled with motion, speed. To the innocent, who had never seen it before, it seemed discorded and inconsequent, bizarre and paradoxical like the frantic darting of the weightless bugs which run on the surface of stagnant pools. Then it would break, coalesce through a kind of kaleidoscopic whirl like a child's toy, into a pattern, a design almost beautiful, as if an inspired choreographer had drilled a willing and patient and hard-working troupe of dancers—a pattern, design which was trying to tell him something, say something to him urgent and important and true in that second before, already bulging with the motion and the speed, it began to disintegrate and dissolve.

Readers familiar with Faulkner's various texts cannot fail to note here the preponderance of phrases and ideas that are central to Faulkner's views on life and art. Life as motion, speed; the historical process as discordant and paradoxical; the compelling human need to find pattern and meaning amidst confusion and even absurdity; the difficulty of communication—these are important motifs that recur throughout Faulkner's corpus of fiction. So, too, is the notion of the transforming and transcendent power of art, although, as elsewhere in Faulkner, that power is always transient and partial. On occasion, Faulkner notes, the hockey players appear as a "troupe of dancers" trained by "an inspired choreographer" to bring order and beauty out of chaos. That such an achievement is only momentary, that the created design all too quickly begins "to disintegrate and dissolve," is to be expected from an author who was greatly saddened by the transitory nature of human experience and, partly for that reason, whose favorite poem was Keats's "Ode on a Grecian Urn."

What Faulkner has introduced, therefore, with his first two paragraphs is a hockey match as a text to be read; and the ultimate meaning of that text, as with all of Faulkner's texts, is to be found in its mythic dimension. It is not this particular game, and certainly not the score of the game, but the universal significance of all games, which engages Faulkner's interest.

Once Faulkner has established the initial scene in terms of the polarities of motion versus order, or life versus art, he moves on to examine the contest before him in greater detail. He is immediately struck by the difference between hockey, in which "individual players" can triumph, and football, which is played by "sweating barehanded behemoths from the troglodyte mass." Here again is a familiar Faulkner theme: a greater respect for the individual than for the faceless masses. Less than four years earlier Faulkner had told the Oxford University High graduating class, of which his daughter Jill was a member, "Our danger is the forces in the world today which are trying . . . to rob [man] of his individuality, his soul, trying to reduce him to an unthinking mass." He went on to assert, "It is not men in the mass who can and will save Man. It is Man himself . . . , men and women" (*ESPL* 123). And in *A Fable*, published just five months before he accepted the *Sports Illustrated* assignment, Faulkner celebrates the lives of a select group of courageous individuals who seek to rise above the "vast seething moiling spiritless mass" of mankind (*F* 30).

The individuals who command Faulkner's attention as the Rangers play the Canadiens are Maurice Richard, Bernard "Boom Boom" Geoffrion, and Edgar Laprade. Richard possesses "something of the passionate glittering fatal alien quality of snakes"; Geoffrion plays "like an agile ruthless precocious boy"; and "the veteran Laprade," with whom the fifty-seven-year-old Faulkner undoubtedly identified, lacks the force and power of the younger players but still performs "with the know-how and the grace."

With the description of Laprade, Faulkner introduces the negative theme of time. He writes of the older player: "But he had time too now, *or rather time had him* [emphasis added], and what remained was no longer expendable that recklessly, heedlessly, successfully; not enough of it left now to buy fresh passion and fresh triumph with." Faulkner was sounding a similar note at this stage of his life with regard to his own productivity. Within the year he would write his good friend and editor Saxe Commins about his next book, *The Town*: "Have not taken fire in the old way yet, so it goes slow." Then again, a short while later: "I still have the feeling that I am written out . . . , and all remaining is the craftsmanship, no fire, force."[6] It is small wonder that Faulkner was impressed with an aging hockey player who skillfully and grace-fully held time at bay as he continued to play the game.

In Faulkner's view, time is not the only enemy working to restrain and defeat the individual—whether player or artist. Space is another. "Had we but world enough and time," Andrew Marvell's famous poem "To His Coy Mis-tress" begins; and the line could well serve as the epigraph to Faulkner's essay on hockey. Just as the hockey match is played out under the judgment of time, so too is it restricted in space. Hence, Faulkner complains that hockey, like many other games invented for the out-of-doors, is now played indoors. The result is presented in a smothering image of claustrophobia:

> He watched it—the figure-darted glare of ice, the concentric tiers rising in sections stipulated by the hand-lettered names of the individual fan-club idols, vanishing upward into the pall of tobacco smoke trapped by the roof—the roof which stopped and trapped all that intent and tense watching, and concentrated it downward upon the glare of ice frantic and frenetic with motion; until the by-product of the speed and the motion—their violence—had no chance to exhaust itself upward into space.

This image of entrapment, an image Faulkner frequently employs to connote human limitation and finitude,[7] leads Faulkner to generalize about what he considers an unfortunate trend in American sports. "Something is happen-ing to sport in America . . . ," he observes, "and that something is the roof we are putting over it and them. Skating, basketball, tennis, track meets and even steeplechasing have moved indoors; football and baseball function beneath covers of arc lights and in time will be rain- and coldproofed too." Only fish-ing and hunting, Faulkner notes, have been spared from this mausoleum-like fate. "But not for long," he laments; "in time that will be indoors too beneath lights and the trapped pall of spectator tobacco, the concentric sections bear-ing the name and device of the lion or the fish as well as that of the Richard or Geoffrion of the scoped rifle or four-ounce rod."

By this point the reader has become aware of the partial irony contained in the word "Innocent" in the title. The narrator may be naive and uninformed about the technical nature of the sport of hockey, but he possesses vast expe-rience in—and considerable wisdom about—the nature of the life process that is symbolized by the game on the ice. He knows, for example, from the advanced perspective of age, how youthful exuberance and excitement must ultimately succumb to the ravaging effects of time and the eventual suffocation of death. Looking back, the reader recognizes that this foreknowledge of tragic finality was there from the very beginning: "the vacant ice" of the opening paragraph is compared to "the mirror simulating ice in the Christmas store window, not before the miniature fir trees and reindeer and cosy lamplit cottage were arranged upon it, but *after they had been dismantled and cleared away*" [emphasis added]. Even before the match, the reader now recognizes, Faulkner has already been thinking about the end.

But Faulkner's literary genius, like that of any truly great writer, is not merely tragic but also comic. And if sport is to mirror life truthfully and accurately, it must reflect both views. Thus, following the symbolic references to time and death, Faulkner shifts to a more positive emphasis. Significantly, he finds this dimension not in the final score which declares one team the winner, and thus the symbolic (if illusionary) victor over time and space, but rather in the fact that among the spectators are "little boys" who are "frantic with the slow excruciating passage of time, panting for the hour when they would be Richard or Geoffrion or Laprade." These dreaming youngsters (the real Innocents of the narrative, since they want time to pass quickly) are identified as "the same little Negro boys whom the innocent has seen shadowboxing in front of a photograph of Joe Louis in his own Mississippi town, the same little Norwegian boys he watched staring up the snowless slope of the Holmenkollen jump one July day in the hills above Oslo." Countering the narrator's awareness of time and death, therefore, is his knowledge of what may be called the Myth of Eternal Recurrence; and as Faulkner's simultaneous reference to children in New York, Mississippi, and Norway makes clear, this myth is universal. Like his use of biblical archetypes in such novels as *Absalom, Absalom!, Go Down, Moses*, and *A Fable*, Faulkner's essay on hockey depicts history as cyclical, an ongoing contest, from generation to generation, between life and death, between nature's obliterating forces and man's heroic efforts to defy those forces in order to "endure and prevail."[8]

Similar themes will be noted in Faulkner's description of the 1955 Kentucky Derby (*ESPL* 52–61). Here, too, the sporting event is presented as a metaphor of human endeavor. As in his treatment of the hockey match, Faulkner's description of the Derby—and the human aspiration and disappointment symbolized by the race—is placed in a historical context that reveals the delimiting factors of time and space. "This saw Boone," Faulkner begins, and he continues by linking the annual reenactment of the Derby to the long-evolving human history that has taken place on this same Kentucky soil:

the bluegrass, the virgin land rolling westward wave by dense wave from the Allegheny gaps, unmarked then, teeming with deer and buffalo about the salt licks and the limestone springs whose water in time would make the fine bourbon whiskey; and the wild men too—the red men and the white ones too who had to be a little wild also to endure and survive and so make the wilderness with proofs of their tough survival—Boonesborough, Owenstown, Harrod's and Harbuck's Stations; Kentucky: the dark and bloody ground.

Once again Faulkner's setting is presented as a place of contradiction, a locale for both tragedy and comedy: Kentucky is not only a "dark and bloody ground" that tests man's capacity for survival; it is also the location that evokes pleasant memories of Abraham Lincoln, who is imagined as "speaking into the scene of his own nativity the simple and matchless prose," and of Stephen Foster, remembered for "the brick mansion of his song."

Faulkner's symbolic linking in his prologue of the running of the Derby with significant events in Kentucky history introduces what will become the major theme of the essay: all human endeavor, like the circuit of horse and jockey around the track, is a frantic race against time. The structure and movement of Faulkner's essay underscore this point. The use of subheadings that stress the ephemeral nature of all experience ("Three Days Before," "Two Days Before," "One Day Before," "The Day," and "4:29 P.M."), as well as the escalating pace of the narrative—from the slow evolutionary historical process of the prologue, through the eager anticipation of the days leading up to the race, to the culmination in the dizzying speed of the Derby itself—both serve to keep the theme of the tyranny of time before the reader.

Within this microcosmic world where history moves to the tick of the stopwatch and time is measured in fifths of seconds, man heroically if absurdly quests for the ideal. In this essay that ideal is symbolized by the statue of Man o' War which stands on the grounds of Churchill Downs:

the golden effigy of the golden horse, . . . looking out with the calm pride of the old manly warrior kings, over the land where his get still gambol as infants, until the Saturday afternoon moment when they too will wear the mat of roses in the flash and glare of magnesium; not just his own effigy, but symbol too of all the long recorded line from Aristides through the Whirlaways and Count Fleets and Gallant Foxes and Citations: epiphany and apotheosis of the horse.

As in the hockey essay (and, indeed, so much of his work), here too Faulkner's vision of the ideal is conveyed as heroic individualism distinguishing itself from the anonymous mass. Thus, Faulkner dramatizes the race as the effort of each horse to separate itself from the pack:

> the clump of horses indistinguishable yet, . . . flowing toward us along the rail until, approaching, we can begin to distinguish individuals, streaming past us now as individual horses . . . , shoot-past and bunching again as perspective diminishes, then becoming individual horses once more around the turn into the backstretch, streaming on, to bunch for the last time into the homestretch itself, then again individuals, individual horses, the individual horse, the Horse. . . .

Into this image of the ideal thoroughbred, "the individual horse, the Horse"—the dream of every owner, trainer, jockey, and fan—man subconsciously pours his deepest desire for survival, heroism, and triumph. Faulkner expresses it,

> It is a sublimation, a transference: man, with his admiration for speed and strength, physical power far beyond what he himself is capable of, projects his own desire for physical supremacy, victory, onto the agent—the baseball or football team, the prize fighter. Only the horse race is more universal because the brutality of the prize fight is absent, as well as the attenuation of football or baseball—the long time needed for the orgasm of victory to occur, where in the horse race it is a matter of minutes, never over two or three, repeated six or eight or 10 times in one afternoon.

As the reference to orgasm makes clear, Faulkner associates the sport's victory with sexuality and hence with the triumph of the life force over death.

In 1955 the avatar of the Big Horse, the hoped-for ideal, was named Nashua, the heavy favorite ridden by Eddie Arcaro. (Arcaro is identified in Faulkner's essay, but the name of his mount is never mentioned.) Faulkner graphically describes the way the excitement and anticipation build among sportswriters and spectators two days before the race. "Y'awl can git out of the way too now," the groom says as he clears the track for Nashua's morning workout; "here's the big horse coming." Then Faulkner and the other onlookers watch admiringly as Nashua races "in full stride" around the track and down the homestretch, "appearing to skim along just above the top rail like a tremendous brown hawk in the flattened bottom of his stoop."

In Faulkner's world, however, like Plato's, the ideal and the real never converge—or, if so, only rarely and fleetingly. On this day, Nashua, the heavy favorite, on a track muddied by a brief afternoon rain, is upset by Swaps expertly ridden down the stretch by Willie Shoemaker. Thus, the ideal, as in so much of Faulkner, remains only a nostalgic memory (as in the statue of Man o' War)—or a future dream. Hence, Faulkner concludes: "So it is not the Day after all. It is only the 81st one." It was a disappointment with which Faulkner was long familiar. All of his books, Faulkner claimed, were failures; none of them lived up to his "dream of perfection" (*LIG* 81). "I think," Faulkner further observed, "the reason that any writer continues to write is that the job, the story, the poem, book, which he has just finished, did not tell the truth that he was moved by in such a manner as suited the dream, the aspiration to tell that dream. So he writes another book, a poem or story" (*LIG* 205). And so, Faulkner might have added, he schedules another Kentucky Derby—and another, and another, and another.

NOTES

1. One notable exception is *The Sporting Spirit: Athletes in Literature and Life*, ed. Robert J. Higgs and Neil D. Isaacs (New York: Harcourt Brace Jovanovich, 1977), which includes Faulkner's essay "An Innocent at Rinkside."

2. To date, the only extended examination of Faulkner's use of sport will be found in Christian K. Messenger's *Sport and the Spirit of Play in American Fiction: Hawthorne to Faulkner* (New York: Columbia University Press, 1981). Other helpful discussions, though brief, are included in Robert J. Higgs, *Laurel & Thorn: The Athlete in American Literature* (Lexington: University Press of Kentucky, 1981), and Michael V. Oriard, *Dreaming of Heroes: American Sports Fiction, 1868–1980* (Chicago: Nelson-Hall, 1982).

3. Johan Huizinga, *Homo Ludens: A Study of the Play Element in Culture* (Boston: Beacon Press, 1955).

4. Whitney Tower, the *Sports Illustrated* staff writer who worked with Faulkner on the Kentucky Derby assignment, has recorded his recollections of the event. As Tower points out, Faulkner was the first of several noted writers enlisted to write about the Derby. He was followed, in successive years, by John P. Marquand, Catherine Drinker Bowen, and Nelson Algren. See "Prose for the Roses," *Sports Illustrated*, April 28, 1986, 38ff.

5. Interestingly, the editors of *Sports Illustrated* elected (perhaps because of space restrictions or perhaps because they thought the antepenultimate paragraph provided a stronger ending) to omit the final paragraph of Faulkner's hockey essay. The complete version has been published in *ESPL*, 48–51.

6. Louis Daniel Brodsky and Robert W. Hamblin, eds., *Faulkner: A Comprehensive Guide to the Brodsky Collection, Volume II: The Letters* (Jackson: University Press of Mississippi, 1984), 187, 189–90.

7. See, for example, the scene in *AILD* in which young Vardaman bores holes in his mother's coffin so she can breathe (67, 73).

8. This phrase, perhaps Faulkner's most famous, appears in his Nobel Prize Acceptance Speech, which is reprinted in *ESPL* (120).

"A Casebook on Mankind"
Faulkner's Use of Shakespeare

Throughout his career William Faulkner acknowledged the influence of many writers upon his work—Twain, Dreiser, Anderson, Keats, Dickens, Conrad, Balzac, Bergson, and Cervantes, to name only a few—but the one writer that he consistently mentioned as a constant and continuing influence was William Shakespeare. Though Faulkner's claim as a fledgling writer in 1921 that "[he] could write a play like *Hamlet* if [he] wanted to" (*FB* 330) may be dismissed as an act of youthful posturing, the statement serves to indicate that from the beginning Shakespeare was the standard by which Faulkner would judge his own creativity. In later years Faulkner frequently acknowledged Shakespeare as a major inspiration and influence, once noting, "I have a one-volume Shakespeare that I have just about worn out carrying around with me" (*FIU* 67). Faulkner's recorded interviews and conversations contain references to a number of Shakespeare's works and characters, including *Hamlet, Macbeth, Henry IV, Henry V, A Midsummer Night's Dream, Romeo and Juliet*, the sonnets, Falstaff, Prince Hal, Lady Macbeth, Bottom, Ophelia, and Mercutio. In 1947 he told an Ole Miss English class that Shakespeare's work provides "a casebook on mankind," adding, "if a man has a great deal of talent he can use Shakespeare as a yardstick."[1] In one of his last interviews shortly before his death in 1962, Faulkner said of all writers, including himself, "We yearn to be as good as Shakespeare" (*LIG* 276).

The parallels in the lives and careers of the two writers are remarkably striking. Both were born in provincial small towns but found their eventual success in metropolitan cities, Shakespeare in London and Faulkner in New York and Hollywood. Both had a great love of nature and the rural outdoors. Neither received a great deal of formal education. Both started out as poets but shortly turned to other narrative forms, Faulkner to fiction and Shakespeare to drama. Both had extramarital affairs that were reflected in some of their writings. Each wrote both tragedies and comedies, and in each case their final work was a comedy, Shakespeare's *The Tempest* and Faulkner's *The Reivers*. A number of dominant themes and emphases are common to both writers, including the imaginative use of historical materials, the incorporation of both tragic and comic views of life, and the paradoxical tension between fate (in Faulkner's case, determinism) and free will. Moreover, both writers exhibit a fascination for experimental form and language, flouting conventional rules to create new narrative structures and delighting in neologisms, puns, and other forms of wordplay. Finally, both writers were acutely interested in the paradoxical relationship of life and art.

It would be impossible, of course, in a short essay to consider all of the possible Shakespearean influences upon Faulkner, so I will cite only three representative examples. These may be grouped according to the following categories:

1. Specific allusions to Shakespeare's plays and characters;
2. A common interest in historical analogues; and
3. An emphasis on the theme of the immortality of art.

ALLUSIONS

Without question the most famous allusion to Shakespeare in all of Faulkner is the title of his 1929 novel, *The Sound and the Fury*. As Faulkner readily acknowledged, the title phrase was borrowed from Macbeth's famous speech,

> Tomorrow, and tomorrow, and tomorrow,
> Creeps in this petty pace from day to day
> To the last syllable of recorded time,
> And all our yesterdays have lighted fools
> The way to dusty death. Out, out brief candle!
> Life's but a walking shadow, a poor player
> Who struts and frets his hour upon the stage
> And then is heard no more: it is a tale
> Told by an idiot, full of sound and fury,
> Signifying nothing. (V.v.19–28)

Not only Faulkner's title phrase, "sound and fury," but also the facts that the opening chapter of Faulkner's novel is narrated through the consciousness of a mentally challenged person, thus "told by an idiot," and that the second chapter presents Quentin Compson very much as "a walking shadow," provide obvious links to this Shakespearean passage. However, as Allen Frye has astutely demonstrated in his study of the bell imagery in *The Sound and the Fury*, Faulkner's use of Shakespeare's play goes far beyond the points just mentioned. Frye traces dozens of references to bells and chimes throughout Faulkner's text. Linking these to Lady Macbeth's bell that provides the signal for Macbeth to murder Duncan ("I go, and it is done; the bell invites me. / Hear it not, Duncan, for it is a knell, / That summons thee to heaven or to hell" [II.i.62–64]), Frye demonstrates that the bells in both *Macbeth* and *The Sound and the Fury* "denote not only time, but opportunities for choices, summonings, even, to choose."[2]

In this connection, Faulkner appears to be using the Shakespearean pattern, much as Joyce uses the Homeric in *Ulysses*, ironically, juxtaposing the heroic, bold, if mistaken, choices of an earlier age with the indecision and impotence often associated with the early twentieth century.

Faulkner employs another significant Shakespearean allusion in *Light in August*. Gail Hightower, a major character in that novel, is, as his name implies, an individual who has sought to escape from actual experience to live in a "high tower" of self-delusion and fantasy. A defrocked clergyman, Hightower has elected to stay on in Jefferson despite the personal scandal that, years earlier, had cost him his marriage, his position as pastor of a church, and finally even his right to the title of ordained minister. When we meet him early in the novel, he is living out his barren existence largely behind the closed doors of his house, entertaining no visitors except one, a mill worker and church layman named Byron Bunch.

As Faulkner's novel unfolds, looping backward as well as forward, we are led to understand the reasons for Hightower's tragic failure. Like many of Faulkner's modern white male southerners, the youthful Hightower had become fixated on an idealistic southern heritage, embodied for Hightower in the image of his grandfather, a Confederate cavalry officer who, the young minister had been led to believe, sacrificially gave his life for region, noblesse oblige, and personal honor. Hightower's worship of this ancestor and the values he supposedly represented come to dominate Hightower's consciousness; the grandfather's legendary exploits even become the focus of Hightower's sermons: "It was as if he couldn't get religion and that galloping cavalry and his dead grandfather shot from the galloping horse untangled from each other, even in the pulpit" (*LIA* 56). When Hightower learns, however, that the fabled grandfather had not died heroically in battle but, quite the contrary, was actually shot while engaged in the ignominious act of stealing chickens, Hightower is robbed of his mythical past; and this loss contributes to his decision to disengage himself from life and action, passing his days "as though the seed which his grandfather had transmitted to him had been on the horse too that night and had been killed too and time had stopped there and then for that seed and nothing had happened in time since, not even him" (59).

Eventually, however, Hightower, inspired by the kindly example and encouraging words of Byron Bunch, elects to climb down from his high tower of retreat and symbolic death to reenter the land of the living. Under Bunch's leadership, Hightower assists first Lena Grove, a young, unwed pregnant woman, and then Joe Christmas, a Black man who is eventually lynched by a white mob. In the case of Christmas, Hightower tries to save the man's life by fabricating an alibi for Christmas. "Men!" he screams at the mob. "Listen to me. He was here that night. He was with me the night of the murder" (439). While Hightower's situational ethics ultimately fail to save Joe Christmas from the hands of the racist mob, his intervention on Christmas's behalf marks a major point in Hightower's progression toward self-awareness, personal responsibility, and social reengagement.

What is interesting and relevant about all this to my purpose is the reading material that Faulkner assigns to Hightower. During his long period of escape and disengagement, we are told, Hightower reads "a great deal" in the large number of books that "line his study wall" (67). One author whom he finds particularly attractive is Alfred, Lord Tennyson.

> He turns from the window. One wall of the study is lined with books. He pauses before them, seeking, until he finds the one which he wants. It is Tennyson. It is dogeared. He has had it ever since the seminary. He sits beneath the lamp and opens it. It does not take long. Soon the fine galloping language, the gutless swooning full of sapless trees and dehydrated lusts begins to swim smooth and swift and peaceful. It is better than praying without having to bother to think aloud. It is like listening in a cathedral to a eunuch chanting in a language which he does not even need to not understand. (301)

Obviously, Hightower finds in Tennyson's mellifluous lines, even more than in prayer, an anodyne to his pain and anguish. But on the day he returns from the cabin where he has served as midwife at the birth of Lena's child, he ignores the "dogeared" Tennyson volume and turns to Shakespeare.

He goes to the study. He moves like a man with a purpose now, who for twentyfive years has been doing nothing at all between the time to wake and the time to sleep again. Neither is the book which he now chooses the Tennyson: this time also he chooses food for a man. It is *Henry IV*, and he goes out into the back yard and lies down in the sagging deck chair beneath the mulberry tree, plumping solidly and heavily into it. (383)

As the words "solidly" and "heavily" imply, Hightower has abandoned the dream world associated with Tennyson's "gutless swooning," "sapless trees," and "dehydrated lusts" to enter the real world of physicality and substance. If I understand Faulkner's allusion correctly, Hightower's choice is not altogether unlike the choice that Shakespeare has Prince Hal make in his transition from youthful irresponsibility to the duties of kingship.

THE USE OF HISTORICAL MATERIALS

A second aspect of Faulkner's work that seems linked to the possible influence of Shakespeare relates to the manner in which both writers make significant use of historical material. Shakespeare, as most readers well know, seldom invented an original plot, choosing rather to take familiar characters and events from older plays or historical chronicles, most notably Raphael Holinshed's *Chronicles of England, Scotland, and Ireland* and Plutarch's *Lives of the Noble Grecians and Romans*, and reworking them to suit his own dramatic purposes. Faulkner, too, drew heavily upon history for his fictional materials, incorporating into his Yoknapatawpha narratives accounts of the settlement of the South, the Civil War and Reconstruction, the racial patterns and conflicts of Jim Crow and segregation, and the displacement of an agrarian lifestyle by mechanization and industrialization.

But it would be a mistake to think that either Shakespeare or Faulkner was primarily interested in history as mere history. They both wrote in what I like to call—accurately, I think, if ungrammatically—"the past-present tense," that is, in a way that utilizes the past as an analogue to or even a commentary on the present situation. Here, it will be helpful to take a brief excursion into contemporary literary theory. Recent advancements in literary criticism and linguistics have helped us to understand better the always-complex relationship existing between a writer, and that writer's world, and any literary text. We now acknowledge that there can never be a definite demarcation between a literary work and its creator, between objectivity and subjectivity, or between the past as lived and the past as perceived by one looking back on it from the altered perspective of the present. To use the term popularized by Mikhail Bakhtin, the interrelationship between these pairs is "dialogical." [3] One of the best illustrations of this point is Arthur Miller's great play *The Crucible*, on the literal level a treatment of the mass hysteria evidenced in the Salem witchcraft trials of 1692 but through contextual parallels an exposé of the McCarthyism that was rampant in America at the time Miller published the play, 1953. There can be no denying that *The Crucible* is an "historical" play; but it would certainly be a mistake to view the play as merely or even primarily historical: the ultimate meaning of the play can be grasped only by placing the historical elements alongside the contemporary event—the McCarthy hearings—that provided the motivation for Miller's writing of the play. In Miller's case, we know, the use of the past-present tense was conscious and calculated; but modern theorists would argue that even had it been unconscious and coincidental, Miller's choice of historical subject and his treatment of it would still have been influenced by his present situation, that is, by his summons to appear as a witness before the House Committee on Un-American Activities.

While Shakespeare's main purpose in his repetitions of history was in all likelihood to tell a good story, or, more precisely, to convert the old stories into poetic form, there can be little doubt that he was very much aware of the parallels between the historical narratives he chose to dramatize and his contemporary Elizabethan world. To cite only two examples: think of Shakespeare's presentation in the great comedies of the pastoral lifestyle that was disappearing with the development and spreading influence of the metropolitan culture of London; or, better, think of Shakespeare's obsession with the history of kingship, even the divine right of kings, at a time when the contemporary wearers of the crown, Queen Elizabeth and King James, were continually being challenged and even threatened with insurrection.

Perhaps the best example of Shakespeare's using the past as a mirror to contemporary events is *Richard II*. Here, Shakespeare deals with one of the most crucial episodes in English history, the deposing of King Richard by Henry Bolingbroke, afterwards King Henry IV. This event had occurred in 1399, nearly two hundred years before Shakespeare wrote about it; and from his later perspective Shakespeare knew that the ultimate outcome of Richard's overthrow was the long and tragic War of the Roses, the civil war between the royal houses of York and Lancaster that lasted for thirty years. Before writing *Richard II*, Shakespeare had already written four plays about the War of the Roses—the three parts of *Henry VI* and *Richard III*. Now, having already dramatized the national calamity of the war, he explores the source of that conflict in Bolingbroke's usurpation of Richard's crown. Yes, Shakespeare acknowledges in his play, Richard was a weak king, a dreamer and an aesthete, out of touch with his subjects; and Henry was a doer, a man of action, and the crowd's favorite—but there was still the huge question, towering large for Shakespeare and others of the Renaissance, of whether any degree of ineffi- ciency or even wickedness could justify the overthrow of God's anointed ruler and the political chaos that would ensue. As Richard states the case,

> Not all the water in the rough, rude sea
> Can wash the balm from an anointed king.
> The breath of worldly men cannot depose
> The deputy elected by God. (III.ii.54–57)

In the deposition scene Shakespeare has Richard compare himself to the cruci- fied Christ: "you Pilates / Have here delivered me to my sour cross, / And water cannot wash away your sin" (IV.i.240–42). Clearly, if Richard is Christ, then Henry is Judas, the political leaders Pilates, and the British populace the fickle mob that demanded the freeing of Barabbas and the crucifixion of Christ.

The issue of who is the rightful ruler is a universal question of British poli- tics, but Shakespeare's interest in the question, as indeed in the entire history of the War of the Roses, was being fueled by particular events of his own day, not unlike the way Arthur Miller's interest in the witchcraft trials was fueled by the McCarthy hearings, or in our own time the revival of interest in Pres- ident Andrew Johnson's impeachment was brought about by the impeach- ments of Presidents Clinton and Trump. At the time Shakespeare wrote *Rich- ard II*, the Henry/Richard conflict was being repeated in the opposition of the Earl of Essex to Queen Elizabeth. Shakespeare was very close to, if not per- sonally involved in, this issue, since his patron, the Earl of Southampton, was one of the leading supporters of Essex. Modern audiences and readers may not be much aware of this parallel when they view or read Shakespeare's play, but the parallel would have been unmistakable to the Elizabethan audience.

We know that the parallel was obvious to both Essex and the queen. In 1601, when Essex and his followers attempted to overthrow Elizabeth and place Essex on the throne, they arranged to have a performance of *Richard II* staged at the popular Globe Theatre the very night before the attempted coup—a kind of pep rally before the big game the following day. When the coup failed, the conspirators were arrested; and in the trial that followed, Essex was con- demned to death, and Southampton was imprisoned in the Tower, where he remained until the death of Elizabeth two years later. One of the real mysteries in all these developments is how Shakespeare managed to escape censure or worse, since he was such a close personal friend of Southampton and thus probably an acquaintance of Essex.

We also know that Queen Elizabeth was acutely aware of the parallel being drawn between herself and Richard II. "I am Richard II, know ye not that?" she is quoted as saying after the conspiracy trial was over; and her sensitivity to the issue was undoubtedly the reason that the deposition scene in Shakespeare's play—where Henry actually takes the crown from Richard—was officially censored and thus omitted in the first printings of *Richard II*, and indeed did not find its way into print until after the accession of James I.[4]

This question of kingship and right rule is at the very heart of so many of Shakespeare's plays, not only the two tetralogies of the Henrys and the Richards, but also the great tragedies of *Macbeth*, *Hamlet*, and *King Lear*, and even many of the comedies such as *Twelfth Night*, *Much Ado about Nothing*, and *The Tempest*. There can be little doubt, I think, that this theme was of great concern for Shakespeare; and his relating it to both past and present situations—in other words, his effective use of the past-present tense—provided him a means of warning his age about the tragic lessons of history.

Like Shakespeare, Faulkner was an historical writer who courageously explored the past in his attempt to analyze and understand the present. We see this approach operative in Faulkner on the level of both individual characters and southern society as a whole. The best example is Faulkner's most complex, and, many think, greatest, novel: *Absalom, Absalom!*

Published in 1936, *Absalom, Absalom!* expands the story of the suicidal Quentin Compson from *The Sound and the Fury* of seven years earlier. Set during the final year of Quentin's life, 1909–10, *Absalom* presents Quentin's desperate and ultimately unsuccessful attempts to come to understand both himself and his native region. In this quest for understanding and, indeed, salvation, Quentin displaces his own inner guilts and conflicts onto a legendary story that he has heard all his life, the story of the rise and fall of Thomas Sutpen, a rags-to-riches southern planter who carved a plantation out of the Yoknapatawpha wilderness in the 1830s and sought to create a family dynasty, but who saw his dream eventually destroyed by a father/son conflict that parallels the tragic story from which Faulkner draws his title, the biblical account of the conflict between King David and his rebellious son Absalom.

In structuring the plot of his novel, Faulkner moves back and forth from the Quentin narrative of 1909–10 to the Sutpen narrative of the 1810s to the 1860s. In analyzing these time shifts, however, and in seeking to determine whether the main character of the novel is Quentin Compson or Thomas

Sutpen, critics typically overlook the novel's third time dimension, that is, the time of Faulkner, the creator of the novel, which is, of course, 1935–36, when the novel was being written. Thus, not unlike the better-known novel published the same year, Margaret Mitchell's *Gone with the Wind*, *Absalom, Absalom!* is written in past-present tense: it is not only an historical novel of Civil War days; it is also a novel about, and with a message for, the Great Depression.

And what is that message? We can begin the search for an answer to that question, I think, by recognizing that Thomas Sutpen is a character type frequently found in American history and literature but one that in the 1930s was coming under increased scrutiny: an entrepreneurial, laissez-faire capitalist. Like the real-life Benjamin Franklin and John D. Rockefeller and Henry Flagler and the fictional Poor Richard, Horatio Alger's Ragged Dick, and Jay Gatsby, Sutpen is born poor but, through ambition, industriousness, and good fortune (pluck and luck), rises to a position of tremendous wealth and status. With the advent of the Great Depression, however, such character types, as indeed all the business practices of capitalism, were being called into question, the more so since the failures of the Great Depression appeared to be the logical consequences of the excesses of the all-too-recent robber barons and monopolists. As Faulkner's novel demonstrates, it was not merely New Deal politicians like Franklin Roosevelt or Henry Wallace or socialist writers like John Dos Passos and John Steinbeck who were questioning the American economic enterprise. The characterization of Thomas Sutpen is a serious critique of the American Dream at a time of crisis when the traditional values and methods associated with that dream were being challenged.

In dramatizing the reasons for Sutpen's self-destruction, Faulkner stresses Sutpen's ruthless exploitation of other people in his quest to amass wealth and power. He utilizes and brutalizes the slaves who build his mansion, and he holds a French architect in virtual imprisonment until the house is completed. Sutpen marries twice, in each case not for love but for financial and social advancement. A racist as well as a materialist, he rejects his first wife when he learns she is part Black, turns away from his door the son of that union, and eventually provides his white son with a motive to murder his biracial half-brother. As a sad, pathetic old man and a widower, with his plantation gone and his family dead or scattered, he seeks to revitalize his dream by seducing a poor-white teenage girl in the hope of producing a male heir: when the child turns out to be a female, Sutpen rejects both the mother and the child with perhaps the cruelest words in the novel: "Well, Milly; too bad you're not a mare too. Then I could give you a decent stall in the stable" (229). "They did not think of love in connection with Sutpen," the reader is told early in the novel. "They thought of ruthlessness rather than justice and of fear rather than respect, but not of pity or love" (32).

Treating Thomas Sutpen as Faulkner's 1930s portrait of capitalism without any redeeming social consciousness leads one to a very different interpretation of Quentin Compson's obsession with the Sutpen legend than is currently offered by critics. While, like many Americans of every day and time, Quentin envies, perhaps even subconsciously admires, the boldness and the audacity of pragmatic doers and achievers like Sutpen, at the same time Quentin is an idealist, a believer in noblesse oblige, a defender of community and brotherhood and family loyalty and romantic love—indeed, a practitioner (to reverse the negative terms earlier applied to Sutpen) of justice rather than ruthlessness, of respect rather than fear, and of pity and love. Caught between such oppositions, the America of the 1930s sought to find itself. And Faulkner dramatizes the quest.

ART AND IMMORTALITY

A third parallel between Faulkner and Shakespeare is a common interest in the paradoxical relationship between life and art. Most artists have a heightened awareness, some obsessively so, of the tragic brevity of life and a concomitant, perhaps even consequent, desire to create works of art that will far outlast their creators' meager space of life and breath. Picasso, we are told, was so fearful of death terminating his creativity that he would tolerate no mention of the word or any reminder of its harsh reality. And Keats, dying of tuberculosis, penned his "Ode on a Grecian Urn," celebrating the capacity of art to survive and inspire others even centuries after the death of its creator—and thereby expressing his own hope that he as a poet might be as lucky as the maker of the urn. It is not at all surprising that Faulkner and Shakespeare shared this interest in the mortality of the artist and the potential immortality of art.

Death seems to have been an obsession with Faulkner from an early age. Perhaps this fear of death may have derived from his near demise from scarlet fever at age four or from his experience, at age nine, of watching his beloved grandmother ("Damuddy") destroyed by cancer. Whatever its origin, death surfaces as a major subject in Faulkner's early poetry and prose and is seldom again absent from his work. Indeed, among American writers only Edgar Allan Poe seems as obsessed as Faulkner with death, decay, corpses, and cemeteries.

But an existential recognition of the tragic inevitability of death is only one—and not the most important—facet of Faulkner's handling of the subject. For Faulkner the ultimate meaning is to be found in the heroic resistance to death, and from Thomas Sutpen's struggle against time and mortality in *Absalom, Absalom!* onward, this theme becomes an overt motif in Faulkner's work. As Ernest Becker has convincingly argued in *The Denial of Death*, all individuals experience death anxiety and consequently long for immortality, whether natural or supernatural;[5] but Faulkner contends that this psychological conflict is especially acute for the artist. As he once said, "Since man is mortal, the only immortality possible for him is to leave something behind him that is immortal since it will always move. This is the artist's way of scribbling 'Kilroy was here' on the wall of the final and irrevocable oblivion through which he must someday pass" (*LIG* 253). Faulkner's most extended expression of this idea is found in his "Foreword" to *The Faulkner Reader* (1954), in which he contends that the ultimate goal of any writer is "to uplift man's heart" by "saying No to death." "Some day," Faulkner concludes, "[the writer] will be no more, which will not matter then, because isolated and itself invulnerable in the cold print remains that which is capable of engendering still the old deathless excitement in hearts and glands whose owners and custodians are generations from the air he breathed and anguished in" (*ESPL* 181–82).

We know less about Shakespeare's personal life and opinions than we do of Faulkner's, but a number of the sonnets clearly evidence the same mortality vs. immortality theme that we have been exploring in Faulkner. These sonnets are addressed to one or more unidentified individuals whom Shakespeare loved dearly (whether patron, friend, or lover, we cannot be quite sure), and they all set actual experience, "Where wasteful Time debateth with Decay, / To change your day of youth to sullied night," against the poet's desire to write "eternal lines" in which the beloved will be made immortal: "So long as men can breathe or eyes can see," sonnet 18 concludes, "So long lives this and this gives life to thee." One of the most sublime expressions of this idea is sonnet 65:

> Since brass, nor stone, nor earth, nor boundless sea,
> But sad mortality o'er-sways their power,
> How with this rage shall beauty hold a plea,
> Whose action is no stronger than a flower?
> O, how shall summer's honey breath hold out
> Against the wreckful siege of battering days,
> When rocks impregnable are not so stout,
> Nor gates of steel so strong, but Time decays?

O fearful meditation! where, alack,
Shall Time's best jewel from Time's chest be hid?
Or what strong hand can hold his swift foot back?
Or who his spoil of beauty can forbid?
O, none, unless this miracle have might,
That in black ink my love shall still shine bright.

It is a cardinal irony, of course, that an individual whose name or identity we do not know is immortalized in Shakespeare's poetry. But that causes us no concern, since it is the universal and immortal poem that we celebrate and not its particular historical circumstance. Faulkner certainly understood that. As he once said, "[Man] can't live forever. He knows that. But when he's gone somebody will know he was here for his short time. He can build a bridge and will be remembered for a day or two, a monument, for a day or two. but somehow the picture, the poem—that lasts a long time, a very long time, longer than anything" (*LIG* 103). And here, I think, he was stating a principle that he learned at least partly from reading Shakespeare's sonnets.

I hope that these few examples I have cited will serve to suggest that Faulkner's use of Shakespearean materials was both conscious and significant. Given such parallels, it is not altogether unfitting that Faulkner is sometimes called "the American Shakespeare."

NOTES

1. James W. Webb and A. Wigfall Green, eds., *William Faulkner of Oxford* (Baton Rouge: Louisiana State University Press, 1965), 134.

2. W. Allen Frye, "Mythic Imagery in *Absalom, Absalom!, The Sound and the Fury*, and *Light in August*: Faulkner's Structural Motifs" (MA thesis, Southeast Missouri State University, 1995), 27.

3. See Tzvetan Todorov, *Mikhail Bakhtin : The Dialogical Principle*, trans. Wlad Godzich (Minneapolis: University of Minnesota Press, 1984).

4. See A. L. Rowse, *The England of Elizabeth* (New York: Macmillan, 1961), 37; and G. B. Harrison, ed., *Shakespeare: Major Plays and the Sonnets* (Harcourt, Brace, & World, 1948), 188–92.

5. Ernest Becker, *The Denial of Death* (New York: Free Press, 1973).

Faulkner's Hucks and Jims

"All modern American literature comes from one book by Mark Twain called *Huckleberry Finn*," Ernest Hemingway claimed.[1] William Faulkner disagreed with many things that Hemingway said or wrote, but on this point the two men wholeheartedly agreed. "Mark Twain," Faulkner said, "was the first truly American writer, and all of us since are his heirs, we descended from him" (*LIG* 137). On another occasion he observed, "[Sherwood Anderson] was the father of my generation of American writers and the tradition of American writing which our successors will carry on.... [Theodore] Dreiser is his older brother, and Mark Twain the father of them both" (249–50). He added, "People will read *Huck Finn* for a long time" (56).

Faulkner's most revealing discussion of *The Adventures of Huckleberry Finn* can be found in comments he made to the English Club at the University of Virginia in 1958 (*FIU* 241–48). The remarks on Twain's novel appear in the context of Faulkner's extended lament that in the modern world of organizations and bureaucracies and dogmatic creeds, citizens have been robbed of their individuality and uniqueness. The accepted "mythology" of the modern world, Faulkner says, is an almost universal belief "that one single individual man is nothing, and can have weight and substance only when organized into the anonymity of a group where he will have surrendered his individual soul for a number" (242). In such a world human beings are "desouled as the stallion or boar or bull is gelded" (245), and individual values such as "honesty and pity and responsibility and compassion" are displaced by "factional regimented group[s], both filling the same air at the same time with the same double-barreled abstractions of 'peoples' democracy' and 'minority rights' and 'equal justice' and 'social welfare'—all the synonyms which take all the shame out of irresponsibility by not merely inviting but even compelling everyone to participate in it" (242).

Primary among those who stand against such dehumanizing tendencies in the modern world, Faulkner claims, are the artists—not only writers but also painters, musicians, sculptors, and architects—who know the value of individuality because their work is the result of individual, not corporate, effort. Faulkner also commends President Eisenhower's People-to-People Program (for which Faulkner served as cochairman of the Writers' Committee) as an attempt, flawed though it proved to be, to inject a degree of individuality and personhood into the conformist, impersonal modern state. But neither artists, nor even presidents, in Faulkner's view, can be successful in their reforming efforts so long as the powerful, controlling mind-set of the collectivist society remains the accepted and desirable norm.

To underscore his point about the loss of individuality in the modern world, Faulkner contrasts J. D. Salinger's *Catcher in the Rye* with *Huckleberry Finn*. For Faulkner the story of Holden Caulfield is the narrative of a character who "loved man and wished to be a part of mankind, humanity, who tried to join the human race and failed." But the cause of Holden's failure rests not so much in the character as in the milieu he inhabits. "His tragedy," Faulkner says, "was that when he attempted to enter the human race, there was no human race there." Faulkner sees Caulfield's situation as typical of many of the characters in the books written by the young writers of the mid-twentieth-century. Instead of living "in myriad company [with] the anguishes and hopes of all human hearts in a world of a few simple comprehensible truths and moral principles," these characters "exist alone inside a vacuum of facts which [they] did not choose and cannot cope with and cannot escape from like a fly inside an inverted tumbler" (244). In terms of the philosophical and literary history of the first half of the twentieth century, Faulkner, like Joseph Wood Krutch and other humanists of the period, is deploring how deterministic theories of human behavior have displaced the traditional belief in free will, how such forces as circumstance, environment, and heredity are believed to overrule individual choice and control.

In contrast to the dilemma of Holden Caulfield and his compatriots, Faulkner offers the example of Huckleberry Finn:

another youth already father to what will some day soon now be a man. But in Huck's case all he had to combat was his small size, which time would cure for him; in time he would be as big as any man he had to cope with; and even as it was, all the adult world could do to harm him was to skin his nose a little; humanity, the human race, would and was accepting him already; all he needed to do was just to grow up in it. (244–45)

Both Huck and Holden are young individuals seeking meaning in their relationship to the larger world. However, according to Faulkner, Huck succeeds because his quest takes place within a community of shared values and beliefs that are compatible with and prize individuality, whereas Holden fails because his quest takes place "not in individuality but in isolation" (244). In other words, Huck lives and functions in relationship to society (even when he is rebelling against it), while Holden exists, metaphorically at least, in solitary confinement.

Let's examine how this theme plays out in Twain's novel.[2] Huck's adventures are often viewed as a rebel's quest for freedom, but it is not freedom per se that Huck desires. An orphan who has faked his own death to escape his abusive father, Huck goes in search of the father he has lost. Though he does not know it for most of the book, he has found that father in Jim, the runaway slave who is also in need of the family he has lost. Rightly understood (and it is sad that readers obsessed with political correctness cannot get past the n-word to recognize the fact), *Huckleberry Finn* is a love story, one of the finest in all of our literature. Jim's ecstatic embrace of Huck after fearing that Huck is dead and Huck's refusal to turn Jim over to the authorities and then later risking his life to steal Jim out of slavery (to Tom Sawyer, of course, this action of the novel is a mere charade, since he knows that Jim is already free) clearly demonstrate the love that develops between these two rejects and escapees of a society given over to abstractions and platitudes. Though the union is threatened at every point along the river, both Huck and Jim are seeking freedom not for its own sake but for the sake of relationship, acceptance, family, and love.

Too little attention has been paid to Jim's role as mentor to Huck as their relationship develops. All readers note Huck's role as "a low-down Abolitionist" (43) in defense of Jim's freedom, but the benefits of the relationship are reciprocal. Along with the great river and the whole of nature, Jim teaches Huck things that go much deeper than "sivilization" and the community's mores. As Richard Chase has noted, *Huckleberry Finn* is a novel about "exorcism,"[3] and just as Jim instructs Huck about the use of hair balls and other magical objects to counter witches and other malignant forces of the universe, so too does Jim's example of simple, authentic humanity instruct Huck about the hypocrisies and injustices and cruelties of conventional society. Jim's counter to Huck's French lesson, "Is a Frenchman a man? . . . *Well*, den! Dad blame it, why doan' he *talk* like a man" (78), expresses more than a naïve theory of language. From Jim, the "n——r" and enslaved man at the beginning of the book but friend and father to Huck later on, Huck learns what is required of him to be truly "a man." But Huck is a slow learner, and he comes to understand only gradually the lessons Jim teaches him; still, we can easily trace the key points of Huck's moral and humanistic development. Hints of that development appear as early as chapter 11 of the novel, when Huck reports to Jim, "They're after us!"—showing by those words, as Leo Marx has pointed out, that Huck is already—instinctively if not consciously—identifying with Jim's flight for freedom.[4] A further point in Huck's initiation occurs when he observes Jim's homesickness for his wife and children and concludes: "I do believe he cared just as much for his people as white folks does for their'n" (150). Another comes when Huck struggles with his conscience over not turning Jim over to the authorities. On one occasion, heading to the shore to report Jim to the authorities but remembering Jim's expression of gratitude to him ("I'se a free man, en I couldn't ever ben free ef it hadn' ben for Huck" [86]), Huck lies to the vigilantes about the identity of his companion on the raft: "He's white," Huck says (87). Huck's moral (to him, ironically, immoral) education reaches its climax when he destroys the letter he has written informing Miss Watson of Jim's whereabouts: "All right, then, I'll *go* to hell," he says, tearing up the letter (206). From this point on Huck actively and unrepentantly works to steal Jim out of slavery. Huck now accepts his role as rebel and outcast, but in the process of losing the world, he has saved his soul. And the catalyst in this conversion experience has been Jim.

Not surprisingly, given his high regard for Twain's novel and its main character, Faulkner created a number of characters who seem modeled at least in part on the relationship of Huckleberry Finn and Jim. Let's briefly consider three pairs of them: Ike McCaslin and Sam Fathers of "The Bear," Chick Mallison and Lucas Beauchamp of *Intruder in the Dust*, and Lucius Priest and Ned McCaslin/Uncle Parsham of *The Reivers*. In each of these cases, a young white boy's cultural and ethical education is conditioned and influenced by a Black mentor.

In "The Bear" the youthful Ike McCaslin serves his novitiate as a woodsman and hunter under the direction of Sam Fathers, whose name suggests the role that he plays not only for Ike but for all the participants in the annual hunt for the legendary bear Old Ben. Part Native American as well as Black, Fathers, like Jim, is a primitive in touch with truths that lie beyond the boundaries of civilized society. "You aint in town now," the camp cook tells Ike; "you in the woods" (*GDM* 308); and Sam Fathers teaches Ike that he must divest himself of the symbols of civilization—the gun, the watch, the compass—in order to gain a vision of Old Ben, the deity that reigns over the wilderness. But it is not only courage and respect and responsibility that Ike learns under Fathers's guidance: he learns also to accept the tragic realities of mutability and death: the eventual loss of the wilderness and the deaths of its heroes—Old Ben, the great hunting dog Lion, and Sam. Faulkner's woods are the equivalent of Twain's river, and life and values and relationships there are different from the ways of the settlements. And the lessons Ike learns in the woods under the tutelage of Sam Fathers he later applies to his decision to forfeit his inheritance of the family plantation. What Vernon L. Parrington said of *Huckleberry Finn*—that it is "a drama of the struggle between the individual and the village mores"[5]—may also be said of "The Bear," with Ike's decision to relinquish the plantation being the equivalent of Huck's tearing up of the letter to Miss Watson. And it is Sam Fathers who has brought Ike to this decision: "Sam Fathers set me free" (286), Ike tells his cousin Cass.

In *Intruder in the Dust* Faulkner's Huck and Jim are Chick Mallison, a young white town boy, and Lucas Beauchamp, a Black farmer. As in the case of Twain's novel, Faulkner's Huck begins by sharing the racial prejudices of his community. This point becomes abundantly clear in the initial encounter between Chick and Lucas. While hunting on Lucas's property, Chick falls into a frozen creek and winds up in Lucas's house, where the binary oppositions of white and Black are reversed when Chick is ordered by Lucas to strip off his wet clothes and later to eat the food that a Black woman has prepared for him. Unaccustomed to being bossed about by a "n——r," Chick tries to regain the ascendancy by offering to pay Lucas for his trouble. Thus begins a series of actions in which Chick tries to lure Lucas back into the traditional southern roles of subservient and unequal. But each time Lucas declines the gambit.

Gradually, however, as in the case of Huck and Jim, Chick comes to recognize and accept Lucas's humanity and, like Huck, actively works to secure the Black man's freedom. In Lucas's case it is freedom from jail and a threatened lynching after Lucas is charged with a murder he did not commit. Eventually, Chick (with the aid of his Black friend Alex and an elderly spinster, Miss Habersham) proves Lucas's innocence by putting himself in danger by digging up a grave in a country cemetery. As a result of his experience, Chick not only comes to appreciate a Black man's pride, dignity, and independence but also finds himself in rebellion against the traditional racial attitudes and actions of the white citizens of his community. In both cases he is following in the footsteps of Huckleberry Finn.

The Reivers is the Faulkner novel that is most nearly like *Huckleberry Finn*. The central focus of both novels is a journey—Twain's a raft trip down the Mississippi River, Faulkner's an automobile trip to Memphis. And each novel places its protagonist in the midst of disrespectable and immoral characters and forces: Huck must deal with robbers, cutthroats, con men, and fighters of feuds; while Lucius traffics with thieves, gamblers, and prostitutes. But just as Jim assists Huck to discover his humanity amidst the chaos of their world, so does a Black mentor (first Ned and then Uncle Parsham) help Lucius come to terms with his.

Not only does each of Faulkner's Hucks go through an initiation experience in which a Black man serves as both catalyst and teacher, but each of them, like Huckleberry Finn, also learns to prize deeds over words. Ever the pragmatist, Huck finds himself continually in conflict with the bombast and inflated rhetoric of Tom Sawyer, the Widow Douglas, Pap, Emily Grangerford, and the King, to name only a few. Similarly, Ike must find his way to a sense of conscience and duty through the jungle of compromising logic expressed by his cousin Cass Edmonds; Chick Mallison must reject the rationalizations about race and states' rights politics spouted by his Uncle Gavin; and Lucius Priest must learn to trust his own experiences more than the platitudes and pieties of his family and community. Like Twain's prototypical character, Faulkner's Hucks learn to trust their hearts and not their heads, and they learn that lesson through the influence of Black mentors who reprise the role of Twain's Jim.

Still, while there are many strong similarities between Twain's Huckleberry Finn and Faulkner's emulators, there is one monumental difference. At the conclusion of his experiences downriver with Jim, Huck determines "to light out for the territory ahead of the rest, because Aunt Sally she's going to adopt me and sivilize me, and I can't stand it. I been there before" (281). Huck's last act of the novel, therefore, is to plan to keep running. By contrast, Faulkner's Hucks choose family, community, and civilization over freedom and the frontier. Ike McCaslin lives out his life in Jefferson, though he continues to make frequent trips into the Big Woods. Chick Mallison, as his role in later Faulkner novels will reveal, becomes more and more a townsman, with little adult involvement with either hunting or blacks. Lucius Priest ends his Memphis adventure by becoming very homesick and longing to return home, even if that means punishment for his misdeeds.

Part of the explanation for this difference in Huckleberry Finn and Faulkner's Hucks is that Twain was writing in the context of a United States that still had an open frontier, whereas Faulkner's setting (even in "The Bear") is that of a closed frontier. As Harold P. Simonson has noted, the existence of the open American frontier of the nineteenth century promoted a national belief in "political democracy, human infinitude, and philosophical idealism"—all of which found expression in the expansionist policy known as

Manifest Destiny.[6] Thus, Huck's rejection of society is tempered by his ongoing faith in the West, where Tom can find adventures among the "Injuns," and Huck and Jim presumably will continue their quest for dignity, equality, and freedom. Faulkner's characters, on the other hand, inhabitants of the closed frontier, are denied such opportunity for escape and must confront their problems and conflicts *within* society. The disappearance of the physical frontier has significantly narrowed the choices available to Americans of Faulkner's day. They had been narrowed even more significantly, Faulkner thought, in Salinger's day.

NOTES

1. Ernest Hemingway, *Green Hills of Africa* (New York: Charles Scribner's Sons, 1935), 22.

2. Mark Twain, *The Adventures of Huckleberry Finn* (New York: Bantam Books, 1981). Cited parenthetically within the essay.

3. In Richard Lettis, Robert F. McDonnell, and William A. Morris, eds., *Huck Finn and His Critics* (New York: Macmillan, 1962), 405.

4. In Lettis et al., *Huck Finn and His Critics*, 352.

5. Vernon Louis Parrington, *The Beginnings of Critical Realism in America: Main Currents in American Thought*, vol. III (New York: Routledge, 2017), 94.

6. Harold P. Simonson, *The Closed Frontier: Studies in American Literary Tragedy* (New York: Holt, Rinehart, and Winston, 1970), 5.

Faulkner and Steinbeck

Let me begin by saying how pleased and honored I am to be invited to participate in this program—and how hopeful I am that everything I've heard about the friendliness and hospitality of the Steinbeck Festival is true. If what I've heard is not true, then I may have to watch my back, since I face the rather daunting task of defending Steinbeck from some less-than-flattering judgments by Faulkner. Let me demonstrate the challenge by sharing with you three of Faulkner's observations about Steinbeck.

In 1947, speaking to an English class at the University of Mississippi in his hometown of Oxford, Faulkner ranked Steinbeck fifth on his list of contemporary authors (behind Thomas Wolfe, Faulkner himself, John Dos Passos, and Hemingway), then added: "I had great hope for him at one time. Now I don't know" (*LIG* 58).

In 1953, in New York, in a conversation with Budd Schulberg, Faulkner criticized *The Grapes of Wrath* and Steinbeck's view of humankind, arguing that Steinbeck's belief in human progress made him "a sentimental liberal" (*FB* 1470).

And in 1955, in an interview during his US State Department visit to Japan, Faulkner said, "Steinbeck is just a reporter, a newspaper man, not really a writer" (*LIG* 91).

Now, since I don't want to test or try your excellent reputation for hospitality, I want you to know at the outset that I do not agree with Faulkner's opinions about Steinbeck; and furthermore, I'm surprised that Faulkner didn't hold a higher regard for Steinbeck's work, since as I hope to demonstrate, the two writers share a number of artistic and thematic concerns. What are some of these?

First of all, both Faulkner and Steinbeck (Hemingway, too, of course) belong to that early twentieth-century literary movement known as modernism. While Faulkner is generally placed in the "high modernist" tradition of Joyce and Eliot, and Steinbeck is commonly identified as a "low modernist" with, say, F. Scott Fitzgerald and Willa Cather and, some would say,

Hemingway, the fact remains that both Faulkner and Steinbeck were members of that generation of writers, painters, and intellectuals who experienced widespread doubt and disillusion as the result of the collapse of traditional nineteenth-century ideas and values. In Hemingway circles this group is widely discussed as the "Lost Generation," with World War I being considered the principal cause of the problem. In actuality, the war is more symptomatic of the problem than causative; and the Lost Generation crowd is far larger than the small group that socialized with Hemingway and Gertrude Stein in Paris. Faulkner and Steinbeck belonged to this group no less than Hemingway, and all of them, plus many others, were challenged to find new order and meanings in what had become, to use Robert Penn Warren's analogy, a Humpty Dumpty world that seemingly "all the king's horses and all the king's men couldn't put . . . together again."

One place the Lost Generation writers turned for meaning and understanding in the midst of their contemporary chaos was to older myths and stories—whether primitive, Greek and Roman, Christian, or "classical" authors like Chaucer, Shakespeare, and Milton. T. S. Eliot gave this aspect of modernism a name in his famous review of Joyce's *Ulysses*: "Mr. Joyce," Eliot wrote, "is pursuing a method which others must pursue after him. . . . It is a method for which the horoscope is auspicious. Psychology . . . , ethnology, and *The Golden Bough* have concurred to make possible what was impossible even a few years ago. Instead of narrative method, we may now use the mythical method." As Eliot goes on to define the term, "the mythical method" involves an author's "manipulating a continuous parallel between contemporaneity and antiquity," the purpose being to provide, in Eliot's words, "a way of controlling, of ordering, of giving a shape and a significance to the immense panorama of futility and anarchy which is contemporary history."[1]

As Eliot predicted, "the mythical method" would become the storytelling preference of an entire generation of writers. Eugene O'Neill would recast Greek tragedies in modern guise; Robinson Jeffers (with *Tamar*), Archibald MacLeish (with *J. B.*), and Thornton Wilder (with *The Skin of Our Teeth*) would retell biblical myths; Hemingway, like Eliot before him, would utilize material from Frazer's *The Golden Bough*, particularly the story of the Fisher King. Faulkner drew heavily upon biblical materials—using, for example, the Easter story as the backdrop for the tragic collapse of the Compson family in *The Sound and the Fury*, the Christ story as a parallel for the scapegoating of Joe Christmas in *Light in August*, the King David and Absalom narrative for the Thomas Sutpen story in *Absalom, Absalom!*, the Exodus account for his treatment of southern Blacks in *Go Down, Moses*, the Eden story for the lost wilderness theme in "The Bear," and the gospel account of the Passion Week of Christ for the pattern of his World War I novel *A Fable*. Steinbeck, too, recycled biblical narratives, most notably the Exodus and Christ stories in *The Grapes of Wrath* and *Of Mice and Men;* but he also uses primitive myth and the Grail quest in *To a God Unknown*, the Eden story in *Pastures of Heaven* and *East of Eden*, the legend of King Arthur and the Round Table in *Tortilla Flat*, and Milton's *Paradise Lost* as a framework for *In Dubious Battle*.

What is important to note in Eliot's explanation of "the mythical method," as in the application of the technique in almost all early twentieth-century authors, is the irony that lies at the heart of the method. Old myths are retold, but they are typically inverted. Edens in modem American literature are, by and large, lost Edens; Promised Lands are dreamed of but never attained; Christ figures are suffering victims, not redemptive saviors; Fisher Kings and Ulysseses and Arthurs are small and pathetic, not heroic. Such is certainly the case with Faulkner and Steinbeck. Dilsey, who is quite literally a suffering servant and the only genuine Christ figure in *The Sound and the Fury*, cannot save the Compsons from disgrace and ruin; and the Christ figure who tries to stop the war in *A Fable* fails miserably and is executed for his efforts. Likewise, California proves anything but a Promised Land for the Joads; the heavenly dream of George and Lennie and the other ranch hands is revealed to be only that—a dream, an illusion; and Danny turns out to be an ineffectual Arthur, not at all kingly. For Faulkner and Steinbeck, as for so many of their contemporaries, the ancient myths serve as a measure of all that is missing, or at least diminished, in the modern world: order, stability, meaning, significance, honor, heroism, innocence. In a world where everything has been turned upside down, the old myths will be turned upside down as well. "The question," as Robert Frost, another of the modernists, stated it so well in his famous poem "The Oven Bird" "is what to make of a diminished thing."[2]

If Steinbeck and Faulkner share an interest in the uses and applications of myth, they also share some common subjects and themes. I will list three of those.

First, both authors exhibit in their best work a striking sense of place— what Faulkner called that "little postage stamp of native soil" (*LIG* 255). The geographies of both writers are concrete and unmistakable. The division of Yoknapatawpha County into the sparsely settled and barren pine hills of the northeast sector, the out-county settlement of Frenchman's Bend in the southeast, and the rapidly diminishing Big Woods of the western section—all bounded by the Tallahatchie River on the north and the Yoknapatawpha River on the south and linked by narrow, rutted dirt roads to the centrally located county seat—roughly corresponds to Lafayette County as it existed during Faulkner's formative years. And Jefferson, with its small stores and offices lining the central square, its courthouse and lawn, its Confederate statue, its jail, its railroad and depot, its lone hotel, its cemetery, and its roads leading outward toward Memphis and other points, almost exactly parallels Oxford during the early years of the twentieth century.

Steinbeck's principal fictional setting likewise mirrors his home region. His Jefferson is Salinas, also a county seat; his county, Monterey; and his geographical benchmarks are the Salinas Valley, fed by the subterranean Salinas River and bordered by the gently rolling Gabilan Mountains on the east and the rugged Santa Lucia Mountains on the west. As Steinbeck records in *East of Eden*,

> I remember that the Gabilan Mountains to the east of the valley were light gay mountains full of sun and loveliness and a kind of invitation, so that you wanted to climb into their warm foothills almost as you want to climb into the lap of a beloved mother. They were beckoning mountains with a brown grass love. The Santa Lucias stood up against the sky to the west and kept the valley from the open sea, and they were dark and brooding—unfriendly and dangerous.[3]

Beyond the Gabilans farther eastward is the Grand Central Valley, while west of the Santa Lucias is the Pacific coast. One of the coastal towns, Monterey, also plays a prominent role in Steinbeck's fiction.

Many readers have noted similarities between Faulkner's Yoknapatawpha and Steinbeck Country. In fact, it has been pointed out—and I think accurately—that both of these writers proved most successful when they maintained their ties with their native regions, and least successful when they divorced themselves from their roots. Faulkner worked for more than a decade on *A Fable*, which is set in France, and frequently referred to it as his "big book" (*SL* 350–51); yet most critics think it his weakest book, partly because it is utterly lacking in the concrete particularities that make the world of Yoknapatawpha so memorable. Similarly, the Steinbeck works set outside the Salinas/Monterey area, such as *The Winter of Our Discontent*, pale in comparison to the California novels and stories. To adapt an analogy once used by Ward Miner in relation to Faulkner,[4] we may say that both of these writers are like the legendary Antaeus in his fight with Hercules. When Antaeus, a son of the Earth, stayed in contact with his mother, he retained his strength; but when he was lifted into the air and held aloft, he quickly became exhausted. In like manner, when Faulkner and Steinbeck maintain their association with the scenes, characters, and events of their home territory, they are strong writers; when they remove themselves from their artistic roots, they lose much of their strength. Part of this sense of place for both writers is a love and respect for the landscape. Faulkner's love of the north Mississippi countryside is evident throughout his work but nowhere more than in his early poem "Mississippi Hills":

Far blue hills, where I have pleasured me,
Where on silver feet in dogwood cover
Spring follows, singing close the bluebird's "Lover!"
When to the road I trod an end I see,

Let this soft mouth, shaped to the rain,
Be but golden grief for grieving's sake,
And these green woods be dreaming here to wake
Within my heart when I return again.

Return I will! Where is there the death
While in these blue hills slumbrous overhead
I'm rooted like a tree? Though I be dead,
This soil that holds me fast will find me breath.[5]

Steinbeck likewise loved his native region, as is clear from the opening pages of *East of Eden*. "I remember my childhood names for grasses and secret flowers," he writes. "I remember where a toad may live and what time the birds awaken in the summer—and what trees and seasons smelled like—how people looked and walked and smelled even. The memory of odors is very rich" (3). Like the Ash Can painters, Steinbeck also finds a curious beauty even in the grimiest details of his environment: "Cannery Row in Monterey in California is a poem, a stink, a grating noise, a quality of light, a tone, a habit, a nostalgia, a dream."[6] Another aspect of Faulkner's and Steinbeck's sense of place is a heightened interest in regional and family history. In the course of seventeen novels and dozens of short stories, Faulkner presents the history of Yoknapatawpha County from the time of its first white settlers in the early 1800s to the beginnings of the civil rights movement in the 1940s. Major events in this chronicle include the displacement of the Native Americans; the development of a plantation system based on chattel slavery; the Civil War, emancipation, and Reconstruction; the decline of the southern aristocracy and the subsequent rise of the middle class; the transition from an agrarian to an increasingly industrialized society; World Wars I and II, the Great

Migration, and the Great Depression; and the racial conflicts (white vs. red, red vs. Black, Black vs. white) that are ever present and, in Faulkner's view, largely insoluble. Interwoven into almost every aspect of this general history are characters and events from Faulkner's own family—particularly the life and career of his great-grandfather W. C. Falkner (John Sartoris in the fiction), who was a plantation and slave owner (and in all likelihood a miscegenist), a Confederate colonel in the Civil War, a defender of southern honor and tradition during Radical Reconstruction, and, finally, a murder victim at the hands of a former business partner.

Steinbeck, too, presents the history of his place as both general and personal. First, he says, there were the Indians, then "the hard dry Spaniards" (*East* 4) who gave names to so many of the places, and then the Americans. These last came because of their "westering" spirit, which drove them to seek wealth or freedom or adventure that had eluded them back East. Like Yoknapatawpha, Steinbeck Country also has a history closely entwined with issues of class, race, and gender. There are big corporations and village shops and stores, ranchers large and small, laborers and bums; representatives of upper, middle, and lower socioeconomic classes; Caucasians good and bad, Blacks like Crooks, Mexican Americans like Danny and Pepe, Chinese Americans like Lee Chong and the other Lee, Sam Hamilton's friend; decent women like Liza Hamilton, frustrated women like Elisa Allen, and prostitutes and madams like Dora Flood and Cathy Ames. Like Faulkner, too, Steinbeck drew upon his own family history: the three generations of Hamiltons in *East of Eden* are based on Steinbeck's maternal ancestors.

A second theme these two writers share in common is a high regard for individuality. Faulkner, both man and writer, was always an inveterate individualist. In his desire for personal privacy, his preference for small-town Oxford over the literary centers of the nation, his often-eccentric dress and behavior, and his unique writing style, Faulkner celebrated nonconformity. "Only an individualist can be a first-rate writer," Faulkner once said. "He can't belong to a group or a school and be a first-rate writer" (*FIU* 33).

Faulkner's most extended and philosophical defense of individuality is his 1954 novel *A Fable*, but perhaps his most eloquent treatment is found in his essay "On Privacy" (1955). Prompted by a reporter's invasion of his privacy to publish a feature article against his will, this essay represents one of Faulkner's most bitter attacks upon modern America. The piece opens by linking individuality with the American Dream: "This was the American Dream: a sanctuary on the earth for individual man: a condition in which he could be free not only of the old established closed-corporation hierarchies of arbitrary power . . . but free of that mass into which the hierarchies of church and state had compressed and held him individually thralled and individually impotent" (*ESPL* 62). "The point is," Faulkner continues, "that in America today any organization or group, simply by functioning under a phrase like Freedom of the Press or National Security or League Against Subversion, can postulate to itself complete immunity to violate the individualness . . . of anyone who is not himself a member of some organization or group numerous enough or rich enough to frighten them off" (*ESPL* 70).

By 1957, when Faulkner was conducting class conferences with students at the University of Virginia, these ideas had coalesced into a political credo. Faulkner insisted "that the individual is more important than any mass or group he belongs to. That the individual is always more important than any state he belongs to. That the state must be never be the master of the individual, it is the servant of the individual" (*FIU* 100). Faulkner's defense of this position was not always expressed in such somber prose, as when in 1962 he dared to resist the power and influence of the state by declining an invitation by President Kennedy to a White House dinner. Asked to explain what many viewed as a startling response, even an affront, Faulkner said simply, "I'm too old at my age to travel that far to eat with strangers" (*FB* 1821).

While Steinbeck had a much greater involvement and thus, it seems to me, a far better appreciation of mass movements and group psychology, he too staunchly defended individuality. As he writes in *East of Eden*, "This I believe: that the free, exploring mind of the individual human is the most valuable thing in the world. And this I would fight for: the freedom of the mind to take any direction it wishes, undirected. And this I must fight against: any idea, religion, or government which limits or destroys the individual" (132). In the same work, in a passage that echoes Faulkner's sentiments on the modern world, Steinbeck writes:

> There are monstrous changes taking place in the world, forces shaping a future whose face we do not know. . . . When our food and clothing and housing all are born in the complication of mass production, mass method is bound to get into our thinking and to eliminate all other thinking. In our time mass or collective production has entered our economics, our politics, and even our religion, so that some nations have substituted the idea collective for the idea God. This in my time is the danger. (131)

Some would see such statements in *East of Eden*, like so many of Faulkner's comments from the same period, as a knee-jerk response to the Cold War and

the threat of Soviet totalitarianism; but this theme had always been a significant emphasis in Steinbeck's works. *In Dubious Battle,* for example, is not, as
many early readers wanted it to be, a defense of communism in its rebellion
against a failed capitalism, but rather a defense of human dignity and freedom
that are being threatened and destroyed by both capitalism and communism.
Jim Nolan, as Warren French has argued, is the victim of "neither the con-
tending party that exploited him nor the one that curtly rejected him, but
rather an entire society that had wandered into a dehumanized wasteland by
insisting on mindless conformity."[7] Likewise, the struggle by the Joads and
other workers in *The Grapes of Wrath* is only partly for material gain and
security: it is even more a quest for the inalienable right to individual integrity
and self-determination.

A third common denominator in the works of Steinbeck and Faulkner is
a sympathetic concern for the poor and oppressed members of society. For
Faulkner, a southerner with a keen understanding of his region's tragic racial
history, the principally oppressed class is the African American; and the marvelous short story "That Evening Sun," with its powerful depiction of the abuse
and exploitation of the Black prostitute Nancy by the white citizens of Jefferson, is only one of several treatments in Faulkner of how racism and poverty
and injustice conjoin to oppress a large segment of the southern population.
But Faulkner is equally sensitive to the plight of other minorities—Native
Americans, poor whites, and women. In the short story "Lo!" dispossessed
Indians invade the White House to protest injustice; in "Tomorrow" a poor
hill farmer, one of "the lowly and invincible of the earth" (*KG* 104), is victimized by bureaucratic legalism; in *Light in August* Lena Grove is depicted as a
brave and self-reliant pregnant female abandoned by an irresponsible male.

Steinbeck likewise has great sympathy for the underprivileged and ostracized members of society. As Anders Osterling noted in presenting Steinbeck
to the Nobel Prize Awards assembly, "His sympathies always go out to the
oppressed, to the misfits and the distressed."[8] One of Steinbeck's characters provides a more graphic list for such individuals in *Cannery Row*: "whores, pimps,
gamblers, and sons of bitches, by which he meant Everybody" (1). The Joads
on the road, the fruit pickers in the fields, the ranch hands, the *paisanos,* the
Chinese immigrants—all of these are treated honestly but compassionately by
Steinbeck. They are a necessary part of the artistic design that makes Steinbeck
Country, no less than Yoknapatawpha, a microcosm of the human cosmos.

I'd like to add an additional word about gender issues in Steinbeck and
Faulkner. Both of these writers, like Hemingway, are often perceived as chau-
vinists who are insensitive to the rights and concerns of women. But I would

point out that Caddy Compson in *The Sound and the Fury*, whom Faulkner called his "heart's darling" (*FIU* 6), is a strong, loving, independent character who refuses to accept the conventional definitions of femininity and sexuality that her brother Quentin and other characters seek to force upon her. And where can one find, even among female authors, a more sympathetic treatment of the plight of women in a male-dominated culture than the story of Elisa Allen in "The Chrysanthemums"? Both Faulkner and Steinbeck are indisputably "dead white males," but I do not find them at all representative of what is usually meant by that phrase.

I noted at the beginning of my remarks that Faulkner was unduly critical of Steinbeck and seems not to have been much aware of the great similarities in their works. Steinbeck, to his credit, didn't make the same mistake toward Faulkner. In fact, in his Nobel Prize Acceptance Speech, Steinbeck referred to Faulkner as his "great predecessor" and went on to praise Faulkner's work and to quote from the Nobel speech Faulkner had delivered twelve years earlier. "Faulkner, more than most men," Steinbeck said, "was aware of human strength as well as of human weakness. He knew that the understanding and the resolution of fear are a large part of the writer's reason for being."[9] While Faulkner may have been too unappreciative of Steinbeck's work and achievement, I think he would agree with Steinbeck's conclusion in his Nobel remarks, and I believe he would have thought that Steinbeck was speaking accurately for a whole generation of writers, Faulkner included, when he said, "Man himself has become our greatest hazard and our only hope."

NOTES

1. T. S. Eliot, "Ulysses, Order and Myth," *Dial* 75 (November 1923): 483.

2. Robert Frost, "The Oven Bird," in *Selected Poems of Robert Frost* (New York: Holt, Rinehart, and Winston, 1963), 76.

3. John Steinbeck, *East of Eden* (New York: Penguin Books, 1992), 3.

4. Ward Miner, *The World of William Faulkner* (New York: Grove Press, 1959), 113.

5. Faulkner, "Mississippi Hills," in *Faulkner: A Comprehensive Guide to the Brodsky Collection, Volume V: Manuscripts and Documents*, ed. Louis Daniel Brodsky and Robert W. Hamblin (Jackson: University Press of Mississippi, 1988), 80.

6. John Steinbeck, *Cannery Row* (New York: Bantam Books, 1959), 1.

7. Warren French, *John Steinbeck's Fiction Revisited* (New York: Twayne, 1994), 72.

8. Anders Osterling, Presentation Speech for John Steinbeck, https://www.nobelprize.org/prizes/literature/1962/ceremony-speech/.

9. Steinbeck's Nobel Prize Acceptance Speech, https://genius.com/John-steinbeck-nobel-prize-acceptance-speech-annotated.

"The World Is like an Enormous Spider Web"

The Contrasting Legacies of Thomas Sutpen and Cass Mastern

The lives and works of William Faulkner and Robert Penn Warren intersect in a number of interesting and significant ways. Contemporaries, although Warren was nearly a decade younger, both were native southerners, but Faulkner came from the Deep South, and Warren from the Upper. Both wrote, in varying degrees, poetry, short stories, novels, criticism, and social commentary; both were fascinated by the history of their region, particularly as that history had been shaped by slavery, the Civil War, Reconstruction, and Jim Crow. Both men's views on race evolved considerably over their lifetimes, though both remained ambivalent about many of the changes they saw coming. Warren lived to see major changes brought by the civil rights movement; Faulkner did not.

While in many ways they share similar experiences and write about similar subjects, not only race but also nature, socioeconomic issues, politics, and religion, they held highly contrasting views of each other's work. Warren was a great admirer of Faulkner; he wrote a number of influential Faulkner reviews and essays, and even edited a book of Faulkner criticism.[1] Invited to speak at the University of Mississippi during the turmoil of the university's integration crisis, Warren chose Faulkner as the focus of his remarks on race, conflict, and reconciliation.[2] Faulkner, on the other hand, paid very little public notice to Warren. When their mutual friend Albert Erskine brought the two men together in 1952 for dinner and conversation, Faulkner evidenced some knowledge of Warren's novel *At Heaven's Gate* and at least one Warren short story (*FB* 1426); but perhaps more telling is the fact that in the transcriptions of Faulkner's interviews, lectures, and class conferences at the University of

Virginia in 1957–58, in which Faulkner alludes to dozens of authors, there is not a single mention of Warren or any of his writings.[3]

The only extended commentary by Faulkner on Warren is to be found in a letter Faulkner mailed to Lambert Davis, a Harcourt, Brace editor who had sent Faulkner an advance review copy of Warren's *All the King's Men*, hopeful that Faulkner might supply a promotional blurb. What Davis received back was a mixed but largely unfavorable view of Warren's novel. "The Cass Mastern story is a beautiful and moving piece," Faulkner wrote. "That was his novel. The rest I would throw away." Faulkner continued: "The Starke [*sic*] thing is good solid sound writing but for my money Starke and the rest of them are second rate. . . . I didn't mind neither loving him nor hating him, but I did object to not being moved to pity. . . . He was neither big enough nor bad enough. But maybe the Cass story made the rest of it look thinner than it is" (*SL* 239).

I propose that one of the reasons for Faulkner's admiration of the Cass Mastern subplot in *All the King's Men* may perhaps have been his recognition of the parallels between Warren's Cass Mastern story and Faulkner's treatment of Thomas Sutpen, whose tragic story provides the centerpiece of *Absalom, Absalom!* In reading the narratives of these two characters intertextually, we see some of the common concerns of Faulkner and Warren, but also some important differences.

Both Thomas Sutpen and Cass Mastern are white plantation owners in Mississippi whose lives and relationships are radically affected by their interracial attitudes and actions. Those actions for both are closely entwined with slavery and the Civil War. The two men's behaviors not only wreak havoc upon their contemporaries but also strongly affect two young men in the following century, Sutpen's on Quentin Compson and Mastern's on Jack Burden. But the ultimate effects of the two stories, both in their immediate climaxes and their consequences, are quite opposite in nature.

Thomas Sutpen's story belongs with the rags-to-riches narratives that have been so conspicuous in American history and literature—from Benjamin Franklin's Poor Richard, to Horatio Alger's Ragged Dick, to William Dean Howells's Silas Lapham, to F. Scott Fitzgerald's Jay Gatsby. Son of poor mountaineer parents in western Virginia, Sutpen as a young boy moves with his family to Tidewater Virginia, where he first views the huge plantations dependent upon slave laborers; then, as a young man, on to Haiti, where his education in plantation economics and personal relationships is furthered; and finally to Jefferson, Mississippi, where he carves out his own plantation, called "Sutpen's Hundred," and becomes one of the leading landowners in antebellum Yoknapatawpha. None of the several narrators who present

Sutpen's story—the communal narrator, Rosa Coldfield, General Compson, Mr. Compson, Quentin, Shreve—ever question Sutpen's courage, ambition, confidence, industriousness, or perseverance. In these regards he possesses exactly the pragmatic character traits needed to tame a wilderness, build a mansion, and establish a dynasty. But what is missing in Sutpen is a moral or ethical center: as the narrator states, "They did not think of love in connection with Sutpen. They thought of ruthlessness rather than justice and of fear rather than respect, but not of pity or love" (32). In short, Sutpen is a crass materialist, an obsessive, manipulative egomaniac possessing "valor and strength but without pity or honor" (13).

Sutpen's self-serving ruthlessness is dramatized in many ways throughout the novel, most notably in his abandonment of his Haitian wife when he discovers she is part Black; in his cruel and inhumane treatment of his slaves and the French architect; in his arranged marriage with Ellen Coldfield to further his "design"; in his callous proposal to Rosa Coldfield that she produce him a male heir as a precondition to their being wed; in his savage rejection of the teenaged Milly Jones when the child she gives him is a female; and, most importantly, in his rejection of and conspiracy against his son Charles Bon because he is part Black.

I have argued elsewhere that Sutpen's Negrophobia, the dominant trait in his characterization, may be traced back to his childhood, when his first encounters with Blacks left him psychologically bruised, emasculated, angry, and vengeful.[4] The first Black man he ever sees, as his family migrates from the mountains to the Tidewater, manhandles and ridicules the boy's father: "a huge bull of a n——r . . . who emerged [from the tavern] with the old man over his shoulder like a sack of meal and his—the n——r's—mouth loud with laughing and full of teeth like tombstones" (182). Later, in the Tidewater, he and his sister are nearly run over by a carriage driven by a "n——r coachman in a plug hat"; and on another occasion he listens as his father excitedly and proudly recounts the beating of a Black man by a group of night riders. Then, when Thomas is about thirteen or fourteen years of age, he is turned away from the front of a "big house" and ordered to go to the back door by a "monkey-dressed n——r butler" (187). Such frightening and dehumanizing experiences involving Blacks, I contend, lay the basis for Sutpen's racism that is only extended and heightened by the horrors of the racial insurrection in Haiti. It seems predictable, even inevitable, that these childhood and youthful experiences will have continued consequences for the older Sutpen after he arrives in Mississippi. And, of course, they do. Given the horrors of his previous experience with Blackness, Sutpen must resort to all means and measures to prevent Judith's marriage to the biracial Bon. As I stated in my previous discussion of this matter, "The logic of the racist may appear to others to be confused and irrational, but to the racist it has the precision and inevitability of a mathematical equation."[5]

I stress the deterministic nature of Sutpen's fate to emphasize how bleak and pessimistic his story is. That pessimism is underscored and heightened by the end of the man and his dream: his death at the hand of Wash Jones, the eventual destruction of his mansion, the ironic survival of his blood lineage in the "idiot Negro" (301) Jim Bond—and the reader's foreknowledge that the chief inheritor and preserver of Sutpen's narrative, Quentin Compson, will all too soon commit suicide by drowning himself. No better description of the deterministic nature of Sutpen's tragedy can be found than the words used by Jack Burden to describe Cass Mastern's dark night of the soul:

> He learned that the world is like an enormous spider web and if you touch it, however lightly, at any point, the vibration ripples to the remotest perimeter and the drowsy spider feels the tingle and is drowsy no more but springs out to fling the gossamer coils about you who have touched the web and then inject the black, numbing poison under your hide. It does not matter whether or not you meant to brush the web of things. Your happy foot or your gay wing may have brushed it ever so slightly, but what happens always happens and there is the spider, bearded black and with his great faceted eyes glittering like mirrors in the sun, or like God's eye, and the fangs dripping.[6]

This passage is one of the best descriptions in American literature of the deterministic theory that lies at the heart of literary naturalism, and one can readily imagine its being written by Stephen Crane, Frank Norris, or Theodore Dreiser. However, as I shall argue later, Cass Mastern and Jack Burden manage finally to escape the spider's web, and its deterministic implications, but the characters of *Absalom, Absalom!* do not.

Cass Mastern's story begins much like that of Thomas Sutpen's. He was born, as he notes in his journal, "in a log cabin in north Georgia, in circumstances of poverty" (161). Like Sutpen, he eventually becomes a plantation owner in Mississippi. And, like Sutpen in Haiti, he experiences a time of "darkness and trouble" (162) that irrevocably alters his life. Cass's fall into awareness of evil and personal culpability occurs in Lexington, Kentucky, where he is enrolled in Transylvania College; and, like Sutpen's initiatory experience in Haiti, Cass's too involves a woman and an issue of race. While in Lexington, Cass engages in an affair with Annabelle Trice, the wife of his best friend; and when the friend, Duncan Trice, discovers the affair, he commits suicide. Realizing that her personal slave Phebe knows about the affair, and fearing that she might make it known to others, Annabelle sells Phebe to a slave dealer who will ship her "down the river" to New Orleans, thus separating her from her husband and likely condemning her to a life of sexual servitude. When Cass questions this mistreatment of Phebe, Annabelle turns her rage upon him: "Oh, I see, you are concerned for the honor of a black coachman . . . why did you not show some such delicate concern for the honor of your friend?" (177) The cumulative effect of this series of actions is described by Cass in his journal:

> All of these things—the death of my friend, the betrayal of Phebe, the suffering and rage and great change of the woman I had loved—all had come from my single act of sin and perfidy, as the boughs from the bole and the leaves from the bough. Or to figure the matter differently. It was as though the vibration set up in the whole fabric of the world by my act had spread infinitely and with ever increasing power and no man could know the end. (178)

Cass's conscience-driven grief, as well as his recognition and regret that his actions have had serious, unexpected social consequences, contrasts sharply with the attitudes and behavior of Thomas Sutpen. Significantly, Cass's journal entries are laced with the biblical language of temptation, sin, guilt, damnation, shame, repentance, penance, and hope of grace and forgiveness. "I write this down," Cass notes, "with what truthfulness a sinner may attain unto, that if ever pride is in me, of flesh or spirit, I can peruse these pages and know with shame what evil has been in me, or may be in me" (161). In another entry he writes that "hopeless of Grace I yet clung to the hope of Grace" (182), and in yet another he voices a prayer to "God and my Redeemer" (166). The narrator notes that Cass Mastern's schooling has included "a great deal of Presbyterian theology" (163), and his journal reads like a casebook in Calvinism.

A major component of Calvinism, as indeed all Christianity, is a belief in repentance, penance, and salvation. Cass's guilt over his adultery, his betrayal of a friend, and his acquiescence to the cruel treatment of the Black servant drives him to seek to atone for his sinful acts. He ends the affair with Annabelle and engages in a futile quest to locate Phebe, with the intention of buying her and then setting her free. Back home in Mississippi, he resumes operation of his plantation, spends time in prayer and Bible study, and then, to the consternation of his brother Gilbert, frees his slaves. When the Civil War breaks out, Cass feels obligated to join the Confederacy, but with the rank of private rather than that of a major or colonel, as Gilbert had advised, and with a secret promise to himself that he will never take the life of another human being. "How can I who have taken the life of my friend, take the life of an enemy, for I have used up my right to blood" (186). After participating in numerous battles, including those at Shiloh and Chickamauga, he is mortally wounded in a battle outside Atlanta and dies with other soldiers in a military hospital, feeling at the end that he has come to know "the common guilt of man" and accepting of "the Justice of God, that others have suffered for my sin, for it may be that only by the suffering of the innocent does God affirm that men are brothers, and brothers in His Holy Name" (187). The last words of Cass's journal are "Blessed be his Name" (188).

How different is the language used by and about Thomas Sutpen. Unlike Cass Mastern, who learns humility and gentleness through his personal ordeal, and who views his experience in the context of a universal struggle between good and evil, Sutpen resorts to violence and cruelty to effect a selfish goal in a world that he perceives to be amoral. Although to Rosa Coldfield, Sutpen is an "ogre" or "demon" (8), "fiend blackguard and devil" (10)—words that appear to identify Sutpen as immoral, Sutpen is more often associated in the text with the amoral world of "brutehood" (210). As a result of his boyhood experience at "the big house," he comes to view himself and his family "as cattle, creatures heavy and without grace, brutely evacuated into a world without hope or purpose for them, who would in turn spawn with brutish and vicious prolixity" (190). Immediately following his being turned away from the front door by the "monkey n——r," he retreats to the woods, where, animal-like, "he crawled back into the cave and sat with his back against the uptorn roots" (188). Shortly thereafter, overcome by hunger, he returns home, where he observes "his sister pumping rhythmic up and down above a washtub in the yard, . . . broad in the beam as a cow, the very labor she was doing brutish and stupidly out of proportion to its reward: the very primary essence of labor, toil, reduced to its crude absolute which only a beast could and would endure" (190–91). In Haiti, Sutpen is thrown into an atavistic world described as "the halfway point between what we call the jungle and what we call civilization," "a theater for violence and injustice and bloodshed and all the satanic lusts of human greed and cruelty" (202). Arriving in Jefferson, he brings with him a wagon load of slaves "smelling like a wolfden" (27) and a French architect who is the only one of the group "resembling a human creature" (28). Soon the community learns that Sutpen regularly engages in hand-to-hand fights with his slaves, "both naked to the waist and gouging at one another's eyes as if their skins should not only have been the same color but should have been covered with fur too" (20–21). "Horse or mare?" Sutpen asks the midwife who delivers his child by Milly Jones. Then, hearing the disappointing news, he says to Milly, "Too bad you're not a mare too. Then I could give you a decent stall in the stable" (229).

All such animal imagery suggests that Sutpen's story belongs not in the context of Calvinistic (and Augustinian) Christianity, as Cass Mastern's does, but rather in the context of literary naturalism and social Darwinism, which were highly prevalent emphases in American literature during the early years of Faulkner's career. One of the chief proponents of a naturalistic and Darwinian interpretation of life was Theodore Dreiser, a writer Faulkner greatly admired.[7] "On the tiger no responsibility rests," Dreiser writes in *Sister Carrie*; and his Frank Cowperwood, a railway tycoon who as a young boy is persuaded that he has discovered the organizing principle of life—and business—when he observes a lobster devouring a squid,[8] is one of the principal literary forebears of Thomas Sutpen. Like Cowperwood and other robber barons, real and fictional, Sutpen intends to let nothing stand in the way of his desire and design for material success.

The contrasts herein noted between Thomas Sutpen and Cass Mastern—and their respective worlds—also play out in the stories of the narrators who, in the next century, recount the older stories, Quentin Compson and Jack Burden.[9] Quentin Compson, as readers know from *The Sound and the Fury*, is a young idealist who is disillusioned by a world given over to pragmatic and material values. In narrating the Sutpen story in *Absalom, Absalom!*, Quentin expresses sympathy for Charles Bon, the son rejected by his father. Quentin identifies with Bon in part because he too, in a sense, has been rejected by his father. Yes, Quentin possesses incestuous desires toward his sister Caddy, just as Charles Bon pursues an incestuous relationship with his half-sister Judith Sutpen; but it can be argued in both cases that it is principally the father/son relationship that pushes each story to its fateful climax.

"Father said" is a constant refrain that runs throughout the Quentin section of *The Sound and the Fury*, from the first page until the last. And everything that Mr. Compson tells Quentin is grounded in the father's alcoholic, nihilistic condition. "No battle is ever won he said. They are not even fought. The field only reveals to man his own folly and despair, and victory is an illusion of philosophers and fools" (76). Thus, according to Mr. Compson, nothing matters—neither honor ("people cannot do anything that dreadful, they cannot do anything dreadful at all" [80]), nor morality ("Purity is a negative state and therefore contrary to nature" [116]), nor virginity ("Because it means less to women" [78]), nor time ("the reducto absurdum of all human experience"

[76]), nor even life itself ("stalemate of dust and desire" [124]). "But to believe that it doesn't matter," Quentin objects, only to have his father respond that "nothing is even worth the changing of it" (78).

Just as Bon desires recognition from his father, and possibly pursues the marriage with Judith partly (or even only) as revenge for his father's rejection (as Sutpen's life has been a revenge against his being turned away from a door), so too is Quentin's suicide related to Mr. Compson's indifference to Caddy's pregnancy and loveless marriage. Both fathers turn their sons away in a moment of personal crisis and thus are complicit in the sons' deaths. In this regard Quentin's story parallels and repeats the tragic pattern of the Sutpen narrative. On the last day of his life, Quentin recalls the times when "I seemed to be lying neither asleep nor awake looking down a long corridor of grey halflight where all stable things had become shadowy paradoxical all I had done shadows all I had felt suffered taking visible form antic and perverse mocking without relevance inherent themselves with the denial of the significance they should have affirmed" (170). This is Quentin's version of the Humpty Dumpty experience that his world has become, and in his case, truly, "all the king's horses and all the king's men / couldn't put Humpty Dumpty together again." The phrase "all stable things had become shadowy paradoxical" links to all those passages in *Absalom, Absalom!* that describe the Sutpen narrative as a clouded mystery, indecipherable and incomprehensible. And Quentin's ultimately futile role as a detective trying to unravel that mystery and make sense of it can be read as an analogue to his failure to order and control his own life. The end result of both stories, for Quentin, is "Nevermore of peace. Nevermore of peace. Nevermore Nevermore Nevermore" (298–99).

Jack Burden likewise has a vicarious involvement in the story he tells about Cass Mastern. Like Mastern, Jack has a personal history marked by irresponsibility, infidelity, betrayal, and guilt. A history student and journalist, Burden becomes the "dirty tricks" man for Governor Willie Stark, using his research skills to supply the corrupt and amoral governor with information that Stark then uses to bully or blackmail his political enemies into submission. Unwittingly, however, in one crucial instance, in what he calls "The Case of the Upright Judge," Jack uncovers information that leads to startling revelations that, when exposed, cause a series of tragic events for himself, his family, and his best friends. Ordered to find some type of scandalous behavior by Judge Irwin, close friend to the Burdens when Jack was a boy, Jack succeeds in discovering that the Judge, as attorney general under Governor Stanton, the father of Jack's best friends Anne and Adam, had accepted a lucrative bribe from a utilities company and that Governor Stanton had assisted him in covering up the crime. When threatened with the public exposure of his actions, Judge Irwin commits suicide. Additionally, the disillusionment Anne Stanton feels over her father's cover-up of Irwin's crime makes it easier for her to become Willie Stark's mistress; and when Anne's brother Adam learns of Stark's affair with his sister, he assassinates Stark. Burden experiences still another shock amid these catastrophes when his mother informs him that Judge Irwin, the next-door neighbor who was her lover, is Jack's actual father. Like Cass Mastern, Burden recognizes that an action of his has had far-reaching, unexpected, and tragic consequences. He has touched the edge of the spider's web, and the entire web has been shaken. And like Mastern, and Quentin Compson as well, Burden "felt that the world outside of me was shifting and the substance of things, and that the process had only begun of a general disintegration of which I was the center" (177).

For a time Burden seeks to deny any personal responsibility for this string of events, finding comfort and escape in the philosophy that he calls the Great Twitch. He gets the idea from observing an old man with an uncontrollable twitch in his face.

> You would suddenly see a twitch in the left cheek, up toward the pale-blue eye. You would think he was going to wink, but he wasn't going to wink. The twitch was simply an independent phenomenon, unrelated to the face or to what was behind the face or to anything in the whole tissue of phenomena which is the world we are lost in. (313)

A wink, of course, would be an act of will, chosen behavior; whereas a twitch is involuntary, the effect of a natural cause over which one has no control. A twitch, therefore, is a useful symbol for the theory of determinism, and Burden, for a while, finds that philosophy to be very comforting, since if there is no free will, there can be no responsibility, and thus no consequent guilt, for one's actions. "But later," Jack observes, "much later, he woke up one morning to discover that he did not believe in the Great Twitch any more." He has seen "too many people live and die," he says; and he has heard Willie Stark say at the end of his life, "It might have been all different, Jack. You got to believe that" (436).

In his rejection of the Great Twitch and his acceptance of personal responsibility, Burden has moved from a deterministic philosophy of human behavior to an existential one that insists on human freedom. "History is blind," Hugh Miller tells Jack, "but man is not" (436). In other words, even in a world that is confusing and unpredictable and even absurd, and one in which the consequences of individuals' actions can never be assured or even foretold, one still must make choices and assume responsibility for those choices. This is the lesson that Cass Mastern learned, and it is the one that Jack Burden likewise learns. And just as the Thomas Sutpen story serves as an analogue for the tragic experience of Quentin Compson, so does the Cass Mastern story stand as an analogue for the redemptive experience of Jack Burden.

I have sought to demonstrate that there are a number of intertextual connections between *Absalom, Absalom!* and *All the King's Men*, but I want to conclude by noting what I perceive to be the principal difference in the two novels. The key to that difference is found in the epigraph that Warren appends to his story: "*Mentre che la speranza ha fior del verde*" ("while hope has speck of green"), from Canto III of the Purgatory section of Dante's *Divine Comedy*.[10] The full quotation from which Warren takes these words reads, "one is not so lost that the Eternal Love cannot return, while hope has speck of green." This concept is echoed on the next-to-last page of the novel, in the words of the tract that the Scholarly Attorney is writing—words that Jack Burden confesses that, in his own way, he possibly too believes:

> Separateness is identity and the only way for God to create, truly create, man was to make him separate from God Himself, and to be separate from God is to be sinful. The creation of evil is therefore the index of God's glory and His power. That had to be so that the creation of good might be the index of man's glory and power. But by God's help. By His help and in His wisdom. (437)

All the King's Men is a novel about things gone wrong, about human mistakes and sins and their consequences. But it is also a novel about redemption, about *felix culpa*, the good that can be made to come out of evil. The novel is a tragedy, but it ends in hope. Like Dante's "Purgatory," or Milton's *Paradise Lost* (which is perhaps alluded to in the last paragraph of the novel), or Shakespeare's *The Tempest*, Warren offers the possibility of a future that can be better than the mistaken past. That depends, of course, on individuals' making better choices than they have done previously.

Absalom, Absalom! is an altogether different type of book. It is unquestionably one of the greatest tragedies ever written, belonging in the company of such classic works as *Oedipus Rex, King Lear*, and *Moby-Dick*. But even these dark tragedies contain a greater degree of hope than is to be found in Faulkner's greatest novel. Simply put, *Absalom, Absalom!*, like the biblical story of David and Absalom upon which it is based, is not a work that posits hope for the future. Its principal character, Sutpen, is an individual who not only cannot escape his past but also is fated to repeat it; and the principal narrator, Quentin Compson, is a young man who likewise has no future—in fact, is already dead when he narrates the story.[11] The Sutpen story ends in holocaust and ruin:

> it was all finished now, there was nothing left now, nothing out there now but that idiot boy to lurk around those ashes and those four gutted chimneys and howl until someone came and drove him away. They couldn't catch him and nobody ever seemed to make him go very far away, he just stopped howling for a little while. Then after a while they would begin to hear him again. (301)

The "idiot boy" is Jim Bond, "the scion, the last of his race" (300), the one remaining Sutpen. His howl is the only aspect of the Sutpen story to last into the future, and it is projected "to conquer the western hemisphere" (302). Unlike *All the King's Men*, *Absalom, Absalom!* contains no Purgatory, and certainly no thought of Paradise. The characters Faulkner gives us in *Absalom, Absalom!* all live in Hell. And that Hell encompasses the entire universe: "the single profound suspiration of the parched earth's agony rising toward the imponderable and aloof stars" (290).

NOTES

1. Warren's review of Malcolm Cowley's *The Portable Faulkner* helped launch the academic interest in Faulkner's work. See also Robert Penn Warren, ed., *Faulkner: A Collection of Critical Essays* (Englewood Cliffs, NJ: Prentice-Hall, 1966), which includes Warren's essay "Faulkner, the Negro, the South, and Time." For a detailed and enlightening survey of Warren's ongoing dialogue with Faulkner's texts, see Joseph Millichap, "Warren's Faulkner," *Mississippi Quarterly* 60, no. 2 (2007): 351–67.

2. See Robert W. Hamblin, "The 1965 Southern Literary Festival: A Microcosm of the Civil Rights Movement," *Journal of Mississippi History* 53 (May 1991): 83–114.

3. *FB*, 1426. Millichap (353) speculates that the Warren story Faulkner had read may have been "Prime Leaf," since both it and Faulkner's story "Ad Astra" appeared in the same issue of *The American Caravan* in 1931.

4. See Robert W. Hamblin, "'Longer than Anything': Faulkner's 'Grand Design' in *Absalom, Absalom!*" included in this volume.

5. Cleanth Brooks has argued that Sutpen's acceptance and treatment of Clytie, his other biracial child, evidences that he is not particularly concerned with race (*William Faulkner: The Yoknapatawpha Country* [New Haven: Yale University Press, 1963], 298–99). But, as Brooks acknowledges, Clytie is no threat to Sutpen's design, whereas Bon is. In my view, Sutpen's design, like the antebellum, pro-slavery South it mirrors, is at heart racist. Sutpen is tolerant of

Clytie because she accepts her role as a domestic servant and never makes any demands to be treated as an equal or a member of the Sutpen family.

6. Robert Penn Warren, *All the King's Men* (New York: Bantam Books: 1973), 188–89. Hereafter cited parenthetically within the text.

7. See, for example, *LIG*, 167, 250.

8. *Sister Carrie* (New York: Dell, 1960), 90; *The Financier* (New York: Dell, 1961), 21–23.

9. For an interesting comparison of Quentin Compson's and Jack Burden's respective searches into the past, see Mary Ann Wilson, "Search for an Eternal Present: *Absalom, Absalom!* and *All the King's Men*," *Connecticut Review* 8, no. 1 (1974): 95–100.

10. Alighieri Dante, *The Divine Comedy*, trans. Charles Eliot Norton (Chicago: Encyclopedia Britannica, 1952), 57.

11. I mean by this statement that Faulkner, and readers who have previously read *The Sound and the Fury*, already know that Quentin committed suicide in that novel. Interestingly, in the original "Chronology" that Faulkner appended to *Absalom, Absalom!* (altered in the "Corrected Edition" of the novel), Quentin and Rosa Coldfield make their trip to Sutpen's Hundred in September 1910, although Quentin in the earlier novel committed suicide on June 2, 1910. Thus, according to Faulkner's original chronology, Quentin was already dead when he narrated the Sutpen story!

"Did You Ever Have a Sister?"
Holden Caulfield and Quentin Compson

J. D. Salinger's *The Catcher in the Rye*, as the title suggests, is a novel built on literary parallels and allusions; as a result, its hero, Holden Caulfield, has been compared to a host of other characters, from both American and world literature.[1] The closest of Holden's blood brothers, as even a cursory survey of the criticism of Salinger's novel will reveal, is generally thought to be Huckleberry Finn.[2] And certainly there are notable likenesses between Huck and Holden: both are troubled adolescents on the run—psychologically, linguistically, and geographically—from an adult world that they find pretentious, hypocritical, shallow, cruel, and dangerous. But the most significant details of Holden Caulfield's characterization—his paralyzing fear of sexuality, his overly protective attitude toward his sister, and his unhealthy preoccupation with death—are missing in Twain's portrait of Huck.[3] Interestingly, though, these anxieties and obsessions are precisely the ones exhibited by William Faulkner's Quentin Compson, one of the protagonists of *The Sound and the Fury*. The key to the neurotic behavior of both characters can be found in the Freudian theory of anality, particularly as that theory has been amplified and reinterpreted by such later psychologists as Norman O. Brown and Ernest Becker. Both Holden and Quentin exhibit character traits that are associated with individuals whose development has been arrested at the anal stage.

The surface similarities between the two characters are easily established, and striking. Both are intelligent, sensitive, introspective, well-informed young men: Holden is a seventeen-year-old prep school student who reads "a lot" and whose best subject is English;[4] Quentin is an eighteen-year-old freshman at Harvard who knows Latin and quotes St. Francis. Both have highly ambivalent feelings about sex: while they talk or think about sex almost constantly, and even boast to others about their sexual knowledge and experience, both are actually fearful of sex, indeed are self-confessed virgins.[5] Moreover, both Holden and Quentin project their sexual anxiety onto their sisters, adopting a defensive, "big brother" attitude and seeking to bar the sisters' entrance into carnal knowledge. Finally, their confused and disturbed mental states lead both Holden and Quentin to contemplate suicide.[6] Quentin, of course, unlike Holden, actually follows through on his death wish, purchasing a pair of flat-irons for body weights and then hurling himself from a bridge into the Charles River.

As suggested earlier, the unifying psychological factor underlying both Holden's and Quentin's anxieties regarding sexuality, females, and death is to be found in the Freudian theory of anality. According to Freud, the explanation of all adult neurosis is to be found in the repressed sexual desires of childhood. Freud posited three stages of infantile sexual development: the oral (birth to twelve months), involving the activities of sucking and biting; the anal (one to three years), focusing on the child's fascination with the anus and feces; and the phallic (two and a half to six years), centering on the child's discovery of the genitals. If the child's passage through each of these phases is not negotiated successfully and happily, the repressed drives will resurface in adulthood in the form of various neuroses. According to Freud, the adult character traits that are associated with denial and repression during the anal stage are orderliness (including neatness), obstinacy, and parsimony (or possessiveness).[7]

For Freud, anal curiosity and play, like the child's actions during the other phases of infantile development, are primarily assertions of the pleasure principle over the reality and morality principles—what can be viewed in retrospect as the futile attempts of the child to cling to an Edenic world of innocent freedom and play in the face of impending exile into the adult world of work and responsibility. But later psychologists such as Norman O. Brown and Ernest Becker have helped us to understand that the issue is somewhat more complicated than even Freud had recognized. In his insightful and influential book *Life against Death*, Brown argues that what is really being stamped on the consciousness of each of us during the anal stage is nothing less than "the conflict between our animal body, appropriately epitomized in the anal function, and our pretentious sublimations, more specifically the pretensions of sublimated or romantic-Platonic love."[8] In other words, the anal condition represents the child's first encounter with mortality and decay. As Becker notes, echoing Brown,

> With anal play the child is already becoming a philosopher of the human condition. But like all philosophers he is still bound by it, and his main task in

life becomes the denial of what the anus represents: that in fact, he is nothing but body where nature is concerned. Nature's values are bodily values, human values are mental values, and though they take the loftiest flights they are built upon excrement, impossible without it, always brought back to it.[9]

The conflict experienced by the child at the anal stage, therefore, is that of the body versus the mind or spirit, the real versus the ideal.

Sometimes, as Brown demonstrates in his brilliant analysis of "The Excremental Vision" of Jonathan Swift, the repugnance that one comes to feel for the anus and its foul-smelling product is displaced onto other parts of the body, particularly the genitals. Such displacement, Brown argues, explains Lemuel Gulliver's rejection of the body after observing the "strange Disposition to Nastiness and Dirt" of the Yahoos, as well as the madness of the lover in one of Swift's poems, who explains to his friend: "Nor wonder how I lost my wits; / Oh! Caelia, Caelia, Caelia shits." Such passages have led a number of biographers to suspect that Swift was sexually dysfunctional in his personal life. As one of those biographers has written, "One gets the impression that the anal fixation was intense and binding, and the genital demands so impaired or limited at best that there was a total retreat from genital sexuality in his early adult life."[10]

Swift, of course, is not the only one to associate the anus with genitalia. Freud, too, was horrified that "we are born between urine and feces"; and William Butler Yeats's character Crazy Jane, echoing Swift's young lover, complains that "Love has pitched his mansion in / The place of excrement."[11] Two others who are obsessed with this paradoxical condition, as I shall now seek to demonstrate, are Holden Caulfield and Quentin Compson.

Holden's attitudes and actions clearly fit the above description of the anal character. Like Swift's Gulliver, he is both fascinated and repulsed by "Nastiness and Dirt," particularly any that is associated with body parts and functions. This attitude is seen not only in the degree to which his vocabulary is characterized by such words as "crap" (1, 11, 56, 57), "manure" (3), "vomity" (81), "snot" (103), and "puke" (128, 139) but also in his specific descriptions of his classmates Ackley and Stradlater. Of Ackley, Holden observes: "His teeth were always mossy-looking, and his ears were always dirty as hell, but he was always cleaning his fingernails. I guess he thought that made him a very *neat* guy" [Holden's emphasis] (22). When Ackley picks up a knee supporter and asks, "Who belongsa this?" Holden notes: "That guy Ackley'd pick up *anything*. He'd even pick up your jock strap or something" (22). Later, Holden says, "That guy had just about everything. Sinus trouble, pimples, lousy teeth, halitosis, crumby fingernails" (39). While conversing with Stradlater in the bathroom as Stradlater shaves, Holden observes: "You should've seen the razor he shaved himself with. It was always rusty as hell and full of lather and hairs and crap. He never cleaned it or anything" (27).

Such passages reveal the extreme discomfort and uneasiness that Holden feels toward all things physical. That this repulsiveness embraces sexuality is underscored not only by his own virginity (which is made more revealing by the fact that it is undesired) but also by his overly protective attitude toward females. Holden idealizes women and seeks to protect them from sexual knowledge and experience. Thus, he expresses grave concern about Jane's being out on a date with Stradlater. "I kept thinking about Jane, and about Stradlater having a date with her and all. It made me so nervous I nearly went crazy. I already told you what a sexy bastard Stradlater was" (34). Later, when Holden observes the man and woman in the hotel squirting water in each other's faces, he says, "I think if you don't really like a girl, you shouldn't horse around with her at all, and if you do like her, then you're supposed to like *her face* [emphasis added], and if you like her face, you ought to be careful about doing crumby stuff to it, like squirting water all over it" (62). Consistent with this idealized, unsexed view of women, Holden declines to engage in sex with the hotel prostitute; and when Luce refers to one of his former girlfriends as "the Whore of New Hampshire," Holden objects: "That isn't nice. If she was decent enough to let you get sexy with her all the time, you at least shouldn't talk about her that way" (145).

A similar attitude is evidenced in the interpretation Holden puts upon the Robert Burns poem that provides the title of the novel. As several critics have pointed out, the text of the original poem (and even more the dozens of parodies of Burns's poem) strongly suggests that the bodies meeting in the rye field are there to engage in sex.[12] But Holden reshapes what in actuality is a bawdy poem into an idealized story of a chivalric knight who rescues children from the danger of falling over a cliff. To the reader who knows Burns's poem, it is clear that the "cliff"' that represents a threat to the children is their "fall" into sexual awareness and experience. Holden's idealized characterization of himself as one who saves the children from falling over the cliff is thus to be understood as an unconscious desire to deny the fact of human sexuality.

This chivalric, unrealistic, and ultimately unhealthy attitude explains Holden's obsession with the word "fuck." When he visits Phoebe's school, he observes,

Somebody'd written "Fuck you" on the wall. It drove me damn near crazy. I thought how Phoebe and all the other little kids would see it, and how they'd wonder what the hell it meant, and then finally some dirty kid would tell

them—all cockeyed, naturally—what it meant, and how they'd all *think* about
it and maybe even *worry* about it for a couple of days. I kept wanting to kill
whoever'd written it. I figured it was some perverty bum that'd sneaked in the
school late at night to take a leak or something and then wrote it on the wall.
I kept picturing myself catching him at it, and how I'd smash his head on the
stone steps till he was good and goddam dead and bloody. (201)

The overreaction in this scene demonstrates, as perhaps no other scene in
the book does so well, the extent of Holden's neurosis regarding sex. Making the act of scribbling an obscenity on a schoolhouse wall into a capital
offense, with himself as the happy executioner of the vile offender, is hardly
the behavior of an individual who is comfortable with sexuality, whether his
own or someone else's.

It is, of course, Holden's subconscious fear of sexuality which explains
his overly protective attitude toward children, particularly his sister Phoebe.
Ideally, Holden would prefer a world without "fuck," not merely the word but
also the act. Thus he erases the obscenity from the wall—only to discover
a second one, "*scratched* on," and hence impossible to remove (202). Becker
states: "The upsetting thing about anality is that it reveals that all culture, all
man's creative life-ways, are in some basic part of them a fabricated protest
against natural reality, a denial of the truth of the human condition, and an
attempt to forget the pathetic creature that man is" (33). Holden's version of
this idea is just as tragic, and just as universal: "It's hopeless, anyway. If you
had a million years to do it in, you couldn't rub out even *half* the 'Fuck you'
signs in the world. It's impossible" (202).

Like Holden Caulfield, Faulkner's Quentin Compson represents a classic
case of the anal character. He too is repulsed by sexuality because he associates it with "Nastiness and Dirt." This attitude is established in the childhood
episode in which Quentin and the other children look at "the muddy bottom
of [Caddy's] drawers" (39) as she climbs the pear tree to look through the parlor window to view the wake being held for their grandmother.[13] It is hardly
coincidental that Faulkner here symbolically links Caddy's stained bottom
and death. Not only does the scene foreshadow Caddy's later "fall" into sexual
experience, which she identifies with death ("*When they touched me I died*,"
she tells Quentin [149]); the stain also symbolizes original sin, which many of
the characters of the novel (as indeed many individuals since St. Augustine
have done) identify with sexuality. What is important for my purpose here,
however, is to note how this scene captures so perfectly the essence of the anal
condition. An innocent child, with panties soiled by contact with the physical

earth, climbs the Tree of Knowledge in her childhood Eden to become one with the adult gods. Observing, Quentin is already beginning (unconsciously, of course) to develop the neurosis that will characterize his adult attitude toward sexuality.

Quentin's personal identification with Caddy's muddy drawers is made clear in another childhood scene in which Caddy chastises him for "hugging" Natalie (137). Quentin's embarrassment and guilt over being caught with "*a dirty girl like Natalie*" (134) is both interesting and revealing: "*I jumped hard as I could into the hogwallow the mud yellowed up to my waist stinking I kept on plunging until I fell down and rolled over in it*" (136–37). In the quarrel with Caddy which continues, Quentin covers her with mud: "*I wiped mud from my legs smeared it on her wet hard turning body*" (137). Later, when they wash themselves in the branch, Quentin observes "*the sloughed mud stinking sur-faceward*" (138). Such passages are typical of the Quentin section. Like Hold-en's, Quentin's language is filled with references to filthiness, and most such phrases relate to sexuality, particularly female.[14] Women are "little dirty sluts" (78), "bitches" (160), and "whore[s]" (159) who "*have an affinity for evil*" (96) which is symbolized by the menstrual cycle, described as the "delicate equi-librium of periodical filth between two moons balanced" (128). These last two quotes Quentin recalls from his father, who must bear the primary responsi-bility for teaching his son that female sexuality is synonymous with all impu-rity and evil. "Purity is a negative state and therefore contrary to nature," Mr. Compson tells Quentin. "It's nature is hurting you not Caddy" (116). Quen-tin also remembers that his father's one-word characterization of the human condition was, significantly, "Excrement" (77).

Such negative views of sexuality account for Quentin's desire for castration. "Versh told me about a man who mutilated himself. He went into the woods and did it with a razor, sitting in a ditch" (115–16). But Quentin would prefer a state even more startling and unnatural. "But that's not it. It's not not having them. It's never to have had them then I could say O That That's Chinese I dont know Chinese" (116). In this passage, the reader will soon discover, is to be found the essence of Quentin's character and fate. His self-imposed virgin-ity represents his identification with the eunuch, as his suicide represents his desire to enter a world where sexuality is not even a possibility. Like Holden Caulfield, Quentin Compson would prefer a world without "Fuck."

Like Holden, too, Quentin exhibits the obsessive concern for neatness and cleanliness that Freud associated with anal retentive behavior. Even on the day that will end in the irrationality of suicide, Quentin bathes, shaves, puts on his new suit, packs his trunk, writes letters to his father and his roommate, and even takes time to clean the watch he has intentionally broken. Observing such fastidiousness, his roommate Shreve asks, "Is it a wedding or a wake?" (82)—not knowing it is both. At the end of the day, following his fight with Gerald Bland, Quentin worries about the shape of his collar, cleans the blood off his vest with gasoline, changes shirts and collars, gets a fresh handkerchief, brushes his hair and teeth, and repacks his bag. Significantly, the last action Faulkner has him perform before leaving his room to drown himself in the river underscores his obsession for neatness and order: "Before I snapped the light out I looked around to see if there was anything else, then I saw that I had forgotten my hat. . . . I had forgotten to brush it too, but Shreve had a brush, so I didn't have to open the bag any more" (179).

Also as in the case of Holden, Quentin's sexual anxieties lead him to be overly protective of his sister Caddy. In the stream episode it is Quentin, the oldest child, who feels that he must assume the responsibility for Caddy's muddy drawers, as he also later seeks to take responsibility for her adolescent promiscuity. To characterize Quentin's feelings concerning the latter, one might paraphrase Swift's observation on Caelia: "Poor Quentin! such sad, sad news: / Caddy, Caddy, Caddy screws." Driven to near madness by this discovery, he threatens to kill Dalton Ames to avenge his sister's seduction and disgrace. Quentin's failure in this scene further underscores his sexual impotence. When Ames hands him a gun (an obvious phallic symbol) and invites him to make good on his threat, Quentin faints, "just passed out like a girl" (162), he says. Having thus failed to protect Caddy from Ames, Quentin next seeks to negate Caddy's promiscuity by persuading his father that he has committed incest with his sister. His father knows better, however, and, unfortunately for Quentin's ultimate well-being, responds to his son's "confession" with ridicule and sarcasm.

Quentin's subsequent attempt to rescue the little lost Italian girl, another "little dirty girl" (146), in Cambridge is an obvious attempt to atone for his failure to protect Caddy. To make the parallel unmistakable, Faulkner not only has Quentin repeatedly call the little girl "sister" (125ff) but also repeats in this episode many of the symbols and motifs employed earlier in the Quentin/Caddy scenes: for example, flowers, trees, water, fences, and gates. Ironically but predictably, Quentin is no more successful in his chivalric treatment of the little stranger than he was with Caddy: his possessive behavior being misunderstood as attempted child molestation, he is detained for a time by policemen and must himself be rescued by his friends. None of these friends, though—only the reader—understands the disappointment and frustration and rage that Quentin directs toward Caddy and the world she represents when he attacks Gerald Bland while shouting, "Did you ever have a sister? did you?" (166). It is the same disappointment and frustration and rage that Holden Caulfield feels when he wants to murder the individual who wrote "Fuck you" on Phoebe's schoolhouse wall.

NOTES

1. As Carl F. Strauch has noted, Holden, in his alienation from society and his quest for personal identity, "is observed to keep company not only with Huck Finn but also with Ulysses, Aeneas, Ishmael, Alyosha, Stephen Dedalus, and Hans Castrop" (in Joel Salzberg, ed., *Critical Essays on Salinger's* The Catcher in the Rye [Boston: G. K. Hall, 1990], 65). Other critics have found similarities between Holden and David Copperfield, Eugene Gant, Nick Adams, Jay Gatsby, and even an occasional female character such as Carson McCullers's Frankie Addams.

2. See, for example, Edgar Branch, "Mark Twain and J. D. Salinger: A Study in Literary Continuity," *American Quarterly* 9 (Summer 1958):144–58; Charles Kaplan, "Holden and Huck: The Odysseys of Youth," *College English* 18 (November 1956): 76–80; and John Pilkington, "About This Madman Stuff," *University of Mississippi Studies in English* 7 (1966): 65–75.

3. Huck's involvement with death, particularly his faking his own death, is symbolic, not literal.

4. J. D. Salinger, *The Catcher in the Rye* (Boston: Little, Brown Books, 1991) 18, 110. Hereafter cited parenthetically within the text.

5. "The thing is," Holden admits, "most of the time when you're coming pretty close to doing it with a girl . . . she keeps telling you to stop. The trouble with me is, I stop. Most guys don't. I can't help it" (92). "Poor Quentin," his sister Caddy tells him, "you've never done that have you" (151).

6. "I felt so lonesome, all of a sudden," Holden says at one point. "I almost wished I was dead" (48). This death wish is objectified in Holden's sympathetic viewing of the museum mummies (204), as it is also in the body of James Castle, the classmate who, clad in the turtleneck sweater Holden has lent him (thus making him Holden's alter ego), kills himself by leaping from a dormitory window (170).

7. See Raymond J. Corsini, ed., *Encyclopedia of Psychology*, 2nd ed. (New York: John Wiley and Sons, 1994), 3:143, 247.

8. Norman O. Brown, *Life against Death: The Psychoanalytic Meaning of History* (Middleton, CT: Wesleyan University Press, 1959), 186.

9. Ernest Becker, *The Denial of Death* (New York: Free Press, 1973), 31.

10. Qtd. in Brown, *Life against Death*, 183.

11. Sigmund Freud, *Civilization and Its Discontents*, qtd. in Becker, *Denial of Death*, 33; and William Butler Yeats, *Collected Poems*, 2nd ed. (New York: Macmillan, 1951), 254.

12. See references to the poem in Salzberg.

13. Significantly, Faulkner identified this scene as the genesis of his novel. See, for example, *FIU*, 31–32.

14. Sometimes the disparaging words are spoken by characters other than Quentin, but since they are presented to the reader through Quentin's stream of consciousness, they come to represent his own thoughts as well.

The International Faulkner

For much of his writing career, William Faulkner was considered primarily if not exclusively a "southern" author, focusing on the characters, conflicts, and history unique to his native region, the American South, specifically Mississippi. His first literary advocate and promoter, Phil Stone, set the tone for this characterization in the preface he wrote for Faulkner's first book, *The Marble Faun* (1924). "The author of these poems," Stone wrote, "is a man steeped in the soil of his native land, a Southerner by every instinct, and, more than that, a Mississippian. . . . The sunlight and mocking-birds and blue hills of North Mississippi are a part of this young man's very being" (7). Actually, there is great irony in Stone's claim, since the poems in the book he is prefacing show more parallels with Algernon Swinburne, A. E. Housman, and T. S. Eliot than they do with the southern local colorism of, say, Irwin Russell or Sidney Lanier.

One of the first Faulkner critics to propose breaking Faulkner out of his southern box, Hyatt H. Waggoner, pointed out that this initial emphasis upon Faulkner as a regionalist was quite understandable, given the provincial orientation of American literature at the time:

> In the mid-twenties regionalism seemed to promise a more luxuriant flowering in American literature than its later development actually produced. Not only [Sherwood] Anderson with his *Winesburg, Ohio* but [Edgar Lee] Masters with his *Spoon River Anthology*, [Vachel] Lindsay with his poems about mid-western figures written in mid-western accents, [Willa] Cather with her novels of the Nebraska frontier and [Robert] Frost with his New England poems all seemed to be following the regionalist's way.[1]

The subject matter and settings of Faulkner's earliest novels encouraged his identification with the American South—the story of a World War I soldier's return to his small Georgia hometown (*Soldiers' Pay*), the description of a group of New Orleans dilettantes (*Mosquitoes*), and the opening chapters of his long-running narrative of the life of the Sartorises, Snopeses, and Compsons in his imaginary Jefferson, Yoknapatawpha County, Mississippi. Once Faulkner settled on Yoknapatawpha County as the principal setting for his stories, he seldom ventured elsewhere—only to New Orleans again in *Pylon*, to Louisiana, Chicago, and Utah in *The Wild Palms*, to Hollywood in "Golden Land," and to France for *A Fable*. As the title of Edouard Glissant's book *Faulkner, Mississippi* indicates, for most readers the name Faulkner was, and remains, synonymous with Mississippi.[2]

In addition to the use and re-use of the same Mississippi town and county as his setting, another factor that has kept Faulkner planted so firmly in southern soil is the primacy of race as a subject of his novels and stories. The rich, creative life of the African American characters as a foil to the declining white aristocracy in *Flags in the Dust/Sartoris*, the enduring qualities of Dilsey and her clan in *The Sound and the Fury*, the tragic lynchings of Joe Christmas in *Light in August* and Will Mayes in "Dry September," the miscegenation in *Absalom, Absalom!* and *Go Down, Moses*, and the threatened lynching of Lucas Beauchamp in *Intruder in the Dust* are all aspects that appear uniquely southern in their geography, characterization, and presentation.

The time in which he lived furthered the link between Faulkner and race. In the 1940s, '50s, and '60s, especially, as the civil rights movement began to gain momentum in the United States, Faulkner and his works were widely employed in the national crusade for Black civil rights and justice. His *Intruder in the Dust* (1948) and the highly successful movie based on the novel (1949) became clarion calls for revision in both attitudes and laws affecting African Americans. College literature anthologies from this period habitually included Faulkner stories that deal primarily with race: for example, "That Evening Sun," "Dry September," and "The Bear." The July 17, 1964, issue of *Time* magazine focusing on race features Faulkner on the cover and includes a discussion of his work as an index to race relations in the South.

There were, of course, exceptions to this general approach, even early on. Because of Faulkner's use of experimental narrative techniques, such as stream of consciousness, shifting viewpoints, disrupted chronology, and counterpointing of incident and character, there has built up a considerable body of criticism that examines his narrative methods as opposed to his content and themes. Books such as Richard P. Adams's *Faulkner: Myth and Motion* and Walter J. Slatoff's *Quest for Failure: A Study of William Faulkner* and essays such as Warren Beck's "William Faulkner's Style," Conrad Aiken's

"William Faulkner: The Novel as Form," and Karl E. Zink's "William Faulkner: Form as Experience" initiated a strand of Faulkner criticism quite independent of place.[3] French critics, in particular, among them Jean-Paul Sartre, André Bleikasten, Michel Gresset, and François Pitavy have been more interested in Faulkner's literary technique than in his historical or sociological context. Belonging also to this school of Faulkner criticism are those critics like Hyatt H. Waggoner, Michael Millgate, Donald Kartiganer, Karl Zender, Daniel Singal, Philip Weinstein, and more recently John T. Matthews, Patrick O'Donnell, and Joseph Urgo, who treat Faulkner as a "modernist" or even "postmodernist" rather than as a "southern" writer.[4]

Still, the bulk of Faulkner criticism, which has averaged more than one hundred articles and books for each year since his winning of the Nobel Prize for Literature in 1950,[5] has focused on Faulkner's works as expressions of his link to the American South; and that approach has been perpetuated by the deconstructionist critics who examine literature primarily in relation to the issues of race, gender, and socioeconomic class.

In recent years, however, there has been a groundswell of interest in viewing Faulkner from an international rather than a regional perspective. I can speak of this topic firsthand. Because of the steady stream of international scholars who come to the Center for Faulkner Studies at Southeast Missouri State University, I have been made increasingly aware of Faulkner's global appeal and relevance. In some respects Faulkner will always remain a quintessential southern novelist, but such a label is becoming less and less useful in analyzing Faulkner's works. For one thing, the American South that Faulkner describes has pretty much disappeared. Cotton is no longer king in the southern states; the "Great Migration" northward has given way to a reverse migration that has brought huge numbers of citizens to the South from other parts of the country, all speaking a different form of American English and bringing a new set of histories and attitudes; urban life and values have displaced rural and small-town ones; the rampant invasions of Walmart and McDonald's and other national business chains have robbed southern towns of their down-home distinctiveness; and the long-held regional prejudices regarding race, gender, and class are greatly diminished. To insist today that Faulkner is a "southern" writer is to relegate his works in large measure to historical curiosities, since the South described in his novels has quite literally "gone with the wind" and has a decreasing correspondence to today's Sun Belt.

For another thing, the label "southern" was never a totally accurate label for Faulkner even from the very beginning. While Faulkner acknowledged that his "own little postage stamp of native soil" (*LIG* 255) was crucial to his art, he understood it only as "somewhere to start from" (*ESPL* 8), a means to a greater end. "I'm inclined to think that my material, the South, is not very important to me," he wrote to Malcolm Cowley. "I just happen to know it, and don't have time in one life to learn another one and write about it at the same time" (*FCF* 14–15). In 1955 Faulkner said in Manila:

> I think that the setting of a novel is just incidental, that the novelist is writing about truth; I mean by truth, the things that are true to all people, which are love, friendship, courage, fear, greed. . . . I write about American Mississippi simply because that is what I know best. The Filipino would write about his country because it is what he knows best. The Chinese about his country because that's what he knows best. The fact that one speaks Spanish, another Japanese, another English, is only incidental; that what they are talking about are the primary basic truths which everyone recognizes. (*LIG* 202–3)

On another occasion Faulkner stated that the writer "is simply trying to tell you the same story of the human heart in conflict with itself for the eternal verities which haven't changed too much since man first found how to record them" (*FWP* 59). Significantly, in his Nobel Prize Acceptance Speech Faulkner said nothing of his "southernness" but spoke rather about "the old verities and truths of the heart, the old universal truths lacking which any story is ephemeral and doomed" (*ESPL* 120).

One way to demonstrate the international aspect of Faulkner is to note the number of languages into which his novels and stories have been translated. In his 1972 study *The Literary Career of William Faulkner*, James Meriwether listed twenty-nine countries that had published one or more Faulkner works in translation;[6] that number has since increased significantly. The 1982 Faulkner and Yoknapatawpha Conference, titled "Faulkner: International Perspectives," featured presenters who discussed the growing Faulkner influence in England, France, Germany, Latin America, Spain, Russia, Japan, and China.

Another way to demonstrate the accuracy of the phrase "the international Faulkner" is to trace his influence on writers in other countries. This influence has been especially strong in Latin America. Peruvian novelist Mario Vargas Llosa, Mexican novelists Juan Rulfo and Carlos Fuentes, Argentinean novelist Jorge Luis Borges, and the Columbian novelist Gabriel García Márquez have all commented on Faulkner's influence on both the techniques and themes of their novels. But writers in other regions of the globe have been similarly influenced by Faulkner. Two Nobel Prize winners—Kenzuburo Oe of Japan and Mo Yan of China—have repeatedly acknowledged their indebtedness to

Faulkner. Another contemporary Japanese author, Haruki Murakami, who is frequently mentioned as a strong candidate for the Nobel Prize, likewise seems strongly influenced by Faulkner. His *Hard-Boiled Wonderland and the End of the World* interweaves two separate plots that are contrapuntally related in the same manner as the two narratives in Faulkner's *The Wild Palms*. Didi-Ionel Cenuser has written about the parallels and affinities of Romanian author Marin Preda's novels to the works of Faulkner, and Ana-Karina Schneider has analyzed the influence of Faulkner upon both communist and postcommunist Romania.[7]

Many of the international writers who have acknowledged Faulkner's influence have been more interested in his narrative techniques than in his subject matter. This is quite understandable, since it is Faulkner's relationship to modernism and postmodernism, not his relationship to the American South, that authors worldwide share with him. The literary movement called modernism, as T. S. Eliot explained, grew out of the desperate desire to reestablish a sense of order and certitude following the perceived breakup of nineteenth-century values and traditions. The writers of Faulkner's generation were keenly conscious of the crisis, uncertainty, and seeming chaos that came to characterize the early twentieth century and, as the postmodernists demonstrate, has become increasingly prevalent even to the present day. Faulkner's literary technique mirrors this reality. Unlike the well-made novel of the nineteenth century (the form of which clearly exhibits the confidence and absolutism of the age that produced it), Faulkner's works utilize radical disruptions of standard chronology, numerous plot intersections, multiple narrators, and countless ambiguities and unresolved conflicts. Like a cubistic painting by Pablo Picasso, the Faulkner novel images a world that has become disjointed and fragmented. These are characteristics that are not unique to Faulkner's South, or the United States, or Europe, where modernism had its beginning, but have been replicated in countries across the globe throughout the twentieth and into the twenty-first century. So it is not surprising that writers in all parts of the world have found in Faulkner's narrative methods analogs by which to describe their own cultural crises, upheavals, and transitions.

I would like now to consider some of those themes and characteristics of Faulkner's works that can be labeled as "international" or "universal" rather than "southern" or even "American." It is such universal aspects, of course, that elevate every great writer to greatness: Sophocles and Plato are not, in any ultimate sense, merely Greek writers, just as Shakespeare is not in the final analysis Elizabethan, or Dickens Victorian, or Tolstoy Russian, or Mo Yan Chinese. While admittedly universal truths can be expressed only in terms of the particular, nevertheless it is the universal qualities and not the local that enable authors to transcend time and place to achieve classic greatness. I will list four of Faulkner's universal themes; and to illustrate their international relevance, I will relate them to novels by four prominent Chinese authors. I choose Chinese authors for this comparison in order to cast the net of Faulkner interest and influence as wide as possible—to Asia, which is outside the Western world that is historically associated with the United States.

1. FATE VS. FREEDOM

One of the most universal themes—not just in literature but in religion, philosophy, politics, and indeed every area of human life—is the conflict of fate versus freedom. Are human beings responsible for their own destiny through the choices they make, or are they at the mercy of forces and circumstances over which they have no control? Faulkner expresses this theme as "the human heart in conflict with itself" (*ESPL* 119). As he told the cadets at West Point, the primary purpose of the writer is "to tell you a true and moving and familiar old, old story of the human heart in conflict with itself for the old, old verities and truth, which are love, hope, fear, compassion, greed, lust" (*FWP* 59).

Faulkner came of age as a writer during the time when deterministic theories of human behavior were undermining the traditional belief in free will. The expanding influence of such major thinkers as Charles Darwin, Karl Marx, and Sigmund Freud had led to the late nineteenth-and early twentieth-century movement known as literary naturalism, in which such elements as natural selection, chance, heredity, economic and other environmental conditions, and the unconscious mind were thought to direct human destiny more than human freedom of choice. Writers such as Stephen Crane, Frank Norris, Jack London, and Theodore Dreiser portrayed characters victimized by situations or circumstances or impulses beyond their control.[8] So, too, does Faulkner in the early stages of his career. Whether it be a Joe Christmas trapped in the racist views and behavior of the Jim Crow South, or a Caddy Compson scandalized and rejected by the attitudes and actions of a sexist society, or a Mink Snopes victimized by poor-white poverty, or a Thomas Sutpen controlled by the Negrophobia of the Old South—so many of Faulkner's characters are overwhelmed by external forces—victims, not heroes, persons (to borrow a line from Shakespeare's *King Lear* [III.ii.60]) "more sinn'd against than sinning."

At the same time, however, Faulkner, like other writers of the Southern Renaissance, was a product of the region of the country known as the Bible

Belt; and his immersion in biblical narratives and themes, I would argue, prohibited his complete allegiance to a naturalistic or deterministic view of human behavior. The Bible stresses a significant degree of human freedom, and in it nations and individuals are accorded free will and held accountable for their actions. Even in those Faulkner works that critics find to be most deterministic, there are characters who rise above their circumstances to direct and control their own destinies—for example, Dilsey Gibson, Lena Grove, Byron Bunch, Gail Hightower, and Judith Sutpen. One way to read the Snopes trilogy at the end of Faulkner's career is to view V. K. Ratliff and Gavin Stevens as the defenders of traditional morality and human freedom against the encroaching deterministic (and atavistic) behavior of the Snopes clan. As Faulkner expressed the matter in his Nobel Prize speech, it is a matter of privileging "the heart" over "the glands" (*ESPL* 120). Faulkner does not deny the role of fate in human experience, but he also insists on a considerable degree of human freedom of choice. Faulkner's characters are not as free as Shakespeare's or Milton's, but they are considerably freer than those of Crane or Dreiser.

An interesting treatment of this same issue is found in Su Tong's Chinese novel *The Boat to Redemption*.[9] Winner of the Man Asian Literary Prize and a nominee for the Man Booker International Prize, this satiric novel recounts the coming-of-age story of the narrator, Ku Dongliang, nicknamed "Kongpi" (or "empty ass"), at the height of Chairman Mao's Cultural Revolution. Dongliang's father, formerly an important official in the Communist government, has been removed from his position and exiled to live among the boat people who operate the industrial barges on the Golden Sparrow River. Thus, Dongliang grows up on the river, where he experiences a degree of freedom unknown to the people who live on shore and are more subject to the bureaucratic rules and collectivist mentality of the Maoist government. Not surprisingly, Kongpi spends much of his time in the novel running and hiding—not only from the local enforcers of Mao conformity but also from the repressive actions and dictates of his father. A nonconformist and rebel from beginning to end, Kongpi represents the universal human urge toward individuality and freedom. It is an attitude he shares with William Faulkner.

2. INDIVIDUAL VS. COMMUNITY

A genuine respect for the individual and self-reliance is one of Faulkner's strongest convictions. One of the frightening things about the world he lived in, he thought, was the emergence of totalitarian and bureaucratic and conformist states that would rob humans of their uniqueness. There is, Faulkner warned his contemporaries, a widespread belief that "individual man can no longer exist," that "man himself can hope to continue only by relinquishing and denying his individuality into a regimented group" (*ESPL* 161). This notion, Faulkner insists, is mistaken, for "it is not men in the mass who can and will save Man. It is man himself . . . ; Man, the individual, men and women" (*ESPL* 123). These views are consistent with Faulkner's political credo, which he once defined as the belief "that the individual is more important than any mass or group he belongs to. That the individual is always more important than any state he belongs to" (*FIU* 100).

As much as Faulkner celebrated individualism, however, he never advocated a rampant or licentious individualism that operates outside social awareness and responsibility. Faulkner frequently spoke of "the family of mankind" (*LIG* 200) or "the human family" (*FIU* 80; *LIG* 202), and he stressed that man is "responsible, terribly responsible" (*LIG* 70). Freedom, Faulkner cautioned, is never to be confused with ruthlessness and license. A person "must be free within a pattern of responsibility always" (*LIG* 206). As John Pilkington has observed, at the heart of Faulkner's literary creation is a genuine concern for "man's potential for right living within the context of human brotherhood."[10]

Faulkner, of course, recognized that not every individual possesses an ethical sense. Some, like his characters Flem Snopes, Jason Compson, and Popeye Vitelli, are amoral nihilists. But others, like Dilsey Gibson, Sarty Snopes, V. K. Ratliff, Ike McCaslin, and Chick Mallison, are heroic individuals who recognize and demonstrate their responsibility to others. One of Faulkner's most undervalued heroes of this type is Byron Bunch of *Light in August*.

An ordinary, nondescript citizen, Bunch is a hardworking, morally upright, and religiously devout individual who works six days a week at a planing mill in Jefferson and travels every Sunday into the countryside to lead the singing at a small rural church. He first befriends and then falls in love with the wandering Lena Grove, and he is the sole link to society for the ostracized, defrocked minister, Gail Hightower. It is through their relationship with Bunch that Lena finds acceptance and protection for herself and her unborn child, and Hightower is emboldened to leave his seclusion and reengage the world in his assistance to Lena and his attempted defense of Joe Christmas. The conclusion of the novel, which depicts Lena, her child, and Byron's traveling together into Tennessee, stands as a stark contrast to the tragic rejection of Christmas and privileges the value of family and community over isolation and alienation. Bunch is one of Faulkner's unsung heroes, and it is his genuine concern for others that makes him heroic.

A classic Chinese novel that treats the importance of community is *Border Town* by Shen Congwen.[11] First published in 1934, this novel describes life in a small frontier town in West Hunan Province, far removed from the turmoil and conflicts of the teeming urban areas. Typically read as a pastoral set in an idyllic time before war and revolution overwhelmed the nation, *Border Town* is also the story of the customs, commerce, and relationships that sustain and perpetuate the sense of community among the simple, ordinary folks in the small town of Chadong. An old ferryman who takes great pride in his work and refuses to take tips from his passengers; his teenaged granddaughter whose courtship by two brothers engages the interest of the entire town; the two brothers whose competition for the love of the same woman never becomes angry or confrontational; the father of the two courtiers, a wealthy dockmaster who is well known for his generosity to those who are in need—these principal characters are typical of the hard-working, peaceful, and kind citizens of Chadong.

When the river floods, the inhabitants of the community band together to assist those in danger. As the narrator explains,

> When they spied a head of livestock, a piece of lumber, or a cargoless boat rising and falling in the waves midstream perhaps with a crying and screaming woman or child on board, they urgently paddled out, and after meeting the object of rescue downstream, lashed it to the sampan with a long rope, than rowed back to shore. These daring souls typified the local people: they had an eye for their own gain, but also for helping other folks. (10)

The narrator further notes of the town: "Commerce on land and water never had to stop on account of warfare or banditry; good order was the rule, and people were satisfied" (23).

Symbolizing the unity and harmony of the town are the annual festivals, a principal one being the Dragon Boat Festival in which teams of oarsmen race their boats along the river to the finish line in front of the customs house in the heart of town. Townsmen line the banks to cheer on their favorite heroes. When the race is completed, townsmen are treated to a fireworks display, after which a flock of drakes is released onto the river and citizens are invited to swim out to claim one for their family's meal. Throughout the entire novel, as its title indicates, individual stories are subsumed in the grand narrative of the town and its traditions. Like Faulkner, Shen Congwen dramatizes the necessity of one's finding a healthy balance between individualism and social responsibility.

3. THE USABLE PAST

In what is perhaps Faulkner's best-known and most frequently repeated quotation, Gavin Stevens of *Requiem for a Nun* says, "The past is never dead. It's not even past" (80). This statement contains both positive and negative qualities. In the Nobel Prize address Faulkner identified one of the roles of the writer as the privilege of "reminding [the reader] of the courage and honor and hope and pride and compassion and pity and sacrifice which have been the glory of his past" (*ESPL* 120). At the same time Faulkner recognized that there are some aspects of the past, both personal and cultural, that, brought forward into the present, become harmful and self-defeating. Some traditions are worthwhile, deserving of respect and continuance, while others, such as slavery and Jim Crow and their abhorrent legacies, must be discarded as outmoded and even destructive. The challenge is in finding a usable past within a history that is so contradictory and troublesome.

Every culture, of course, and every individual within it, must go through a similar process of assessment and engagement. And writers who represent these cultures dramatize the process. Thus, Mo Yan, the Chinese author who is the recipient of the Nobel Prize for Literature, presents in his novel *Red Sorghum* (1987) a modern China that is emerging still from its past that reaches back to the Cultural Revolution of Mao Tse-tung, the civil war between the communists and the Chiang Kai-Shek loyalists, and the Japanese occupation of China during World War II.[12] The sorghum fields themselves become the symbol of this cultural evolution. The narrator, a city dweller who is the grandson of a legendary Chinese freedom fighter and who is unhappy with his bland, mechanistic, and anonymous existence, laments that fields of hybrid sorghum, "ugly bastards" that "never seem to ripen" and "are devoid of the dazzling sorghum color" (358), have now replaced the rich red sorghum that he recalls from his boyhood days in Northeast Gaomi Township. "Surrounded by hybrid sorghum, whose snakelike leaves entwine themselves around my body, whose pervasive green poisons my thoughts, I am in shackles from which I cannot break free, I gasp and groan, and because I cannot free myself from my suffering I sink to the depths of despair" (359). A way out of his despair is provided, however, in the recollections of his family's heroic past.

> Then a desolate sound comes from the heart of the land. It is both familiar and strange, like my granddad's voice. . . . The ghosts of my family are sending me a message to point the way out of this labyrinth.

You pitiable, frail, suspicious, stubbornly biased child, whose soul has been spellbound by poisonous wine, go down to the Black Water River and soak in its waters for three days and three nights . . . to cleanse yourself, body and soul. Then you can return to your real world. Besides the yang of White Horse Mountain and the yin of the Black Water River, there is also a stalk of pure-red sorghum which you must sacrifice everything, if necessary, to find. When you have found it, wield it high as you re-enter a world of dense brambles and wild predators. It is your talisman, as well as our family's glorious totem and a symbol of the heroic spirit of Northeast Gaomi Township! (359)

Like Bayard Sartoris, Ike McCaslin, and other Faulkner characters, the narrator of *Red Sorghum* finds in his personal and cultural past useful lessons for dealing with the difficulties and uncertainties of the present. His choice is not an either-or decision; he must sift and sort and weigh both the advantages and disadvantages of both eras to arrive at an appropriate and acceptable synthesis.

4. ENDURANCE

In his "Appendix" to *The Sound and the Fury* Faulkner writes of Dilsey and her African American sisters and brothers, "They endured" (*PF* 721). In the Nobel Prize speech he expressed an even greater faith in humanity's future, stating, "I decline to accept the end of man. . . . I believe that man will not merely endure: he will prevail" (*ESPL* 120). While Faulkner frequently identifies the will and strength to survive and endure with the struggles of African Americans to survive slavery and Jim Crow persecution, he also demonstrates these qualities in a number of his white characters as well. A prime example is the Bundren family in *As I Lay Dying*. A poor-white, farm family, the Bundrens undertake a long and arduous journey with the corpse of their wife and mother, Addie, fulfilling the promise to her that she will be buried with her family in Jefferson. To complete this journey the Bundrens must overcome the age-old obstacles of flood and fire, as well as the family's internal quarrels and conflicts. Though described in a mock-heroic style infused with a considerable degree of dark humor, the Bundrens' odyssey in *As I Lay Dying* concludes with Addie's successful burial, the Bundren family still intact, and the husband Anse having acquired not only a new set of false teeth but also a new wife. The Bundrens, like Dilsey and her family in *The Sound and the Fury*, have endured.

Endurance is likewise the theme of Yu Hua's outstanding novel *To Live* (1993).[13] The protagonist, Yu Fugui, the son of a wealthy landowner, wastes his family fortune in gambling and dissolute living. He is then conscripted into the Chinese Nationalist army to fight in the country's civil war. Two years later he returns home to find that his mother has died and his daughter has become mute and nearly deaf as a result of a fever. Reduced now to the hard, simple life of a farmer, Fugui experiences a life of deprivation and, Job-like, watches one after another of his family die: first his wife, then his son, then his daughter, then his son-in-law, and finally, his last surviving family member, his beloved grandson. At the end he is left with only one companion, an old ox that he has purchased to save it from slaughter and that he uses to plow his field. Fittingly, he gives this beast of burden his own name, Fugui, since both have known nothing throughout their entire lives but suffering and want. Still, despite his succession of personal losses and the failed promises of the civil war, the land reforms of the new republic, and the tyranny of Mao's Cultural Revolution, Fugui clings to life, finding in survival itself the only existential meaning of life. Yu Hua said of Fugui:

> After going through much pain and hardship, Fugui is inextricably tied to the experience of suffering. So there is really no place for ideas like "resistance" in Fugui's mind—he lives simply to live. In this world I have never met anyone who has as much respect for life as Fugui. Although he has more reason to die than most people, he keeps on living. (244)

Interestingly, Yu Hua said he found the inspiration for his story of Fugui in the story of an American enslaved person recounted in an old folk song, "Old Black Joe," and in the narrative practices of William Faulkner and other American authors.

CONCLUSION: THE NECESSITY OF STORYTELLING

I want to conclude by noting an overarching emphasis that Faulkner shares with other writers from every country and every culture: a conviction that storytelling is an essential part of the human experience. "The most important thing," Faulkner once said, "is that man continues to create, just as woman continues to give birth. Man will keep on writing on pieces of paper, on scraps, on stones, as long as he lives" (*LIG* 73). In Manila, Faulkner observed: "It is the writer's duty to show that man has an immortal soul. The writer, the artist, the musician is the one factor which can show him the shape of his hope and aspirations of the future by reminding him of what he has accomplished in the past" (*LIG* 202). The most moving and explicit statement of Faulkner's credo of art is his "Foreword" to *The Faulkner Reader*, published in 1954. There he explains how, as a young reader, he discovered in a book by Polish author Henryk Sienkiewicz the idea that the purpose of literature is "to uplift men's hearts" (*ESPL* 180). This is the goal of all authors, Faulkner goes on to say: "for the ones who are trying to be artists, the ones who are trying to write simple entertainment, the ones who write to shock, and the ones who are simply escaping themselves and their own private anguishes." While there is a social dimension to such purpose, Faulkner acknowledges that the primary motivation for an author is "completely selfish, completely personal." He continues: "He would lift up man's heart for his own benefit because in that way he can say No to death. He is saying No to death for himself by means of the hearts which he has hoped to uplift, or even by means of the mere base glands which he has disturbed to that extent where they can say No to death on their own account" (181). For Faulkner, a writer's work becomes his immortality.

> So he who, from the isolation of cold impersonal print, can engender this excitement, himself partakes of the immortality which he has engendered. Some day he will be no more, which will not matter then, because isolated and itself invulnerable in the cold print remains that which is capable of engendering still the old deathless excitement in hearts and glands whose owners and custodians are generations from even the air he breathed and anguished in; if it was capable once, he knows that it will be capable and potent still long after there remains of him only a dead and fading name. (182)

Thus, Faulkner expresses the universal hope and dream of every writer, whatever his or her nationality, ethnicity, race, class, or gender—and of whatever time and place. And at this conference, here in Sibiu, far removed from "the air [Faulkner] breathed and anguished in," it is that universality that we remember and celebrate.

NOTES

1. Hyatt H. Waggoner, *William Faulkner: From Jefferson to the World* (Lexington: University of Kentucky Press, 1959), 56.

2. Edouard Glissant, *Faulkner, Mississippi*, trans. Barbara B. Lewis and Thomas C. Spear (Chicago: University of Chicago Press, 1999).

3. Richard P. Adams, *Faulkner: Myth and Motion* (Princeton, NJ: Princeton University Press, 1968); Walter J. Slatoff, *Quest for Failure: A Study of William Faulkner* (Ithaca: Cornell University Press, 1960); Warren Beck, "Faulkner's Point of View," *College English* 2 (May 1941): 736–49, and "William Faulkner's Style," *American Prefaces* 6 (Spring 1941): 195–211; Conrad Aiken, "William Faulkner: The Novel as Form," *Atlantic Monthly* 164 (November 1939): 650–54; Karl E. Zink, "William Faulkner: Form as Experience," *South Atlantic Quarterly* 53 (July 1954): 384–403.

4. I exclude in this discussion textual studies conducted by such critics as Gerald Lankford, Noel Polk, and Judith Sensibar.

5. As of May 24, 2013, the web version of the MLA International Bibliography listed 7,247 items relating to Faulkner.

6. James B. Meriwether, *The Literary Career of William Faulkner: A Bibliographical Study* (Princeton: Princeton University Press, 1961).

7. Didi-Ionel Cenuser, in papers presented at literary conferences and in emails to me; Ana-Karina Schneider, "William Faulkner and the Romanian 'Criticism of Survival,'" *Faulkner Journal* 24, no. 1 (2008): 99–117.

8. See Rod W. Horton and Herbert W. Edwards, "Literary Naturalism," in *Backgrounds of American Literary Thought* (New York: Appleton-Century-Crofts, 1952), 246–61.

9. Su Tong, *The Boat to Redemption*, trans. Howard Goldblatt (New York: Overlook Press, 2010). Quotations from this and the other Chinese novels treated in the essay are cited parenthetically within the text.

10. John Pilkington, *The Heart of Yoknapatawpha* (Jackson: University Press of Mississippi, 1981), xiii.

11. Shen Congwen, *Border Town*, trans. Jeffrey C. Kinkley (New York: Harper Perennial, 2009).

12. Mo Yan, *Red Sorghum*, trans. Howard Goldblatt (New York: Viking Penguin, 1993).

13. Yu Hua, *To Live*, trans. Michael Berry (New York: Anchor Books, 2003).

"Like a Big Soft Fading Wheel"
The Triumph of Faulkner's Art

Upon the occasion of his receiving the Nobel Prize for Literature in Stockholm in 1950, William Faulkner responded with a speech which is now generally acknowledged to be the best (certainly it is the most famous) ever given by a Nobel recipient. In the memorable phrasing of that speech Faulkner celebrated both finished works of art and the artists who craft them, calling attention to artistic achievement that is made even more impressive and ennobling because it is produced through "anguish and travail," "in the agony and sweat of the human spirit" (*ESPL* 119). Few in Faulkner's 1950 audience could know how much of his own personal history was embodied in such words as "anguish" and "agony." Today, of course, because we have read biographies of Faulkner, we are better able to understand and appreciate not only the greatness of his art but also his greatness as an individual artist, one whose literary genius and unswerving dedication to his craft conjoined to enable him to transform personal misfortune and disappointment and tragedy and grief—to use his words, "anguish" and "agony"—into novels and stories that continue to give every evidence, even in a world much different from the one Faulkner lived in, that they will "endure and prevail" (120).

Even though Faulkner once claimed it was "[his] ambition to be, as a private individual, abolished and voided from history, leaving it markless, no refuse save the printed books" (*FCF* 126), I believe it is incumbent upon us, as we gather here in Faulkner's birthplace to commemorate the one hundredth anniversary of his birth, to recall and celebrate both the work and the man, not only the monumental work that survives to delight and instruct its readers but also the dedicated artist who struggled and sacrificed and suffered to create that work. In the hope of accomplishing this dual purpose, I shall frame my remarks with a discussion of the text and context of a short story Faulkner wrote in 1942 entitled "Shall Not Perish." While no one, I think, would contend that this is one of Faulkner's greatest stories, and while Faulkner himself labeled the story as "topical, not too good" (SL 274), "Shall Not Perish" serves my intention well because it includes some of Faulkner's most serious reflections on the nature of art and the artist.

In "Shall Not Perish," Faulkner movingly describes the reaction of a small boy from rural Mississippi upon observing for the first time the paintings that hang in a town museum much like the Mary Buie Museum in Oxford. There the youngster views paintings like the one executed by William Dunlap as part of this Centennial celebration; as Faulkner describes them,

> pictures from all over the United States, painted by people who loved what they had seen or where they had been born or lived enough to want to paint pictures of it so that other people could see it too; pictures of men and women and children, and the houses and streets and cities and the woods and fields and streams where they worked or lived or pleasured, so that all the people who wanted to, people like us from Frenchman's Bend or from littler places even than Frenchman's Bend in our county or beyond our state too, could come without charge into the cool and the quiet and look without let at the pictures of men and women and children who were the same people that we were even if their houses and barns were different and their fields worked different, with different things growing in them. (CS 110–11)

Later, after leaving the museum and boarding a bus for the return trip home, the boy cannot forget the paintings he has viewed, and through them he feels an intimate kinship with the places and people he has seen depicted in the art. Faulkner writes:

> And so, even though the bus ran fast again, when the road finally straightened out into the long Valley stretch, there was only the last sunset spoking out across the sky, stretching all the way across America from the Pacific ocean, touching all the places that the men and women in the museum whose names we didn't even know had loved enough to paint pictures of them, like a big soft fading wheel. (111)

Faulkner emphasizes the importance of this wheel metaphor by returning to it at the end of the story, as the boy recalls again the way the museum paintings have created in him a recognition of the identity between his small provincial world and the larger world beyond.

It was like the wheel, like the sunset itself, hubbed at that little place that don't even show on a map, that not two hundred people out of all the earth know is named Frenchman's Bend or has any name at all, and spoking out in all the directions and touching them all, never a one too big for it to touch, never a one too little to be remembered:—the places that men and women have lived in and loved whether they had anything to paint pictures of them with or not, all the little places quiet enough to be lived in and loved and the names of them before they were quiet enough and the names of the deeds that made them quiet enough and the names of the men and the women who did the deeds, who lasted and endured (114).

The passages I have just quoted are among Faulkner's most powerful tributes to artists and the art they create. Here, Faulkner pays homage to the capacity of art to both record and transcend the life it captures and, as a result, to inspire its participants to a greater awareness and understanding of the human condition. In "Shall Not Perish" the artists celebrated are painters, but that detail hardly disguises the fact that Faulkner's comments embrace his own specialty of literary art as well. In fact, as I hope to demonstrate, there are some deeply personal elements encoded in Faulkner's text.

First of all, we should note the context in which the Grier boy's visit to the museum occurs. "Shall Not Perish" takes place during the first few months of World War II; and the boy's older brother, Pete, the reader learns, has been the first casualty of that war from Yoknapatawpha County. Now word has just been received that a second soldier, the son of Major de Spain of Jefferson, has also been killed. Mrs. Grier, accompanied by her remaining son, who is only nine years old, goes to Jefferson to offer sympathy and comfort to Major de Spain in his bitterness and despair. Following the visit to de Spain, Mrs. Grier takes her young son to the town museum, where he views the paintings that, like his mother's commiseration with Major de Spain, celebrate human empathy and solidarity. Not insignificantly, Faulkner's text identifies the museum as "a house like a church" (110), an altogether appropriate description since in the museum the young boy experiences something very like a religious epiphany, a rush of sudden insight in which he comes to understand his kinship with human beings from other places and times. Thus, we note, Faulkner encapsulates a tribute to art, and the humanizing effect of that art, within a text that treats the personal and communal tragedies of war, death, and grief.

This merging of art and death is hardly coincidental. In numerous interviews and public statements, Faulkner expressed his belief that all artistic endeavors are ways of "saying No to death" (FR ix), of "scratch[ing] 'Kilroy was here' on the last wall of the universe" (*LIG* 227), or, as he expressed it in *Absalom, Absalom!*, of leaving an "undying mark on the blank face of the oblivion to which we are all doomed" (102). But art is not only the artist's personal protest against time and death; it is also, as Faulkner noted in his Nobel Prize Acceptance Speech, "one of the props, the pillars to help [humanity] endure and prevail." It accomplishes that goal, as do the paintings in "Shall Not Perish," "by lifting [man's] heart, by reminding him of the courage and honor and hope and pride and compassion and pity and sacrifice which have been the glory of his past" (*ESPL* 120).

Moreover, it is important to note that Faulkner wrote "Shall Not Perish" not only during a time of national catastrophe but also during a period of extreme artistic, financial, and personal distress. His letters of this period to his agent Harold Ober and others reflect the desperation of his situation. For example, when he sought Ober's assistance in placing the story "Knight's Gambit" with a magazine, he enclosed a letter which stated: "As always, I am broke. If and when this sells, will you get the check to me as soon as you can." A short while later, in agreeing to rewrite another story, "Snow," according to Ober's request, Faulkner wrote: "Thank you for advance two weeks ago. If you have anything else of mine which any editor ever intimated he might buy if it were simplified, send that back too. As usual, I am not quite a boat's length ahead of the sheriff" (*SL* 148–49).

An index of how terribly low Faulkner's spirits had sunk is the letter he wrote to Whit Burnett, the noted editor, who had asked Faulkner to recommend one of his stories for an anthology Burnett was compiling. Faulkner wrote:

> Choose anything of mine you want to and that is convenient. I have become so damned frantic trying to make a living and keep my grocer etc. from putting me in bankruptcy for the last year that nothing I or any body else ever wrote seems worth anything to me anymore. Sorry I couldn't have helped you and best wishes for [the] anthology. I thought I had written you before to this effect, but I have been so worried lately with trying to write pot-boilers and haunting the back door of the post-office for checks that dont come to keep a creditor with a bill from catching me on the street, that I dont remember anything anymore. (*SL* 152)

Faulkner's inability to earn a living from his writing at this stage of his career led him to seek a commission in the naval reserve, which he anticipated would secure him a desk job with the Bureau of Aeronautics in Washington, DC, at a salary of $3,200 a year. While the patriotic and militaristic side of

Faulkner's nature was attracted to the possibility of serving his country during wartime, the projected salary was far less than that needed to satisfy his debtors. For this reason Faulkner had also initiated a search for a screenwriting job in Hollywood. In late June 1942 Faulkner described his rapidly deteriorating financial situation in a letter to Bennett Cerf, one of his publishers at Random House.

> I have 60c in my pocket, and that is literally all. I finished a story and sent it in yesterday, but with no real hope it will sell. My local creditors bother me, but so far none has taken an action because I began last year to give them notes for debts. But the notes will come due soon and should I be sued, my whole house here will collapse: farm, property, everything. (154–55)

Within a month of writing this letter, Faulkner had found temporary relief from his dire financial circumstances by signing a lengthy movie contract with Warner Bros. He began work for the studio on July 27, 1942, at a salary of $300 a week, considerably less than the salaries writers of Faulkner's stature usually commanded in Hollywood, but somewhat more than the "anything above $100" weekly figure Faulkner had indicated to Harold Ober that he would be willing to take in order to obtain a regular salary (155). Faulkner spent much of the next three years in Hollywood, working on more than a dozen film projects; and while he resented the time movie work took away from his fiction, he was nevertheless grateful that the money he made ($500 a week by 1945) enabled him to pay off most of his debts. But the fact that he made this money from what he called "the salt mines" (*SL* 182) in Hollywood rather than through the sales of his novels and stories led him to question even more his stature and future as a serious writer. For example, in early 1944 he wrote Malcolm Cowley: "My mail consists of two sorts: from people who dont write, asking me for something, usually money, which being a serious writer trying to be an artist, I naturally dont have; and from people who do write telling me I cant." A little later in the same letter, Faulkner lamented that he seemed destined "to leave no better mark on this our pointless chronicle than I seem to be about to leave" (*FCF* 6–7).

Looking back on Faulkner's doleful situation in the early forties from our perspective over a half century later, with our knowledge of his eventual triumph over both critical neglect and financial difficulty, his Nobel Prize award, his ever-expanding international fame and reputation, his now-familiar picture adorning a commemorative stamp, and this month his centennial birthday being celebrated by events like this all around the world, we are struck with amazement and incredulity that this writer, the one who is unquestion-ably the greatest American novelist of the twentieth century, the one who has been called "the American Shakespeare," should, at age forty-five, with his greatest work already accomplished, have found himself largely unread, unap-preciated, unmarketable, and unrewarded.

Our amazement and incredulity become even greater when we consider the nature of the artistic achievement Faulkner had already accomplished by age forty-five. In little more than a single decade, beginning with *The Sound and the Fury* in 1929 and continuing through *Go Down, Moses* in 1942, Faulkner produced, initially at the rate of one per year, a succession of truly outstanding novels, nearly every one of which has been advanced by one critic or another as his masterpiece. In keeping with our desire to pay tribute to Faulkner during this centennial celebration, let's briefly recount the history of those marvelous years of creativity.

In 1929, following a somewhat unimposing apprenticeship that included a volume of rather mediocre poems and three promising but largely undis-tinguished novels, Faulkner burst upon the literary scene like a giant meteor, producing *The Sound and the Fury*, the novel that would always remain Faulkner's personal favorite because, he said, it represented his "most mag-nificent failure" (*FIU* 61). *The Sound and the Fury* recounts the tragic story of the collapse of the once-aristocratic Compson family, a poignant story made even more remarkable by the experimental strategy of narrating the action from four different perspectives, the first three of which are brilliant interior monologues of the type utilized by James Joyce and T. S. Eliot. The next year, 1930, Faulkner stretched this narrative device to its ultimate in *As I Lay Dying*, employing fifteen different characters to narrate the mock-epic journey of the rural Bundren family to transport the corpse of Addie, the wife and mother, to her burial place in Jefferson. In 1931 Faulkner published *Sanctuary*, which traces the moral corruption of an Ole Miss coed who is abducted and con-trolled by an amoral Memphis gangster. *Sanctuary* is one of the great horror stories in American literature and, interestingly, a novel that French critics have always championed as one of Faulkner's finest.

Light in August followed in 1932, with its brilliant counterpointing of the tragic lynching of Joe Christmas and the happy resolution of Lena Grove's search for a father for her newborn child. *Light in August* is not only a power-ful indictment of racial hatred and religious fanaticism but also a testament, through Lena's successful quest, of humankind's ability, as Faulkner later expressed it, to "endure" and "prevail." In 1936 appeared *Absalom, Absalom!*, which many critics, including the present speaker, now rank as Faulkner's greatest novel. In this story of miscegenation and the Civil War, readers meet Thomas Sutpen, unquestionably one of the supreme tragic heroes in all of literature. To speak of Sutpen is to speak of a character who belongs in the rare company of the biblical David, Hamlet, Lear, Adam of *Paradise Lost*, Faust, Ahab, Roskolnikov, or Kurtz—those individuals who seem to possess almost unlimited potential but tragically self-destruct because of significant weaknesses of character. It is one of the great ironies of American literary history that *Absalom, Absalom!*, which was ridiculed in the *New Yorker* by the influential Clifton Fadiman[1] and generally ignored by the reading public, was published the same year as a far lesser novel of the Civil War, Margaret Mitchell's *Gone with the Wind*, which went on to become an international bestseller and a world-famous movie.

In 1940 Faulkner published *The Hamlet*, the comic masterpiece which emulates the tradition of Mark Twain and the southwestern humorists to trace the rise to power of the shrewd and rapacious Flem Snopes, surely one of the most despicable characters in modern literature. As Sinclair Lewis had done with "Babbit" and Joseph Heller would later do with "Catch-22," Faulkner with "Snopes" succeeded in adding a new term to the common vocabulary of the English language. In 1942 Faulkner closed out his greatest period of creativity with *Go Down, Moses*, dedicated to his beloved Black mammy, Caroline Barr, and presenting his most passionate plea for racial justice and equality. The climax of this narrative is the section entitled "The Bear," which has been frequently printed as a separate story and is now universally acclaimed as one of the finest short narratives in the English language.

In addition to the seven masterpieces listed above, the period 1929–42 also saw the publication of four additional novels; two impressive collections of short stories, including such world-renowned ones as "Red Leaves," "A Rose for Emily," "That Evening Sun," "Dry September," and "Wash"; and a second volume of poems. All in all, this period of Faulkner's career, which Melvin Backman has called "The Major Years" and John Pilkington has called "The Heart of Yoknapatawpha,"[2] represents a magical run of creativity that, in the aggregate, is unmatched in the annals of American, and perhaps world, literature. Merely to list the names of a few of the major characters that Faulkner invented during this period is to call attention to the monumentality of his achievement: Compson, Sutpen, Sartoris, McCaslin, Beauchamp, Snopes, Hightower, Varner, Dilsey, Temple Drake, Popeye, Ratliff, Stevens, Sam Fathers, Old Ben. Among novelists perhaps only Charles Dickens and Leo Tolstoy supply us with as lengthy a list of memorable characters.

Now, having reviewed the remarkable artistic successes during his miracle years, as well as the critical neglect and financial distress that Faulkner was experiencing, I'd like to return to "Shall Not Perish" to consider what it reveals about Faulkner's ideas concerning his own artistic creation. First of all, it seems quite evident that Faulkner, whether consciously or unconsciously, is paralleling the descriptions of the paintings that the young Grier boy views in the Jefferson museum to his own fiction. The wheel metaphor alluded to earlier is one that Faulkner often applied to his artistic creation, most notably in *Requiem for a Nun*, *The Town*, and the maps he drew of Yoknapatawpha County—the "hub" being the courthouse and Jefferson Square, the "spokes" being the roads and rivers leading outward, as he put it, "from Jefferson to the world" (*T* 315). Moreover, all of the paintings are characterized by their particularity, by their relation to specific places, that is, the homes of the individual artists, "the houses and streets and cities and the woods and fields and streams where they worked or lived or pleasured." The same observation, of course, may be made of Faulkner's Yoknapatawpha novels and stories. Indeed, like Thomas Hardy's Wessex or James Joyce's Dublin or Nathaniel Hawthorne's New England, Faulkner's Yoknapatawpha County is inextricably rooted in the actual landscape and history of its creator's native region.

Faulkner himself recognized the degree to which his best work was identified with his "own little postage stamp of native soil," and he dated the beginning of his genuine success from the time he realized that this native region "was worth writing about and that [he] would never live long enough to exhaust it" (*LIG* 255). In this conclusion he was partly following the advice of Sherwood Anderson, who told him in New Orleans in 1925, "You're a country boy; all you know is that little patch up there in Mississippi where you started from" (*ESPL* 8). Faulkner probably also learned a great deal from his older contemporary Willa Cather, whose *My Antonia* and other novels set on the Nebraska frontier provided models for the use of native materials. And, of course, looming like a mountain peak over Faulkner and all the writers of his generation was the example of Mark Twain's *Adventures of Huckleberry Finn*, which elevated local-color realism from subgenre into genuine literature. "In my opinion," Faulkner once observed, "Mark Twain was the first truly American writer, and all of us since are his heirs" (*LIG* 137).

Whether from Anderson, Cather, Twain, and/or others, Faulkner learned well the lesson that wider, even universal, concerns may be expressed in the language, geography, and customs of a particular locale. Open any Yoknapatawpha novel or story at random, and you'll quickly discover descriptions of places, persons, and events that are easily recognizable as unique to Faulkner's native region. Consider, for example, the famous description of the mule pow-ering the sorghum mill in *Flags in the Dust*:

> Round and round the mule went, setting its narrow, deerlike feet delicately down in the hissing cane-pith, its neck bobbing limber as a section of rubber hose in the collar, with its trace-galled flanks and flopping, lifeless ears and its half-closed eyes drowsing venomously behind pale lids, apparently asleep with the monotony of its own motion. Some Homer of the cotton fields should sing the saga of the mule and of his place in the South. . . . Father and mother he does not resemble, sons and daughters he will never have; vindictive and patient (it is a known fact that he will labor ten years willingly and patiently for you, for the privilege of kicking you once). (289–90)

Or consider the following description of a landscape in *The Mansion*:

> The road had ceased some time back to be even gravel and at any moment now it would cease to be passable to anything on wheels; already, in the fixed glare . . . of the headlights, it resembled just one more eroded ravine twisting up the broken rise crested with shabby and shaggy pine and worthless blackjack. The sun had crossed the equator, in Libra now; and in the cessation of motion and the quiet of the idling engine, there was a sense of autumn after the slow drizzle of Sunday and the bright spurious cool which had lasted through Monday almost; the jagged rampart of pines and scrub oak was a thin dike against the winter and rain and cold, under which the worn-out fields overgrown with sumac and sassafras and persimmon had already turned scarlet, the persimmons heavy with fruit waiting only for frost and the baying of potlicker possum hounds. (417)

Or, to cite just one more example, consider the authentic southern idiom employed by characters such as Anse Bundren in *As I Lay Dying*:

> Durn that road. . . . A-laying there, right up to my door, where every bad luck that comes and goes is bound to find it. I told Addie it wasn't any luck living on a road when it come by here, and she said, for the world like a woman, "Get up and move, then." But I told her it wasn't no luck in it, because the Lord put roads for travelling: why He laid them down flat on the earth. When He aims for something to be always a-moving, He makes it long ways, like a road or a horse or a wagon, but when He aims for something to stay put, He makes it up-and-down ways, like a tree or a man. (34–35)

How thoroughly Faulkner's work is linked to the people, places, sights, and sounds of his native region is demonstrated each year, of course, by the legions of visitors from around the world who tour Oxford, New Albany, Ripley, and other settings utilized in Faulkner's books.

In considering the close ties of Faulkner's fiction to the region of his birth and residence, we cannot ignore, even on this day of celebration and triumph, the negative characterizations that Faulkner sometimes presents of the South. As a realist, of course, Faulkner well understood that an honest and accurate depiction of life—anywhere, anytime, not merely in the twentieth-century South—must include the ugly and the ignoble as well as the beautiful and the admirable. But many of Faulkner's contemporaries were not inclined to view his work from such a detached philosophical perspective, and they responded to his incidents of violence, murder, racism, incest, sodomy, and fanaticism with the same question that Shreve asks Quentin at the end of *Absalom, Absalom!*: "Why do you hate the South?" (303). Today, I think, readers, even loyal southerners, are more prepared, more willing to view Faulkner's work in the context he intended, that is, as a critical reassessment of southern mores and traditions, the bad as well as the good. In this regard it is helpful to recall that such fellow southerners as Hodding Carter and Robert Penn Warren defended Faulkner from charges of perversity and cruelty and, indeed, quite to the contrary, saw in his novels and stories the striving of a moral conscience under siege by the forces of darkness. In this regard, too, we should recall Faulkner's own words at the end of his loving tribute to Mississippi, published in *Holiday* magazine in 1954: "Loving all of it even while he had to hate some of it because he knows now that you dont love because: you love despite; not for the virtues, but despite the faults" (*ESPL* 42–43). As this statement makes clear, Faulkner did not belong to the "love it or leave it" school of thought; rather, he practiced what Adlai Stevenson once called "the hard kind of patriotism,"[3] that is, a love of homeland that is so honest and intense that it compels one to identify, expose, and hopefully eradicate the evils that threaten its continuance. Admittedly, it is a tough kind of love that Faulkner directs toward his native land, but it is nonetheless a love that is genuine and sincere.

While Faulkner is in many ways the most southern of our southern writers, it is also paradoxically true that had he been *merely* a southern writer, his work would be relegated to the level of minor regionalists like, say, James Branch Cabell, Donald Davidson, and Erskine Caldwell, and we would not be here celebrating his life and work. But Faulkner's regional elements, like those of Twain and Hawthorne, whom he equals in ability and stature, are always employed in the interest of larger concerns. The fact that the Faulkner

Centennial is being celebrated in places as diverse as Moscow, Tokyo, Beijing, Venice, and Paris, as well as various sites in the United States, both south and north, attests to the universality of Faulkner's appeal.

Faulkner himself well understood and acknowledged that it was not the regional aspects but the universality of his art upon which his achievement must ultimately be judged. As he wrote to Malcolm Cowley in 1944, "I'm inclined to think that my material, the South, is not very important to me. I just happen to know it, and dont have time in one life to learn another one and write at the same time" (*FCF* 14–15). He was still voicing this opinion when he visited the Philippines a decade later: "I write about American Mississippi simply because that is what I know best. The Filipino would write about his country because it is what he knows best. The Chinese about his country because that's what he knows best" (*LIG* 202–3). But for any writer to be truly great, Faulkner believed, he must subordinate the local, regional, or even national particularities to the greater service of universal truth. As Faulkner told the cadets at West Point just weeks before his death,

> The writer is simply trying to use the best method he possibly can find to tell you a true and moving and familiar old, old story of the human heart in conflict with itself for the old, old human verities and truths, which are love, hope, fear, compassion, greed, lust . . . eternal verities which haven't changed too much since man first found how to record them. (*FWP* 59)

Faulkner's insistence that there are only a relatively few basic story lines that are repeated over and over down through the centuries places him with other writers of his time—notably Joyce, Eliot, Cather, Hemingway, O'Neill, MacLeish, Steinbeck, and Warren—who interwove their poems and narratives of contemporary life with ancient stories that have survived from primitive folklore, Greek or Roman mythology, or the Bible. Eliot gave this distinctly modern way of writing a name, calling it "the mythical method,"[4] and Faulkner became one of the method's greatest practitioners.

For instance, in the monumental compendium of primitive man's religious customs, James George Frazer's *The Golden Bough*, one of the most influential books upon modern literature, Faulkner read the account of the killing of the sacred bear—an account he drew upon years later in writing "The Bear." In *Light in August* Faulkner incorporated the ancient Greek notion of an earth goddess into his characterization of Lena Grove. And, of course, on numerous occasions Faulkner retold biblical material, using, for example, the story of King David and his rebellious son in *Absalom, Absalom!*, the story of the

Exodus in *Go Down, Moses*, and the Eden and Christ stories in *The Sound and the Fury* and various other works. In all of these instances, Faulkner seems clearly intent on reminding his readers that human nature has not changed a great deal down through the centuries, that humanity's deepest needs and desires, what he called "the old verities and truths of the heart" (*ESPL* 120), are the same in the modern world as they have been from the beginning. And, as Faulkner well knew, it is only a literature that treats these universal concerns that deserves to "endure and prevail." In the paintings in "Shall Not Perish" the people live in different kinds of houses, and build different types of barns, and grow different crops; but they are still "the same people," because they all share a common humanity that, even as it confronts the ravages of war, injustice, suffering, grief, and death, nevertheless longs and quests for identity, peace, love, and community. And, in Faulkner's view, it is only an art that expresses these universal conflicts and values that can ever possess the power to truly move its viewers and readers. Faulkner's choosing to emphasize that point through the responses of a nine-year-old boy, I would submit, merely demonstrates just how fundamental, indeed how elementary, he considers the point to be.

There is one other aspect of Faulkner's work that persuades readers that it deserves the claim of universality. I have reference here to his blending of pathos and comedy. All of our truly greatest writers—Shakespeare of course being the best example—possess both a tragic and comic sense, enabling them to be true to the contradictions and polarities of existence. As Shakespeare's genius ranged from the despair and pessimism of *King Lear* to the madcap comedy of *A Midsummer Night's Dream* to the Utopian vision of *The Tempest*, so too did Faulkner's muse express itself in a wide variety of tones and moods—tragic, comic, grotesque, fantastic, satiric, elegiac. And such moods, like the character types and plots in Faulkner's work, are universal, not limited by geography or era.

I conclude my remarks with a few comments suggested by Faulkner's title "Shall Not Perish." Faulkner lifted this phrase from Lincoln's Gettysburg Address, and readers should not forget that the lines offering such great hope and promise for our nation—the proposition "that government of the people, by the people, and for the people shall not perish from the earth"—were first delivered at a military cemetery marking the battlefield of an earlier conflict when the American nation had faced perhaps an even greater peril than World War II.[5] Like Lincoln's speech, Faulkner's story treats the death of soldiers but also presents those individual tragedies in the context of a corporate history that could, hopefully and possibly, have a happy ending. The mythic pattern here is the ancient and oft-repeated one of *felix culpa*, "the fortunate fall," which dramatizes how positive results of a greater good can sometimes evolve from negative situations. It is a pattern that Faulkner employed again and again in his books, not only because he recognized it as a central myth of human desire and history but also because he lived out that recurring story in his own personal life and career. As noted earlier, Faulkner was often plagued by serious doubts about his ultimate place in literary history; yet at the same time he continued to find the inner strength and courage to maintain his faith in himself as an artist and to produce stories like "Shall Not Perish" that hold out at least the hope of an ultimate triumph over apparent defeat and failure. And on December 10, 1950, in Stockholm, he received into his hands from King Gustaf Adolf of Sweden the tangible proof that his faith in himself and his work had not been mistaken.

And this week, here and at similar events being held around the world, we and readers like us are reminded that we have received from Faulkner's hands a double legacy—an impressive number of literary masterpieces that rank among the best the world has ever produced, and the inspirational example of a dedicated writer who demonstrated that a life devoted to imagination and creativity is well worth the "anguish and travail," all the "agony and sweat." And both of these legacies, we can be quite sure, "shall not perish," because, to rephrase the ending of that story, "North and South and East and West . . . the name of [who he was and what he did] became just one single word, louder than any thunder. It was [Faulkner], and it covered all the . . . earth" (*CS* 115).

NOTES

1. See Clifton Fadiman, "Faulkner, Extra-Special, Double-Distilled," *New Yorker* 12 (October 31, 1936): 62–64.

2. Melvin Backman, *Faulkner: The Major Years* (Bloomington: Indiana University Press, 1966); John Pilkington, *The Heart of Yoknapatawpha* (Jackson: University Press of Mississippi, 1981).

3. Adlai Stevenson, "The Hard Kind of Patriotism," *Harper's Magazine*, July 1963.

4. T. S. Eliot, "Ulysses, Order and Myth," *Dial* 75 (November 1923): 483.

5. "Shall Not Perish" is not the only work in which Faulkner draws upon Lincoln's life and example. His 1943 screenplay "Battle Cry" makes use of "Abe Lincoln Comes Home," a musical cantata by Earl Robinson and Millard Lampell (subsequently published as *A Cantata: The Lonesome Train* (New York: Sun Music, 1945).

Index

Pages in **bold** indicate significant and extensive treatment of a topic.

About the Author

Photo courtesy of the author

A native of northeast Mississippi, Robert W. Hamblin holds a bachelor's degree from Delta State University and master's and doctor's degrees from the University of Mississippi. He is Emeritus Professor of English at Southeast Missouri State University and the founding director of the school's Center for Faulkner Studies. He has directed Faulkner seminars for the National Endowment for the Humanities and the Missouri Humanities Council and lectured on Faulkner throughout the United States and overseas. He has published poetry, fiction, and personal essays as well as critical and biographical studies.